Employment Law
for Business Students

Visit the *Employment Law for Business Students, third edition* Companion Website at **www.mylawchamber.co.uk/nairns** to find regular updates on major legal changes affecting the book.

We work with leading authors to develop the strongest
educational materials in law, bringing cutting-edge thinking
and best learning practice to a global market.

Under a range of well-known imprints, including Longman,
we craft high quality print and electronic publications
which help readers to understand and apply their content,
whether studying or at work.

To find out more about the complete range of our
publishing please visit us on the World Wide Web at:
www.pearsoned.co.uk

Third Edition

Employment Law
for Business Students

Janice Nairns

LLB (Hons), LLM, PGCE (HE), Barrister
Formerly Senior Lecturer in Law, University of Teesside

PEARSON
Longman

Harlow, England • London • New York • Boston • San Francisco • Toronto
Sydney • Tokyo • Singapore • Hong Kong • Seoul • Taipei • New Delhi
Cape Town • Madrid • Mexico City • Amsterdam • Munich • Paris • Milan

Pearson Education Limited

Edinburgh Gate
Harlow
Essex CM20 2JE
England

and Associated Companies throughout the world

Visit us on the World Wide Web at:
www.pearsoned.co.uk

First published 1999
Second edition published 2004
Third edition published 2008

© Pearson Education Limited 1999, 2004, 2008

ISBN: 978-1-4058-3276-2

British Library Cataloguing-in-Publication Data
A catalogue record for this book is available from the British Library.

10 9 8 7 6 5 4 3 2 1
11 10 09 08 07

Typeset in 9/12 pt Stone Serif by 30.
Printed in Great Britain by Henry Ling Ltd., at the Dorset Press, Dorchester, Dorset.

The publisher's policy is to use paper manufactured from sustainable forests.

This book is dedicated to Trinny Gresham Taylor,
who brought her own brand of charm into our lives,
and whom we loved very much. xxxxx

Brief contents

Contents

Supporting resources

Visit **www.mylawchamber.co.uk/nairns** to find valuable online resources

Companion Website for students
● Regular updates on major legal changes affecting the book

For more information please contact your local Pearson Education sales representative or visit **www.mylawchamber.co.uk/nairns**

Preface

There have been many developments in employment law since the publication of the second edition of this text. Again, it is true to say that employment law is a fast-moving and fascinating subject. The government continues to outline various proposals for change that are likely to take effect over the next few years. Many of the proposed changes outlined in the second edition are now fully in force.

There has been a major development in the discrimination law field. The Equality Act 2006 established the new Commission for Equality and Human Rights. The CEHR is likely to become operational in October 2007, taking over the work of the EOC and DRC at that time. The work of the Commission for Racial Equality is due to be integrated within the CEHR by April 2009.

The Employment Equality (Age) Regulations 2006 are now in force, meaning that it is now unlawful to discriminate on the grounds of age. There has recently been an increase in what are termed 'family rights'. The Work and Families Act 2006 (and associated Regulations) provide for (amongst other things) increased maternity leave and payments.

The statutory discipline and grievance procedure is now well established. However, the DTI have recently stated that it may be scrapped in the near future. Their research has shown that the procedures have done little to improve the way that discipline and grievance are handled within the workplace and cannot be said to have been a successful addition to the guidance that was already in place.

This text retains the format of the first edition. I have endeavoured to ensure that the text remains accessible to those students who have studied little or no law before. Case scenarios appear at the end of most chapters, as do checklists, self-test questions and guidance on further reading. There is also an enhanced list of Internet references, current ET and EAT forms and details of online specialist employment law services. The text has been fully updated with regards to case law and existing and forthcoming developments. I hope that you find the text both interesting and useful.

Janice Nairns

Guided tour

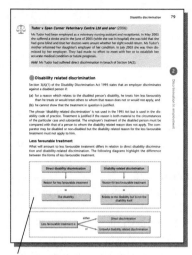

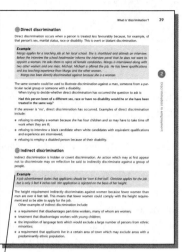

Diagrams clearly illustrate more complicated legal processes or principles.

Examples highlight how the law works in real life by applying the legal principle under discussion to everyday scenarios.

Facsimile documents are reproduced to give you a flavour of what a statute, law report or legal form looks like. Guidance on reading legal documents is also offered to make sure that you get the most out of your study.

Located at the end of each chapter, **self-test questions** allow you to test your understanding of topics following your reading.

Located at the end of each chapter, the **summary checklist** draws out the key issues from the chapter allowing you to check whether you understand all of the main points.

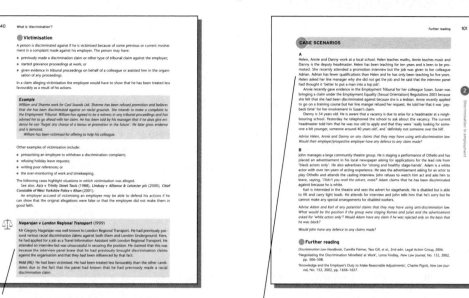

Case summaries: summaries and commentary of selected cases throughout highlight the key facts, legal principle and context underlying important legal cases.

Located at the end of each chapter, **case scenarios** allow you to practise applying the law you have learnt to real life problems and situations.

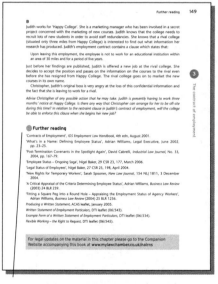

End of chapter **further reading** offers useful additional sources for extended essays, course work and exam preparation.

Located at the end of the book, the **glossary** offers clear and straightforward definitions of employment law terminology used throughout the book.

Acknowledgements

I would like to thank all copyright holders who kindly gave permission for the publication of their material (please see details below, under 'Publisher's acknowledgements'). I would also like to thank those people who have supported me while I completed this edition of the text. Thanks to Zoe Botterill, Cheryl Cheasley, Philippa Fiszzon and Kay Holman at Pearson for their support and patience. Thanks to my friends Janet Dowson-Bell and Marie Drake for their friendship and support. Finally, I would like to thank my husband Chris and the rest of our family for their continued love and support.

PUBLISHER'S ACKNOWLEDGEMENTS

We are grateful to the following for permission to reproduce copyright material:

LexisNexis Butterworths for *Malik* v *Bank of Credit and Commerce International SA (in liquidation)*, *Mahmud* v *Bank of Credit and Commerce International SA (in liquidation)* [1997] 3 All ER 1, and for *Faccenda Chicken Ltd* v *Fowler and others* [1986] IRLR 69, (our Figures 1.3 and 1.4), Reproduced by permission of Reed Elsevier (UK) Limited trading as LexisNexis Butterworths; the Equal Opportunities Commission for *EOC Code of Practice on Equal Pay: Section 3: An equal pay policy* (our Figure 4.2); the Advisory, Conciliation and Arbitration Service (ACAS) for 'Handling discipline: an overview', 'Informal disciplinary action', 'The disciplinary meeting', 'Disciplinary appeals', 'Taking disciplinary action', 'The grievance procedure', 'The statutory discipline and dismissal procedure' and 'Appendix 2 – ACAS Model Disciplinary Procedure' from the ACAS handbook *Discipline and Grievances at Work*, and downloaded from www.acas.org.uk, and for permission for 'Claims settled, withdrawn or sent to an Employment Tribunal 2005/6' from the ACAS Annual Report and Accounts 2005/6 (our Figures 5.1, 5.3, 5.5, 5.6, 5.7, 5.8, 5.10, and Table 10.2), this material belongs to ACAS and is subject to Crown Copyright, Crown Copyright material is reproduced with the permission of the Controller of Her Majesty's Stationery Office and the Queen's Printer for Scotland; the Employment Tribunals Service for Forms ET1 and ET3 from www.employmenttribunals.gov.uk, and for 'Tribunal jurisdictions made in 2005/6' from Employment Tribunals Service *Annual Report 2005/6*, page 27 (accessed via website), (our Figures 10.3, 10.4, and Table 10.1); the Employment Appeal Tribunal for Forms EAT1 and EAT3 from www.employmentappeals.gov.uk (our Figures 10.5 and 10.6); the Controller of Her Majesty's Stationery Office and the Queen's Printer for Scotland for permission to reproduce the Equal Pay Act 1970, and extracts from other HMSO copyright material, including the Sex Discrimination Act 1975, Race Relations Act 1976, Employment Equality (Sexual Orientation) Regulations 2003, Disability Discrimination Act 1995, Employment Equality (Age) Regulations 2006, Employment Equality (Religion or Belief) Regulations 2003, Employment Relations Act 2004, The Transfer of Undertakings (Protection of Employment) Regulations 2006, and the TULR(C)A 1992.

In some instances we have been unable to trace the owners of copyright material, and we would appreciate any information that would enable us to do so.

List of abbreviations

Acas	Advisory, Conciliation and Arbitration Service
All ER	All England Law Reports
CA	Court of Appeal
CAC	Central Arbitration Committee
CEHR	Commission for Equality and Human Rights
CHRFF	[European] Convention for the Protection of Human Rights and Fundamental Freedoms
CO	Certification Officer
COIT	Central Office of Industrial Tribunals
CRE	Commission for Racial Equality
DDA	Disability Discrimination Act 1995
DPA	Data Protection Act 1998
DRC	Disability Rights Commission
DTI	Department of Trade and Industry
EA 2002	Employment Act 2002
EA 2006	Equality Act 2006
EAT	Employment Appeal Tribunal
ECHR	European Court of Human Rights
ECJ	European Court of Justice
EDT	Effective date of termination
EOC	Equal Opportunities Commission
EPA	Equal Pay Act 1970
ERA 1999	Employment Relations Act 1999
ERA 2004	Employment Relations Act 2004
ERA 1996	Employment Rights Act 1996
ET	Employment Tribunal
ETS	Employment Tribunals Service
HL	House of Lords
HRA	Human Rights Act 1998
HSC	Health and Safety Commission
HSE	Health and Safety Executive
HSAWA	Health and Safety at Work Act 1974
IC	Information Commissioner
ICR	Industrial Cases Reports
IRLR	Industrial Relations Law Reports
IT	Industrial Tribunal
LPC	Low Pay Commission
NMWA	National Minimum Wage Act 1998
PIDA	Public Interest Disclosure Act 1998
RRA	Race Relations Act 1976

RRAA	Race Relations Amendment Act 2002
SDA 1975	Sex Discrimination Act 1975
SDA 1986	Sex Discrimination Act 1986
TULR(C)A	Trade Union and Labour Relations (Consolidation) Act 1992
TURERA	Trade Union Reform and Employment Rights Act 1993
WFA	Work and Families Act 2006
WLR	Weekly Law Reports

Table of cases

Table of statutes

Table of statutory instruments

Table of European Directives and other materials

1

Courts and tribunals, sources and institutions of employment law

Before beginning the study of individual areas of employment law, it is useful to explore the forum in which employment disputes are settled: the courts and tribunals. The employment law student should also appreciate the sources of that law and the role of the institutions which oversee its operation.

An aggrieved employee, union or employer initially brings a claim in the County Court, High Court or Employment Tribunal. This chapter begins by highlighting the reasons for a claim being brought in either a court or the Employment Tribunal and considers the roles of the:

- County Court and High Court
- Employment Tribunal
- Employment Appeal Tribunal.

Thorough knowledge and appreciation of the sources of employment law are essential in a subject that is constantly changing. The sources of employment law are:

- common law
- legislation
- European law
- codes of practice
- regulations.

Guidance is given on how to read and interpret employment law reports and statutes. Other sources such as textbooks, case books, journal articles and the use of the Internet are explored.

Workplace relations are governed by various bodies or 'institutions'. The composition and roles of these institutions are discussed below. The institutions that oversee and assist in the application of employment law are the:

- Advisory, Conciliation and Arbitration Service (Acas)
- Central Arbitration Committee (CAC)
- The Department of Trade and Industry and related government departments (DTI)
- Commission for Equality and Human Rights (CEHR)
- Equal Opportunities Commission (EOC)
- Commission for Racial Equality (CRE)
- Disability Rights Commission (DRC)
- Low Pay Commission (LPC)

- Certification Officer (CO)
- Health and Safety Commission (HSC)
- Health and Safety Executive (HSE)
- Information Commissioner (IC).

COURTS AND TRIBUNALS

Employment law disputes are initially heard either in the County Court, High Court or the Employment Tribunal. Whether the aggrieved party brings his claim in a court or tribunal will depend on the nature of the dispute. Claims concerning breach of contract, wrongful dismissal and applications for injunctions are brought in the courts. Claims involving unfair dismissal, discrimination, equal pay, redundancy pay, deductions from wages and maternity rights (amongst others), are heard in the Employment Tribunal.

In other words, claims involving breach of the common law or contract are brought in the courts and claims involving a breach of a statute are brought in the Employment Tribunal.

The exception to this is that there are some claims for breach of contract that can be brought either in the courts or the Employment Tribunal. Before 1994, claims for breach of contract could only be brought in the courts. The Employment Tribunals Extension of Jurisdiction (England and Wales) Order 1994 changed this rule and extended tribunal jurisdiction to include some claims for breach of contract. Employees may not issue a breach of contract claim in the Employment Tribunal until their employment has ended but they do not have to make a concurrent statutory claim. When dealing with contractual claims the Employment Tribunal is only able to make awards of up to £25000. It is also important to note that the Employment Tribunal is unable to deal with claims concerning:

- personal injury;
- the breach of a term requiring an employer to provide living accommodation for their employee;
- the breach of a term relating to intellectual property (including copyright, rights in performances, moral rights, design rights, registered designs, patents and trade marks;
- the breach of a term imposing an obligation of confidence; or
- the breach of a term which is a covenant in restraint of trade.

Such claims are able to be heard only in the courts. (See further pages 366–367)

County Court or High Court?

Most claims are heard in the County Court. Whether a claim is brought there or in the High Court will depend on the monetary value attached to the claim. There is a presumption that claims involving possible damages of £25000 or less will be tried in the County Court. There is a presumption that claims involving damages of over £50000 will be heard in the High Court. The High Court will not hear cases involving claims of less than £15000. In personal injury claims the High Court deals with cases involving claims for £50000 or more. The High Court deals with applications from employers seeking an injunction to prevent strike action. It should be noted that judges in the High Court are able to transfer a case to the County Court (and vice versa) either following an application from one of the parties or by taking the decision to do so themselves.

Figure 1.1 highlights the possible stages involved in a claim for breach of contract.

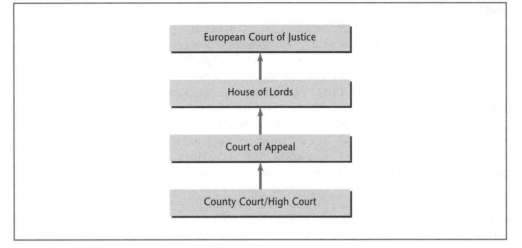

Figure 1.1 Barney's claim for breach of contract

> **Example**
> *Barney has been injured at work. He has broken his ankle and alleges that his employer is in breach of contract for having failed to provide a safe working environment. Barney would bring his claim for damages for personal injury in the County Court (claim could not be brought in the Employment Tribunal because, even though it is a breach of contract action, it involves personal injury and so is excluded).*

Any appeal against the County Court's decision would be heard in the Court of Appeal and then the House of Lords. If the case involved a question of European law, it might be referred to the European Court of Justice.

The European Court of Justice (ECJ)

The European Court is staffed by 25 judges, each one representing a member state of the European Union. They are assisted by 8 Advocates General. The court sits in Luxembourg. Any national court or tribunal can refer a case to the European Court for a ruling if it involves a question of European law. Decisions of the ECJ have a great impact on national employment law. They are binding on our courts/tribunals and form 'precedents' for future cases. The ECJ is not bound by its own previous decisions.

The European Court of Human Rights (ECHR)

The European Court of Human Rights sits in Strasbourg. It is composed of a number of judges equal to that of the contracting states. At the time of writing there are 45 judges. These judges are elected by the Parliamentary Assembly of the Council of Europe. They are appointed for a term of 6 years. Applications to have a case heard by the ECHR may be made by either an individual or a contracting state. Either applies stating that they believe themselves to have suffered due to a violation of the European Convention on Human Rights.

Human rights

The Human Rights Act 1998 came into force on 2 October 2000. It gives effect to the European Convention for the Protection of Human Rights and Fundamental Freedoms (CHRFF). The role of the European Court of Human Rights (ECHR) is further discussed above.

The 1998 Act has provided a framework for the operation of the CHRFF in domestic law. It enables individuals to enforce CHRFF rights against public authorities through the domestic courts. The Act imposes a duty on public authorities or any person whose functions are 'functions of a public nature' to act in a way which is compatible with Convention rights. It does not, however, give private individuals or companies the right to take action against other private individuals or companies. Since its enactment in 2000 the Human Rights Act has generally been found to have struck the correct balance between the rights of the individual and that of the wider public interest. However, at the time of writing both the Lord Chancellor and the Leader of the Opposition have suggested that the time has come to amend the Act. It will be interesting to see how this debate develops and to monitor what changes are actually made.

If a court or tribunal is asked to determine a question which has arisen in connection with a right existing under the CHRFF then it must take into account any judgment, decision, declaration or advisory opinion of the ECHR. The court or tribunal must take any earlier decision into account but then has a discretion as to whether or not to follow that decision. This is outlined in Section 2 of the 1998 Act. Section 3 of the 1998 Act states that the legislation must be interpreted as far as possible in a way which is compatible with the Convention. Courts and tribunals should decide all cases compatibly with Convention rights unless they are prevented from doing so by primary legislation.

The CHRFF consists of 18 articles and 11 protocols. Not all of the detail contained in the Convention is relevant to employment law. The articles that do relate to employment law are summarised in the following paragraphs. The CHRFF is set out in Schedule 1 to the 1998 Act.

Article 8 - right to respect for private and family life

This article states that 'everyone has a right to respect for his private and family life, his home and his correspondence'. In the context of employment law this article has been considered in cases relating to sexual orientation and gender reassignment. See further: **Smith and Grady v United Kingdom** (1999), **MacDonald v Ministry of Defence** (2001). Both of these cases concerned complaints from individuals who had been dismissed from the RAF due to their homosexuality. Discrimination on the basis of sexual orientation is now prohibited by the Employment Equality (Sexual Orientation) Regulations 2003.

Article 8 was also considered in the case of **Halford v United Kingdom** (1997). Here, Ms Halford had pursued a sex discrimination claim against her employer, Merseyside police force. During the time leading up to her tribunal hearing the force intercepted telephone calls being made by her from her office. It was held that this interfered with her right to a private life under article 8. The court held that she was entitled to privacy and that as she had been told that she could use her work telephone in order to discuss her claim with, for example, her lawyer that this right had been infringed. Ms Halford had not been given any indication that her telephone calls might be intercepted.

The right under article 8 is subject to qualification. These are:

where the interference is by a public authority in accordance with the law, and is necessary in a democratic society in the interests of national security, public safety or the economic well-being of the country, for the prevention of disorder or crime, for the protection of health or morals, or for the protection of rights and freedoms of others.

This right would also cover interception of Internet usage and emails. Here, in order to justify any such interception an employer would have to show that his actions were based on one of the above reasons or that they informed their employees that such communication was likely to be intercepted.

This situation has also been regularised by the Telecommunications (Lawful Business Practice) (Interception of Communications) Regulations 2000. These regulations were made under the Regulation of Investigatory Powers Act 2000. Under the regulations employers are able to legitimately monitor telephone calls, emails or other telecommunications transmitted over their systems. This can be done without the consent of the employees involved in order to, for example, check whether the communications are relevant to the employer's business. There is obviously a contradiction between this and the right to privacy under the Human Rights Act 1998.

Article 9 - right to freedom of thought, conscience and religion

This article states that:

> everyone has the right to freedom of thought, conscience and religion [and that] this right includes freedom to change ... religion or belief and freedom either alone or in community with others and in public or private, to manifest ... religion or belief, in worship, teaching, practice and observance.

The justifications discussed in relation to article 8 (above) also apply to article 9. In *Ahmad* v *United Kingdom* (1981) Mr Ahmad, a Muslim, was employed as a teacher. He asked his employer if he could take 45 minutes off work every Friday in order to attend prayers at his local mosque. His employer refused this request and instead offered to reduce his working week to four and a half days meaning that he would be free to attend the mosque on a Friday afternoon. He refused this offer and resigned claiming constructive dismissal. The ECHR rejected his appeal stating that by offering to reduce his hours his employer had not infringed his right to practise his religion.

Article 10 - freedom of expression

This article states that:

> everyone has the right to freedom of expression ... and that this right shall include freedom to hold opinions and to receive and impart information and ideas without interference by public authority and regardless of frontiers.

The justifications discussed in relation to article 8 (above) also apply to article 10.

Article 11 - freedom of assembly and association

This article states that:

> everyone has the right to freedom of peaceful assembly and to freedom of association with others, including the right to form and join trade unions for the protection of his interests.

The justifications discussed in relation to article 8 (above) also apply to article 11. The Convention also allows the use of restrictions on the exercise of these rights by members of the armed forces and the police. In January 2002 the ECHR held that the prohibition of a strike can amount to a restriction on the freedom of assembly and association. See: *University College Hospital NHS Trust* v *UNISON* (1999).

Article 14 - prohibition of discrimination

This article states that:

> the enjoyment of the rights and freedoms set forth in this Convention shall be secured without discrimination on any ground such as sex, race, colour, language, religion, political or other opinion, national or social origin, association with a national minority, property, birth or other status.

This article reinforces the other rights in the Convention and can only be relied upon insofar as it relates to the rights set out elsewhere in the Convention.

Use of other courts

The High Court may become involved in the control of industrial action. It has the power to issue injunctions to restrain unlawful industrial action. The Magistrates' Court and Crown Court hear cases concerning the enforcement of health and safety legislation.

EMPLOYMENT TRIBUNAL (ET)

Employment tribunals were established under the Industrial Training Act 1964. They are now governed by the Employment Tribunals (Constitution and Rules of Procedure) Regulations 2004/1861 as amended by the Employment Tribunals (Constitution and Rules of Procedure) (Amendment) Regulations 2004/2351, the Employment Tribunals (Constitution and Rules of Procedure) (Amendment) (No.2) Regulations 2004/1865 and the Employment Tribunals Act 1996. Employment Tribunals were previously referred to as Industrial Tribunals. Their name was changed by s 1 of the Employment Rights (Dispute Resolution) Act 1998 which took effect on 1 August 1998. In April 2006 the Employment Tribunals Service joined the 'Tribunals Service'. This is a new government agency within the Department of Constitutional Affairs. The Tribunals Service provides administrative support to the main central government tribunals. Further detail on the role of the Service can be found at www.tribunals.gov.uk/. A link to the Employment Tribunals website can be accessed from the Tribunal Service home page.

Cases are heard by a panel of three people: a legally qualified chairman and two lay members. One lay member is drawn from a list representing employer organisations and the other from one representing employee organisations. Legal Aid is not available for representation in the Employment Tribunal. In 2000 the term 'legal aid' was renamed 'legal help' (referring to legal advice), and 'legal help at court' (referring to representation). At this time the Legal Services Commission replaced the Legal Aid Board. The Community Legal Service was also set up in order to supply details of advisers who may be able to assist the individual with employment law problems. It has long been thought that legal help at court should be extended to include representation in the Employment Tribunal. In January 2001 an extension for such representation was given in Scotland. This has been extended to cover 'complex cases' only. This extension does not apply to the rest of the United Kingdom. Legal help at court is available for representation in the Employment Appeal Tribunal. Applicants to the Employment Tribunal may seek funding and/or representation from their trade union. Law Centres and Citizens' Advice Bureaux may also be of assistance. In cases concerning sex, race or disability discrimination, the Equal Opportunities Commission, the Commission for Racial Equality and the Disability Rights Commission may assist either financially or by providing representation. The new Commission for Equality and Human Rights will also be able to provide this type of assistance.

Tribunals are bound by the earlier decisions of the Employment Appeal Tribunal (EAT). This means that these have to be taken into account when dealing with new cases. Tribunals are also bound by the decisions of the Court of Appeal, the House of Lords and the European Court of Justice.

Appeals against tribunal decisions are heard in the EAT. The role and composition of the Employment Tribunal is discussed in more detail in Chapter 10.

Figure 1.2 highlights the possible stages involved in a claim alleging breach of statute.

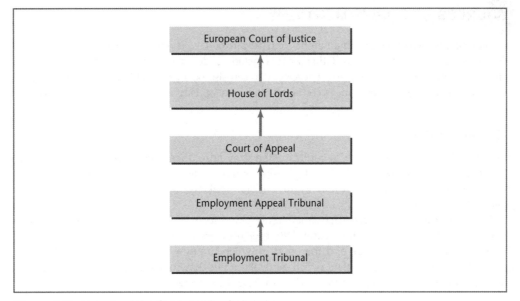

Figure 1.2 Jenny's claim for breach of statute

> **Example**
> *Jenny alleges that she has been discriminated against at work because she is a woman. She alleges that her employer has directly discriminated against her in breach of the Sex Discrimination Act 1975. Jenny would bring her claim in the Employment Tribunal for breach of a statute.*

Any appeal from the Employment Tribunal would be heard in the EAT, from there by the Court of Appeal and then the House of Lords. If the case involves a question of European law, it may be referred to the European Court of Justice. Claims involving allegations of breach of contract that are brought in the tribunal would follow the same pattern.

EMPLOYMENT APPEAL TRIBUNAL (EAT)

The EAT was originally set up in 1975. It is based in London and hears appeals from decisions of the Employment Tribunal generally on points of law only. It can hear appeals based on fact in only two situations, namely when the appeal concerns the decision of the Certification Officer (CO), or where the CO has refused to list a union. (See page 32) Cases are heard by a chairman who is a High Court judge, and either two or four lay members drawn from lists representing employer and employee organisations.

The EAT is not bound by its own previous decisions. This means that it does not have to follow its earlier decisions when looking at new cases. It does, however, have to follow decisions made in the Court of Appeal or the House of Lords.

If a lone chairman has presided over the Employment Tribunal hearing, the appeal need not be heard by a full panel. One High Court judge chairman is nominated to be the President of the EAT. The EAT is also part of the Tribunals Service (The role of the EAT is discussed further at page 364)

SOURCES OF EMPLOYMENT LAW

Employment law can be found in a number of different sources. The main sources are the common law, legislation and European law. Other sources include codes of practice and regulations. Journal articles, the Internet and employment encyclopedias can also be an invaluable source of information. The study of employment law can also be aided by the use of textbooks, case and statute books.

Common law

Common law is the law made by judges when they announce their decisions in each case. Common law is entirely separate from legislation. Judges may consider sections from legislation during the case and use them to aid in the decision-making process, but their decision forms part of the common law.

Important decisions are recorded in law reports and form precedents. This means that they may have to be followed in new cases. Whether they are followed depends on the court in which the decision was made and the court in which the new case is being heard. This rule relates to the doctrine of precedent which generally states that courts have to take the decisions of more important courts into account when making their decisions.

Legislation

Legislation is also referred to as statute law or Acts of Parliament. Legislation is drafted and enacted by the government. Their proposals appear in a Bill and this Bill goes through a reading and committee procedure in both the House of Commons and the House of Lords before it becomes law. Legislation may govern either the civil or criminal law.

The main statutes encountered on employment law courses are:

- Employment Act 2002 (EA 2002).
- Employment Relations Act 1999 (ERA 1999).
- Employment Relations Act 2004 (ERA 2004).
- Employment Rights Act 1996 (ERA 1996) (contains most of the law on individual employment rights).
- Trade Union and Labour Relations (Consolidation) Act 1992 (TULR(C)A 1992) (contains most of the law on collective employment rights).
- Equal Pay Act 1970 (EPA 1970).
- Sex Discrimination Act 1975 (SDA 1975).
- Sex Discrimination Act 1986 (SDA 1986).
- Race Relations Act 1976 (RRA 1976).
- Disability Discrimination Act 1995 (DDA 1995).
- Disability Discrimination Act 2005 (DDA 2005).
- Health and Safety at Work Act 1974 (HSAWA 1974).
- Employment Rights (Dispute Resolution) Act 1998.
- Trade Union Reform and Employment Rights Act 1993 (TURERA 1993).
- Human Rights Act 1998 (HRA 1998).
- National Minimum Wage Act 1998 (NMWA 1998).
- Race Relations (Amendment) Act 2000 (RRAA 2002).
- Data Protection Act 1998 (DPA 1998).

- Public Interest Disclosure Act 1998 (PIDA 1998).
- The Equality Act 2006 (EA 2006).
- Work and Families Act 2006 (WFA 2006).

The role of European law

The United Kingdom joined the European Community under the European Communities Act of 1972. It became a member state of the Community on 1 January 1973. Section 2(2) of the 1972 Act states that from that date European law will have legal effect in the United Kingdom.

European law has had a major impact on national employment law particularly in the areas of sex discrimination, equal pay, the transfer of undertakings and health and safety regulation. The following is a basic outline of the sources of European law. Where appropriate the application of specific forms are discussed within this text. Students should refer to a specific European law textbook for more detailed information.

In the event of a conflict between national and European law, the latter takes precedence and must be followed by our courts. If a case is brought before our courts involving a question of European law, it must either be decided in accordance with European principles or referred to the European Court of Justice for further deliberation.

The sources of European Community law are:

- Treaties
- Directives
- Regulations
- Decisions
- Recommendations and Opinions.

Treaties

The main treaties are the European Community Treaty (Treaty of Rome), the Treaty of the European Union (Maastricht Treaty) and the Amsterdam Treaty. Treaties contain articles which list the legal principles involved. Any national law that conflicts with a treaty can be challenged in the courts. The Amsterdam treaty inserted the Social Chapter into the Treaty of Rome. This treaty came into force on 1 May 1999 and (amongst other amendments) was responsible for the renumbering of the articles of the Treaty of Rome. What was article 119 (relating to equal pay for equal work) is now referred to as article 141.

Directives

Directives issued by Europe have to be followed by member states and they have a duty to implement them within a specified time limit. This means that they have to take the principles contained in the Directive and create national legislation that adheres to it. Member states can choose how to implement the Directive. In this country implementation may take the form of legislation or statutory instrument. Directives must be followed by member states from the time of their issue and bind individuals once incorporated into national law.

Examples of Directives influential in employment law are the Equal Pay Directive and the Equal Treatment Directive.

Regulations

Regulations apply to member states without them having to pass additional implementing legislation. They are binding and enforceable once drafted. The health and safety at work regulations are an example of European Regulations.

Decisions

Decisions have to be followed only by those to whom they are addressed. They can be addressed to member states, individuals or companies.

Recommendations and Opinions

Recommendations and Opinions have no binding force and so do not have to be followed. However, they may be of persuasive authority, meaning that they can be followed as examples of good practice in courts and tribunals. An example of a Recommendation influential in employment law is that on the 'Protection of the Dignity of Women and Men at Work' of 1991.

Codes of practice

Codes of practice do not have the same legal significance as legislation. If a party breaches a code, he will not be liable for any civil or criminal wrong. However, as the codes in employment law are meant to guide the parties as to what is and is not good practice, the breach of a code will be considered in evidence in the court or tribunal. The court or tribunal will not look favourably on a party who has ignored the guidance of a code of practice.

Draft codes of practice have to be approved by the Secretary of State (DTI). Codes of practice can be produced by the:

- Advisory, Conciliation and Arbitration Service
- Equal Opportunities Commission
- Commission for Racial Equality
- Disability Rights Commission
- Health and Safety Commission.

The new Commission for Equality and Human Rights will also be able to issue codes of practice relevant to equality issues.

The Secretary of State (DTI) also has the power to draft and implement codes of practice. Codes of practice exist in the areas of, for example sex, race, disability and age discrimination, equal pay, the employment of immigrants, data protection, industrial action ballots, disciplinary and grievance procedures, disclosure of information to trade unions for collective bargaining purposes and time off for trade union duties and activities.

Regulations

General regulations are not to be confused with the European Regulations (outlined above). General regulations are laws that are made in addition to the main principles contained in legislation. An example of regulations in employment law are the health and safety regulations made under the Health and Safety at Work Act 1974. The Act sets down the general principles of health and safety provision and the regulations apply to specific hazards, such as noise in the workplace.

HOW TO READ EMPLOYMENT LAW REPORTS AND STATUTES

All law libraries keep copies of law reports and statutes. While employment law students may be able to rely on a textbook, statute, online provision or a case book during some of their course, the time will inevitably come when they will be expected to locate and read a case or statute for themselves. As the law changes, books become out of date and for this reason students should ensure that they are able to do effective library research. The following provides guidance on how to locate and interpret employment law reports and statutes.

Employment law reports

Employment cases can be found in standard law reports. There are also two types of specialist report devoted only to employment cases. The general law reports containing employment cases are:

- *All England Law Reports* (All ER)
- *Weekly Law Reports* (WLR).

The specialist reports are:

- *Industrial Relations Law Reports* (IRLR)
- *Industrial Cases Reports* (ICR).

Most cases are reported in one or more report and the reader is able to select one to read. Appeal cases and decisions from the European Court are also found in the above volumes. Cases are also reported on a selective basis in *The Times* and *The Independent* newspapers.

Case citation

The term 'citation' is that given to the way the name and location of a case is written down. The citation of a case provides information on where it can be located within the law reports.

> **Example**
> **Shepherd & Co Ltd v Jerrom** [1986] 3 WLR 801; [1986] ICR 802; [1986] 3 All ER 589; [1986] IRLR 358.

This citation shows the names of the parties involved in the case, Shepherd and Jerrom. It also shows that the case was reported in 1986 in:

- the third volume of the *Weekly Law Reports* at page 801;
- the *Industrial Cases Reports* at page 802;
- the third volume of the *All England Law Reports* at page 589;
- *Industrial Relations Law Reports* at page 358.

Most cases are to be found in either the *All England Law Reports* or the *Industrial Relations Law Reports*. For this reason the following examples concentrate on these two types of report and give guidance on how to read and interpret a law report.

An *All England* law report

The case in Figure. 1.3 is an extract from **Malik v Bank of Credit and Commerce International SA** [1997] 3 All ER 1.

This citation shows that the case was reported in 1997 in the third volume of the *All England Law Reports* at page 1. The key explains what is meant by each number reference on the case.

An *Industrial Relations* law report

Figure 1.4 is an extract from the case of **Faccenda Chicken v Fowler** [1986] IRLR 69 (CA).

This citation shows that the case was an appeal case (CA), and that it was reported in 1986 in the *Industrial Relations Law Reports* at page 69. The key explains what is meant by each number reference on the case.

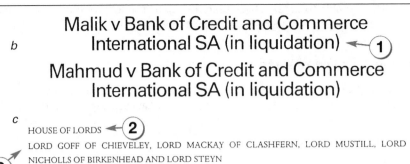

b

Malik v Bank of Credit and Commerce International SA (in liquidation) ← ①

Mahmud v Bank of Credit and Commerce International SA (in liquidation)

c

HOUSE OF LORDS ← ②

LORD GOFF OF CHIEVELEY, LORD MACKAY OF CLASHFERN, LORD MUSTILL, LORD NICHOLLS OF BIRKENHEAD AND LORD STEYN

③

24, 25, 26 FEBRUARY, 12 JUNE 1997 ④

d

⑤ *Employment – Contract of service – Implied term – Implied term in contract of employment that employer would not conduct itself in manner likely to damage relationship of trust and confidence between employer and employee – Bank employees– Bank involved in fraudulent activities – Employees made redundant by liquidators – Employees claiming damages for stigma suffered in search for future employment as*
e *former employees of bank – Whether damages recoverable in law.*

⑥ The two appellants were long-serving employees of a bank which collapsed as the result of a massive and notorious fraud perpetrated by those controlling the bank. The appellants were unaware of and had no part in the fraud. After the bank
f went into liquidation the appellants were made redundant by the liquidators and thereafter they found difficulty in obtaining employment in the banking field because of their association with the bank. The appellants lodged a claim in the liquidation for 'stigma compensation' arising out of the fact that they had been put at a disadvantage in the employment market. The appellants appealed to the court against the liquidators' rejection of their claim, contending that it was an
g implied term of their contracts of employment that an employer would not conduct his business in a manner calculated or likely to destroy or seriously damage the relationship of confidence and trust between the employer and employee. The judge held on the trial of a preliminary issue that a claim for stigma compensation did not disclose a reasonable cause of action or a sustainable claim for damages because the term contended for could not be
h implied in a contract of employment as it was not part of that contract that the employer should prepare an employee for employment with future employers or that he should ensure that employees were not put at a disadvantage in the employment market in the event of their employment being terminated. On
j appeal, the Court of Appeal held that although the employees had an arguable case that there had been a breach of the implied mutual obligation of trust and confidence the employees had no remedy as damages were not recoverable in contract for damage to or loss of an existing reputation except in certain limited situations which did not apply. The Court of Appeal accordingly dismissed the appeal. The appellants appealed to the House of Lords. The liquidators contended that injury to reputation was protected by the law of defamation, that

Figure 1.3 An *All England* law report

Source: [1997] 3 All ER 1. Reproduced by permission of Reed Elsevier (UK) Limited trading as LexisNexis Butterworths.

Key

1 Names of the parties involved in the case
2 Court in which the case was heard
3 Judges who heard the case
4 Year in which the case was reported
5 Summary of the main legal issues of the case
6 The headnote, brief statement of the case and the nature of the claim

7 Court's decision, with a summary of reasons
8 Other cases that were referred to during the hearing
9 This is an appeal case: details of appeal
10 Lawyers who represented the parties
11 Judgments of the Law Lords, setting out the reasons for their decision

the implied obligation of trust and confidence was not breached if the employer's
dishonest behaviour was directed at defrauding third parties, not the employees,
and that the employee had to have been aware of such conduct while he was an
employee.

(7) **Held** – The appeal would be allowed for the following reasons—

(1) In appropriate cases damages could in principle be awarded for loss of
reputation caused by breach of contract. Furthermore, provided a relevant
breach of contract was established and the requirements of causation,
remoteness and mitigation were satisfied, financial loss in respect of damage to
reputation caused by breach of contract could be recovered for breach of a
contract of employment (see p 3 *j* to p 4 *a*, p 11 *h*, p 21 *d e h j* and p 22 *d e*, post).

(2) An employer was under an implied obligation that he would not, without
reasonable and proper cause, conduct his business in a manner likely to destroy
or seriously damage the relationship of confidence and trust between employer
and employee, and an employer who breached the trust and confidence term
would be liable if he thereby caused continuing financial loss of a nature that was
reasonably foreseeable. Thus, if it was reasonably foreseeable that conduct in
breach of the trust and confidence term would prejudicially affect employees'
future employment prospects and loss of that type was sustained in consequence
of a breach, then in principle damages in respect of the loss would be recoverable.
The trust-destroying conduct need not be directed at the employee, either
individually or as part of a group, in order to attract liability, nor was it necessary
that the employee must have been aware of the employer's trust-destroying
conduct while he was an employee (see p 3 *j* to p 4 *a*, p 5 *f* to *j*, p 6 *g h*, p 7 *g*, p 11 *h*,
p 15 *d*, p 16 *a*, p 17 *a* and p 22 *e*, post); *Addis v Gramophone Co Ltd* [1908–10] All ER
Rep 1 explained; *Marbe v George Edwardes (Daly's Theatre) Ltd* [1927] All ER Rep
253 approved; *Withers v General Theatre Corp Ltd* [1933] All ER Rep 385 overruled.

(3) Since the bank had promised, in an implied term, not to conduct a
dishonest or corrupt business the promised benefit being employment by an
honest employer which benefit did not materialise the appellants were entitled to
damages if they proved that they were handicapped in the labour market in
consequence of the bank's corruption (see p 3 *j* to p 4 *a*, p 7 *e f*, p 11 *h* and p 22 *e*,
post).

Decision of the Court of Appeal [1995] 3 All ER 545 reversed.

Notes
For damages recoverable for breach of contract of employment, see 16 *Halsbury's
Laws* (4th edn reissue) paras 306–307, and for cases on the subject, see 20(1)
Digest (2nd reissue) 394–401, *1749–1785.*

(8) **Cases referred to in opinions**
Addis v Gramophone Co Ltd [1909] AC 488, [1908–10] All ER Rep 1, HL.
Aerial Advertising Co v Batchelors Peas Ltd (Manchester) [1938] 2 All ER 788.
Anglo-Continental Holidays Ltd v Typaldos Lines (London) Ltd [1967] 2 Lloyd's Rep
61, CA.
Brandt v Nixdorf Computer Ltd [1991] 3 NZLR 750, NZ HC.
Clayton (Herbert) & Jack Waller Ltd v Oliver [1930] AC 209, [1930] All ER Rep 414,
HL.
Cointax v Myham & Son [1913] 2 KB 220.
Foaminol Laboratories Ltd v British Artid Plastics Ltd [1941] 2 All ER 393.
GKN Centrax Gears Ltd v Matbro Ltd [1976] 2 Lloyd's Rep 555, CA.

Figure 1.3 continued

a *Hadley v Baxendale* (1854) 9 Exch 341, [1843–60] All ER Rep 461, 156 ER 145.
Imperial Group Pension Trust Ltd v Imperial Tobacco Ltd [1991] 2 All ER 597, [1991] 1
    WLR 589.
Lewis v Motorworld Garages Ltd [1986] ICR 157, CA.
Lonrho plc v Fayed (No 5) [1994] 1 All ER 188, [1993] 1 WLR 1489, CA.
Marbe v George Edwardes (Daly's Theatre) Ltd [1928] 1 KB 269, [1927] All ER Rep
b   253, CA.
Maw v Jones (1890) 25 QBD 107, DC.
Norton Tool Co Ltd v Tewson [1973] 1 All ER 183, [1973] 1 WLR 45, NIRC.
O'Laoire v Jackel International Ltd (No 2) [1991] ICR 718, CA.
*Scally v Southern Health and Social Services Board (British Medical Association, third
    party)* [1991] 4 All ER 563, [1992] 1 AC 294, [1991] 3 WLR 778, HL.
c *Spring v Guardian Assurance plc* [1994] 3 All ER 129, [1995] 2 AC 296, [1994] 3 WLR
    354, HL
Vivian v Coca-Cola Export Corp [1984] 2 NZLR 289, NZ HC.
Vorvis v Insurance Corp of British Columbia (1989) 58 DLR (4th) 193, Can SC.
Whelan v Waitaki Meats Ltd [1991] 2 NZLR 74, NZ HC.
d *Withers v General Theatre Corp Ltd* [1933] 2 KB 536, [1933] All ER Rep 385, CA.
Woods v WM Car Services (Peterborough) Ltd [1981] ICR 666, EAT; *affd* [1982] ICR
    693, CA.

⑨

e **Appeal**
Qaiser Mansoor Malik and Raihan Nasir Mahmud appealed with leave granted by
the Appeal Committee from the decision of the Court of Appeal (Glidewell,
Morritt and Aldous LJJ) ([1995] 3 All ER 545, [1996] ICR 406) delivered on 9 March
1995 dismissing their appeal from the decision of Evans-Lombe J ([1994] TLR 100)
delivered on 16 February 1994 whereby, on the trial of a preliminary issue, the
judge held that proofs of debt submitted to the respondents, the provisional
f liquidators of Bank of Credit and Commerce International SA, did not disclose a
reasonable cause of action or a sustainable claim for damages and had been
properly rejected by the liquidators. The facts are set out in the opinions of Lord
Nicholls of Birkenhead and Lord Steyn.

g *Eldred Tabachnik QC* and *Andrew Stafford* (instructed by *Manches & Co*) for the
    appellants.
⑩ *Patrick Elias QC* and *Christopher Jeans* (instructed by *Lovell White Durrant*) for the
    liquidators.

h Their Lordships took time for consideration.

12 June 1997. The following opinions were delivered.

⑪ **LORD GOFF OF CHIEVELEY.** My Lords, for the reasons given in the speeches
to be delivered by my noble and learned friends Lord Nicholls of Birkenhead and
j Lord Steyn, which I have read in draft and with which I agree, I would allow these
appeals.

LORD MACKAY OF CLASHFERN. My Lords, I have had the privilege of
reading in draft the speeches prepared by my noble and learned friends Lord
Nicholls of Birkenhead and Lord Steyn. I agree that this appeal should be allowed
for the reasons that they give.

Figure 1.3 continued

LORD MUSTILL. My Lords, for the reasons given in the speech to be delivered by my noble and learned friend Lord Steyn, which I have read in draft and with which I agree, I would allow this appeal.

a

LORD NICHOLLS OF BIRKENHEAD. My Lords, this is another case arising from the disastrous collapse of Bank of Credit and Commerce International SA (BCCI) in the summer of 1991. Thousands of people around the world suffered loss. Depositors lost their money, employees lost their jobs. Two employees who lost their jobs were Mr Raihan Nasir Mahmud and Mr Qaiser Mansoor Malik. They were employed by BCCI in London. They claim they lost more than their jobs. They claim that their association with BCCI placed them at a serious disadvantage in finding new jobs. So in March 1992 they sought to prove for damages in the winding up of BCCI. The liquidators rejected this 'stigma' head of loss in their proofs. Liability for notice money and statutory redundancy pay was not in dispute.

b

c

Mr Mahmud had worked for the bank for 16 years. At the time of his dismissal he was manager of the bank's Brompton Road branch. Mr Malik was employed by the bank for 12 years. His last post was as the head of deposit accounts and customer services at BCCI's Leadenhall branch. On 3 October 1991 they were both dismissed by the provisional liquidators, on the ground of redundancy.

d

Mr Mahmud and Mr Malik appealed to the court against the liquidators' decision on their proofs. The registrar directed the trial of a preliminary issue: whether the applicants' evidence disclosed a reasonable cause of action or sustainable claim for damages. The judge, Evans-Lombe J, gave a negative answer to this question. So did the Court of Appeal ([1995] 3 All ER 545, [1996] ICR 406), comprising Glidewell, Morritt and Aldous LJJ.

e

Before this House, as in the courts below, the issue is being decided on the basis of an agreed set of facts. The liquidators do not admit the accuracy of these facts, but for the purpose of this preliminary issue it is being assumed that the bank operated in a corrupt and dishonest manner, that Mr Mahmud and Mr Malik were innocent of any involvement, that following the collapse of BCCI its corruption and dishonesty became widely known, that in consequence Mr Mahmud and Mr Malik were at a handicap on the labour market because they were stigmatised by reason of their previous employment by BCCI, and that they suffered loss in consequence.

f

g

In the Court of Appeal and in your Lordships' House the parties were agreed that the contracts of employment of these two former employees each contained an implied term to the effect that the bank would not, without reasonable and proper cause, conduct itself in a manner likely to destroy or seriously damage the relationship of confidence and trust between employer and employee. Argument proceeded on this footing, and ranged round the type of conduct and other circumstances which could or could not constitute a breach of this implied term. The submissions embraced questions such as the following: whether the trust-destroying conduct must be directed at the employee, either individually or as part of a group; whether an employee must know of the employer's trust-destroying conduct while still employed; and whether the employee's trust must actually be undermined. Furthermore, and at the heart of this case, the submissions raised an important question on the damages recoverable for breach of the implied term, with particular reference to the decisions in *Addis v Gramophone Co Ltd* [1909] AC 488, [1908–10] All ER Rep 1 and *Withers v General Theatre Corp Ltd* [1933] 2 KB 536, [1933] All ER Rep 385.

h

j

Figure 1.3 continued

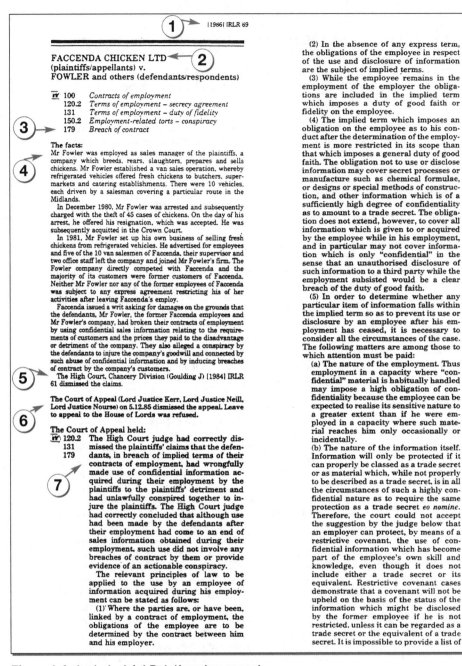

① [1986] IRLR 69

FACCENDA CHICKEN LTD ②
(plaintiffs/appellants) v.
FOWLER and others (defendants/respondents)

③
irr 100   Contracts of employment
120.2   Terms of employment – secrecy agreement
131   Terms of employment – duty of fidelity
150.2   Employment-related torts – conspiracy
179   Breach of contract

The facts:

④ Mr Fowler was employed as sales manager of the plaintiffs, a company which breeds, rears, slaughters, prepares and sells chickens. Mr Fowler established a van sales operation, whereby refrigerated vehicles offered fresh chickens to butchers, supermarkets and catering establishments. There were 10 vehicles, each driven by a salesman covering a particular route in the Midlands.

In December 1980, Mr Fowler was arrested and subsequently charged with the theft of 45 cases of chickens. On the day of his arrest, he offered his resignation, which was accepted. He was subsequently acquitted in the Crown Court.

In 1981, Mr Fowler set up his own business of selling fresh chickens from refrigerated vehicles. He advertised for employees and five of the 10 van salesmen of Faccenda, their supervisor and two office staff left the company and joined Mr Fowler's firm. The Fowler company directly competed with Faccenda and the majority of its customers were former customers of Faccenda. Neither Mr Fowler nor any of the former employees of Faccenda was subject to any express agreement restricting his or her activities after leaving Faccenda's employ.

Faccenda issued a writ asking for damages on the grounds that the defendants, Mr Fowler, the former Faccenda employees and Mr Fowler's company, had broken their contracts of employment by using confidential sales information relating to the requirements of customers and the prices they paid to the disadvantage or detriment of the company. They also alleged a conspiracy by the defendants to injure the company's goodwill and connected by such abuse of confidential information and by inducing breaches of contract by the company's customers.

⑤ The High Court, Chancery Division (Goulding J) [1984] IRLR 61 dismissed the claims.

⑥ The Court of Appeal (Lord Justice Kerr, Lord Justice Neill, Lord Justice Nourse) on 5.12.85 dismissed the appeal. Leave to appeal to the House of Lords was refused.

The Court of Appeal held:

irr 120.2   The High Court judge had correctly dis-
131   missed the plaintiffs' claims that the defen-
179   dants, in breach of implied terms of their
⑦   contracts of employment, had wrongfully
made use of confidential information acquired during their employment by the
plaintiffs to the plaintiffs' detriment and
had unlawfully conspired together to injure the plaintiffs. The High Court judge
had correctly concluded that although use
had been made by the defendants after
their employment had come to an end of
sales information obtained during their
employment, such use did not involve any
breaches of contract by them or provide
evidence of an actionable conspiracy.

The relevant principles of law to be
applied to the use by an employee of
information acquired during his employment can be stated as follows:

(1) Where the parties are, or have been,
linked by a contract of employment, the
obligations of the employee are to be
determined by the contract between him
and his employer.

(2) In the absence of any express term, the obligations of the employee in respect of the use and disclosure of information are the subject of implied terms.

(3) While the employee remains in the employment of the employer the obligations are included in the implied term which imposes a duty of good faith or fidelity on the employee.

(4) The implied term which imposes an obligation on the employee as to his conduct after the determination of the employment is more restricted in its scope than that which imposes a general duty of good faith. The obligation not to use or disclose information may cover secret processes of manufacture such as chemical formulae, or designs or special methods of construction, and other information which is of a sufficiently high degree of confidentiality as to amount to a trade secret. The obligation does not extend, however, to cover all information which is given to or acquired by the employee while in his employment, and in particular may not cover information which is only "confidential" in the sense that an unauthorised disclosure of such information to a third party while the employment subsisted would be a clear breach of the duty of good faith.

(5) In order to determine whether any particular item of information falls within the implied term so as to prevent its use or disclosure by an employee after his employment has ceased, it is necessary to consider all the circumstances of the case. The following matters are among those to which attention must be paid:

(a) The nature of the employment. Thus employment in a capacity where "confidential" material is habitually handled may impose a high obligation of confidentiality because the employee can be expected to realise its sensitive nature to a greater extent than if he were employed in a capacity where such material reaches him only occasionally or incidentally.

(b) The nature of the information itself. Information will only be protected if it can properly be classed as a trade secret or as material which, while not properly to be described as a trade secret, is in all the circumstances of such a highly confidential nature as to require the same protection as a trade secret *eo nomine*. Therefore, the court could not accept the suggestion by the judge below that an employer can protect, by means of a restrictive covenant, the use of confidential information which has become part of the employee's own skill and knowledge, even though it does not include either a trade secret or its equivalent. Restrictive covenant cases demonstrate that a covenant will not be upheld on the basis of the status of the information which might be disclosed by the former employee if he is not restricted, unless it can be regarded as a trade secret or the equivalent of a trade secret. It is impossible to provide a list of

Figure 1.4 An *Industrial Relations* law report

Source: [1986] IRLR 69. Reproduced by permission of Reed Elsevier (UK) Limited trading as LexisNexis Butterworths.

Key

1 Citation, the 1986 volume of cases at page 69
2 Name of the case
3 Details of the legal principles involved in the case
4 Facts of the case
5 Decision from the previous High Court hearing
6 Decision of the Court of Appeal and the names of the judges who made the decision
7 Summary of the Court's decision
8 Cases referred to during the hearing
9 Lawyers who represented the parties
10 Beginning of the first judgment in the case from Lord Justice Neill

matters which will qualify as trade secrets or their equivalent. Secret processes of manufacture provide obvious examples, but innumerable other pieces of information are *capable* of being trade secrets, though the secrecy of some information may be only short-lived. In addition, the fact that the circulation of certain information is restricted to a limited number of individuals may throw light on the status of the information and its degree of confidentiality.

(c) Whether the employer impressed on the employee the confidentiality of the information. Thus, though an employer cannot prevent the use or disclosure *merely* by telling the employee that certain information is confidential, the attitude of the employer towards the information provides evidence which may assist in determining whether or not the information can properly be regarded as a trade secret.

(d) Whether the relevant information can be easily isolated from other information which the employee is free to use or disclose. The separability of the information in question is not conclusive, but the fact that the alleged "confidential" information is part of a package and that the remainder of the package is not confidential is likely to throw light on whether the information in question is really a trade secret.

In the present case, neither the sales information as a whole which the defendants had acquired while in the employ of the plaintiffs – the names and addresses of customers, the most convenient routes to be taken to reach individual customers, the usual requirements of individual customers, the days of the week and times of day when deliveries were made to individual customers, and the prices charged to individual customers – nor their knowledge of the prices charged to individual customers looked at by itself, fell within the class of confidential information which an employee is bound by an implied term of his contract of employment or otherwise not to use or disclose after his employment has come to an end. The argument on behalf of the plaintiffs that any information about the prices charged to individual customers was confidential, and that, as this information formed part of the package of sales information, the package taken as a whole was confidential too could not be accepted. Although in certain circumstances information about prices can be invested with a sufficient degree of confidentiality to render that information a trade secret or its equivalent, in the present case the following factors led to the conclusion that neither the information about prices nor the sales information as a whole had the degree of confidentiality necessary to support the plaintiffs' case: the sales information contained some material which the plaintiffs conceded was not confidential if looked at in isolation; the information about the prices was not

clearly severable from the rest of the sales information; neither the sales information in general, nor the information about prices in particular, though of some value to a competitor, could reasonably be regarded as plainly secret or sensitive; the sales information, including the information about prices, was necessarily acquired by the defendants in order that they could do their work and each salesman could quickly commit the whole of the sales information relating to his own area to memory; the sales information was generally known among the van drivers who were employees, as were the secretaries, at quite a junior level, so that this was not a case where the relevant information was restricted to senior management or to confidential staff; there is no evidence that the plaintiffs had ever given any express instructions that the sales information or the information about prices was to be treated as confidential.

Cases referred to:
United Indigo Chemical Co v Robinson (1932) 49 RPC 178
E Worsley & Co v Cooper (1939) 1 AER 290
Amber Size & Chemical Co v Menzel (1913) 2 Ch 239
Herbert Morris Ltd v Saxelby (1916) 1 AC 688
Sir W C Leng & Co v Andrews (1909) 1 Ch 763
Thomas Marshall (Exports) Ltd v Guinle [1978] IRLR 174
Vokes Ltd v Heather (1945) 62 RPC 131
Robb v Green (1895) 2 QB 315
Wessex Dairies Ltd v Smith (1935) 2 KB 80
Reid and Sigrist Ltd v Moss and Mechanism Ltd (1932) 49 RPC 461
Printers & Finishers Ltd v Holloway (1965) RPC 239
Littlewoods Organisation Ltd v Harris (1977) 1 WLR 1472

Appearances:
For the Plaintiffs/Appellants:
Mr C F DEHN QC and Mr J TRENCH, instructed by Messrs Penningtons (agents for Messrs Shoosmiths & Harrison)
For the Defendants/Respondents:
Mr P J CRAWFORD QC and Mr J F GIBBONS, instructed by Messrs Johnson & Gaunt

1   LORD JUSTICE NEILL: This is the judgment of the court.

2   In these two appeals it will be necessary to consider the interaction of three separate legal concepts:
(1) The duty of an employee during the period of his employment to act with good faith towards his employer: this duty is sometimes called the duty of fidelity.
(2) The duty of an employee not to use or disclose after his employment has ceased any confidential information which he has obtained during his employment about his employer's affairs.
(3) The *prima facie* right of any person to use and to exploit for the purpose of earning his living all the skill, experience and knowledge which he has at his disposal, including skill experience and knowledge which he has acquired in the course of previous periods of employment.

3   The two appeals are against the orders of Mr Justice Goulding dated 8.11.83, whereby he rejected the claims by Faccenda Chicken Ltd ('Faccenda') that the respondents to the appeals had improperly used confidential information obtained during their employment by Faccenda and had conspired together to injure Faccenda.

4   The events which gave rise to the claims which are the subject-matter of these appeals are set out with admirable clarity in the judgment of Mr Justice Goulding (reported in [1984] IRLR 61).

Figure 1.4 continued

5   We propose therefore from time to time in the course of this judgment to adopt passages from the judge's recital of the facts. In this case such a course is particularly appropriate because we were not referred to any transcript of the evidence, and both sides accepted before us that, for the purpose of ascertaining any matter of fact, we should not look beyond the judge's judgment.

6   Faccenda carry on the business of breeding, rearing, slaughtering and selling chickens. Faccenda's premises are at Brackley in the county of Northampton. The chickens are sold as fresh chickens which means that, though after being slaughtered they are chilled in refrigerators until sale, they are not actually frozen.

7   At all material times Mr Robin Michael Faccenda has been the chairman and managing director of Faccenda. In about 1973 Faccenda engaged Mr Barry Fowler (the first respondent) as sales manager.

8   The judge described the subsequent development of the business of Faccenda in these terms:
'At that time (1973), and for some time afterwards, the company sold its chickens to wholesalers, and did not approach retailers directly. Mr Fowler, who is agreed to be a businessman of considerable ability, proposed to Mr Faccenda the establishment of what he called a van sales operation, whereby itinerant refrigerated vehicles would daily offer fresh chickens to such traders as butchers, supermarkets and catering establishments. Starting at first in a small way, Mr Fowler built up this branch of the business until it came to represent a substantial part, though always the smaller part, of the company's trade. There were in all 10 refrigerated vehicles, each driven by a salesman and travelling in a particular sector of the Midlands. The sectors radiated in different directions from Brackley in Northamptonshire, where Faccenda Chicken Ltd has its factory. Each salesman followed a different round within his sector on each of the five working days of the week, some customers receiving a call once a week and others twice a week, according to their requirements and the possibilities of the van sales organisation. Thus, the whole operation was based on 50 journeys or rounds, one for each vehicle on each working day of the week. The journeys were, of course, not rigidly fixed, but variable from time to time as particular customers were gained or lost or their requirements changed. It is clear from the evidence that the weekly standing orders of customers were not contractually binding upon them. The evidence shows in my judgment that each customer was freely permitted to take less than his standing order when the salesman called, or to increase, or vary the composition of, his order if the goods he wanted on the particular day were available in the van when it called. Firm orders were placed on special occasions or by large customers by telephoning to the office of Faccenda Chicken Ltd at Brackley, but the van salesman played no part in their negotiation.'

9   It seems clear that by 1980 the van sales operation was prospering. The average weekly profit for the period which covered approximately the second half of 1980 was about £2500.

10   On 11.12.80, however, Mr Fowler was arrested, together with another man, on a charge of stealing some of Faccenda's chickens. Mr Fowler resigned immediately as sales manager, and, though at his trial in September 1981, he was acquitted of the charge of theft, his work at Faccenda was at an end.

11   During the early part of 1981 Mr Fowler considered the purchase of an hotel in Cornwall, but the project fell through. Shortly afterwards he decided to set up his own business of selling fresh chickens from refrigerated vehicles.

12   This business was to be carried on in the Brackley area.

13   Though he had no source of supply under his own control, there was no shortage of fresh chickens available for bulk purchase.

14   In about May 1981 Mr Fowler advertised for employees under a box number in a local newspaper. As a result of this advertisement eight employees of Faccenda applied to join Mr Fowler's new organisation. This was not surprising, because, although a box number was used, the eight employees knew of Mr Fowler's intentions before the advertisement appeared.

15   The applications were successful; Mr Fowler was pleased to be able to obtain staff whom he knew to be experienced and competent and who had worked with him before. In the course of the next few weeks the eight employees, consisting of a supervisor (Mr Finch), five van salesmen (that is, half the van salesmen then employed by Faccenda) and two ladies who had been employed in the offices of Faccenda, gave notice and joined Mr Fowler.

16   The new business started its operations on 6.7.81, although Mr Fowler's company (Fowler Quality Poultry Products Ltd) was not incorporated until August.

17   The loss of such a high proportion of their experienced staff had a serious effect on Faccenda. Indeed, ever since Mr Fowler had left at the end of 1980, the operations of the van sales division of Faccenda had been much less profitable, and after July 1981 the position deteriorated further.

18   Mr Faccenda, not surprisingly, was dismayed by what had happened, and on 10.9.81, the date (it seems) of Mr Fowler's acquittal, an action was started by Faccenda in the Chancery Division against Mr Fowler and his company and the eight former employees of Faccenda.

19   In these proceedings two alleged causes of action were relied upon:
(a) Breaches of implied terms of the contracts of employment that the nine employees would faithfully serve Faccenda and 'would not use confidential information and/or trade secrets gained by them and each of them whilst in [Faccenda's] employment to the disadvantage or detriment of [Faccenda], whether during the currency of such employment or after its cessation'.
(b) An unlawful conspiracy 'together to injure [Faccenda's] goodwill and connection by unlawfully making use of the said confidential information and/or trade secrets of [Faccenda] gained by the individual defendants whilst in [Faccenda's] employment'.

20   A year later, on 16.9.82, Mr Fowler issued a writ in the Queen's Bench Division claiming nearly £23,000 in respect of commission which he said was due to him. In these proceedings Faccenda served a counterclaim which in effect repeated the allegations of breaches of contract and conspiracy and also included a claim for £435 in respect of the chickens which it was said Mr Fowler had wrongly converted in 1980 and which had been the subject-matter of the criminal proceedings in which Mr Fowler had been acquitted.

21   The Queen's Bench action was transferred to the Chancery Division in March 1983.

22   On 27.6.83 the two actions came on for hearing together before Mr Justice Goulding. After a hearing lasting 39 days, the learned judge, in a reserved judgment delivered on 8.11.83, dismissed the claims by Faccenda for damages for breach of contract and for conspiracy. At the same time he gave judgment for Mr Fowler for £15,316 in respect of his claim for commission and interest after making a deduction in respect of the amount claimed by Faccenda in conversion, where a sum was conceded by way of set-off without an admission of liability.

Figure 1.4 continued

23   At the trial the claims for injunctions which had been included in the writ in the Chancery action were not pursued owing to the lapse of time. An injunction had been granted and certain undertakings had been given at an interlocutory stage, but it is not necessary for us to make any further reference to these matters, as it is agreed that the interlocutory orders have no relevance to the issues now before the court.

24   Moreover, we need only make passing reference to the fact that at the trial a substantial amount of time was taken to deal with allegations put forward on behalf of Faccenda to the effect that documents in the possession of some of the employees during the period of their employment had been wrongfully used or copied.

25   The learned judge came to the conclusion that none of these allegations had been satisfactorily proved.

26   We can therefore concentrate our attention on the matters round which the argument before us principally revolved.

27   The main case put forward on behalf of Faccenda before Mr Justice Goulding, and the only factual basis for the claims relied upon before us, was that Mr Fowler and the other former employees of Faccenda as well as the new Fowler company had wrongfully made use of confidential information which Mr Fowler and his colleagues had acquired while in the employment of Faccenda.

28   This information, which was described by the judge compendiously as 'the sales information', can be listed under five headings:
(1) the names and addresses of customers;
(2) the most convenient routes to be taken to reach the individual customers;
(3) the usual requirements of individual customers, both as to quantity and quality;
(4) the days of the week and the time of the day when deliveries were usually made to individual customers;
(5) the prices charged to individual customers.

29   It was submitted on behalf of Faccenda that this sales information could be regarded as a package which, taken as a whole, constituted 'confidential information' which could not be used to the detriment of Faccenda.

30   In addition, however, particular attention was directed to the prices charged to individual customers, because, it was submitted, information as to prices was itself 'confidential information', quite apart from the fact that such information formed a constituent element of the package of sales information. Thus our attention was drawn to the following passage in the judgment:
'Counsel for Faccenda . . . , in the course of evidence and argument, paid special attention to the importance of knowing the prices paid by the respective customers . . . There has been much controversy regarding the extent to which one trader's prices are generally known to his rivals in the fresh chicken market. I find that an experienced salesman quickly acquires a good idea of the prices obtained by his employer's competitors, but usually such knowledge is only approximate; and in this field accurate information is valuable, because a difference of even a penny a pound may be important.'

31   It was further said on behalf of Faccenda that by wrongfully making use of this confidential sales information Mr Fowler and his colleagues had seriously damaged Faccenda's business.

32   We understand that at the trial it was suggested that the damages amounted to no less than about £180,000, though it may be noted that the judge concluded that, even if he had decided the issue of liability in favour of Faccenda, he would have assessed the damages at £5000.

33   In his judgment Mr Justice Goulding dealt with the allegations made by Faccenda in these terms:

Figure 1.4 continued

● Employment legislation

Statutes can be found on the Office of Public Sector Information website (www.opsi.gov.uk/acts.htm) or in libraries in volumes sorted by year. Statutes are normally referred to by a shortened version of their title and the year of publication: for example, the Equal Pay Act 1970.
  This Act is cited as:

Equal Pay Act 1970
1970 Chapter 41

Every Act published in a year is given a 'chapter number'. The chapter number 41 means that the Act was the forty-first to become law in 1970.
  The extract in Figure 1.5 is a copy of the first two pages from the Equal Pay Act 1970. The key explains what is meant by each number reference on the statute.

1

Courts and tribunals, sources and institutions of employment law

Equal Pay Act 1970

CHAPTER 41 ◄─②

ARRANGEMENT OF SECTIONS

Section

1. Requirement of equal treatment for men and women in same employment.
2. Disputes as to, and enforcement of, requirement of equal treatment.
3. Collective agreements and pay structures.
4. Wages regulation orders.
5. Agricultural wages orders.
6. Exclusion from ss. 1 to 5 of pensions etc.
7. Service pay.
8. Police pay.
9. Commencement.
10. Preliminary references to Industrial Court.
11. Short title, interpretation and extent.

Figure 1.5 The first two pages of the Equal Pay Act 1970

(Crown Copyright 1970. Parliamentary copyright material from Acts of Parliament is reproduced with the permission of the Controller of Her Majesty's Stationery Office and the Queen's Printer for Scotland.)

Key

1 The short title – Equal Pay Act 1970
2 Chapter number – the 41st Act of 1970
3 List of the Sections contained in the Act
4 Date of Royal Assent – 29th May 1970

5 Enacting formula
6 Section number and subsection
7 Marginal explanatory note
8 Subsection

1970 CHAPTER 41

An Act to prevent discrimination, as regards terms and conditions of employment, between men and women.

[29th May 1970] ← 4

BE IT ENACTED by the Queen's most Excellent Majesty, by and with the advice and consent of the Lords Spiritual and Temporal, and Commons, in this present Parliament assembled, and by the authority of the same, as follows:—

5

6   1.—(1) The provisions of this section shall have effect with a view to securing that employers give equal treatment as regards terms and conditions of employment to men and to women, that is to say that (subject to the provisions of this section and of section 6 below)—

Requirement of equal treatment for men and women in same employment.   7

    (*a*) for men and women employed on like work the terms and conditions of one sex are not in any respect less favourable than those of the other ; and

    (*b*) for men and women employed on work rated as equivalent (within the meaning of subsection (5) below) the terms and conditions of one sex are not less favourable than those of the other in any respect in which the terms and conditions of both are determined by the rating of their work.

The following provisions of this section and section 2 below are framed with reference to women and their treatment relative to men, but are to be read as applying equally in a converse case to men and their treatment relative to women.

8   (2) It shall be a term of the contract under which a woman is employed at an establishment in Great Britain that she shall be given equal treatment with men in the same employment, that is to say men employed by her employer or any associated employer at the same establishment or at establishments in Great Britain which include that one and at which common terms and conditions of employment are observed either generally or for employees of the relevant classes.

Figure 1.5 continued

Courts and tribunals, sources and institutions of employment law   1

OTHER SOURCES OF INFORMATION

Apart from cases and statutes, there are many secondary sources of employment law that can be an aid to study. There are various employment law textbooks available. Where appropriate, guidance on extra reading is given at the end of each chapter in this book. Apart from textbooks, the employment law student may also find the use of a case and statute book beneficial.

Case books contain copies of all of the relevant cases on each employment law topic. Comment is also made on the decisions made in the cases. There are several good case books on the market, the most recent being *Cases and Materials on Employment Law* by Richard Painter and Ann Holmes (Oxford University Press, 2006).

Statute books contain copies of the relevant sections from both national and European legislation. Again there are several on the market. One that also includes copies of codes of practice is *Blackstone's Statutes on Employment Law*. This is compiled by Richard Kidner and is updated annually.

Journals

Journal articles are an invaluable source of up-to-date employment law information. Most libraries stock at least some of the journals listed below. Guidance on extra reading from journals is given at the end of each chapter in this text. The main sources of employment law articles are found in:

- *Business Law Review*
- *Industrial Law Journal*
- *IDS Brief*
- *Labour Market Trends*
- *Equal Opportunities Review*
- *Employers' Law*
- *The New Law Journal*
- *Legal Action*
- *Industrial Relations Law Bulletin*.

Some journal articles can be complex and difficult to follow. Those in the *Business Law Review, IDS Brief* and *The New Law Journal* tend to set out the law in a very accessible way. Incomes Data Services, publishers of the *IDS Brief*, also produce handbooks which accompany the *Brief*. These concentrate on individual areas of employment law and are very comprehensive and easy to follow.

The Legal Journals Index

The Legal Journals Index provides details on all employment law articles which have been published over the last two decades. The index may be found in paper format in the library or more often appears as part of networked information. It can often be accessed as part of the Current Legal Information package noted below.

Online resources

Current Legal Information

Depending on the type of computer facilities available, students may be able to access the Current Legal Information package. This database is normally accessible on the network and provides current information on journal articles, cases and legislation. The system allows searches to be made specifically on employment law and is able to convey recent cases and developments in minutes.

IDS Brief

IDS Brief is a journal which is published every two weeks. It contains articles and case reports. There is also an online service. In order to access the full range of facilities you need access to a subscription password. This gives you access to case reports and information on all sections of employment law. However, even without a password the site provides useful information on employment law topics, and contains articles on recent developments – www.idsbrief.co.uk/.

Lexis Nexis

This service is part of the Butterworths online information services. It can be accessed via subscription using a password. It contains an online employment law service giving access to cases, legislation and references to journal articles.

Westlaw

This online service provides access to cases, articles, newspaper reports and legislation. This is a subscription service, which requires a password in order to gain entry to the site.

Athens

You will often find access to the above services via an 'Athens' password. This is an academic network which allows access to various sites. It is worth finding out what services are provided by your university or college.

www.emplaw.co.uk

This site deserves a particular mention. It provides user-friendly information on employment law. There is a 'free section' which can be accessed without a password. You can also purchase a password to gain entry to the 'professional' section of the site. Although it does not provide references to articles it is a very comprehensive and easy to follow site. You can also register for 'What's new?' email updates. I would strongly recommend that you make yourself familiar with this site early in your study of employment law.

Useful websites

There are various websites containing information on employment law in general, recent cases and legislation. The following list reflects only some of those available:

www.dti.gov.uk The Department of Trade and Industry: link to the 'Employment Matters' section which contains information on employment law topics, information on proposed new legislation/campaigns, access to leaflets and other publications and a link to the Directgov/employees site (www.direct.gov.uk/Employment/Employees). The site provides a link to the interactive 'tiger' website.

www.tiger.gov.uk Provides interactive information on the minimum wage, maternity, paternity and adoption rights, written in a user-friendly manner, easy to understand and apply.

www.dfes.gov.uk The Department for Education and Skills: mainly concerned with education issues but does contain employment law information under 'employers' link and provides useful links to other sites.

Courts and tribunals, sources and institutions of employment law

www.dwp.gov.uk The Department for Work and Pensions: information on benefits, statistics and current research.

www.opsi.gov.uk The Office of Public Sector Information: contains information on a wide range of official publications, links to other government sites and access to UK Acts of Parliament.

www.parliament.uk The Parliament site: contains information: on the bills before Parliament, Acts of Parliament, committees, lists of MPs and detail on the working and organisation of the House of Commons and the House of Lords.

www.eoc.org.uk Equal Opportunities Commission: source of press releases, leaflets and other publications. Also contains general information on the role of the Commission and on sex discrimination, equal pay legislation and maternity/paternity rights. Promotes 'good practice' in the workplace.

www.equalitydirect.org.uk Equality Direct: designed for managers but does provide accessible information on equality legislation.

www.cre.gov.uk Commission for Racial Equality: source of press releases, leaflets and other publications. Also contains general information on the role of the Commission and on race discrimination legislation. Promotes 'good practice' in the workplace.

www.drc-gb.org Disability Rights Commission: source of press releases, leaflets and other publications, information on recent policy and campaigns. A useful 'know your rights' section detailing information on legislation and regulations, promotes the rights of disabled people.

www.hse.gov.uk Health and Safety Executive: source of press releases, leaflets and other publications, information on recent safety campaigns, enforcement action and the role of the Executive. Also, a useful 'workers' webpage' containing links to information on health and safety law. This website also provides links to information on the role of the Health and Safety Commission.

www.tribunals.gov.uk The Tribunals Service: provides administrative support to both the Employment Tribunals Service and the Employment Appeal Tribunal. Provides information on the service's role and functions. Also provides useful addresses and links to both the Employment Tribunals and Employment Appeal Tribunal websites.

www.employmenttribunals.gov.uk Employment Tribunals: information on how to apply to the Employment Tribunal, leaflets and publications, locations of tribunal offices, information on tribunal hearings. There is also a facility by which you can apply to a tribunal online or complete a 'notice of appearance'.

www.employmentappeals.gov.uk The Employment Appeal Tribunal: information on procedure, forms and judgments.

www.hmcourts-service.gov.uk The Court Service: provides guidance on how to make a claim, outlines the role of various courts and explains some legal terminology.

www.legalservices.gov.uk Legal Services Commission: provides information on the role of the Commission which administers the Community Legal Service and Criminal Defence Service.

www.clsdirect.org.uk Community Legal Service: provides information on civil 'legal aid' and on the location of various advice agencies.

www.europa.eu.int The European Union: information on the Institutions, an overview on the composition and workings of the EU, access to official documents and news stories.

www.echr.coe.int The European Court of Human Rights: information on the role and composition of the court, pending cases, judgments and decisions.

www.curia.eu.int The European Court of Justice: information on the composition and role of the court, procedures, judgments and press releases.

www.acas.co.uk Advisory, Conciliation and Arbitration Service: a really useful site which outlines the role of Acas and provides advice on the main employment law topics. Also gives access to publications, handbooks, leaflets and codes of practice.

www.tuc.org.uk Trades Union Congress: outlines the role of the TUC, provides information on a range of employment law issues, campaigns, recent developments and publications. Site also contains a free registration 'email update' facility.

www.lowpay.gov.uk Low Pay Commission: Commission was formed to advise the Government on the National Minimum Wage, provides information on minimum wage rates, reports and publications.

www.incomesdata.co.uk Incomes Data Services: information on a wide range of employment related issues including international comparisons, comment on legislation and procedure and a link to the *IDS Brief* site.

www.cac.gov.uk Central Arbitration Committee: information on the role and membership of the Committee, annual reports, hearings, decisions and publications.

www.certoffice.org Certification Officer: information on the role of the Officer, reports, guidance and decisions.

www.statistics.gov.uk National Statistics: government statistics on a wide range of employment related topics.

www.efa.org.uk Employer's Forum on Age: information promoting 'age diversity' in the workplace.

www.agepositive.gov.uk Age Positive: information on age discrimination and flexible working for older workers.

www.venables.co.uk Delia Venables: information on online legal resources in the UK and Ireland.

www.ico.gov.uk Information Commissioner: information on the role of the Commissioner, the Data Protection Act, news and publications.

www.workingfamilies.org.uk Working Families: the United Kingdom's 'leading work–life balance organisation'. Contains factsheets on issues such as maternity/paternity rights and flexible working.

www.cehr.org.uk The Commission for Equality and Human Rights: information on the CEHR and the Equality Act 2006.

INSTITUTIONS OF EMPLOYMENT LAW

The operation and development of employment law is regulated and assisted by selected government departments and other institutions working in specific fields.

Various government departments are responsible for employment law issues. These include the Department of Trade and Industry (Employment Relations Directorate), the Department for Work and Pensions and the Department for Education and Skills. Each Department is headed by a Secretary of State. The Employment Relations Directorate of the DTI is responsible for the development of legislation on employment issues.

Advisory, Conciliation and Arbitration Service (Acas)

The 2004/5 Acas annual report states that its mission is 'to improve organisations and working life through better employment relationships'. The report states that Acas provides 'up-to-date information, independent advice, high quality training', and that the organisation works with 'employers and employees to solve problems and improve performance'.

Acas was established in 1974 to improve industrial relations. It is now governed by s 247 of the Trade Union and Labour Relations (Consolidation) Act 1992. The service is headed by a chairman and overall guidance is provided by the Acas Council. At the time of writing the Acas Council has 11 part-time members. Several members represent employee organisations such as trade unions. Several represent employer organisations and the remainder are those with particular experience in employment issues such as personnel officers and academics. The Acas Council is responsible for determining the strategic direction, policies and priorities of Acas and for ensuring that its statutory duties are carried out effectively.

Appointments are initially for a period of five years but can be reviewed after this time. The chairman is appointed by the Secretary of State and although the Service is funded by the government, it remains independent. Acas is based in London but has offices in all of the major regions.

As its name suggests, the functions of Acas are threefold. It provides advice, conciliation and arbitration in employment cases.

Advice

Acas gives general employment advice over the telephone, and produces a mass of leaflets on employment law and personnel-related issues. Copies of these leaflets can be obtained from the Acas address noted in the Appendix. Copies of Acas publications are also available on their website. These can be ordered online. Many can also be printed direct from the site. Since December 2002 Acas have also administered a national public helpline. At the time of writing the telephone number for this service is 0845 7474747.

Acas is able to give advice on collective matters and run conferences and seminars dealing with industrial relations issues. It may charge for some services including handbooks. It does not, however, charge for advice on employment matters.

Acas produces codes of practice, advisory booklets and handbooks. The main advisory handbooks are: *Discipline and Grievances at Work*, and the *A–Z of Work* which provide details on most employment issues. Acas also publishes a *Model Workplace* booklet which is described as 'a one-stop guide which identifies the features of an organisation which manages people effectively.' The booklet contains information on issues such as health and safety, equal pay, discipline and grievance procedures and equality and discrimination. The three Acas codes of practice are:

- No. 1 Disciplinary and Grievance Procedures (2004)
- No. 2 Disclosure of Information to Trade Unions for Collective Bargaining Purposes (revised 1997)
- No. 3 Time Off for Trade Union Duties and Activities (revised 2003).

Conciliation

In 2004/5 Acas conciliated in almost 87000 applications to employment tribunals. The majority of tribunal applications are sent to Acas. When an application is received by Acas, it appoints a conciliation officer to the case. This person tries to negotiate between the parties to promote a settlement of the dispute before it is heard in the tribunal. Either party to a dispute may also ask Acas to intervene before any application is made to the tribunal. Conciliation is voluntary and both parties have to agree to the involvement of Acas. The 2004/5 Acas annual report states that 77 per cent of cases were resolved before going to a tribunal hearing.

Acas may also conciliate in collective disputes involving employers and unions. The aim of such conciliation is to prevent or stop industrial action. In such cases one party must ask for conciliation to take place.

The Employment Act 2002 modified the role of the conciliation officer. Since 1 October 2004 their duty to conciliate has been limited to 7 weeks for certain claims, e.g. breach of contract and redundancy, and 13 weeks for most other claims. At the end of these periods, the conciliation officer can exercise a discretionary power to offer conciliation. It is likely that the time period will only be extended if the officer believes that an early settlement of the case is likely. Once this fixed period has expired it will then be left to the officer to decide whether to continue to conciliate or pass the claim on to the Employment Tribunal for deliberation. The time restraints are designed to encourage and promote the early settlement of claims. It should be noted that claims relating to discrimination, equal pay and public interest disclosure are excluded from these fixed consultation periods.

Arbitration

If both parties consent, their dispute may be referred to Acas for arbitration. This will only happen if the possibility of reaching a settlement by way of conciliation has been pursued and was unsuccessful.

Acas officers do not arbitrate themselves, but appoint an independent arbitrator to hear the case. The arbitrator is selected from a list kept by Acas or the Central Arbitration Committee. The arbitrator will hear both sides to the dispute and attempt a compromise between the parties that will lead to settlement of the case. The decision of the arbitrator is not binding and the parties may choose not to accept it and pursue the case further. Cases may also be referred to the Central Arbitration Committee.

Acas also administer an arbitration scheme relating only to complaints involving alleged unfair dismissal or flexible working disputes. This scheme initially became operational in 2001 and is further discussed at page 254.

Central Arbitration Committee (CAC)

The Central Arbitration Committee was established under the Employment Act 1975. It is an independent source of arbitration and is now governed by s 259 of the Trade Union and Labour Relations (Consolidation) Act 1992. The Committee is staffed by a chairman, 11 deputy chairmen and 44 representatives from both sides of industry. Twenty-three of these representatives are 'experienced representatives of employers' and the other 21 'members experienced as representatives of workers'.

All members of the Committee are appointed by the Secretary of State for Trade and Industry following consultation with Acas. The Committee's main function is to adjudicate on applications relating to the statutory recognition or derecognition of trade unions for collective bargaining purposes. The Committee also hears complaints from trade unions alleging that an employer has failed to disclose information for collective bargaining purposes and also adjudicates on certain disputes arising out of the provisions of the Information and Consultation Regulations 2004 and the Transnational Information and Consultation of Employees Regulations 1999. It also has a statutory role in disposing of claims and complaints regarding the establishment and operation of European Works Councils. The Central Arbitration Committee encourages parties to reach a settlement by suggesting solutions to their dispute. It can also arbitrate over matters concerning industrial disputes referred to it by Acas. However, the parties in the dispute have to agree to the Committee becoming involved. A decision of the Committee cannot be appealed.

The Department of Trade and Industry and related government departments (DTI)

The DTI and other government departments (see page 25) are each staffed by a Secretary of State. These are government ministers appointed to deal with and be a spokesperson for employment issues. They may issue codes of practice and approve draft codes. The minister also receives notification of proposed redundancies and approves agreements concerning the allocation of redundancy payments. They also review financial limits, for example, on unfair dismissal payments.

Commission for Equality and Human Rights (CEHR)

The Equality Act 2006 received Royal Assent on 16 February 2006. This Act established the new Commission for Equality and Human Rights (CEHR). The CEHR will replace the Equal Opportunities Commission, the Commission for Racial Equality and the Disability Rights Commission.

At the time of writing it is estimated that the new Commission will become operational in October 2007. The work of the EOC and the DRC will be integrated into the new Commission from that time. The work of the CRE will be integrated from April 2009. From October 2007 the new Commission will also be responsible for promoting equality and tackling discrimination in relation to sexual orientation, age and religion or belief. It will also be responsible for the promotion of human rights, providing institutional support for the Human Rights Act 1998.

The CEHR vision statement states that the Commission will 'be an independent, influential champion whose purpose is to reduce inequality, eliminate discrimination, strengthen good relations between people and protect human rights'.

Section 3 of the Equality Act 2006 covers the 'general duty' of the CEHR. This section states that the Commission shall 'exercise its functions ... with a view to encouraging and supporting the development of a society in which –

(a) people's ability to achieve their potential is not limited by prejudice or discrimination,

(b) there is respect for and protection of each individual's human rights,

(c) there is respect for the dignity and worth of each individual,

(d) each individual has an equal opportunity to participate in society, and

(e) there is mutual respect between groups based on understanding and valuing of diversity and on shared respect for equality and human rights.'

The Commission will be staffed by up to 15 Commissioners including a Chair, and a Commissioner for Scotland and a Commissioner for Wales. There is also a requirement that one Commissioner be a disabled person. The Commission will also have the power to appoint advisory committees and will be able to issue codes of practice. The Commission will be based at two main sites in Manchester and London. There will also be offices in Glasgow and Cardiff and others located throughout the country.

The duties of the CEHR will include:

● providing information, advice and assistance on equality and diversity and human rights;

● issuing guidance and good practice that will help employers, service providers, voluntary organisations and trade unions embrace equality and human rights;

- conducting formal inquiries and investigations where there are persistent inequalities, human rights issues or where there is evidence of unlawful discrimination; and

- providing support for individuals making anti-discrimination claims, intervening in cases where equality and human rights arguments need to be made and where appropriate providing conciliation.

The Commission will also publish a 'state of the nation' report every three years. This will outline those areas in which Britain is failing on equality and human rights issues. The report will also put forward proposals for improvement.

At the time of writing the government is also under pressure to pass a single discrimination Act to replace the various anti-discrimination statutes currently in existence. This proposal has been debated several times over the last decade but it seems inevitable that it will receive serious consideration once the new CEHR is operational.

The amalgamation of the existing Commissions into one 'super-Commission' is widely anticipated. It is thought that having a single Commission will have many benefits. These include the bringing together of experts on all forms of discrimination and the provision of a single point of contact for anyone requiring advice or assistance with discrimination issues.

The CEHR website will contain updated information on the setting up and role of the Commission prior to October 2007. It will then expand to include information on the constitution, role and work of the Commission. At the time of writing there is a link to the CEHR 'vision statement' from the website. This statement contains a wealth of information on the anticipated role and organisation of the new Commission. The CEHR website can be accessed at **www.cehr.org.uk**.

● Equal Opportunities Commission (EOC)

The Equal Opportunities Commission was established under the Sex Discrimination Act 1975. The EOC is staffed by 8–15 members. The duties of the EOC are to:

- work towards the elimination of discrimination on the grounds of sex;
- promote equality of opportunity between men and women;
- review the operation of the Sex Discrimination Act and the Equal Pay Act;
- submit proposals for amendment of the above legislation;
- act against discriminatory job advertisements;
- conduct enquiries into discriminatory practices.

The EOC may assist in individual sex-discrimination or equal-pay cases if the case is a 'test case'. This means that it must involve a new legal principle or argument that has not been discussed before. Under s 75 of the Sex Discrimination Act 1975 the EOC may also assist an individual in the bringing of an action where it would be unreasonable to expect the individual to be able to handle the case alone. This could be where the case is complex or where, for whatever reasons, the applicant is perceived to be unable to take the matter further without help.

Assistance may involve the giving of advice or paying for representation in a tribunal. The EOC may also attempt to secure a settlement of the case before any formal action is taken. The EOC's financial resources are limited, so it is unable to assist in every case that is brought to its attention.

The EOC may also investigate the practices taking place within a company. However, it can only organise an investigation where it has some suspicion that discriminatory acts are taking place. The EOC may also act to prevent the use of discriminatory job advertisements.

Where the EOC finds evidence of the use of discriminatory practices or job advertisements it may issue non-discriminatory notices ordering the employer not to discriminate in the future. Employers must comply with the notice and provide the EOC with evidence as to how they have done so. If employers do not comply with the notice, the EOC is able to apply to the County Court for an injunction to prevent them from discriminating further.

The EOC has also produced two codes of practice to guide employers as to what is good practice in the field of equality. These codes are:

- The Elimination of Discrimination on the Grounds of Sex and Marriage and the Promotion of Equality of Opportunity in Employment (1985);
- Equal Pay (2003).

From October 2007 the Equal Opportunities Commission will cease to exist as an independent body and its work will be undertaken by the Commission for Equality and Human Rights.

Commission for Racial Equality (CRE)

The CRE was established under the Race Relations Act 1976. Its duties are to:

- work towards the elimination of racial discrimination and to promote equality of opportunity;
- encourage good relations between people from different racial backgrounds;
- monitor the way the Race Relations Act 1976 is working and recommend ways in which it can be improved.

The CRE can advise and assist individuals who complain of racial discrimination. It may assist in individual cases where under s 66 of the Race Relations Act 1976 it is 'unreasonable to expect the individual to deal with the application unaided' or if there are any 'special circumstances'.

The CRE may conduct a formal investigation of a company suspected of discriminating on the basis of race. If it finds that a company is discriminating on racial grounds, it can order the company to change its policies. This is done by the issue of a non-discriminatory notice inform-ing the employer that it must not discriminate or use discriminatory practices in the future. If the employer does not comply with the notice the CRE can apply to the County Court for an injuction to prevent them from discriminating further.

The CRE can take legal action if it sees a job advertisement that discriminates on the grounds of race. It may issue a non-discrimination notice or can apply to the County Court and request an injunction to prevent the advertisement from being used or the company from repeating such use in the future.

The CRE may also issue codes of practice to promote good practice in the field of race relations. The CRE issued a code of practice in 2006. This code is referred to as 'The Statutory Code of Prac-tice on Racial Equality in Employment' (2006). The code came into force on 6 April 2006 and replaces the 1984 code of practice on the 'elimination of racial discrimination and the promotion of equality of opportunity in employment'. The 2006 code contains a set of recommendations and guidance on how to avoid unlawful racial discrimination and harassment in employment.

The CRE also issued a code of practice in 2002. This code is concerned with 'The Elimination of Unlawful Racial Discrimination and Promotion of Equality of Opportunity and Good Race Relations'. This code was brought into effect in May 2002 and relates to the duties imposed on public authorities under the Race Relations (Amendment) Act 2000. The 2006 code remains the most important source of guidance on race relations. From April 2009 the Commission for Racial Equality will cease to exist as an independent body and its work will be undertaken by the Com-mission for Equality and Human Rights.

Disability Rights Commission (DRC)

The Disability Rights Commission was established under the Disability Rights Commission Act 1999. This Act abolished the National Disability Council. The Commission became operational in April 2000 and is staffed by 10–15 members, the majority of whom must be disabled. The duties of the DRC are to:

- work towards the elimination of discrimination against disabled persons;
- promote equality of opportunity for disabled persons;
- encourage good practice in the treatment of disabled persons;
- review the operation of the Disability Discrimination Act 1995;
- submit proposals or give advice to the government on the improvement and amendment of legislation;
- provide advice and information on disability rights.

The DRC can advise and assist individuals who complain of discrimination on the grounds of disability. It may provide legal advice or fund representation in the tribunal. The Commission may assist in individual cases where under s 7 of the Disability Rights Commission Act 1999 the case 'raises a question of principle' (a test case), where it would be 'unreasonable to expect the applicant to deal with the case unaided', or if there are other 'special considerations'.

The Commission may conduct a formal investigation where it believes that either an individual or a company may be discriminating against disabled persons. If, having completed an investigation they find that discrimination is taking place they are able to issue a non-discrimination notice. This notice requires the individual/company to stop using discriminatory practices at the time of issue and in the future. If the notice is not complied with the Commission can apply to the County Court for an injunction to prevent those concerned from being able to continue to discriminate.

Under s 5 of the 1999 Act the Commission may suspend a formal investigation to seek to reach a statutory agreement rather than issue a non-discrimination notice. This right does not apply to the Equal Opportunities Commission or the Commission for Racial Equality. Unlike the EOC and the CRE the DRC does not have the power to make a complaint following the publication of a discriminatory job advertisement.

The DRC has produced a code of practice to guide employers as to what is good practice in the field of equality. The code is referred to as that on: 'Employment and Occupation' (2004). There is also an accompanying guidance document entitled 'Guidance on matters to be taken into account in determining questions relating to the definition of disability' (2006). This revised guidance came into force on 1 May 2006. From October 2007 the Disability Rights Commission will cease to exist as an independent body and its work will be undertaken by the Commission for Equality and Human Rights.

Low Pay Commission (LPC)

The Low Pay Commission was formed in 1997 and given legal status under the National Minimum Wage Act 1998. It is staffed by a Chairman and 8 other members. The function of the Commission is to monitor and evaluate the impact of the national minimum wage. It can also recommend that the set minimum wage be increased. Its current terms of reference are:

- to continue to monitor and evaluate the impact of the national minimum wage, with particular reference to the effect on pay, employment and competitiveness in low paying sectors and small firms; the effect on different groups of workers; the effect on pay structures; and the interaction between the national minimum wage and the tax and benefit systems; and

● to review the levels of both the main national minimum wage rate and the development rate and make recommendations, if appropriate, for change.

The government does not have to accept any of the Commission's recommendations but in practice many of them are followed.

The permanent status of the Commission was confirmed by the government in 2002 and it was then given a remit for a programme of longer-term research.

Certification Officer (CO)

This position was established in 1975 and is governed by s 254 of the Trade Union and Labour Relations (Consolidation) Act 1992. The role of the Certification Officer is to maintain a list of independent trade unions and to issue certificates of independence to such unions. The CO also keeps records of union annual membership, financial returns, and copies of union rules.

The CO may investigate complaints concerning the election of trade-union officials, allegations that proper membership records have not been kept or where there is alleged discrepancy in the balloting procedures for setting up political funds. The CO may also appoint an inspector to investigate union practices where fraud is suspected. The role of the CO was enhanced by Schedule 6 of the Employment Relations Act 1999. Under this provision a union member can complain to the CO if they think that there has been a breach or threatened breach of union rules. The CO has the power to require the union to remedy any such breach.

The Health and Safety Commission (HSC)

The Health and Safety Commission was established under s 10 of the Health and Safety at Work Act 1974. It is staffed by a chairman, and 6–9 commissioners. The commissioners represent employer and employee organisations. The HSC is largely an advisory body and although independent of the government is accountable to the Parliamentary Under Secretary for Work and Pensions.

The duties of the Health and Safety Commission are to:

● assist and encourage persons to further the general purposes of the Health and Safety at Work Act 1974;
● arrange research into health and safety issues;
● promote education, training and information on health and safety issues;
● act as an information and advice service;
● submit proposals for health and safety regulations;
● issue codes of practice.

The HSC can organise an investigation of a company that it thinks does not provide adequate levels of safety for its workers. The HSC publishes many informative leaflets and booklets on health and safety issues. Copies can be obtained from the Commission's address in the Appendix.

Health and Safety Executive (HSE)

The Health and Safety Executive was established under s 10 of the Health and Safety at Work Act 1974. It is staffed by a director, two deputy directors and many administrative and technical employees. The HSE is answerable to the Health and Safety Commission on all matters except the enforcement of health and safety legislation.

The HSE is largely an enforcement agency. It may investigate and report on accidents at work. It uses local authority inspectors to report on and inspect incidents in shops, hotels, catering and sports facilities. Its inspectors report and inspect incidents in factories, building sites, mines, quarries, railways, chemical plants and fairgrounds.

The HSE enforces the provisions of the Health and Safety at Work Act 1974 and the regulations made under it. It may issue improvement or prohibition notices to improve safety standards and may prosecute where employers refuse to raise standards.

● The Information Commissioner (IC)

The Office of the Information Commissioner was established by the Data Protection Act 1998. The office was previously referred to as that of the Data Protection Commissioner. The IC is there to enforce and oversee the Data Protection Act 1998 and the Freedom of Information Act 2000.

The IC is a United Kingdom independent supervisory authority which reports directly to Parliament. It is responsible for 'the promotion of good information handling and the encouragement of codes of practice for data controllers'. Data controllers are defined as 'anyone who decides how and why personal data is processed'. The Commissioner issued a draft code of practice for employers in December 2000.

The final code of practice was issued in four stages. A complete consolidated version of the code of practice on 'Data Protection in the Employment Field' was published in June 2005. The code is comprised of four parts:

- Part 1 – 'Recruitment and Selection: An Employer's Guide'.
- Part 2 – 'Employment Records'.
- Part 3 – 'Monitoring of Employees'.
- Part 4 – 'Information about Workers' Health'.

SUMMARY CHECKLIST

- **Employment cases are brought in either the County Court, High Court or Employment Tribunal.**
- **The sources of employment law are the common law, legislation, European law, codes of practice and regulations.**
- **Various institutions regulate and monitor employment law.**
- **Cases concerning breach of contract, wrongful dismissal or injunctions are brought in the courts.**
- **Cases concerning claims of e.g. unfair dismissal, discrimination, equal pay and redundancy payments are brought in the Employment Tribunal.**
- **Some breach of contract claims can be brought in either a court or a tribunal.**
- **Employment Tribunals are administered by the Employment Tribunals Service, through Regional Offices.**
- **Appeals from a tribunal decision can be made on a point of law only to the Employment Appeal Tribunal.**
- **Common law is the law made by judges when they announce their decision in each case.**

- Important decisions are reported in law reports.
- Legislation is drafted by the government.
- Legislation may govern either the civil or criminal law.
- European law has had a major impact on our national employment law.
- The sources of European law are Treaties, Directives, Regulations, Decisions, Recommendations and Opinions.
- Codes of practice do not have the same legal significance as legislation but are important reflections of what is good practice.
- Employment law cases are reported in the *All England Law Reports*, the *Weekly Law Reports*, the *Industrial Relations Law Reports* and the *Industrial Cases Reports*.
- The citation given to a case shows its location within the law reports.
- Other sources of information include textbooks, case and statute books, journals and the Internet.
- Acas provide advice, conciliation and arbitration.
- The Central Arbitration Committee hears complaints from trade unions and arbitrates in cases referred by Acas.
- The Equal Opportunities Commission works to combat gender discrimination.
- The Commission for Racial Equality works to combat racial discrimination.
- The Disability Rights Commission works to combat disability discrimination.
- The EOC, CRE and DRC can issue non-discriminatory notices to stop employers from using discriminatory practices or apply for an injunction where they refuse to do so.
- From October 2007 there will be a Commission for Equality and Human Rights.
- The Low Pay Commission monitors and evaluates the impact of the national minimum wage.
- The Health and Safety Commission advises on health and safety matters, promotes education and training and issues codes of practice.
- The Health and Safety Executive enforces the Health and Safety at Work Act 1974, can issue improvement or prohibition notices or instigate prosecution.
- The Information Commissioner enforces and oversees the Data Protection Act 1998 and the Freedom of Information Act 2000.

SELF-TEST QUESTIONS

1 In which courts and tribunals are employment cases heard?

2 What are the sources of employment law?

3 What are the sources of European law?

4 What type of legal significance do codes of practice have?

5 In which law reports are you likely to find reports of employment cases?

6 If a case citation is '[1998] 1 All ER 33' where will it be found?

7 What is the role of the Advisory, Conciliation and Arbitration Service?

8 What will be the role of the Commission for Equality and Human Rights?

9 What is the role of the Low Pay Commission?

10 What are the roles of the Health and Safety Commission and the Health and Safety Executive?

Further reading

On general principles of English law

Introduction to the English Legal System, Martin Partington, 3rd edn. Oxford University Press, 2006.

On European law

Law of the European Union, John Fairhurst, 6th edn. Pearson Education, 2007.

On the use of a law library

How to use a law library, Jean Dane and Philip A. Thomas, 4th edn. Sweet & Maxwell, 2001.

For legal updates on the material in this chapter please go to the Companion Website accompanying this book at **www.mylawchamber.co.uk/nairns**

Courts and tribunals, sources and institutions of employment law

2 Discrimination in employment

Discrimination in the workplace may take various forms. When new job vacancies arise employers may discriminate in the way that they choose to advertise them. Their application forms or selection tests may be drafted in such a way so as to discriminate against some applicants. When selecting candidates to interview they may discriminate by rejecting a category of person without even reading their forms.

At the interview itself questions that discriminate may be asked and these may result in the employer deciding not to offer a job to a particular candidate. When the employer does select the successful candidate offering that person the job, the employer may have discriminated against the others for reasons not related to their suitability or previous experience. An employer may also discriminate against existing employees. This may take place when the employer refuses an employee training or promotion, or dismisses an employee for reasons unrelated to his work record or skill.

Discrimination is not confined to the workplace and we all experience it at some stage in life for whatever reason. Whilst the law cannot prevent employers from making subjective decisions based on their perceptions of an applicant or employee, it does attempt to regulate those areas in which discrimination is known to be widespread.

Discrimination on the basis of sex, race or disability are the most common forms but a person can also be discriminated against on the grounds of age, religious beliefs, political persuasion, trade-union membership, sexual orientation or for having a criminal record.

Anti-discrimination legislation makes it unlawful to discriminate both during the recruitment and selection process and after appointment. It provides individuals who feel that they have experienced discrimination with the right to complain to an Employment Tribunal.

The Equal Opportunities Commission, the Commission for Racial Equality and the Disability Rights Commission play a significant role in the enforcement of anti-discrimination law and the promotion of equal opportunities in the workplace. The role of the EOC, CRE and DRC are discussed in Chapter 1 at pages 29–31. These paragraphs should be re-read as an introduction to this chapter. Note also the comment on the role of the new Commission for Equality and Human Rights at page 28.

By first giving an overview of existing anti-discrimination law and defining what is meant by the term 'discrimination' this chapter goes on to discuss:

- the types of discrimination, direct, indirect and victimisation;
- direct and indirect sex discrimination;
- direct and indirect racial discrimination;
- victimisation;
- the stages at which discrimination may take place;
- possible defences – justification, genuine occupational qualifications;

- other unlawful acts such as the use of discriminatory job advertisements;
- positive discrimination;
- European sex discrimination law;
- discrimination on the grounds of sexual orientation and transsexualism;
- discrimination on the grounds of pregnancy;
- sexual and racial harassment;
- the Equal Opportunities Commission, Commission for Racial Equality and Disability Rights Commission codes of practice;
- disability discrimination, stages at which discrimination may take place, the duty to make reasonable adjustments, justification;
- discrimination on the grounds of age, political persuasion, religion or belief, trade-union involvement, and the rehabilitation of offenders;
- the Fixed-term Employees (Prevention of Less Favourable Treatment) Regulations 2002 and the Part-time Workers (Prevention of Less Favourable Treatment) Regulations 2000;
- making a discrimination claim to the Employment Tribunal, remedies and awards;
- the use of equal opportunities in the workplace and proposals for the reform of anti-discrimination law.

ANTI-DISCRIMINATION LAW

The law aims to control discrimination mainly on the grounds of sex, race and disability. The main statutes are:

- **Sex Discrimination Act 1975**
- **Sex Discrimination Act 1986**
- **Race Relations Act 1976**
- **Disability Discrimination Act 1995**
- **Disability Discrimination Act 2005**
- **Equality Act 2006**.

The law aims to ensure that all people are treated equally at work irrespective of their sex, race or disability. The Sex Discrimination Act 1975 also prohibits discrimination on the grounds of marital status.

The Acts protect both those people applying for jobs and those already employed. An employee is protected from the first day of employment. There is no need for the employee to have worked for a particular employer for any length of time before making a tribunal claim. The Acts also extend protection to independent contractors and agency workers employed on a temporary basis.

The following statutes prohibit discrimination in the areas of trade-union membership and the rehabilitation of those people with criminal records:

- **Trade Union and Labour Relations (Consolidation) Act 1992**
- **Rehabilitation of Offenders Act 1974**.

European law has played a significant role in the development of the areas of sex discrimination and sexual harassment. The most significant piece of European law with regard to discrimination to date is the Equal Treatment Directive, referred to as the: 'EC Council Directive No. 76/207 on the implementation of the principle of equal treatment for men and women as regards access to employment, vocational training and promotion, and working conditions'. Over the last few years there has also been an expansion of European law in this area, a wider approach that takes into account more than just the problems of sex discrimination and sexual harassment. Article 13 of the Amsterdam Treaty states that appropriate action should be taken to 'combat discrimination based on sex, racial or ethnic origin, religion or belief, disability, age or sexual orientation'.

A new framework Equal Treatment Directive (EC 2000/78) was adopted in November 2000. This Directive is concerned with preventing discrimination on the grounds of religion or belief, disability, age or sexual orientation. The provisions in relation to religion or belief and sexual orientation were to be implemented by December 2003. The provisions were given legislative effect by the Employment Equality (Sexual Orientation) Regulations 2003 and the Employment Equality (Religion or Belief) Regulations 2003. A time extension was given with regard to provisions on age and disability discrimination. They were to be given legislative effect by 2006. The Disability Discrimination Act 1995 (Amendment) Regulations 2003 came into force on 1 October 2004. The Employment Equality (Age) Regulations 2006 came into force on 1 October 2006.

The EC Race Discrimination Directive (EC 2000/43) was adopted in June 2000. This Directive was to be implemented by the end of July 2003. The Race Relations Act 1976 (Amendment) Regulations 2003 came into force on 19 July 2003.

The Equal Treatment Amending Directive (EC 2002/73) amends the Equal Treatment Directive (EC 76/207). The Directive was to be implemented by 5 October 2005. These amendments make minor changes to the Sex Discrimination Act 1975 (in relation to harassment and indirect discrimination), and were implemented in the form of the Employment Equality (Sex Discrimination) Regulations 2005. These regulations came into force on 1 October 2005.

In summary the Regulations issued in response to these imposed changes are the:

- **Disability Discrimination Act 1995 (Amendment) Regulations 2003**
- **Employment Equality (Religion or Belief) Regulations 2003**
- **Employment Equality (Sexual Orientation) Regulations 2003**
- **Race Relations Act 1976 (Amendment) Regulations 2003**
- **Employment Equality (Sex Discrimination) Regulations 2005**
- **Employment Equality (Age) Regulations 2006**

These developments are discussed where appropriate in this chapter and summarised alongside other proposals for reform at page 98.

WHAT IS 'DISCRIMINATION'?

The dictionary definition of 'to discriminate' is 'to single someone out for a special favour or disfavour'. To single someone out for a special favour is to positively discriminate. (This is discussed further at page 64.) Here, we are concerned with the other form of discrimination, negative discrimination. To single someone out for disfavour means to come to a decision which disadvantages that person in some way. If this decision is made, for example, on the basis of gender, race or disability, it discriminates against the individual and is unlawful.

The law recognises three forms of discrimination:

- direct discrimination
- indirect discrimination
- victimisation.

Direct discrimination

Direct discrimination occurs when a person is treated less favourably because, for example, of that person's sex, marital status, race or disability. This is overt or blatant discrimination.

> ### Example
> *Margo applies for a teaching job at her local school. She is shortlisted and attends an interview. Before the interview the school headmaster informs the interview panel that he does not want to appoint a woman. He asks them to reject all female candidates. Margo is interviewed along with two other women and one man, Michael. Michael is offered the job. He has fewer qualifications and less teaching experience than Margo and the other women.*
> *Margo has been directly discriminated against because she is a woman.*

The same scenario could be used to illustrate discrimination against a man, someone from a particular racial group or someone with a disability.

When trying to decide whether direct discrimination has occurred the question to ask is:

Had this person been of a different sex, race or have no disability would he or she have been treated in the same way?

If the answer is 'no', direct discrimination has occurred. Examples of direct discrimination include:

- refusing to employ a woman because she has four children and so may have to take time off work when they are ill;
- refusing to interview a black candidate when white candidates with equivalent qualifications and experience are interviewed;
- refusing to employ a disabled person because of their disability.

Indirect discrimination

Indirect discrimination is hidden or covert discrimination. An action which may at first appear not to discriminate may on reflection be said to indirectly discriminate against a group of people.

> ### Example
> *A job advertisement states that applicants should be 'over 6 feet tall'. Christine applies for the job but is only 5 feet 4 inches tall. Her application is rejected on the basis of her height.*

The height requirement indirectly discriminates against women because fewer women than men are over 6 feet tall. This means that fewer women could comply with the height requirement and so be able to apply for the job.

Other examples of indirect discrimination include:

- a requirement that disadvantages part-time workers, many of whom are women;
- treatment that disadvantages workers with young children;
- the imposition of language tests which would exclude a large number of persons from ethnic minorities;
- a requirement that applicants live in a certain area of town which may exclude areas with a predominantly ethnic population.

● Victimisation

A person is discriminated against if he is victimised because of some previous or current involvement in a complaint made against his employer. The person may have:

● previously made a discrimination claim or other type of tribunal claim against the employer;

● started grievance proceedings at work; or

● given evidence in tribunal proceedings on behalf of a colleague or assisted him in the organisation of any proceedings.

In a claim alleging victimisation the employee would have to show that he has been treated less favourably as a result of his actions.

> ### Example
> William and Sharma work for Cool Sounds Ltd. Sharma has been refused promotion and believes that she has been discriminated against on racial grounds. She intends to make a complaint to the Employment Tribunal. William has agreed to be a witness in any tribunal proceedings and has advised her to go ahead with her claim. He has been told by his manager that if he does give evidence he can 'forget any chance of a bonus or promotion in the future'. He later gives evidence and is demoted.
>   William has been victimised for offering to help his colleague.

Other examples of victimisation include:

● pressurising an employee to withdraw a discrimination complaint;

● refusing holiday leave requests;

● writing poor references; or

● the over-monitoring of work and timekeeping.

The following cases highlight situations in which victimisation was alleged.

See also: *Aziz v Trinity Street Taxis* (1988), *Lindsay v Alliance & Leicester plc* (2000), *Chief Constable of West Yorkshire Police v Khan* (2001).

An employer accused of victimising an employee may be able to defend his actions if he can show that the original allegations were false or that the employee did not make them in good faith.

> ### Nagarajan v London Regional Transport (1999)
>
> Mr Gregory Nagarajan was well known to London Regional Transport. He had previously pursued various racial discrimination claims against both them and London Underground. Here, he had applied for a job as a Travel Information Assistant with London Regional Transport. He attended an interview but was unsuccessful in securing the position. He claimed that this was because the interview panel knew that he had previously brought discrimination claims against the organisation and that they had been influenced by that fact.
>
> *Held (HL)* He had been victimised. He had been treated less favourably than the other candidates due to the fact that the panel had known that he had previously made a racial discrimination claim.

Northants County Council v Dattani (1994)

Dattani had complained of racial discrimination. Northants County Council (NCC) began an internal investigation into the allegations. It began to interview witnesses and collect evidence but when Dattani made a complaint to the Industrial Tribunal, NCC's attitude changed. It halted the internal investigation and refused to discuss the matter further.

Held The stopping of the investigation amounted to victimisation because it would have been allowed to continue had Dattani not made the tribunal claim.

Sex, race and disability discrimination

The Sex Discrimination Act 1975 and the Race Relations Act 1976 recognise all three forms of discrimination. The Disability Discrimination Act 1995 only recognises direct discrimination and victimisation. The 1995 Act outlines another way in which an employer may discriminate against disabled persons. This is the employer's duty to make reasonable adjustments to their premises and is further discussed below.

The Acts also create other offences relating to, for example, the use of discriminatory job advertisements. The 1975 and 1976 Acts also recognise the possible defence to a job being specifically offered to a man, woman or person from a particular racial group where this is a genuine occupational qualification. All three Acts recognise situations where an employer may be able to justify their discriminatory actions.

Whilst the areas of direct and indirect sex and race discrimination are discussed separately below the other areas concerning victimisation, justification and genuine occupational qualification are discussed under one heading. Disability discrimination is discussed separately towards the end of the chapter.

SEX DISCRIMINATION

The Sex Discrimination Act 1975 states that it is unlawful to discriminate against a person on the basis of that individual's sex or marital status.

It recognises direct and indirect discrimination and victimisation. Whilst sex discrimination is usually thought of as being discrimination against women, s 2 of the Act states that it applies equally to discrimination against men.

The 1975 Act makes it unlawful for an employer to discriminate either during the recruitment and selection process or after appointment. It does not apply to any special treatment given to women in connection with pregnancy or childbirth or for health and safety reasons.

The Sex Discrimination Act 1986 amended the 1975 Act. It is concerned mainly with discrimination in collective bargaining and retirement ages. This section deals exclusively with the 1975 Act. A new s 1 and s 3 were inserted into the 1975 Act by the Sex Discrimination (Indirect Discrimination and Burden of Proof) Regulations 2001. The general scope of the sections remains unaffected. The changes were made to bring the legislation into line with the EC Directive on the Burden of Proof in Sex Discrimination Cases (77/80/EC). The Sex Discrimination Act 1975 (Amendment) Regulations 2003 came into force on 19 July 2003. These regulations state that:

(a) Chief Constables will be liable for sex discriminatory acts committed by officers in their force which were committed 'in the course of their employment', and that

(b) sex discriminatory acts which are committed by an employer after the affected employee's employment has ended will be unlawful.

Note also that the Employment Equality (Sex Discrimination) Regulations 2005 provided new definitions of 'indirect discrimination' and 'harassment'.

● A sex discrimination claim

Figure 2.1 outlines the possible stages involved in deciding whether or not a claim can be made for sex discrimination.

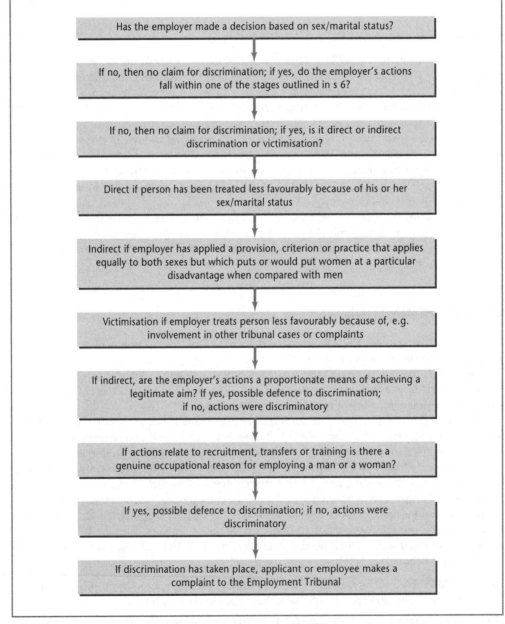

Figure 2.1 Is there a valid claim for sex discrimination?

Discrimination on the grounds of marital status

Section 3 of the Sex Discrimination Act 1975 states that it is unlawful to discriminate against a person because he or she is married. This means that a person cannot be discriminated against on the basis of her sex or marital status. In *Graham v Chief Constable of the Bedfordshire Constabulary* (2002) the EAT held that a police officer had been discriminated against due to the fact that she was married to a fellow officer. Had she been given the promotion she desired it would have meant that she would have been working in the same division as her husband. This was the only reason why she had not been successful in her application.

Until recently it was not unlawful to discriminate against single people. In *Bick v School for the Deaf* (1976) a female teacher was dismissed just before she was due to be married. The school had a policy of not employing married staff. She was unable to make a discrimination claim because at the time of her dismissal she was not married and so was not protected by the 1975 Act. However, a recent ruling now seems to differentiate between single people and those who are engaged to be married. The ruling in **Bick** was not followed in the case of *Turner v Turner* (2005). Here, the claimant brought an action against her former employer. Her claim was for unfair dismissal on the grounds of discrimination on the basis of her marital status. Her employer had dismissed her from her job when she became engaged to his son. The Employment Tribunal held in her favour stating that s 3 of the Sex Discrimination Act 1975 should be interpreted in light of s 3 of the Human Rights Act 1998 and Art. 8 and 12 of the Convention. The Tribunal held that the 1975 Act must be interpreted as encompassing discrimination not only against married persons but also against those who were about to marry.

It would seem, therefore, that s 3 of the 1975 Act will now be interpreted as applying to persons who can show that they are engaged to be married. The position in relation to single persons who are not engaged remains the same. This question of applicability will inevitably come before the Employment Tribunal again in the near future.

Direct sex discrimination

Section 1(1)(a) of the Sex Discrimination Act 1975 states that a person discriminates against another if:

> on the ground of her sex he treats her less favourably than he treats or would treat a man.

The employer's motive for treating a person 'less favourably' is irrelevant and there is no defence to a claim of direct discrimination once it has been proved.

Direct sex discrimination is overt or blatant discrimination. The following cases highlight situations in which direct sex discrimination was alleged.

R v Birmingham City Council, ex parte Equal Opportunities Commission (1989)

The City Council allocated 390 of 600 available school places to boys and only 210 to girls.

Held (HL) This was an example of direct discrimination as the girls would not have received the same treatment had they been boys.

Hereford County Council v Clayton (1996)

A Council manager was held to have directly discriminated against a female employee when he announced to his other staff the 'bad news' concerning her appointment because she was a woman.

Less favourable treatment

In order to prove that there has been direct discrimination, an individual has to show that he or she has been treated less favourably because of their sex. This means that the individual has been disadvantaged in some way because of being female or male. This is often referred to as the 'but for' test. Would the individual have been treated less favourably 'but for' their gender? See: *James v Eastleigh Borough Council* (1990). A person may also be treated less favourably due to the fact of being married. Not all actions will amount to less favourable treatment. In *Shamoon v Chief Constable of the Royal Ulster Constabulary* (2003) the House of Lords stressed that when carrying out a comparison in order to show less favourable treatment it is important that any actual comparators are in the same circumstances as the complainant. Where there is no actual comparator the tribunal may try to assess the way in which a hypothetical comparator would have been treated.

In *Stewart v Cleveland Guest (Engineering) Ltd* (1994) the Employment Appeal Tribunal held that there had been no discrimination when female nude pin-ups were displayed in a factory. Even though her employers knew that she found such material offensive, Ms Stewart had not been treated any less favourably. The pictures could be seen by all of the workforce.

In *British Telecom Plc v Roberts* (1996) it was held that there had been no discrimination when a woman returning from maternity leave was told that she could not return to her job on a job-share basis. She had not been treated any less favourably than a man would have been in the same circumstances. Her employers had refused her request on the basis that the job needed to be done by a full-time employee and not because she was a woman.

In the recent case of *Moyhing v Barts and London NHS Trust* (2006) the Trust's policy of requiring a male student nurse to be accompanied by a female colleague when administering an ECG to a female patient (because the procedure involved touching the patient's breasts) was held to be direct discrimination. Mr Moyhing had claimed direct sex discrimination as there was no requirement for a female nurse to have a male chaperone when dealing with male patients. He had been treated less favourably because of his sex. Compensation for injury to feelings was limited to £750 because the policy was unlawful only because statute specifically provides that there is no defence of justification in direct discrimination cases.

It could be said that the decision in *Smith v Safeway Plc* (1996), below, is unfair because had Mr Smith been a woman the length and appearance of his ponytail would have been acceptable!

In 2003 there were two interesting 'dress code' cases concerning the wearing of ties at work. In both cases it was questioned whether or not it was discriminatory to force a man to wear a tie in the workplace. In March 2003 Exeter Employment Tribunal held that it was not discriminatory for the prison service to require an employee (Mark Coldicott) to wear a tie at work.

Smith v Safeway Plc (1996)

Mr Smith worked as a delicatessen assistant. Safeway Plc dismissed him because they said that his ponytail breached their 'dress code' rules. The rules stated that male staff should have 'tidy hair not below collar length and no unconventional styles'. Mr Smith alleged direct discrimination saying that he had been treated less favourably than female employees who were allowed to wear their hair long. Although successful when his claim was heard by the EAT Mr Smith eventually lost his claim in the Court of Appeal.

Held (CA) The dress code did not discriminate just because the employer had a 'conventional outlook'. Judge Phillips stated that he did not 'believe that this renders discriminatory an appearance code which applies a standard of what is conventional'.

In the same month a Manchester Employment Tribunal held that it was discriminatory for Stockport Job Centre to require an employee (Matthew Thompson) to wear a tie at work.

On appeal the Employment Appeal Tribunal remitted this case back to a different Employment Tribunal, stating that in considering whether a requirement of an employer's dress code imposed on men but not on women, e.g. to wear a collar and tie, is sex discrimination, the question must be considered in the overall context of the code as a whole, such as an over-reaching requirement for staff to dress in a professional and businesslike way. In the light of the EAT ruling the Department for Work and Pensions withdrew from the case and allowed men to work without ties when they were not in direct contact with the public. This ensured that the 7,000 other applications made by male workers following Mr Thompson's claim were withdrawn. This case is reported at *Thompson* v *Department for Work and Pensions* (2004).

Other conflicting (but interesting) decisions on the use of dress codes include: *Schmidt* v *Austicks Bookshops Ltd* (1977), *Burrett* v *West Birmingham Health Authority* (1994), *Fuller* v *Mastercare Service & Distribution (EAT)* (2001).

A specific definition of direct discrimination is included in the amendments made to the Equal Treatment Directive (2002/73/EC). This defines direct discrimination as 'where one person is treated less favourably on grounds of sex than another is, has been or would be treated in a comparable situation'.

Indirect sex discrimination

Section 1(2)(b) of the Sex Discrimination Act 1975 was initially amended by the Sex Discrimination (Indirect Discrimination and Burden of Proof Regulations) 2001. Recently, a new s 1(2)(b) was inserted into the 1975 Act by regulation 3 of the Employment Equality (Sex Discrimination) Regulations 2005. From 1 October 2005 a person indirectly discriminates against a woman ... if:

(b) he applies to her a provision, criterion or practice which he applies or would apply equally to a man, but –

  (i) which puts or would put women at a particular disadvantage when compared with men,

  (ii) which puts her at that disadvantage, and

  (iii) which he cannot show to be a proportionate means of achieving a legitimate aim.

In most cases the new definition will be of little practical significance but it is hoped that it will make it easier for claimants to bring indirect discrimination claims. From 1 October 2005 there is no longer a need to consider what is a 'considerably smaller group' or who should be included in the 'pool of comparison'. The claimant now has to show that the employer applied a provision, criterion or practice which would apply equally to men but which puts women at a disadvantage compared to men and which put her at that disadvantage.

An employer may be able to defend an indirect discrimination claim by showing that their actions were justified, or a 'proportionate means of achieving a legitimate aim'.

The examples below are cases that dealt with the old terminology. However, as the new changes do not make any real difference to the application of the law they will still be relevant. It remains to be seen how much of an improvement (if any) the new wording will make to those bringing a claim for indirect sex discrimination.

Indirect discrimination is hidden discrimination. What may or may not constitute indirect discrimination may often be difficult to grasp. The easiest way to work out whether there is a possible case of indirect discrimination is to take the situation where it may have occurred and apply it to the above definition.

Taking the height example noted above (page 39), we can see that there is clear evidence of indirect discrimination. In this example Christine has read a job advertisement. It does not say that she cannot apply because she is a woman, but it does say that she cannot apply unless she is over 6 feet tall.

On the face of it, the advertisement **applies to both sexes**. However, due to the fact that fewer women than men are over 6 feet tall the advertisement puts women at a particular disadvantage when compared with men.

In order to dispute any claim of indirect discrimination, an employer would have to show justification in imposing the height qualification, showing that his actions were a proportionate means of achieving a legitimate aim (see page 56)

Applies in principle to both sexes ...

Here, an applicant or employee would have to show that in principle the provision, criterion or practice, for example, to work particular shifts or be of a certain weight, applies to both sexes.

... which puts or would put women at a particular disadvantage when compared with men

Here, an applicant or employee would have to show that the provision, criterion or practice puts or would put women at a particular disadvantage when compared with men.

In *Jones* v *University of Manchester* (1993) the court laid down guidelines to assist in the identification of the 'pool for comparison'. The guidelines show that the correct 'pool' is identified by highlighting those people who could comply with the condition, for example 70 per cent of the population. Then you would ask which proportion of that 70 per cent are male and which are female. If, for instance, the statistics show that 60 per cent of men could comply with the condition as opposed to 10 per cent of women, then the condition is discriminatory.

This is a rather simplified account of the guidelines but serves as an illustration of the way in which statistics can be used to isolate the 'pool' of comparison and so prove that there has been indirect discrimination. The new terminology also requires the applicant to identify a 'pool for comparison'.

Puts her at that disadvantage

In order to prove indirect discrimination, the applicant or employee must be able to show that the actions of the employer put her at a disadvantage. Often this will mean having been deprived of the chance of applying for a job or an application being rejected for not meeting the imposed requirement. Alternatively, it could mean a refusal relating to training or promotion. To be put at a disadvantage is similar to the concept of less favourable treatment in direct discrimination.

The following cases highlight situations where indirect sex discrimination was alleged.

Price v Civil Service Commission (1978)

Ms Price was a 35-year-old mother. She wanted to apply for a job as a Civil Service executive officer. The job advertisement stated that only people aged 17–28 years could apply. She claimed that she had suffered indirect discrimination because she could not comply with the age requirement.

Held As a woman she had suffered indirect discrimination; fewer women than men could comply with the age barrier. This was because a large number of women from that age group were occupied in the bearing and bringing up of children.

London Underground v Edwards (No. 2) (1999)

Ms Edwards was employed as a tube train driver. She was a single mother and had worked for London Underground (LU) for almost ten years. She had worked a shift system which allowed her to take care of her son outside of school hours. LU then introduced a new variable shift system which prevented her from being able to organise regular childcare. She asked LU to help her by rearranging her shifts to fit in with her parental responsibilities. LU refused and she was forced to resign. She claimed that she had been indirectly discriminated against because as a female she was less likely to be able to comply with the new shift system than her male colleagues.

Held (CA) There had been indirect discrimination. There were only 21 women train drivers employed as part of a workforce of over 2000. The new shift system had had a far greater impact on female drivers than it did on male drivers.

See also, *R v Secretary of State for Employment, ex parte Seymour-Smith* (2000), *Meade-Hill v British Council* (1995), *R v Secretary of State for Employment, ex parte Equal Opportunities Commission* (1995), *Coker & Osamor v The Lord Chancellor, Lord Irvine* (2002).

RACIAL DISCRIMINATION

The Race Relations Act 1976 states that it is unlawful for a person to discriminate against another on the basis of the other person's: colour, race, nationality, ethnic origin or national origin.

The Act recognises direct and indirect discrimination and victimisation. It is unlawful for an employer to discriminate on the grounds of race either during the recruitment and selection process or after appointment.

A racial discrimination claim

Figure 2.2 outlines the possible stages involved in deciding whether there can be a claim for racial discrimination.

What is a racial group?

Section 3 of the Race Relations Act 1976 states that it applies only to people who belong to a recognised racial group. A racial group is defined as being:

a group of persons defined by reference to colour, race, nationality or ethnic or national origins.

In some situations a tribunal may have to decide on whether or not an applicant or employee belongs to a particular racial group. If a person cannot show that he belongs to such a group, he will not be protected under the Act and so will not be able to proceed with a claim for racial discrimination.

In *Mandla v Lee* (1983) Mr Mandla, a Sikh, complained of racial discrimination when his local school refused to admit his son. He said that his son had been refused entry because he was a Sikh. He could only bring a claim under the 1976 Act if being a Sikh was taken to mean that he belonged to a particular racial group.

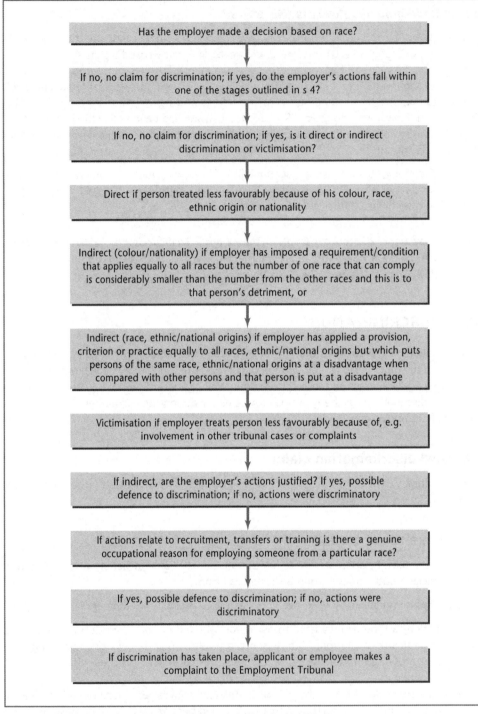

Figure 2.2 Is there a valid claim for racial discrimination?

Using the s 3 definition, the House of Lords held that being a Sikh did constitute being part of a particular racial group. Their lordships defined a racial or ethnic group as being identifiable by things such as:

- a long shared history;
- a cultural tradition of its own including family and social customs;
- a common geographical origin;
- a common language;
- a common religion.

In *Seide* v *Gillette Industries* (1980) the tribunal held that people belonging to the Jewish faith could be classed as belonging to a particular racial group. Similarly in *Commission for Racial Equality* v *Dutton* (1989) Gypsies were also held to belong to a particular racial group. See also, *Catton* v *Hudson Shribman* (2002).

The Scots and English are covered by the Race Relations Act 1976 but only in relation to 'national origins', not 'ethnic origins'. See: *BBC Scotland* v *Souster* (2001), *British Airways* v *Boyce* (2001). In the following case, however, a Rastafarian was held not to be part of a particular racial group.

See also, *Gwynedd County Council* v *Jones* (1986), *J H Walker Ltd* v *Hussain* (1996).

Crown Suppliers v *Dawkins* (1993)

Mr Dawkins complained to the Industrial Tribunal stating that he had not been given a job as a van driver because he was a Rastafarian with dreadlocks. Crown Suppliers had offered him the job if he would cut his hair but he had refused to do so. The tribunal had to decide whether, as a Rastafarian, Dawkins belonged to a particular racial group.

Held Although Rastafarianism was a 'twentieth-century movement with an irregular and uncertain history which might be a religious sect', it could not be a racial group. Consequently, Dawkins could not make a claim for racial discrimination because he was not protected under the 1976 Act.

Direct racial discrimination

Section 1(1)(a) of the Race Relations Act 1976 states that a person discriminates against another if:

> on racial grounds he treats that other less favourably than he treats or would treat other persons.

Direct racial discrimination is overt or blatant discrimination. The following case highlights a situation in which direct discrimination was alleged.

Owen & Briggs v *James* (1982)

James advertised regularly for new staff. Ms Owen had applied for a job as a secretary on two occasions but had been rejected. She was black and on the second occasion the job was offered to a white girl who had fewer qualifications and less experience. When the white girl was offered the job one of the interview panel said, 'why take on coloured girls when English girls are available?' Owen complained to the Industrial Tribunal, stating that she had been discriminated against on the grounds of race.

Held (CA) The discriminatory statement showed that the employers had deliberately not offered her the job because she was not white. They directly discriminated against her because she had been treated less favourably than she would have been had she been white.

The employers' motive for treating a person 'less favourably' is irrelevant and there is no defence to a claim of direct discrimination once it has been proved.

Less favourable treatment

In order to prove that there had been direct racial discrimination, an individual has to show that he has been treated less favourably because of his race. This means that he will have been disadvantaged in some way because of being from a particular racial group.

In the recent decision in *Serco Ltd* v *Redfearn* (2006) it was held that where an employee who is a member of a racist group (here the British National Party) is dismissed because of the danger that his continued employment might lead to violence in the workplace, the dismissal was properly regarded as being for health and safety reasons and was not unlawful racial discrimination.

Indirect racial discrimination

The Race Relations Act 1976 (Amendment) Regulations came into force on 19 July 2003. These regulations brought the terminology used in racial discrimination claims in line with those of sex discrimination. The regulations inserted a new s 1(1A) into the Race Relations Act 1976 and consequently there are now two definitions of what will amount to indirect racial discrimination.

The original definition from s 1(1)(b) of the Act still applies to claims that relate to colour or nationality. The new definition in s 1(1A) applies to claims on the basis of 'race, ethnic origins or national origins'.

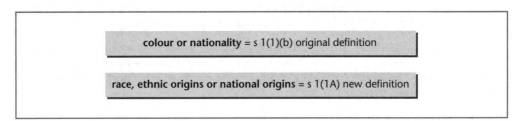

colour or nationality = s 1(1)(b) original definition

race, ethnic origins or national origins = s 1(1A) new definition

It is unfortunate that we now have two separate definitions of what will amount to racial discrimination. However, in practice it is thought that most claims will be made under the s 1(1A) definition. Both the original and the new definitions are outlined below.

Section 1(1)(b) RRA 1976 - colour or nationality

Section 1(1)(b) of the Race Relations Act 1976 states that a person discriminates against another on the grounds of race if:

he applies to that other a requirement or condition which he applies or would apply equally to persons not of the same racial group as that other, but –

(i) which is such that the proportion of persons of the same racial group as that other who can comply with it is considerably smaller than the proportion of persons not of that racial group who can comply with it, and

(ii) which he cannot show to be justifiable irrespective of the colour, race, nationality or ethnic or national origins of the person to who it is applied; and

(iii) which is to the detriment of that other because he cannot comply with it.

Applies in principle to all races

An applicant or employee would have to show that in principle the requirement or condition applies to all races.

But only a considerably smaller group of one race can comply

Here, it has to be shown that even though the requirement or condition applies to all races only a considerably smaller group from a particular race are able to comply. This can be done with the aid of statistics. The applicant or employee must choose the correct 'pool' for comparison. See *Perera* v *Civil Service Commission* (below) and *TNT Express Worldwide (UK) Ltd* v *Brown* (2001).

Suffering a detriment

In order to prove indirect discrimination, the applicant or employee must be able to show that he has suffered a detriment. Often this will mean having been deprived of the chance of applying for a job or an application having been rejected for not meeting the imposed requirement.

Alternatively, it could mean a refusal for training or promotion. To suffer a detriment is similar to the concept of less favourable treatment in direct discrimination.

The following case highlights a situation where indirect racial discrimination was alleged.

Perera v *Civil Service Commission* (1982)

Mr Perera had been born in Sri Lanka and emigrated to the United Kingdom as an adult. He worked for the civil service as an executive officer. He had applied for promotion on several occasions but had been rejected despite the fact that he had numerous accountancy and legal qualifications. He alleged racial discrimination and during tribunal proceedings it was shown that it was civil service policy not to promote anyone from Perera's grade who was over 32 years old.

Held (EAT) There had been indirect racial discrimination. The age limit was a requirement or condition that had indirectly discriminated against the large number of black people who had emigrated to Britain as adults. This meant that a considerably smaller percentage of blacks than whites could comply with the age requirement.

Section 1 1(A) RRA 1976 – race, ethnic origins or national origins

Section 1 1(A) of the Race Relations Act 1976 states that a person discriminates against another on the grounds of race, ethnic or national origins if:

he applies to that other person a provision, criterion or practice which he applies or would apply equally to persons not of the same race or ethnic or national origins as that other,

but –

(a) **which puts or would put persons of the same race or ethnic or national origins as that other at a particular disadvantage when compared with other persons,**

(b) **which puts that other at a disadvantage, and**

(c) **which he cannot show to be a proportionate means of achieving a legitimate aim.**

Provision, criterion or practice

The provision, criterion or practice applies to persons of all races and ethnic/national origins.

Puts at a disadvantage when compared with other persons

Here, it has to be shown that the provision, criterion or practice puts or would put persons from a particular race or ethnic/national origin at a particular disadvantage when compared with other persons.

Is put at a disadvantage

The applicant/employee is put at a disadvantage. Often this will mean having been deprived of the chance of applying for a job, or an application being rejected for not meeting the required provision, criterion or practice.

As with cases of indirect sex discrimination, indirect racial discrimination can often be difficult to define. Again the applicant or employee must work through the definition in stages, collecting evidence to support any claim. Consider the example again at page 39. The same logic would apply if Christine was Chinese and so unable to comply with the height restriction because people from her race are less likely to be of the required height.

In order to dispute any claim of indirect discrimination, an employer has to show justification in imposing the requirement or condition. Under the new definition he has to show that his actions were justified as a proportionate means of achieving a legitimate aim. (See page 56).

Discrimination on the grounds of another's race

Whilst the Sex Discrimination Act relates to discrimination aimed at the individual, the Race Relations Act states that discrimination claims may be made by a person even where the discrimination was aimed at someone else. The following cases highlight situations where such claims have succeeded.

In *Wilson v TB Steelworks* (1979) a job offer to a white woman was withdrawn when she revealed that her husband was black. In *Zarcynska v Levy* (1978) a barmaid was dismissed because she refused to follow orders not to serve black customers. Similarly, in *Showboat Entertainment Centre v Owens* (1984) Owens, a white amusement arcade manager was sacked after refusing to obey an order to exclude black people from the arcade.

In these cases, even though the discrimination was actually aimed at a third party or group of people, those instructed were also able to make successful claims. A more recent case on this point is detailed below.

Weathersfield (Van and Truck) Rentals v Sargent (1999)

Ms Sargent began to work as a receptionist for Weathersfield Rentals. She was told by her manager that if any coloured or Asian person visited the premises asking to hire a car or van they should be told that no vehicles were available. She resigned after a few days because she found the above instruction to be very distasteful.

Held (CA) The 'orders' given by the manager were discriminatory. Ms Sargent had suffered a detriment as a result of her refusal to carry out a policy, which involved unlawful race discrimination and so was successful in her claim.

VICTIMISATION

Victimisation was discussed at page 40. Section 4 of the Sex Discrimination Act 1975 and s 2 of the Race Relations Act 1976 state that victimisation will occur where a person treats another less favourably because:

- he has begun tribunal or grievance proceedings against the discriminator or any other person under the Act; or

- he has given evidence in any such proceedings.

Victimisation may also occur where, for instance, an employee has done neither of the above but the employer mistakenly believes that he has done so or will do so in the future.

Section 4(2) of the 1975 Act and s 2(2) of the 1976 Act state that an employer will be able to defend a claim of victimisation where he can show that any allegations involved were 'false and not made in good faith'.

WHAT IF AN EMPLOYER DOES NOT INTEND TO DISCRIMINATE?

An employer may not intentionally discriminate against an applicant or employee. However, the law is not concerned with motive and the employer may still be found to have discriminated unlawfully even where he did not intend to do so.

The following cases highlight a situation where no discrimination was intended but was nevertheless found to have occurred.

In relation to racial discrimination, in *Hafeez* v *Richmond School* (1981) Mr Hafeez's application to work in the school was rejected because he was not English. The position involved teaching English and the students made it known that they would rather be taught by an English teacher. Even though the school's headmaster had not meant to discriminate, he was found to have acted unlawfully.

See also, *Thorndyke* v *Bell* (1979), *Ministry of Defence* v *Jeremiah* (1979), *R* v *Birmingham City Council, ex parte Equal Opportunities Commission* (1989), *Din* v *Carrington Viyella Ltd* (1982).

James v Eastleigh Borough Council (1990)

Mr and Mrs James both went swimming at their local pool. They were both 61 years of age. Mrs James was allowed a free swim because she was a pensioner but her husband was asked to pay 75p because he was not. The Council had not intended to discriminate against male pensioners; it was merely observing the ages at which people received their pension.

Held (HL) Although the Council did not intend to discriminate on the grounds of sex, its actions amounted to direct discrimination. As a man Mr James had been treated less favourably than he would have been had he been a woman.

Greig v Community Industries (1979)

Two women were offered jobs working as part of a team of painters and decorators. On the first day one woman did not turn up. Greig did attend but she was dismissed because her employer thought that it would be 'for her own good'. He genuinely believed that it would not be good for her to work as the only female on the team.

Held Although the employer's intentions were honest, he was found to have discriminated against Greig on the ground of her sex.

Discrimination in employment

STAGES AT WHICH DISCRIMINATION MAY TAKE PLACE

Section 6 of the Sex Discrimination Act 1975 and s 4 of the Race Relations Act 1976 recognise that discrimination may take place either during the recruitment and selection process or when a person is already employed. These sections state that it is unlawful for an employer to discriminate on the grounds of sex, marital status or race in the following situations:

- in the arrangements made for the purpose of deciding who should be employed;
- on the terms on which a person is offered a job;
- by refusing to employ a person because of his sex/marital status or race;
- by refusing access to opportunities at work such as promotion, transfers, training, benefits, facilities or services;
- by dismissing a person or subjecting him to any other detriment.

In the arrangements made for the purpose of deciding who should be employed

This relates to discrimination that may take place during the recruitment and selection process. Employers should not discriminate on the grounds of sex, marital status or race during this process. Selection procedures should focus on the suitability of the candidate as regards previous experience and aptitude for the job and not on the candidate's gender or race.

Employers should take care when drafting application forms and conducting interviews. Likely acts of discrimination at this stage would include rejecting an application form on the basis that it was sent by a woman or because it was sent by someone from an ethnic minority. Employers may also discriminate during the interview stage by asking discriminatory questions.

In *Hurley v Mustoe* (1981) it was held that to assume that a woman with young children would be an unreliable employee was direct sex discrimination.

As a general guideline, employers should only ask questions in interviews that they could put to both male and female applicants. The questions should also be capable of being asked to applicants from all races. For example, a woman should not be asked questions about her childcare arrangements if the same questions are not asked to a man with a family. Applicants from ethnic minorities should not be asked questions such as 'were you born in England?'.

Not all questions will be discriminatory. In *Saunders v Richmond-upon-Thames Borough Council* (1977) a female golfer had applied for a job as a golf professional. At her interview she was asked questions such as 'are there any other female golf professionals?' and 'are you blazing a trail?' When she did not get the job she alleged that the questions had been discriminatory. It was held that in this case the questions were not discriminatory. On this occasion this may be because they were asked by a woman.

When selecting employees for interview, employers should not discriminate in their choices. The following cases highlight situations in which blatant racial discrimination occurred.

Similarly in *Hussein v Saints Complete House Furnishers* (1979) Saints were held to have discriminated during the recruitment and selection process when they stipulated that when selecting candidates for interview they would not choose people who lived in the city-centre area of Liverpool. The tribunal held that this discriminated on racial grounds because the people who lived in that area were predominantly from ethnic minorities.

Johnson v *Timber Tailors (Midlands)* (1978)

Mr Johnson, a black Jamaican, applied for a job as a wood machinist. A manager at Timber Tailors told him that he would be contacted a few days after interview and told whether or not he had been successful. After a week during which he was not contacted, he rang Timber Tailors and was told that the vacancy had been filled. Later that day he noticed that another advert for the same job had appeared in his local newspaper. He applied for the same job again and was again told that the position had been filled. Yet another advert for the same job appeared in the newspaper a few days later.

Held (IT) Johnson had suffered blatant racial discrimination. Timber Tailors had discriminated against him during the recruitment and selection process because he was Jamaican.

On the terms on which a person is offered a job

Employers should not discriminate in the terms on which they offer employment. For example, if an employer employs one male and one female employee to the same job, they should be given the same holiday entitlement. To offer the man two extra weeks just because he is male would be discriminatory. This relates to both sex and race discrimination.

By refusing to employ a person on the basis of his/her sex or marital status or race

It is unlawful for an employer to refuse to employ a person just because of being female, male or married. In *Batisha* v *Say* (1971) a woman was refused a job as a cave guide because the employer thought that it was 'a man's job'. This was held to be direct discrimination. It is also discriminatory to refuse to employ a person on the basis of their race.

By refusing access to opportunities at work

The refusal may relate to promotion, transfers, training, benefits, facilities or services. Access to all of these things should be available equally to both sexes and irrespective of marital status or race. In *Timex Corporation Ltd* v *Hodgson* (1987) a male employee was made redundant and was not offered an alternative position. The alternative job was given to a female employee. The EAT held that the refusal was capable of falling within the definition of a transfer and that consequently Timex's refusal to appoint Hodgson amounted to discrimination.

By dismissing a person or subjecting him/her to any detriment

An employer should not dismiss or subject an employee to any other detriment on the basis of his sex, race or marital status. To 'put to a detriment' simply means to disadvantage the employee in some way.

2

Discrimination in employment

Coleman v Skyrail Oceanic Ltd (1981)

Ms Coleman worked as a booking clerk for Skyrail Oceanic Ltd, a travel agency. She married an employee from a rival firm and was dismissed by Skyrail because it was thought that she might leak confidential information to her husband. Skyrail assumed that her dismissal was reasonable because her husband was the higher earner and so could continue to support their family.

Held (CA) In dismissing Coleman, Skyrail had directly discriminated against her on the basis that she was female. In the circumstances, had she been a man, Skyrail would have perceived her as the family 'breadwinner' and she would not have been dismissed.

DOES AN EMPLOYER HAVE ANY DEFENCE TO A DISCRIMINATION CLAIM?

There can be no defence to a claim of direct discrimination but in cases of indirect discrimination employers may be able to show that they were justified in attaching a requirement or condition/provision, criterion or practice to, for example, a job advertisement.

Section 1(1)(b) of both the Sex Discrimination Act 1975 and the Race Relations Act 1976 state that an employer does not indirectly discriminate where he can show that there was a justifiable reason for using the requirement or condition/provision (race), criterion or practice (sex), and that that reason does not relate to gender or race.

In relation to sex discrimination the employer must be able to show that his actions were a proportionate means of achieving a legitimate aim.

Section 1(1A) of the Race Relations Act 1976 states that an employer does not indirectly discriminate where he can show that there was a justifiable reason for applying a provision, criterion or practice and that his actions were a proportionate means of achieving a legitimate aim.

In practice the differing terminology makes little difference to the way in which the tribunal will consider the claim.

It is a question of fact as to what a tribunal would consider to be justifiable. It is not sufficient that the employer believes his actions to be justified. An employer would have to produce evidence to support such a defence.

The tribunal will consider the requirement or condition/provision, criterion or practice and balance the effect of the discrimination on the individual involved against the reasonable needs of the employer. This was discussed in the case of *Hampson v Department of Education and Science* (1989). Here, the House of Lords held that in order to prove justification, an employer must show that there was a real need to impose the requirement or condition. This need can be either economic or administrative and must relate to the running of the employer's business.

This means that in order to prove that their actions were justified employers must show that:

- the requirement or condition/provision, criterion or practice was objectively justified regardless of sex or race; or
- that it served a real business need and the need was justifiable on economic or administrative grounds.
- In cases of sex discrimination and racial discrimination under s 1(1A) (race, ethnic/national origins) that his actions were a proportionate means of achieving a legitimate aim.

The following cases highlight situations in which employers have tried to show that their requirements or conditions were justified.

Home Office v Holmes (1984)

The Home Office had refused to employ women on a part-time basis. It said that if it did employ part-time workers, accommodation and insurance costs would rise. On this basis it said that its actions were justified.

Held (EAT) There was no justification for the Home Office's actions. The EAT had considered a report which showed that the civil service was losing valuable trained workers when they left to have a family. The report also showed that in some departments efficiency increased when part-timers were introduced. There could be no justification for imposing such a condition.

Panesar v Nestlé Co Ltd (1979)

A rule at the Nestlé factory stated that workers were not allowed to have beards or excessively long hair. This was held to indirectly discriminate against Sikhs because they had beards for religious reasons and so could not cut them to comply with the condition.

Held Even though the condition did discriminate, the employers were justified in imposing it on health and safety grounds and in the interests of hygiene. The rule against the wearing of beards was essential in a factory making chocolate to prevent it from becoming contaminated by bacteria.

A similar decision was made in the case of *Singh v Rowntree Mackintosh Ltd* (1979).

In *Singh v British Rail Engineering Ltd* (1986) British Rail rules stated that safety headgear had to be worn in designated areas. Mr Singh objected to this because he was unable to wear headgear whilst wearing his turban. The tribunal held that British Rail was justified in imposing this condition. Again, this decision was taken on health and safety grounds.

GENUINE OCCUPATIONAL QUALIFICATIONS

An employer may be able to discriminate against one sex or race if appointing a man, woman or someone from a particular racial group to the job is a genuine occupational qualification. This exception applies only to recruitment, transfers and training.

Sex genuine occupational qualifications

The Sex Discrimination Act 1975 recognises eight situations where an employer is able to discriminate by favouring someone from a particular sex. In these situations being either a man or a woman is a genuine occupational qualification for the job. Section 7 of the Act states that it will be possible for an employer to discriminate where:

1 The job needs to be done by a man or woman for reasons of physiology (excluding physical strength or stamina) or in dramatic performances or other entertainment for reasons of authenticity.

Examples
- *Employing a man to play Romeo or a woman to play Juliet in Romeo and Juliet.*
- *Employing a woman to model wedding dresses.*

2

Discrimination in employment

2 The job needs to be done by a man or woman to preserve decency or privacy because it is likely to involve physical contact with men or women, and these people would object to the presence of someone of the opposite sex.

> ### Example
> *A job working in an all-male or all-female retirement home, working as a live-in carer.*

3 The job involves working or living in a private home and there may be either a degree of physical/social contact with the person living in the home or the worker may acquire intimate knowledge of the person's life.

> ### Example
> *A job working as a home-help for an elderly woman.*

4 The nature of the job means that the employee will have to live at his place of work and the accommodation provided is only suitable for either men or women, and it is not reasonable to expect the employer to make adjustments to that accommodation.

5 The job involves working in a single-sex prison or hospital.

6 The holder of the job will be expected to provide individuals with personal services promoting welfare or education, and those services could most effectively be provided by a man or a woman.

> ### Example
> *Employing a woman to counsel victims in a rape crisis centre.*

7 The job needs to be held by a man because it is likely to involve duties outside of the United Kingdom in a country where laws or customs would prevent a woman from being able to carry out their duties effectively or at all.

> ### Example
> *Appointing a man where the job involves a posting to a Middle Eastern country where women are not allowed to drive.*

8 The job is one of two to be held by a married couple.

> ### Example
> *Housekeeper/gardener or jobs involving the looking after of children where one person from each sex is required.*

The following cases highlight situations in which employers have argued that employing either a man or woman was a genuine occupational qualification for the job.

In *Wylie v Dee* (1978) a woman was refused employment in a tailoring establishment because she would have to take men's inside leg measurements. In these circumstances it was held that being a woman was not a genuine occupational qualification for the job. Had she been offered the job her manager could have asked one of her male colleagues to deal with all measurements.

Similarly, in *Etam plc v Rowan* (1989) it was held to be discriminatory not to employ a man in a shop selling only female clothing. Etam's argument had been that appointing women only

Sisley v Britannia Security Systems (1983)

Sisley's application for a job at Britannia's security station was rejected. Britannia had a policy of only employing women. The women at the station worked 12-hour shifts. During rest breaks they undressed down to their underwear, rested and slept on the beds provided. Sisley claimed that he had been discriminated against because he was a man. Britannia claimed that for reasons of privacy and to preserve decency, being a woman was a genuine occupational qualification for the job.

Held (EAT) In the circumstances and to preserve decency and privacy employing a woman was a genuine occupational qualification.

was a genuine occupational qualification because men would not be able to assist customers in the changing rooms. The tribunal said that, whilst this may have been the case, the store manager could have asked female employees to perform those tasks whilst Mr Rowan was, for example filling shelves or dealing with customer queries. There was no genuine occupational qualification for Etam offering employment only to women.

Lasertop Ltd v Webster (1997)

Mr Webster had applied for a job in a women's health club. He was told that only female staff would be employed and refused employment. He claimed that he had been discriminated against on the grounds of his sex. The health club defended this claim, stating that being a woman was a genuine occupational qualification for the job.

Held (EAT) The employer was entitled to rely on this defence and that it was lawful to appoint a woman to preserve privacy and decency. It could not be said that the post-holder's duties, which would include showing prospective club members around the premises, could be undertaken by male employees without undue disruption.

Racial genuine occupational qualifications

The Race Relations Act 1976 recognises four situations where an employer is able to discriminate by favouring someone from a particular race. In these situations being from a particular race is a genuine occupational qualification for the job.

Section 5 of the 1976 Act states that it will be possible for an employer to discriminate where:

- The job involves participation in a dramatic performance or other entertainment in a role where a person of a particular racial group is required for reasons of authenticity.

Example
Employing a black actor to play Othello.

- The job involves participation as an artist's or photographic model and a person from a particular race is needed for reasons of authenticity.
- The job involves working in a place where food or drink is provided for and consumed by the public in a particular setting in which a person of a particular race is required for reasons of authenticity.

> **Example**
> Advertising for a Chinese chef and waiting staff to work in a Chinese restaurant.

● The holder of the job provides persons of a particular racial group with personal services promoting their welfare, and those services can be most effectively provided by a person from that racial group.

> **Example**
> Advertising for or appointing an Asian welfare or legal adviser to provide advice in an area with a predominantly Asian population.

An illustration of the application of this last exception appears in the **Tottenham Green** case below.

> **Tottenham Green Under Fives Centre v Marshall** (1989)
>
> The Centre had a policy of maintaining an ethnic balance between its staff and children. An Afro-Caribbean worker had resigned and the recruitment advertisement for a replacement specified that the position was only open to Afro-Caribbean applicants. Mr Marshall's application was rejected on the basis that he was not Afro-Caribbean. He complained to the Industrial Tribunal alleging racial discrimination. The Centre stated that there had been no discrimination because they had a genuine occupational reason for advertising for an Afro-Caribbean worker. This was because the new employee would be expected to provide personal services, read and talk to the children in Afro-Caribbean dialect.
>
> *Held (EAT)* The requirement that the worker was of Afro-Caribbean origin was a genuine occupational qualification for the job and so there had been no discrimination.

In *London Borough of Lambeth* v *Commission for Racial Equality* (1990) the Council advertised for two people to work in the housing department. The advertisements stated that the jobs were only open to Asian or Afro-Caribbean candidates. At the bottom of the advertisement there was a statement that it was made in accordance with s 5(2)(d) of the Race Relations Act, meaning that it was covered by the exception of genuine occupational qualification relating to welfare.

The Borough's argument was that as half of its council-house tenants were from those particular racial groups, workers from the same groups would be most effective in the roles.

The Commission for Racial Equality complained to the Industrial Tribunal. The Commission argued that the jobs were not covered by the genuine occupational exclusion and so discriminated against people who did not belong to the ethnic groups mentioned in the advertisement. The tribunal agreed with them, saying that, for the type of work that the new employees would be expected to do, their racial group was irrelevant. The Borough had discriminated on the grounds of race.

Racial 'genuine occupational requirement'

Regulation 7 of the Race Relations (Amendment) Regulations 2003 inserted a new s 4A into the Race Relations Act 1976. This section refers to exceptions for 'genuine occupational requirements' and states that the rules will not apply if:

(a) being of a particular race or particular ethnic or national origin is a genuine and determining occupational requirement;

(b) it is proportionate to apply that requirement in the particular case; and

(c) either –

(i) the person to whom that requirement is applied does not meet it, or

(ii) the employer is not satisfied, and in all the circumstances it is reasonable for him not to be satisfied, that that person meets it.

The Regulations amend s 5 of the 1976 Act, meaning that a genuine occupational qualification exception will only be available if a genuine occupational requirement is not. At the time of writing these changes have not yet been tested by case law. It remains to be seen how much effect they will have on the way in which the genuine occupational qualification exception is used.

OTHER DISCRIMINATORY ACTS

Both the Sex Discrimination Act 1975 and the Race Relations Act 1976 recognise other discriminatory offences. Employers may also discriminate by:

- using discriminatory job advertisements
- using discriminatory practices
- instructing others to discriminate
- pressurising another to discriminate
- aiding unlawful discriminatory acts.

Using discriminatory advertisements

Section 38 of the Sex Discrimination Act 1975 and s 29 of the Race Relations Act 1976 state that it is unlawful for employers to discriminate when advertising job vacancies. They state that it is unlawful:

to publish or cause to be published an advertisement which indicates or might reasonably be understood to indicate an intention to sexually or racially discriminate.

Employers should take care not to discriminate when drafting advertisements to ensure that they do not include any words with sexual or racial connotations. Examples of potentially discriminatory advertisements are:

- those with pictures of existing employees who are all from one sex or race;
- those which use male connotations, for example, suggesting that the employer only intends to employ a man, e.g. 'salesman', 'waiter', 'postman'.

An interesting example of a situation where an employer tried to get around this rule is the case of *Equal Opportunities Commission* v *Robertson* (1980). Here, the employer advertised for a 'good bloke (or blokess to satisfy fool legislators)'. It was held that this advertisement could reasonably be understood to indicate that the advertiser intended to employ a man and so discriminated against women.

If there is a genuine occupational reason for advertising for applicants from a particular sex or race, this should be stated at the bottom of the advertisement. Any use of this exception should

2

Discrimination in employment

be explained to the publishers before publication to ensure that they are fully aware of the reasons why the advertisement is drafted in a particular way.

This is because ss 38 and 29 impose liability both on the employer who drafts the advertisement and on those who publish it. Both parties are liable to be fined if discrimination can be proved. This means that newspapers or magazines which publish job advertisements could also be said to have discriminated by allowing a discriminatory advert to appear in their publication.

A publisher will have a defence to a discrimination claim if it can be shown that the publisher relied on a statement from the employer stating that there was no intention to discriminate.

Employers may also indicate in the advertisement that there is no intention to discriminate by stating that they are an 'equal opportunities employer'.

Only the Equal Opportunities Commission and the Commission for Racial Equality can bring proceedings for a breach of these sections. Individuals cannot complain to an Employment Tribunal on this basis, but they are able to use copies of advertisements in tribunal proceedings. Such copies would support a claim for discrimination after they have applied for a job and been rejected.

Using discriminatory practices

Section 37 of the Sex Discrimination Act 1975 and s 28 of the Race Relations Act 1976 state that it is unlawful for employers to use discriminatory practices. This would cover things such as having a policy of not employing women or people from ethnic minorities. Individuals cannot make a complaint to the Employment Tribunal under these sections.

Actions can only be brought by the EOC or the CRE. Both may issue a non-discrimination notice to an employer warning him not to use discriminatory practices in the future. If an employer does not adhere to this notice, the EOC/CRE may apply for a court injunction to prevent further discrimination. (See further Chapter 1 at pages 29 and 30.)

Instructing someone to discriminate

Section 39 of the Sex Discrimination Act 1975 and s 30 of the Race Relations Act 1976 state that it is unlawful to instruct someone to discriminate. An example of this offence would be an employer instructing an employment agency not to send it workers from ethnic minorities.

Pressurising someone to discriminate

Section 40 of the Sex Discrimination Act 1975 and s 31 of the Race Relations Act 1976 state that it is unlawful to pressurise or attempt to induce a person to discriminate. Employers should not offer an employee incentives to discriminate or threaten them with, for example, demotion or dismissal if they do not.

Aiding unlawful discriminatory acts

Section 42 of the Sex Discrimination Act 1975 and s 33 of the Race Relations Act 1976 state that it is unlawful to assist someone in the commission of discriminatory acts.

ARE EMPLOYERS LIABLE FOR THE DISCRIMINATORY ACTIONS OF THEIR EMPLOYEES?

Section 41 of the Sex Discrimination Act 1975 and s 32 of the Race Relations Act 1976 state that employers may be vicariously liable for the discriminatory actions of their employees. For a general discussion on vicarious liability, see Chapter 9 at page 341.

Generally, employers will only be liable for those actions of their employees which take place in the 'course of their employment'. However, in discriminatory situations employers may be liable even where employees act outside the scope of their employment. An employer may be able to defend such a claim if he can show that he took all reasonable steps to prevent the discrimination from taking place.

The following cases highlight situations where employers have been held to be vicariously liable for the actions of their employees.

Burton & Rhule v *De Vere Hotels* (1996)

Ms Burton worked as a waitress at a De Vere Hotel. A 'comedian' began to make an after dinner speech while she was clearing tables. His 'jokes' and remarks were racially motivated and directed at herself and the other black waitresses. She became very distressed. She made a claim to the Industrial Tribunal alleging racial discrimination, stating that her employers had created a discriminatory environment by inviting the particular 'comedian' on to the premises.

Held The employers were responsible for the discrimination as they had known that this particular 'comedian' was likely to be offensive and even when alerted to the situation had done nothing to prevent him from continuing. They should have taken all reasonable steps to prevent the discrimination from either continuing or taking place.

Jones v *Tower Boot Co Ltd* (1997)

Jones, a 16-year-old boy of mixed race, was severely racially abused by his colleagues. They had called him names, stuck offensive notes to his back, assaulted him, branded him with a hot screwdriver, whipped him and generally made his time at work unbearable. He alleged that his employers were vicariously liable for the racial abuse.

Held For an employer to be vicariously liable for their acts, the employees have to be acting 'in the course of their employment'. Whilst it was admitted that the acts here were not done within the 'course of employment', the Court of Appeal said that it would be wrong to allow racial harassment on this scale to go unpunished. In this case the actions were so severe that the employers were held to be vicariously liable.

The decision in **Burton** was disapproved by the House of Lords in *Pearce* v *Governing Body of Mayfield School* (2003). Here, the House of Lords suggested (obiter) that an employer will not be liable for unlawful sexual or racial discrimination unless the reason why they failed to prevent the harassment was related to the sex or race of the employee.

See also, *Irving* v *Post Office* (1987), *Waters* v *Commissioner of Police of the Metropolis* (1997), *Chief Constable of the Lincolnshire Police* v *Stubbs* (1999), *Bennett* v *Essex County Council & ors* (1999).

2

Discrimination in employment

POSITIVE DISCRIMINATION

It is unlawful to positively discriminate in favour of one particular sex or racial group. This means that although advertisements may explicitly encourage applications from, for example 'women, or persons from ethnic minorities', an employer cannot refuse to send out job information to men or persons from a different racial group.

In relation to training while at work s 45 of the Sex Discrimination Act 1975 states that an employer can encourage people from one sex to train for a particular job if in the preceding 12 months the job has been done exclusively by people from the opposite sex. This exception also applies to situations where the number of persons from one sex doing a particular job is so small that it creates a sexual imbalance in the workforce.

Section 38 of the Race Relations Act 1976 contains a similar provision allowing employers to encourage the training of employees from a particular racial group if in the preceding 12 months the job has been done exclusively by people from another racial group or where the number of ethnic employees are under-represented in the workplace. Where any such preferential treatment is afforded to those of one sex or race, employers should take care to document their reasoning carefully. A more recent example of a case involving positive discrimination is *Arnold* v *Barnfield College* (2004). Here, the college had a deliberate policy of encouraging job applications from persons from ethnic minorities. The college appointed Mrs Akhtar who was of Pakistani origin rather than Ms Arnold who was white but had more experience. Ms Arnold brought a racial discrimination claim against the college. She alleged that the college had been affected by 'unconscious discrimination' from a desire to improve the proportion of staff from ethnic minorities.

The Employment Tribunal found that Ms Arnold had been discriminated against but on appeal the EAT rejected this decision, stating that there had been no discrimination. This was because the college was able to show that it had conducted interviews properly and that they had genuinely appointed Mrs Akhtar because she was found to be the most suitable candidate for the job.

The position in relation to EC sex discrimination law is worthy of note here. Article 2(4) of the Equal Treatment Directive permits an employer to use measures designed to remove inequalities 'which affect women's opportunities'. For a discussion on 'positive discrimination' in this context see: *Kalanke* v *Freie Hansestadt Bremen* (1995), *Marschall* v *Land Nordrhein Westfalen* (1998), *Abrahamsson & Anderson* v *Fogelqvist* (2002).

EUROPEAN SEX DISCRIMINATION LAW

European law has had a major impact on our national sex discrimination law. Many of the sex discrimination cases referred to in this chapter have been referred to the European Court of Justice. In the context of discrimination law, the Equal Treatment Directive has widened the scope of our national law.

The Equal Treatment Directive of 1976 establishes the principle of equal treatment for men and women 'as regards access to employment, vocational training and promotion, and working conditions'.

Article 2 of the Directive states that there shall be 'no discrimination whatsoever on grounds of sex either directly or indirectly by reference in particular to marital or family status'.

Individuals are able to rely on the Directive in tribunal proceedings but only where their employer is a state authority. This decision stems from the case of *Marshall* v *Southampton & South West Hampshire Area Health Authority* (1986). In *Foster* v *British Gas* (1991) the European

Court of Justice held that state employers include local governments, health authorities, the police force, the post office and nationalised industries. Private-sector workers cannot use the Directive to claim against their employer.

However, under the principles laid down in *Francovich* v *Italian Republic* (1992), where employees suffer loss as a direct result of the government's failure to implement the Directive, they may be able to sue the government for compensation.

The Directive has also been used to clarify the provisions surrounding retirement and pensions. In the **Marshall** case noted above the health authority dismissed Mrs Marshall because she had reached the normal retirement age of 60. The health authority was following the provision of its retirement policy and accepted that she would not have been dismissed had she been a man. Men were not forced to retire until they were 65. Marshall claimed discrimination under European law as at the time the Sex Discrimination Act 1975 did not cover retirement provisions. This situation has now been remedied by the Sex Discrimination Act 1986.

The European Court of Justice held that the health authority had breached the Equal Treatment Directive and discriminated against Marshall.

See also: *Barber* v *Guardian Royal Exchange Assurance Group* (1990).

Note also:

- Article 13 Amsterdam Treaty
- Framework Equal Treatment Directive 2000/78
- Race Discrimination Directive 2000/43
- Equal Treatment (Amending) Directive 2002/73.

DISCRIMINATION ON THE GROUNDS OF PREGNANCY

It is unlawful to discriminate against a woman because she is pregnant or for any reason connected to her pregnancy. Discrimination on the grounds of pregnancy will constitute direct sex discrimination. The following cases highlight situations in which discrimination on the grounds of pregnancy has been alleged.

Webb v *EMO Air Cargo (UK) Ltd (No. 2)* (1995)

Ms Webb was employed on a temporary basis to cover the work of another employee who was on maternity leave. Webb then became pregnant and, as she would then need to take maternity leave and be unable to cover for the absent employee, she was dismissed. She alleged sex discrimination. The case was eventually referred to the ECJ and such discrimination was held to be in breach of the Equal Treatment Directive and capable of amounting to direct sex discrimination.

See also: *Dekker* v *VJV Centrum* (1991), *Hertz* v *Aldi Marked* (1991) and *Rees* v *Apollo Watch Repairs* (1996).

Recently, the Employment Equality (Sex Discrimination) Regulations 2005 amended the Sex Discrimination Act 1975 with regards to pregnancy discrimination.

The Regulations inserted two new sections into the 1975 Act. Section 3A relates to 'discrimination on the grounds of pregnancy or maternity leave', and s 6A relates to 'terms and conditions during maternity leave'.

Section 3A states that:

'a person discriminates against a woman if –

(a) **at a time in a protected period, and on the ground of the woman's pregnancy, the person treats her less favourably than he would treat her had she not become pregnant; or**

(b) **on the ground that the woman is exercising or seeking to exercise, or has exercised or sought to exercise, a statutory right to maternity leave, the person treats her less favourably than he would treat her if she were neither exercising nor seeking to exercise and had neither exercised nor sought to exercise, such a right.'**

The 'protected period' begins when the woman becomes pregnant and ends at the time at which her maternity leave ends.

The Regulations have put into statute form what had already been held in the courts in cases such as *Webb*, namely that it is unlawful to discriminate against a woman because she is pregnant or for a reason connected to her pregnancy.

The 2005 Regulations specifically extend protection to women who miscarry before becoming entitled to maternity leave.

THE EOC'S AND CRE'S CODES OF PRACTICE

The Equal Opportunities Commission and the Commission for Racial Equality have both published codes of practice with the objective of preventing discrimination and promoting equal opportunities in the workplace. Whilst the codes do not contain any legal sanctions, they can be used as evidence in tribunal proceedings.

EOC code (1985)

This code is referred to as the 'Code of Practice for the elimination of discrimination on the grounds of sex and marriage and the promotion of equal opportunity in employment'.

It provides guidance to employers, trade unions and employment agencies on measures that can be taken to achieve equality in the workplace. It provides guidance on advertising job vacancies, selection methods, interviews, the use of appraisal schemes and disciplinary and grievance procedures. It also provides guidelines on the drafting of equal opportunities policies and on the ways in which equal opportunity in the workplace can be monitored.

CRE code (2006)

This code is referred to as the 'Statutory Code of Practice on Racial Equality in Employment'. It came into force on 6 April 2006.

The Code provides guidance to employers, trade unions and employment agencies on measures that can be taken to promote racial equality in the workplace. It provides advice on how to implement an equal opportunities policy and how best to advertise job vacancies, interview candidates and implement disciplinary and grievance procedures.

The 2006 code replaces the original 1983 code of practice 'for the elimination of racial discrimination and the promotion of equality of opportunity in employment.'

The CRE has also produced a second code of practice aimed at public authorities. This gives guidance in connection with their new general duties under the Race Relations (Amendment)

Act 2000. This code was published in 2002. The 2006 Code remains the main source of guidance for employers.

SEXUAL AND RACIAL HARASSMENT

The law also recognises situations in which discrimination occurs in the form of sexual and racial harassment. Until recently there was no statutory definition of what types of action can amount to sexual or racial harassment but various cases and, in relation to sexual harassment, European law did provide some guidelines.

Historically sexual or racial harassment could amount to direct discrimination. This is still the case where the harassment is on the grounds of colour/nationality. If an employee wants to bring a claim on the grounds of colour/nationality, he must show that he has suffered less favourable treatment and that this treatment has caused him to suffer a detriment.

The following cases highlight those situations in which both sexual and racial harassment has been alleged. As noted above, the situation remains the same with regards to complaints involving harassment on the basis of colour or nationality.

However, with regards to sexual harassment and harassment on the grounds of race, ethnic or national origin, regulations have recently inserted new 'harassment' definition sections into both the Sex Discrimination Act 1975 and the Race Relations Act 1976. These developments are outlined at the end of this section.

Porcelli v *Strathclyde Regional Council* (1986)

Ms Porcelli worked for the Council as a laboratory technician. She had been subjected to a persistent campaign of verbal and physical sexual harassment by two of her male colleagues. They wanted her to transfer to another department. She claimed that she had been discriminated against because she was female. The Council argued that she had been treated badly, not because she was a woman but because the other employees did not like her.

Held The men had sexually harassed Porcelli because she was a woman and the actions of the other employees would not have been the same had she been an equally disliked man. She had been treated less favourably on the grounds of her sex.

In *Bracebridge Engineering* v *Darby* (1990) the EAT held that one act of harassment could constitute 'suffering a detriment'. Consequently, one isolated incident may amount to harassment in the same way as would a continued and lengthy campaign. In **Bracebridge**, a worker had been sexually assaulted by two supervisors. Bracebridge Engineering had argued that a single incident could not amount to harassment. The EAT disagreed with this saying that 'whether or not harassment is a continuing course of conduct, there was here an act which was an act of discrimination against a woman because she was a woman'.

The victim of harassment in claims involving harassment on the basis of colour or nationality must show that he has suffered a detriment. In other words he must show that the harassment has disadvantaged him in some way. This principle is the same as that in general discrimination claims and could relate, for example, to an employee having been refused promotion, training or being dismissed.

Various forms of sexual and racial harassment may be discriminatory, for instance:

● suggesting that sexual activity may help to further a career, or that refusal may mean that an employee is dismissed, or that it might hinder his career;

- unwelcome sexual attention;
- sustained obscene racist language, insults or discriminatory behaviour;
- the display of sexually suggestive or racially discriminatory material in the workplace.

If an employer has reason to believe that sexual harassment is taking place he has a duty to investigate the matter, and to take some action if necessary. He should not wait for a formal complaint to be made. See: ***Reed & Bull Information Systems Ltd v Stedman*** (1999).

There have been several European developments in relation to sexual harassment. In 1991 the European Commission issued a Recommendation on the Protection of the Dignity of Women and Men at Work. It does not impose direct legal obligations but encourages the development of policies to prevent and combat sexual harassment.

The code of practice on Protecting the Dignity of Women and Men at Work attached to the Recommendation defines sexual harassment as 'unwanted conduct of a sexual nature, or other conduct based on sex affecting the physical, verbal or non-verbal conduct'.

As noted above, regulations have recently inserted new 'harassment' definition sections into both the Sex Discrimination Act 1975 and the Race Relations Act 1976. Regulations 5 and 6 of the Race Relations Act 1976 (Amendment) Regulations 2003 inserted a new s 3A and amended s 4 of the 1976 Act. Section 3A(1) of the 1976 Act provides that:

> '**an employer will be unlawfully discriminating against a job applicant or employee if on grounds of race or ethnic or national origins, he engages in unwanted conduct which has the purpose or effect of**
>
> **(a) violating that other person's dignity, or**
>
> **(b) creating an intimidating, hostile, degrading, humiliating or offensive environment for him.'**

The conduct will be regarded as having had the above effect if having regard to all the circumstances it should reasonably be considered as having that effect.

Regulation 5 of the Employment Equality (Sex Discrimination) Regulations 2005 inserted a new s 4A into the Sex Discrimination Act 1975. Section 4A of that Act provides that:

> '**a person subjects a woman to harassment if –**
>
> **(a) on the ground of her sex, he engages in unwanted conduct that has the purpose or effect –**
>
> > **(i) of violating her dignity, or**
> >
> > **(ii) of creating an intimidating, hostile, degrading, humiliating or offensive environment for her,**
>
> **(b) he engages in any form of unwanted verbal, non-verbal or physical conduct of a sexual nature that has the purpose or effect –**
>
> > **(i) of violating her dignity, or**
> >
> > **(ii) of creating an intimidating, hostile, degrading, humiliating or offensive environment for her, or**
>
> **(c) on the ground of her rejection of or submission to unwanted conduct of a kind mentioned in paragraph (a) or (b), he treats her less favourably than he would treat her had she not rejected, or submitted to, the conduct.'**

The conduct will be regarded as having had the above effect if having regard to all the circumstances it should reasonably be considered as having that effect.

At the time of writing there is no significant case law that deals with these new definitions. In practice, the approach to harassment claims is unlikely to change significantly. Existing case law will still have relevance (see above) and it remains to be seen how the Employment Tribunal will deal with harassment claims in the future.

See also: *Snowball* v *Gardner Merchant* (1987), *Insitu Cleaning Co Ltd* v *Heads* (1995), *De Souza* v *Automobile Association* (1986).

OTHER HARASSMENT

The Criminal Justice and Public Order Act 1994 created a new offence of intentional harassment. This offence appears as the new s 4A inserted into the Public Order Act 1986 and carries a penalty of up to six months' imprisonment or a fine not exceeding £5000.

This offence covers harassment on the grounds of sex, race, disability, age and sexual orientation. This means that workplace harassment is covered and that employees who suffer harassment from colleagues or employers are now able to report the matter to the police.

The Protection from Harassment Act 1997 has also created two new criminal offences. This Act was primarily intended as an 'anti-stalking' measure and in some situations victims may suffer this form of harassment by work colleagues. The Act also allows the victim to apply for an injunction to prevent further harassment.

DISCRIMINATION ON THE GROUNDS OF SEXUAL ORIENTATION - THE EMPLOYMENT EQUALITY (SEXUAL ORIENTATION) REGULATIONS 2003

Prior to the implementation of the Employment Equality (Sexual Orientation) Regulations 2003, it was lawful for an employer to discriminate solely on the basis of a person's sexual orientation. The Regulations came into force on 1 December 2003. Following this time, employees who are subjected to homophobic abuse at work will not have to undertake the virtually impossible task of trying to present their case under the Sex Discrimination Act 1975.

The Regulations implemented the sexual orientation aspects of the EC Equal Treatment Framework Directive. The Directive set out a framework for eliminating 'employment inequalities based on religion, belief, disability, age and sexual orientation'.

The Regulations make it unlawful to discriminate against a straight person because they are straight or against a gay man or lesbian because they are a homosexual. There are two exceptions, namely where being of a particular sexual orientation is a genuine occupational requirement or where national security is at risk. Prior to 2003 some successful claims were made by referring cases to the European Court of Justice and the ECHR under the Equal Treatment Directive and the Convention on Human Rights but the decisions both from the courts and tribunals do not form any uniform set of rules or guidelines.

The pre-2003 case law is outlined here mainly for historical reasons but the decisions remain interesting in that we are able to follow the reasoning of the judges at the time. Secondly, the 2003 Regulations only apply to discrimination on the basis of sexual orientation in the employment field. Consequently, the pre-2003 case law is still relevant in cases of discrimination on the grounds of sexual orientation in other fields. Note, however, that in relation to employment matters it is now unlawful to discriminate on the basis of sexual orientation.

Similarly in *Smith* v *Gardner Merchant Ltd* (1996) the EAT held that discriminating against a person for being either a male homosexual or a lesbian was discrimination on the grounds of sexual orientation and not on the grounds of sex. Consequently, as neither the Sex Discrimination Act 1975 nor the Equal Treatment Directive recognised sexual orientation, they provided no protection.

R v Ministry of Defence, ex parte Smith (1996)

The tribunal was asked to consider whether the Ministry of Defence had discriminated against members of the armed forces when it dismissed them on the ground of their homosexuality. In 1994 the Ministry had reaffirmed its policy that being homosexual was incompatible with army life and that persons known to be gay would be dismissed. A soldier who had been discharged argued that this decision breached the Equal Treatment Directive.

Held (CA) Appeal dismissed because the Ministry's policy could not be questioned and the Directive was not intended to protect discrimination on the grounds of sexual orientation.

A year later the High Court held that it was likely that the Equal Treatment Directive did apply to homosexuals. In *R v Secretary of State for Defence, ex parte Perkins* (1997) a Royal Navy officer was discharged from the navy when he revealed that he was homosexual. However, in July 1998 the European Court of Justice ruled that such dismissals were not discriminatory as they did not fall under the remit of the Equal Treatment Directive: See: *R v Secretary of State for Defence, ex parte Perkins (No. 2)* (1998).

In *Grant v South West Trains* (1998) Ms Grant was denied travel concessions for her lesbian partner. Her male predecessor had been given travel concessions for his female partner, regardless of whether they were married. The European Court of Justice held that stable single-sex relationships did not have to be treated in the same way as marriages or relationships between men and women.

On an appeal hearing of *Smith v Gardner Merchant Ltd* (1999) the COA held that the Sex Discrimination Act 1975 would apply to a male homosexual who had been harassed because he was gay. However, it would only apply if he could show that a female homosexual would not have been treated in the same way. In the Scottish case of *MacDonald v Ministry of Defence* (2001) it was held that the SDA did not apply to issues of sexual orientation. Mr MacDonald was a RAF Flight lieutenant who had been dismissed because he was homosexual. Whilst it was agreed that he had a viable action under Articles 8 and 14 of the Human Rights Convention, it was said that he had no claim under the 1975 Act. The court reiterated the point that the 1975 Act refers to discrimination against a person because of their gender and not their sexual orientation. These cases provide an interesting analysis of the confusion surrounding the law in this area.

Pearce v Governing Body of Mayfield Secondary School (2002) (CA)

Ms Pearce, a homosexual teacher, had been subjected to regular homophobic taunts and abuse by pupils. These included students referring to her as a 'lesbian' and a 'dyke'. She failed in her claim that the use of those words to describe her (as opposed to gender neutral words such as 'gay') was discrimination on the grounds of her sex. She had alleged this even though she could not show that she had been treated less favourably than a male homosexual. The Human Rights Act was not in force at the time of her original complaint and so the court held that they could not take it into account.

Held Ms Pearce failed in her claim; the Sex Discrimination Act 1975 did not apply to questions of sexual orientation.

Both **Pearce** and **MacDonald** were appealed to the House of Lords. In *Pearce v Governing Body of Mayfield School* (2003) and *MacDonald v Advocate General for Scotland (2003)* the House of Lords made it clear that the Sex Discrimination Act 1975 made it unlawful to discriminate on the basis of gender only and that this did not cover discrimination on the grounds of sexual orientation.

The 2003 Regulations

The Regulations specify four types of discrimination: direct discrimination, indirect discrimination, victimisation and harassment. They protect the rights of workers and apply to all employers/businesses whatever their size and whether in the public or private sector. The Regulations apply to recruitment, terms and conditions, pay, promotion, transfers and dismissals. The Regulations are broadly similar in structure to the Sex Discrimination Act 1975 and the Race Relations Act 1976 and implement the sexual orientation strands of the Framework Directive 200/78/EC.

The scope of the Regulations is wide ranging. Although the law seeks mainly to protect gay men, lesbians and bisexuals, the Regulations also protect every individual from discrimination based on their sexuality. The Regulations also protect against discrimination on the grounds of perceived, as well as actual, sexual orientation.

What is sexual orientation? - Regulation 2(1)

Regulation 2 acts as an interpretation section. Regulation 2(1) states that:

'sexual orientation' means a sexual orientation towards –

(a) persons of the same sex;

(b) persons of the opposite sex; or

(c) persons of the same sex and of the opposite sex.

Direct sexual orientation discrimination - Regulation 3(1)(a)

Regulation 3(1)(a) states that:

For the purposes of these Regulations, a person ('A') discriminates against another person ('B') if –

(a) on grounds of sexual orientation, A treats B less favourably than he treats or would treat other persons.

Direct discrimination is overt or blatant discrimination. It occurs where a person treats another less favourably on the grounds of their sexual orientation.

> **Example**
> Victoria is an accountant. She is interviewed for a new position. Whilst being interviewed she mentions that she has a same-sex partner. Although she has all of the skills required for the job the firm decides not to offer her the position because she is a lesbian.

Direct discrimination may also be based on the grounds of a person's perceived sexual orientation. Direct discrimination may also occur when a person is treated less favourably because they associate with gay friends, or because they refuse to carry out an employer's instruction to discriminate against homosexual persons. In bringing a claim the individual does not have to declare their sexual orientation. They only have to show that they were treated less favourably than a heterosexual person because the employer believed them to be a homosexual.

Direct discrimination cannot be justified. In very limited circumstances an employer may be able to discriminate where a genuine occupational requirement can be shown to apply (see below).

Indirect sexual orientation discrimination - Regulation 3(1)(b)

Regulation 3(1)(b) states that:

(1) a person ('A') discriminates against another person ('B') if –

(b) A applies to B a provision, criterion or practice which he applies or would apply equally to persons not of the same sexual orientation as B, but –

(i) which puts or would put persons of the same sexual orientation as B at a particular disadvantage when compared with other persons,

(ii) which puts B at that disadvantage, and

(iii) which A cannot show to be a proportionate means of achieving a legitimate aim.

Example
A brewery advertises for a couple to run a pub but stipulates that the couple must be married. This preference for a married couple would be a 'provision, criterion or practice' which, although not on the face of it discriminatory, would put homosexual couples at a particular disadvantage as they cannot marry in the legal sense of the word. The brewery would have to show that the requirement pursued a legitimate aim and that it was proportionate to apply it in this instance.

Indirect discrimination is covert or hidden discrimination. If the person claiming indirect discrimination can show that they have suffered a disadvantage, then the provision, criterion or practice is indirectly discriminatory. Indirect discrimination is unlawful whether it is intentional or not.

Indirect discrimination will not be unlawful if it can be shown to be justified. To justify its actions, an employer must show that there was a legitimate aim, e.g. a real business need and that the practice was proportionate to that aim. The practice will be proportionate to the aim if it is necessary and there are no alternative means available.

Victimisation - Regulation 4

Regulation 4(1) states that:

A person ('A') discriminates against another person ('B') if he treats B less favourably than he treats or would treat other persons in the same circumstances, and does so by reason that B has –

(a) brought proceedings against A or any other person under these Regulations;

(b) given evidence or information in connection with proceedings brought by any person against A or any other person under these Regulations;

(c) otherwise done anything under or by reference to these Regulations in relation to A or any other person; or

(d) alleged that A or any other person has committed an action which (whether or not the allegation so states) would amount to a contravention of these Regulations, or by reason that A knows that B intends to do any of those things, or suspects that B has done or intends to do any of them.

An employer will not have victimised an individual where the allegation was false and not made or given in good faith. Victimisation on the basis of a person's sexual orientation takes place where they are treated less favourably because of something they have done, e.g. the person may have made a formal discrimination complaint or given evidence in a tribunal case.

> **Example**
> *Helen gave evidence for her colleague Clare in a sexual orientation discrimination tribunal claim. She is then branded a troublemaker by her boss and her application for promotion is rejected even though she has all of the required experience/skills for the position. Her boss tells her that he would not promote troublemakers and that she would have been promoted had she not given evidence for Clare. Here, Helen has been victimised.*

Harassment - Regulation 5

Regulation 5 states that:

> **a person ('A') subjects another person ('B') to harassment where, on grounds of sexual orientation, A engages in unwanted conduct which has the purpose or effect of –**
>
> **(a) violating B's dignity; or**
>
> **(b) creating an intimidating, hostile, degrading, humiliating or offensive environment for B.**

Conduct will be regarded as violating a person's dignity or creating an intimidating, hostile, degrading, humiliating or offensive environment if having regard to all the circumstances it should reasonably be considered as having that effect.

> **Example**
> *A male worker who has a same-sex partner is continually referred to by female nicknames, which he finds humiliating and distressing. This would amount to harassment.*

Behaviour that is offensive, frightening or distressing is likely to be termed harassment. The Regulations apply equally to the harassment of heterosexual people as they do to the harassment of lesbians, gay men and bisexual persons. Employers may be held to be responsible for any harassment carried out by their employees (see Regulation 22). Individual employees may also be liable for any harassment that they themselves instigate.

Stages at which discrimination may take place

Regulation 6 states that it is unlawful for an employer to discriminate against an individual in:

(a) the arrangements he makes for determining to whom he should offer employment;

(b) the terms on which he offers that person employment;

(c) refusing to offer, or deliberately not offering him employment;

(d) the terms of employment in existence during employment;

(e) the opportunities which he affords for promotion, transfer, training, or the receipt of any other benefit;

(f) refusing to afford or deliberately not affording him such opportunity; or

(g) in dismissing him, or subjecting him to any other detriment.

Discrimination after the employment has ended - Regulation 21

Regulation 21 states that it is unlawful for an employer to discriminate against or harass a former employee after the working relationship between them has ended. The act of discrimination or harassment must be closely linked to the former relationship.

Genuine occupational requirements – Regulation 7

Regulation 7 states that there are two very limited situations in which an employer may discriminate against a person on the basis of their sexual orientation. These are where:

(a) having regard to the nature of the employment being of a particular sexual orientation is a genuine and determining occupational requirement and it is proportionate to apply that requirement, and

(b) the employment is for the purposes of any organised religion.

In relation to (b) an employer may discriminate on the grounds of a person's sexual orientation to either comply with particular religious beliefs or to avoid a situation in which other workers' beliefs conflict with that persons sexual orientation. In *R (Amicus – MSF Section)* v *Secretary for Trade and Industry* (2004) the unions applied for judicial review on the basis that the 2003 Regulations did not properly implement the EC Equal Treatment Directive. Their claim was unsuccessful. Leave to appeal to the Court of Appeal was granted but at the time of writing there is no information on whether the unions intend to appeal.

National security – Regulation 24

This regulation states that an employer may lawfully discriminate on the basis of sexual orientation where they do so to safeguard national security. Their actions must be justified.

Making a sexual orientation discrimination claim to the Employment Tribunal

A person who believes that they have been discriminated against on the grounds of their sexual orientation may make a claim to the Employment Tribunal. The claim must be made within 3 months of the act complained of. The Regulations provide for a questionnaire procedure which allows an applicant to ask their employer/prospective employer to provide information prior to the tribunal hearing. If the claimant is successful the Employment Tribunal may make a declaration or recommendation stating that the employer should take action to prevent or reduce the impact of the discrimination. The tribunal may also make a compensatory award. There is no limit set on the amount of compensation that may be awarded.

Acas have produced a useful guide to the Regulations: *Sexual Orientation and the Workplace – Putting the Employment Equality (Sexual Orientation) Regulations 2003 into practice.* The DTI have also produced a very useful set of explanatory notes: *Explanation of the provisions of the: Employment Equality (Sexual Orientation) Regulations 2003 and Employment Equality (Religion or Belief) Regulations 2003.* Both publications are available via the Acas or DTI websites.

Civil partnerships

The Civil Partnership Act 2004 came into force on 18 November 2004. Under the provisions of this statute, same-sex couples are able to obtain legal recognition of their relationship by registering as 'civil partners'.

Discrimination against transsexuals

Tribunals have also had to consider cases concerning discrimination against transsexuals. In the case of *P* v *S and Cornwall County Council* (1996) P was a manager at a council-run educational department. S was its Chief Executive. P had been born male, but had announced her intention to undergo a sex change. She was then dismissed and claimed that it was because she had made the announcement. The Council argued that the real reason for P's dismissal was redundancy.

It was held that the true reason behind P's dismissal was her intention to undergo a sex change and as such she had been discriminated against. However, she was unable to make a claim as she was not protected by the Sex Discrimination Act 1975. P was not protected by the 1975 Act because it only referred to people of one sex or another and not those in a transsexual condition. The case was referred to the ECJ which held that the Equal Treatment Directive did cover gender reassignment. This meant that P was eventually successful in her claim. The Council was in breach of the Equal Treatment Directive when it dismissed her on the grounds of her gender reassignment.

In the case of *Chessington World of Adventure* v *Reed* (1998) the Employment Appeal Tribunal stated that the Sex Discrimination Act 1975 would apply to cases involving discrimination against transsexuals.

The law on such discrimination is now covered by the Gender Reassignment Regulations 1999 (1999/1102). These Regulations inserted a new s 2A into the Sex Discrimination Act 1975. The Act now states that it is unlawful to discriminate against a person who 'intends to undergo, is undergoing, or has undergone gender reassignment'. It is unlawful to treat them less favourably on the basis of their gender reassignment. If a person is going to be absent from work because they are having treatment which will lead to gender reassignment they should not be treated any less favourably than they would have been had they been absent due to illness or injury.

There are exceptions to this rule which relate to genuine occupational qualifications. If being a man or woman is a genuine occupational qualification for a job, for example, the job involves performing intimate physical searches subject to statutory powers then to refuse to employ a transsexual will not be discriminatory. Details on valid genuine occupational qualifications can be found in Sections 7A–B of the 1975 Act.

In July 2002 the European Court of Human Rights ruled that transsexuals should be legally recognised as having changed sex for all purposes. In December 2002 the government announced that it was committed to changing the law in this area to bring it into line with the European Convention on Human Rights. This was achieved by the introduction of the Gender Recognition Act 2004. This Act came into force on 1 July 2004. Transsexuals are now able to apply for the right (from the date of recognition) to marry in their acquired gender, claim benefits and state pensions at the appropriate age, and request an updated birth certificate.

THE IMMIGRATION, ASYLUM AND NATIONALITY ACT 2006

If an employer employs someone who does not have the right to remain in the United Kingdom or does not have a work permit the employer may be guilty of an offence under this Act. The Immigration, Asylum and Nationality Act 2006 received Royal Assent on 30 March 2006. This Act repeals and replaces s 8 of the Asylum and Immigration Act 1996. At the time of writing there is no information on when the 2006 Act will be fully in force. The 2006 Act imposes new civil penalties on employers who employ illegal workers. An employer found to be employing an illegal worker will be liable to pay a penalty of up to £2,000 per illegal employee. The Act also introduces a new criminal offence of employing a person knowing that they are not legally entitled to work in the United Kingdom. The maximum penalty for contravention of this provision is 2 years' imprisonment and/or a fine.

It is not discriminatory for an employer to ask a job applicant or employee to provide evidence of his residence or work permit. An employer may be able to defend a charge under the Act if they are able to show that such evidence (which appeared to be legitimate) was shown to him before the person was employed/during employment.

Discrimination in employment

Dhatt v McDonald's Hamburgers Ltd (1991)

McDonald's asked Mr Dhatt, an Indian, to provide a work permit. This would not have been required of a British applicant.

Held (CA) This request was not discriminatory but justified in light of British immigration laws.

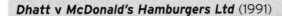

Olatokun v Ikon Office Solutions (2004) EAT

When the claimant stated on her job application that she was Nigerian her prospective employer asked her to produce her passport. She claimed racial discrimination.

Held (EAT) Her claim was unsuccessful. It was not discriminatory for the employer to ask for information which proved that the claimant was legally entitled to work in the United Kingdom.

DISABILITY DISCRIMINATION

The Disability Discrimination Act 1995 has been amended by the Disability Discrimination Act 1995 (Amendment) Regulations 2003. These regulations came into force on 1 October 2004. There has also been an addition to legislation in this area in the form of the Disability Discrimination Act 2005.

The Employment Tribunals Service annual report (2004/5) states that there were 4,942 disability discrimination claims during that year. The Acas annual report (2004/5) states that they dealt with 2,652 claims involving alleged disability discrimination. Most cases concerned dismissal, followed by recruitment and the duty of employers to make reasonable adjustments to the working environment to accommodate a disabled person.

The Disability Discrimination Act 1995 is the main statute on disability discrimination but there is also additional guidance to be found in the:

- Disability Discrimination (Amendment) Regulations 2003;
- Guidance on matters to be taken into account in determining questions relating to the definition of disability (in force 1 May 2006); and
- Disability Discrimination Act Code of Practice on employment and occupation (2004).

As noted above, the 2003 Amendment Regulations made significant changes to the 1995 Act. These regulations implement the disability discrimination provisions within the EC Equal Treatment Framework Directive (2000/78). The guidance notes provide clear information on both the 1995 and 2005 Acts (plus relevant amendments), and the new code of practice replaces the original 1996 code to take into account the new legislation. (The code of practice is discussed further at page 86.)

The scope of the Disability Discrimination Act 1995

The 1995 Act recognises four forms of discrimination:

1 direct discrimination
2 disability related discrimination
3 failure to make reasonable adjustments
4 victimisation.

The Act differs from the sex and race legislation in that it does not recognise indirect discrimination. The Act only protects disabled people. This means that a non-disabled person cannot rely on it to show that discrimination has occurred. An employer is able to positively discriminate in favour of disabled people.

What will be classed as a 'disability'?

A person cannot make a discrimination claim under the 1995 Act unless classed as a 'disabled person' under the definition in s 1. Section 1 of the 1995 Act defines a disabled person as one who:

> **. . . has a physical or mental impairment which has a substantial and long-term adverse effect on his ability to carry out normal day-to-day activities.**

Both physical and mental conditions are recognised. To have a substantial effect the condition must not be minor or trivial and must have a long-term adverse effect on the employee's ability to perform daily activities. This means that it must be likely to last either for 12 months or more or for the rest of a person's life. In *Abadeh* v *British Telecommunications Plc* (2001) it was held that the issue of whether a condition has a 'substantial' effect is a question for the tribunal and not a doctor. This does not mean, however, that the tribunal can ignore medical evidence. Day-to-day activities include things such as the use of memory, concentration, speech, hearing, eyesight, mobility and dexterity.

Rowley v *Walkers Nonsuch Ltd* (1997)

Rowley had suffered a back injury at work and had to go on sick leave for six months.

Held This injury did not constitute a 'disability' under the 1995 Act. It did not have a substantial and long-term adverse effect on Rowley's ability to carry out daily activities.

It used to be the case that a mental illness had to be 'clinically well recognised' in order for it to be regarded as a mental impairment for the purposes of the 1995 Act. The Disability Discrimination Act 2005 removed this requirement from 5 December 2005. This Act also widened the definition of those persons who will be classed as having a disability. The following people are deemed to meet the definition of 'disability' without having to show that they have an impairment that has (or is likely to have) a substantial, adverse, long-term effect on the ability to carry out normal day-to-day activities:

- those with cancer, HIV/Aids, or multiple sclerosis
- those certified blind or partially sighted.

Anyone whose condition does not come under the above will have to show that their particular condition meets the requirements as outlined below.

Both the Disability Discrimination (Meaning of Disability) Regulations 1996 and the 2006 guidance notes define what types of condition will and will not constitute a disability. The following conditions will not be regarded as impairments for the purposes of the 1995 Act:

- addiction to alcohol, nicotine or drugs;
- hay fever;
- pyromania (tendency to set fires);

- kleptomania (tendency to steal);
- tendency to physical or sexual abuse of other persons;
- exhibitionism;
- voyeurism; and
- disfigurements which consist of a tattoo, non-medical body piercing or something attached through piercing.

In *Morgan v Staffordshire University* (2002) it was held that suffering from 'stress' did not amount to a disability. In *Quinn v Schwarzkopf* (2002) it was held that suffering from rheumatoid arthritis did constitute a disability. In *Hewett v Motorola Ltd* (2004) it was held that suffering from autism amounted to having a disability for the purposes of the 1995 Act. Similarly, in *Whitbread Hotel Co Ltd v Bayley* (2006), suffering from dyslexia was held to amount to having a disability. In *Goodwin v The Patent Office* (1999) general guidelines were set out in order to assist the tribunal. These state that the tribunal should ask:

1 whether the applicant has a mental or physical impairment;

2 whether the impairment affects the applicant's ability to carry out normal day-to-day activities;

3 whether the adverse effect is substantial;

4 whether the adverse effect is long term.

Once a person is recognised as being disabled under the Act, this recognition remains with him for the rest of his life. There is no need for him to reapply at any time in the future.

Direct disability discrimination

Section 3A(5) of the Disability Discrimination Act 1995 states that an employer directly discriminates against a disabled person if:

> on the ground of the disabled person's disability, he treats the disabled person less favourably than he treats or would treat a person not having that particular disability whose relevant circumstances, including his abilities, are the same as, or not materially different from, those of the disabled person.

Direct discrimination is blatant or overt discrimination. Here, the comparator must be someone who does not have the same disability and may be someone who is not disabled. Their circumstances must be the same or not materially different to those of the disabled person. A hypothetical comparator may be used. Section 3A(4) of the 1995 Act states that there can be no justification in relation to direct disability discrimination. An employer is unable to justify the fact that they discriminated on the basis of a person's disability.

Paragraph 4.8 of the disability code of practice provides examples of what will amount to direct discrimination. An example from paragraph 4.8 is set out below:

> A blind woman is not shortlisted for a job involving computers because the employer wrongly assumes that blind people cannot use them. The employer makes no attempt to look at the individual circumstances. The employer has treated the woman less favourably than other people by not shortlisting her for the job. The treatment was on the ground of the woman's disability (because assumptions would not have been made about a non-disabled person).

See also the following recent decision on direct disability discrimination.

Tudor v Spen Corner Veterinary Centre Ltd and anor (2006)

Ms Tudor had been employed as a veterinary nursing assistant and receptionist. In May 2005 she suffered a stroke and in the June of 2005 (while she was in hospital) she was told that she had gone blind and that her doctors were unsure whether her sight would return. Ms Tudor's mother informed her daughter's employer of her condition. In July 2005 she was then dismissed by her employer. They had made no effort to meet with her or to establish her accurate medical condition or future prognosis.

Held Ms Tudor had suffered direct discrimination in breach of Section 3A(5).

Disability related discrimination

Section 3(A)(1) of the Disability Discrimination Act 1995 states that an employer discriminates against a disabled person if:

(a) for a reason which relates to the disabled person's disability, he treats him less favourably than he treats or would treat others to whom that reason does not or would not apply, and

(b) he cannot show that the treatment in question is justified.

The phrase 'disability related discrimination' is not used in the 1995 Act but is used in the disability code of practice. Treatment is justified if the reason is both material to the circumstances of the particular case and substantial. The employer's treatment of the disabled person must be compared with that of a person to whom the disability related reason does not apply. The comparator may be disabled or non-disabled but the disability related reason for the less favourable treatment must not apply to him.

Less favourable treatment

What will amount to less favourable treatment differs in relation to direct disability discrimination and disability-related discrimination. The following diagrams highlight the difference between the forms of less favourable treatment.

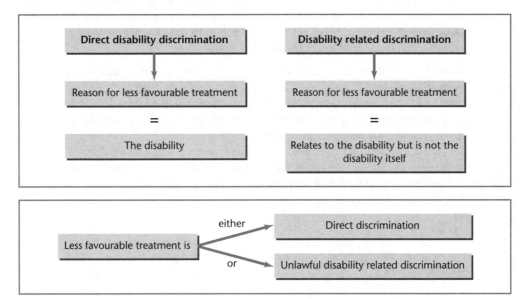

To treat a person less favourably on the grounds of a disability related reason means that the person is refused some advantage, such as employment or training, or e.g. they are dismissed. The key is to compare what has happened to the disabled person with what would have happened had he not been disabled. In *Clark* v *Novacold Ltd* (1999) the Court of Appeal held that the less favourable treatment does not run on a like-for-like comparison of the disabled person and of others in similar circumstances. This means that the correct comparator is someone to whom the reason does not apply. See also, *British Sugar* v *Kirker* (1998). The test of less favourable treatment is based on the reason for the treatment and not the fact of the person's disability.

Paragraph 4.30 of the disability code of practice provides examples of what will amount to disability related discrimination. An example from paragraph 4.30 is set out below:

> **A disabled man is dismissed for taking 6 months' sick leave which is disability related. The employer's policy, which has been applied equally to all staff (whether disabled or not) is to dismiss all employees who have taken this amount of sick leave. The disability related reason for the less favourable treatment of the disabled person is the fact of having to take 6 months' sick leave, and the correct comparator is a person to whom that reason does not apply – that is, someone who has not taken 6 months' sick leave. Consequently, unless the employer can show the treatment is justified, it will amount to disability related discrimination because the comparator would not have been dismissed. However, the reason for the treatment is not the disability itself (it is only a matter related thereto, namely the amount of sick leave taken), so, there is no direct discrimination.**

Duty to make reasonable adjustments

As noted above, s 3A(2) of the 1995 Act states that an employer discriminates against a disabled person if he fails to comply with a duty to make reasonable adjustments. An employer's failure to make reasonable adjustments cannot be justified. Section 4A(1) of the 1995 Act states that:

> **Where –**
>
> **(a) a provision, criterion or practice applied by or on behalf of an employer, or**
>
> **(b) any physical feature of premises occupied by the employer,**
>
> **places the disabled person concerned at a substantial disadvantage in comparison with persons who are not disabled, it is the duty of the employer to take such steps as it is reasonable, in all the circumstances of the case, for him to have to take in order to prevent the provision, criterion or practice, or feature having that effect.**

If an employer fails to make reasonable adjustments, he can be said to have discriminated against the disabled person. This will then form part of an action for direct discrimination. The employer does not have any duty to make reasonable adjustments under s 4A if he did not know, and could not reasonably have known that an applicant for employment is disabled. There is no requirement, however, for an employer to have knowledge of a person's disability in order to treat them less favourably for reasons connected with it. See: *London Borough of Hammersmith* v *Farnsworth* (2000), *HJ Heinz & Co Ltd* v *Kenrick* (2000). Section 18B of the 1995 Act provides a list of examples of what may amount to making reasonable adjustments.

> ### Example
> *Reasonable adjustments might include:*
>
> * *making adjustments to premises, for instance, widening doorways, providing wheelchair ramps or repositioning shelves;*

- *changing working hours; allocating some of the disabled person's duties to another person;*
- *allowing the disabled person to be absent during working hours to attend rehabilitation sessions or obtain medical treatment;*
- *acquiring or modifying equipment;*
- *providing training; providing supervision;*
- *providing a reader or interpreter.*

The extent of the adjustments needed is subject to a test of what is 'reasonable' in the particular circumstances. An employer should carry out an assessment of what steps may be required to aid an employee in carrying out their employment within the workplace. Paragraph 5.3 of the disability code of practice provides the following example of what might be likely to be a reasonable adjustment.

A man who is disabled because he has dyslexia applies for a job which involves writing letters. The employer gives all applicants a test of their letter-writing ability. The man can generally write letters very well but finds it difficult to do so in stressful situations and within short deadlines. He is given longer to take the test. This adjustment is likely to be a reasonable one for the employer to make.

Section 18B(1) of the 1995 Act provides guidance on what would or would not be regarded as 'reasonable' action on the part of the employer.

Section 18B(1) states that:

In determining whether it is reasonable for a person to have to take a particular step in order to comply with a duty to make reasonable adjustments, regard shall be had, in particular to –

- **the extent to which taking the step would prevent the effect in relation to which the duty is imposed;**
- **the extent to which it is practicable for him to take the step;**
- **the financial and other costs which would be incurred by him in taking the step and the extent to which it would disrupt any of his activities;**
- **the extent of his financial and other resources;**
- **the availability to him of financial or other assistance with respect to taking the step;**
- **the nature of his activities and the size of his undertaking;**
- **where the step would be taken in relation to a private household, the extent to which taking it would –**
  - **(i) disrupt that household, or**
  - **(ii) disturb any person residing there.**

The following decisions are illustrative of cases in which it was alleged that an employer failed to make reasonable adjustments.

Tarling v Wisdom Toothbrushes (1997)

Tarling suffered from a club foot and had trouble standing or sitting for long periods of time. He was dismissed because of this disability.

Held He had been discriminated against because his employer had not taken steps to make reasonable adjustments to the workplace. It would not have been prohibitively expensive or inconvenient for the employer to have provided Tarling with special seating.

Meikle v Nottinghamshire County Council (2004)

Gaynor Meikle worked as a schoolteacher for a local authority. She suffered from deteriorating vision. Eventually she lost the sight in one eye and had limited vision in the other. When she arrived at work each morning she was handed a timetable detailing which classes she was to cover that day. Ms Meikle found these timetables very difficult to read. She made several requests to her Head of Department asking for an enlarged copy of the timetable. No arrangements were ever made to provide her with this. Secondly, she was told that she would have to teach in a classroom which was some distance away from the one in which she generally taught. Ms Meikle asked for her timetable to be adjusted so that she would easily be able to find her way to her classroom. She also requested extra preparation time, and that school notices should be provided in enlarged print. No adjustments were ever made following her requests even though it would have been practicable for the school to make such changes. Ms Meikle had to take time off sick due to eye strain and eventually resigned, claiming constructive dismissal and that her employer had failed to make reasonable adjustments.

Held (CA) The school should have made the reasonable adjustments outlined above. They were wrong to reduce Ms Meikle's salary when she took sick leave following their failure to make reasonable adjustments to her working environment.

Archibald v Fife Council (2004)

Ms Archibald had been employed by the council as a road sweeper since 1997. After undergoing surgery she became unable to walk without the aid of sticks and consequently could not continue to do her job. She could do sedentary work and so approached the council asking for a 'desk job'. The council was aware of their need to make reasonable adjustments and sent Ms Archibald on several computer and administration courses. She then applied for over 100 jobs at the council but failed to impress the panel during 'competitive interviews'. It was council policy that candidates had to attend such an interview prior to being offered a job. She was dismissed when the council thought that they had exhausted all possible redeployment measures. Ms Archibald stated that the council should have placed her in a new role without the need for her to attend an interview and that there had therefore been a failure to make reasonable adjustments.

Held (HOL) The council had breached their duty to make reasonable adjustments. In the House of Lords Lady Hale stated that 'The 1995 Act ... does not regard the differences between disabled people and others as irrelevant. It does not expect each to be treated in the same way. It expects reasonable adjustments to be made to cater for the special needs of disabled people. It necessarily entails an element of more favourable treatment.' In some cases the Act obliges employers to treat a disabled person more favourably than others and this may even require transferring them to a higher-level position without the need for a competitive interview.

Williams v J Walter Thomson Group Ltd (2005)

Ms Williams is completely blind. She was appointed as an IT developer in June 1999 and was told that she would be working with Lotus Notes software. It was established that she would need specific training on the use of this software. She was also aware that she would need specialist equipment, e.g. a Braille display to enable her to do her job. This equipment was not provided when she began work and when it arrived four months later it took several weeks to install. She made several requests for training and work to be provided but her requests were ignored. Ms Williams resigned.

Held (CA) Her employer had failed to make reasonable adjustments. They had known when they appointed Ms Williams that she was completely blind and that she would require training in order to be able to do her job. They had failed to provide her with the training or equipment that she needed and had thus failed in their duty.

Rothwell v Pelikan Hardcopy Scotland Ltd (2006) EAT

Mr Rothwell has Parkinson's disease. He was assessed by an occupational doctor and a consultant. However, he was not shown his medical reports. He was invited to a meeting with his employer and was told that he was to be dismissed on health grounds. His employer was not fully aware of his current medical circumstances and did not consult with him before taking the decision to dismiss. There was no discussion as to whether his condition might improve enough to enable him to continue to work.

Held (EAT) The employer's failure to consult with Mr. Rothwell before dismissing him on the grounds of ill health amounted to a failure to make reasonable adjustments. He should have been consulted before the decision was taken and it was not unreasonable to expect his employer to tolerate a delay while this consultation took place.

See also: *High Quality Lifestyles Ltd* v *Watts* (2006) EAT, *British Telecommunications plc* v *Pousson* (2005) EAT.

Victimisation - section 55

Section 55 of the 1995 Act states that a person is victimised on the grounds of disability where he is treated less favourably because:

- he has brought proceedings under the 1995 Act; or
- given evidence in any such proceedings.

An employer may defend such an action if he believes that the original allegations were false or not made in good faith.

Harassment - section 4(3)

The 2003 Regulations inserted a new offence of harassment into the 1995 Act. Harassment is defined in s 3B of the 1995 Act, which states that:

A person subjects a disabled person to harassment where, for a reason which relates to the disabled person's disability he engages in unwanted conduct which has the purpose or effect of

Discrimination in employment

2

(a) **violating the disabled person's dignity, or**

(b) **creating an intimidating, hostile, degrading, humiliating or offensive environment for him.**

The conduct will be taken to be harassment only if having regard to all the circumstances it can reasonably be considered as having the effect of harassment.

The following diagrams highlight the different forms of disability discrimination.

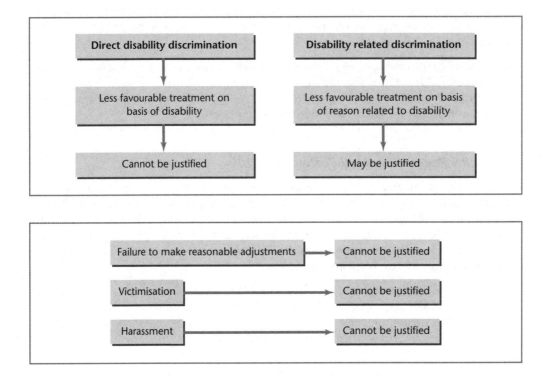

Stages at which discrimination may take place

Section 4 of the 1995 Act states that it is unlawful for an employer to discriminate:

- in the arrangements which he makes for the purpose of determining to whom he should offer employment;
- in the terms on which he offers that person employment; or
- by refusing to offer, or deliberately not offering, him employment;
- in the opportunities which he affords him for promotion, a transfer, training or receiving of any other benefit;
- by refusing to afford him, or deliberately not affording him any such opportunity; or
- by dismissing him or subjecting him to any other detriment.

Job advertisements

The Disability Discrimination Act 1995 did not contain any specific provision relating to job advertisements until it was amended by the 2003 Regulations. Whilst there was no specific rule banning employers from using advertisements that discriminate against disabled people, it was assumed that they would not. Section 11 of the 1995 Act stated that 'if an advertisement blatantly infers that the employer does not intend to employ a disabled person then it is for the employer to show that he did not intend to discriminate'. This section has been replaced by a section which specifically prohibits discriminatory advertisements.

Section 16B of the 1995 Act states that it is unlawful for a person to publish or cause to be published an advertisement which:

(a) invites applications for a relevant appointment or benefit; and

(b) indicates, or might reasonably be understood to indicate, that an application will or may be determined to any extent by reference to-

    (i) the applicant not having any disability, or any particular disability,

    (ii) the applicant not having had any disability, or any particular disability, or

    (iii) any reluctance of the person determining the application to comply with a duty to make reasonable adjustments.

Many advertisements contain statements reinforcing the fact that employers welcome applications from disabled people.

Application forms and interviews

Employers should take care not to discriminate against disabled persons when drafting application forms and when selecting and interviewing potential candidates. Employers should offer disabled applicants assistance during this process. This could mean the changing of interview times, location or the provision of assistance during the interview.

Offers of employment and access to promotion

Employers should not discriminate against disabled persons when making an offer of employment. They should not be disadvantaged in relation to transfers, promotion, terms and conditions, benefits, pension schemes, harassment, victimisation, redundancy or dismissal.

Defences to disability discrimination

As noted above, direct disability discrimination, failure to make reasonable adjustments and victimisation can never be justified. However, in relation to disability related discrimination an employer may be able to show that their conduct was justified. Their treatment will only be justified if the reason for it is both material to the circumstances of the particular case and substantial. It remains to be seen how these provisions will be assessed in the Employment Tribunal.

Employer's liability - section 58

As with sex and race discrimination, s 58 of the 1995 Act states that employers may be vicariously liable for the discriminatory actions of their employees.

Exclusions

When it first became law, the Disability Discrimination Act 1995 did not apply to businesses which employed fewer than 20 employees. In 1998 the law changed and from that time the 1995 Act did not apply to employers with fewer than 15 employees. This exception could still be said to be unfair because, whether an employer with 2000 or 10 employees discriminates against a disabled person, his actions and the consequences remain the same.

From 1 October 2004 the 'exemption for small employers' was removed from the 1995 Act by the Disability Discrimination Act 1995 (Amendment) Regulations 2003. The Disability Discrimination Act 1995 now applies to all employers regardless of the number of persons that they employ.

The Disability Rights Commission

The Disability Rights Commission was set up under the Disability Rights Commission Act 1999. It has a similar role to that of the Equal Opportunities Commission and the Commission for Racial Equality. The Commission can assist individuals in bringing a disability discrimination claim and can investigate where they suspect that discrimination is taking place. (The role of the Commission is further discussed at page 31.) Note that from October 2007 the DRC will cease to exist and its role will be undertaken by the Commission for Equality and Human Rights.

Disability code of practice (2004)

The disability code of practice is referred to as the 'Code of Practice on employment and occupation'.

It came into force on 1 October 2004 and, although it does not impose any legal sanctions, it can be used as evidence in tribunal proceedings. It provides employers with general guidance on issues involving disability discrimination. The code gives examples and explanations of likely interpretations of the Disability Discrimination Act 1995. It also provides assistance on how to make a disability discrimination claim to the employment tribunal. The code is accompanied by a guidance document referred to as 'Guidance on matters to be taken into account in determining questions relating to the definition of disability'. This was produced in 2006.

The Disability Rights Commission also produce other codes of practice such as that on 'Rights of Access, Goods, Facilities, Services and Premises'. Copies of the DRC codes of practice are accessible via the Commission's website. However, it is the 2004 Code that provides the most general and detailed guidance on disability issues.

DISCRIMINATION ON THE GROUNDS OF AGE, POLITICAL PERSUASION OR RELIGION

An employer is able to discriminate on the basis of political persuasion. However, it is now unlawful to discriminate on the basis of a person's religion or belief. The Employment Equality (Religion or Belief) Regulations came into force on 2 December 2003. Following detailed consultation the Employment Equality (Age) Regulations 2006 came into force on 1 October 2006.

Age discrimination

Age discrimination has been unlawful in the United States and Australia for some time. Here in the United Kingdom the issue of age discrimination has been a source of debate for many years. Some employers have already introduced schemes whereby they recruit from the older section of the workforce. The Office of National Statistics has indicated that nearly a third of the labour force will be over 50 by 2020.

There has long been support for some form of anti-age discrimination legislation in this country. However, it has taken until 2006 for any such provisions to materialise. In 1998 a Bill was introduced which sought to combat age discrimination in advertisements. This was the Employment (Age Discrimination in Advertisements) Bill 1998. This Bill would have regulated the way in which employers could have advertised job vacancies. Unfortunately it did not get government support and did not become law.

The Employment Equality (Age) Regulations 2006 have recently been published and came into force on 1 October 2006. The government had until the end of 2006 to implement age discrimination legislation. The regulations stem from the Equal Treatment Directive 2000/78. The 'age' elements of that Directive were to be given legislative effect by the end of 2003 but the government was given extra time in which to consult on and then develop the Regulations. The 2006 Regulations apply to persons of all ages, not just older workers. Younger workers may also experience discrimination on the grounds of their age. The Regulations apply to employment and vocational training.

In summary the regulations:

- remove the current upper age limits for unfair dismissal rights and statutory redundancy;
- provide exemptions for many age-based rules in occupational pension schemes;
- make all retirement ages under 65 illegal unless objectively justified;
- require employers to properly consider an employee's request to continue to work beyond retirement age;
- require employers to give written notice to employees at least 6 months in advance of their intended retirement date;
- provide for a questionnaire procedure to aid a claimant in bringing a discrimination claim;
- remove the age limits for statutory sick pay, statutory maternity pay and statutory adoption pay; and
- make it unlawful to discriminate against someone, in certain circumstances, after the working relationship has ended.

Scope of the Regulations - Regulation 7

Regulation 7(1) states that it is unlawful for an employer to discriminate against a person:

(a) in the arrangements he makes for the purpose of determining to whom he should offer employment;

(b) in the terms on which he offers that person employment; or

(c) by refusing to offer, or deliberately not offering, him employment.

Regulation 7(2) states that it is unlawful for an employer to discriminate against an employee:

(a) in the terms of employment which he affords him;

(b) in the opportunities which he affords him for promotion, transfer, training, or receiving any other benefit;

(c) by refusing to afford him, or deliberately not affording him, any such opportunity; or

(d) by dismissing him or subjecting him to any other detriment.

The 2006 age Regulations also prohibit:

- direct discrimination – reg 3;
- indirect discrimination – reg 3;
- victimisation – reg 4; and
- harassment – reg 6.

Direct discrimination on the basis of age – Regulation 3(1)(a)

Regulation 3(1)(a) states that:

a person ('A') discriminates against another person ('B') if –

(a) on the grounds of B's age, A treats B less favourably than he treats or would treat other persons.

This is overt blatant discrimination in which a person is treated less favourably than another on the basis of their age.

Example
Sally (aged 54) and Jennifer (aged 36) apply for a job at a local firm of IT consultants. They have very similar experience and qualifications. The firm does not want to employ what they perceive to be 'over the hill workers' and so do not invite Sally for interview. She has been directly discriminated against on the basis of her age.

Indirect discrimination on the basis of age – section 3(1)(b)

Regulation 3(1)(b) states that a person ('A') discriminates against another person ('B') if:

A applies to B a provision, criterion or practice which he applies or would apply equally to persons not of the same age group as B, but –

(i) which puts or would put persons of the same age group as B at a particular disadvantage when compared with other persons, and

(ii) which puts B at that disadvantage,

and A cannot show the treatment, or as the case may be, provision, criterion or practice to be a proportionate means of achieving a legitimate aim.

A comparison of B's case with that of another person under this section must be such that the relevant circumstances in the one case are the same, or not materially different, in the other. Note that an employer may be able to justify treating an individual differently because of their age if they can show that the treatment, provision or practice can be objectively justified as a proportionate means of achieving a legitimate aim.

Victimisation – Regulation 4

Regulation 4(1) states that a person ('A') discriminates against another person ('B') if he treats B less favourably than he treats or would treat other persons in the same circumstances, and does so by reason that B has:

(a) brought proceedings against A or any other person under or by virtue of these Regulations;

(b) given evidence or information in connection with proceedings brought by any person against A or any other person under or by virtue of these Regulations;

(c) otherwise done anything under or by reference to these Regulations in relation to A or any other person; or

(d) alleged that A or any other person has committed an act which (whether or not the allegation so states) would amount to a contravention of these Regulations,

or by reason that A knows that B intends to do any of those things, or suspects that B has done or intends to do any of them.

Example

Margaret and Sara work for a local department store. Margaret recently brought an age discrimination claim against her employer in the Employment Tribunal. Sara gave evidence for Margaret during the tribunal hearing. Sara recently asked if she could attend a training course in London. Her boss refused her request, stating that she was a troublemaker and that she would never be taken seriously at work again. Sara has been victimised because she gave evidence for her colleague.

An employer does not victimise an employee if any of the allegations made by the employee, or any information/evidence given by him was false and not made or given in good faith.

Harassment - Regulation 6

Regulation 6(1) states that a person ('A') subjects another person ('B') to harassment where, on grounds of age, A engages in unwanted conduct which has the purpose or effect of:

(a) violating B's dignity; or

(b) creating an intimidating, hostile, degrading, humiliating or offensive environment for B.

The conduct shall only be regarded as having the effect specified if having regard to all the circumstances, including in particular the perception of B, it should reasonably be considered as having that effect.

Genuine occupational requirement - Regulation 8

Regulation 8 provides an exception where possessing a characteristic related to age is a genuine and determining occupational requirement for a post if it is proportionate to apply the requirement in the particular case. Examples of such an occupational requirement may include:

- casting a play which has parts for older or younger characters; or
- an organisation advising on and promoting rights for older people stipulating that its Chief Executive must be of 'certain age'.

Code of Practice

The Age Diversity at Work Code of Practice was issued in 2002 by the Department for Work and Pensions. The code covers recruitment, selection, promotion, training and development, redundancy selection decisions and retirement schemes. As with other codes of practice the code does not have statutory effect. However, its provisions will be taken into account in appropriate cases. It is thought that the code will be updated to take into account the new 2006 Regulations.

In the meantime both Acas and the DTI have produced very useful guidance on the 2006 Regulations. The Acas guidance, *Age and the Workplace*, is a very comprehensive and easy to read guide to the 2006 Regulations. The DTI has produced a series of fact sheets on the Regulations. All of this information is available via the DTI and Acas websites. Another source of useful information is the Age Positive website: **www.agepositive.gov.uk**. Age Positive is a team working within the Department for Work and Pensions. The site provides information on the 2006 Regulations and on age-related matters generally.

2

Discrimination in employment

Political persuasion

At the present time it is lawful for an employer to discriminate on the grounds of political persuasion. However, in Northern Ireland the Fair Employment (Northern Ireland) Acts of 1976 and 1989 prohibit both direct and indirect discrimination on the grounds of religion and political belief. Since 2003 the Employment Equality (Religion or Belief) Regulations have made it unlawful to discriminate on the grounds of religion or belief in the United Kingdom.

Discrimination on the grounds of religion or belief

The Employment Equality (Religion or Belief) Regulations 2003 came into force on 2 December 2003. The Regulations implement the religion/belief strands of the Framework Directive 200/78/EC. The Regulations specify four types of discrimination: direct discrimination, indirect discrimination, victimisation and harassment. They protect the rights of workers and apply to all employers/businesses whatever their size and whether in the public or private sector.

The Regulations prohibit discrimination in the fields of employment and vocational training. They apply to recruitment, terms and conditions, pay, promotion, transfers and dismissals. The Regulations are broadly similar in structure to the Sex Discrimination Act 1975 and the Race Relations Act 1976.

What is classed as a 'religion' or 'belief' – Regulation 2

Under regulation 2(1) 'religion or belief' is defined as meaning 'any religion, religious belief, or similar philosophical belief'.

This section does not really provide much of an explanation as to what will be classed as being either a 'religious or philosophical belief'. However, the Explanatory Notes for the 2003 Regulations state that the definition will include widely recognised religions such as Christianity, Judaism, Islam and Hinduism. Branches or sects within a particular religion will also be covered. For example, Catholics or Protestants would be recognised as being part of the Christian faith.

It will be left to the Employment Tribunal or court to decide on what will or will not be classed as being a valid 'religion' or 'belief'.

Direct discrimination on the grounds of religion or belief – Regulation 3(1)(a)

Regulation 3(1)(a) states that:

> For the purposes of these Regulations, a person ('A') discriminates against another person ('B') if –
>
> (a) on the grounds of religion or belief, A treats B less favourably than he treats or would treat other persons.

Direct discrimination is overt or blatant discrimination. It occurs where a person treats another less favourably on the grounds of their religion or belief.

> **Example**
> *Reshwana is a solicitor. She is interviewed for a new position. While being interviewed she mentions that she is a Muslim. Although she has all the skills required for the job, the firm decides not to offer her the position because they do not employ any Muslims and do not think that she will 'fit in'.*

Direct discrimination may also be based on the grounds of a person's perceived religion or belief. Direct discrimination may also occur when a person is treated less favourably because they associate with persons of a particular religion/belief, or because they refuse to carry out an employer's instruction to discriminate against such persons. In bringing a claim the individual does not have to declare their religion or belief. They only have to show that they were treated less favourably because the employer believed them to be part of a particular religion or to have particular beliefs.

Direct discrimination cannot be justified. In very limited circumstances an employer may be able to discriminate where a genuine occupational requirement can be shown to apply or where there is an issue of national security (see below).

Indirect discrimination on the basis of religion or belief - Regulation 3(1)(b)

Regulation 3(1)(b) states that:

(1) (a) person ('A') discriminates against another person ('B') if –

    (b) A applies to B a provision, criterion or practice which he applies or would apply equally to persons not of the same religion or belief as B, but –

        (i) which puts or would put persons of the same religion or belief as B at a particular disadvantage when compared with other persons,

        (ii) which puts B at that disadvantage, and

        (iii) which A cannot show to be a proportionate means of achieving a legitimate aim.

> **Example**
> *Martin refuses to give his shift employees work breaks between 7 a.m. and 9 a.m. This practice is applied to all employees but may discriminate against Muslim employees who are required to stop work to pray at intervals during the day. A Muslim employee could show that this practice puts him at a disadvantage. It would then be for Martin to show that this practice was justified.*

The reference to religion or belief does not include the employer's religion or belief. A comparison of B's case with that of another person must be such that the relevant circumstances in the one case are the same, or not materially different, in the other.

Indirect discrimination is covert or hidden discrimination. If the person claiming indirect discrimination can show that they have suffered a disadvantage, then the provision, criterion or practice is indirectly discriminatory. Indirect discrimination is unlawful whether it is intentional or not.

Indirect discrimination will not be unlawful if it can be shown to be justified. To justify their actions, an employer must show that there was a legitimate aim, e.g. a real business need and that the practice was proportionate to that aim. The practice will be proportionate to the aim if it is necessary and there are no alternative means available.

Victimisation - Regulation 4

Regulation 4(1) states that:

> A person ('A') discriminates against another person ('B') if he treats B less favourably than he treats or would treat other persons in the same circumstances, and does so by reason that B has –
>
> (a) brought proceedings against A or any other person under these Regulations;
>
> (b) given evidence or information in connection with proceedings brought by any person against A or any other person under these Regulations;

(c) otherwise done anything under or by reference to these Regulations in relation to A or any other person; or

(d) alleged that A or any other person has committed an act which (whether or not the allegation so states) would amount to a contravention of these Regulations.

An employer will not have victimised an individual where the allegation was false and not made or given in good faith. Victimisation on the basis of a person's religion or belief takes place where they are treated less favourably because of something they have done, e.g. the person may have made a formal discrimination claim or given evidence in a tribunal case.

Example
Eve gave evidence for her colleague Sherin in a religious discrimination tribunal claim. She is then branded a troublemaker by her boss and her application to attend a training course is rejected even though all her colleagues are allowed to attend. Her boss tells her that it is 'payback' time for her getting involved in Sherin's claim. Eve has been victimised because she previously gave evidence to support her colleague.

Harassment - Regulation 5

Regulation 5 states that:

a person ('A') subjects another person ('B') to harassment where, on grounds of religion or belief, A engages in unwanted conduct which has the purpose or effect of –

(a) violating B's dignity; or

(b) creating an intimidating, hostile, degrading, humiliating or offensive environment for B.

Conduct will be regarded as violating a person's dignity or creating an intimidating, hostile, degrading or humiliating or offensive environment if having regard to all the circumstances it should reasonably be considered as having that effect.

Behaviour that is offensive, frightening or distressing is likely to be termed harassment. Employers may be held to be responsible for any harassment carried out by their employees (see: Regulation 22). Individual employees may also be liable for any harassment that they themselves instigate.

Stages at which discrimination may take place - Regulation 6

Regulation 6 states that it is unlawful for an employer to discriminate against an individual in:

(a) the arrangements he makes for determining to whom he should offer employment;

(b) the terms on which he offers that person employment; or

(c) refusing to offer, or deliberately not offering, him employment;

(d) the terms of employment in existence during employment;

(e) the opportunities which he affords for promotion, transfer, training, or the receipt of any other benefit;

(f) refusing to afford or deliberately not affording him such opportunity; or

(g) in dismissing him, or subjecting him to any other detriment.

Discrimination after employment has ended - Regulation 21

Regulation 21 states that it is unlawful for an employer to discriminate against or harass a former employee after the working relationship between them has ended. The act of discrimination or harassment must be linked to the former relationship.

Genuine occupational requirements – Regulation 7

Regulation 7 states that there are two very limited situations in which an employer may discriminate against a person on the basis of their religion or belief. These are where:

(a) **having regard to the nature of the employment or the context in which it is carried out being of a particular religion or belief is a genuine and determining occupational requirement, and it is proportionate to apply that requirement, and**

(b) **where an employer has an ethos based on religion or belief and, having regard to that ethos and to the nature of the employment or the context in which it is carried out –**

   (i) **being of a particular religion or belief is a genuine occupational requirement for the job; and**

   (ii) **it is proportionate to apply that requirement in the particular case.**

In the first requirement religion/belief must be a genuine and determining occupational requirement.

Although there is no case law on this area it is likely that the first requirement will cover jobs that are needed to be carried out by Ministers of the church. The second requirement, referring to having an 'ethos' would, for example, apply to a religious school which needs to recruit teachers to fit in with their particular religious outlook and methods/content of teaching.

> **Example**
> *If a care home for elderly Christian gentlemen were to employ a Minister to provide services and prayers for their residents it may specify that that Minister be of the Christian faith.*

National security – Regulation 24

This regulation states that an employer may lawfully discriminate on the basis of religion or belief where they do so to safeguard national security. Their actions must be justified.

Making a religion or belief discrimination claim to the Employment Tribunal

A person who believes that they have been discriminated against on the grounds of their religion or belief may make a claim to the Employment Tribunal. The claim must be made within 3 months of the act complained of. The Regulations provide for a questionnaire procedure which allows an applicant to ask their employer/prospective employer to provide information prior to the tribunal hearing. If the claimant is successful the Employment Tribunal may make a declaration or recommendation stating that the employer should take action to prevent or reduce the impact of the discrimination. The tribunal may also make a compensatory award. There is no limit set on the amount of compensation that may be awarded.

Acas have produced a useful guide to the regulations: *Religion or Belief in the Workplace – Putting the Employment Equality (Religion or Belief) Regulations 2003 into practice.* The DTI have also produced a very useful set of explanatory notes: *Explanation of the provisions of the: Employment Equality (Sexual Orientation) Regulations 2003 and Employment Equality (Religion or Belief) Regulations 2003.* Both publications are accessible via the Acas and DTI websites.

DISCRIMINATION ON THE GROUNDS OF TRADE-UNION INVOLVEMENT

Section 137 of the Trade Union and Labour Relations (Consolidation) Act 1992 states that it is unlawful for an employer to discriminate when making offers of employment because:

2

Discrimination in employment

    (a) he is, or is not, a member of a trade union, or

    (b) because he is unwilling to accept a requirement –

        (i) to take steps to become or cease to be, or to remain or not become, a member of a trade union, or

        (ii) to make payments or suffer deductions in the event of his not being a member of a trade union.

Section 146 extends this protection by stating that it is unlawful for an employer to take any action against an employee, such as preventing him from joining a union or taking part in union activities. It is also unlawful for an employer to force an employee to join a union.

THE REHABILITATION OF OFFENDERS

In some situations it is unlawful for an employer to discriminate against a job applicant or an employee because of a previous criminal record. One of the aims of sentencing an offender is rehabilitation.

The Rehabilitation of Offenders Act 1974 states that a person should not be discriminated against because of 'spent' previous convictions. This is based on the idea that once a person has held the conviction for a specified period of time that conviction then becomes 'spent' and the person is treated as though it never existed. In the case of imprisonment, it is the period of sentence imposed by the court which counts (including any suspended sentence) not the actual time spent in prison. The period of rehabilitation runs from the date of the conviction.

Once a conviction is 'spent' and the ex-offender rehabilitated, potential employers should not ask him about his convictions and there is no requirement to declare spent convictions on any application form (unless, of course, the job in question falls under one of the exceptions noted below). An employer should not exclude or dismiss a person on the basis of his spent convictions.

Property Guards Ltd v *Taylor & Kershaw* (1982)

When applying for a job two security guards signed a statement saying that they had no previous convictions. They were entitled to do this because their minor convictions were 'spent'. After a few months Property Guards found out about the convictions and dismissed the men.

Held The dismissals were unfair. The men had been entitled not to divulge their previous convictions. The convictions were spent and so covered by the 1974 Act.

The time at which a conviction will become 'spent' will depend on the original sentence imposed. Sentences of imprisonment of 30 months or more will never become spent.

If someone over 18 years old is sentenced to a term of imprisonment of between 6 months and $2\frac{1}{2}$ years then their conviction is not spent until 10 years have passed. If they are sentenced to a term of imprisonment of 6 months or less then the rehabilitation period is 7 years. If a person is punished by way of a fine, community punishment order, or community rehabilitation order then the period of rehabilitation is 5 years.

A community punishment order is what was referred to as a 'community service order'. A community rehabilitation order is what was referred to as a 'probation order'.

If a person is given a conditional discharge, bind over, care order or supervision order then the period of rehabilitation is one year, or until the order expires, whichever is the longer. If a person is given an absolute discharge then the rehabilitation period is 6 months. The rehabilitation period for those fined or given prison sentences is halved if the offender was aged 17 or below at the date of conviction.

The 1974 Act does not apply to all types of employment. The Rehabilitation of Offenders Act 1974 (Exceptions) Order 1975 (as amended by the Rehabilitation of Offenders Act 1974 (Exceptions) (Amendment) (England & Wales) Order 2003) states that when applying for some jobs applicants must divulge all previous convictions. Exempted professions include teaching, social work, accountancy, the law and the police force.

THE FIXED-TERM EMPLOYEES (PREVENTION OF LESS FAVOURABLE TREATMENT) REGULATIONS 2002 AND THE PART-TIME WORKERS (PREVENTION OF LESS FAVOURABLE TREATMENT) REGULATIONS 2000

The Fixed-term Employees (Prevention of Less Favourable Treatment) Regulations came into force in October 2002 (under the Employment Act 2002). Under the regulations a worker on a fixed-term contract has the right not to be discriminated against just because they are not a permanent employee. It is unlawful to discriminate against a fixed-term worker in this way. A fixed-term worker is classed as being one who works under a contract for a specific fixed time, for a specific task, or a contract which will terminate on the happening or not happening of some future event.

An employer does have a possible defence to a claim of less favourable treatment if he can show that his actions were objectively justified. The regulations state that a fixed-term contract will automatically become a permanent contract of indefinite length after 4 years. The start date for this provision was 10 July 2002 meaning that the first automatic conversion could not take place until 10 July 2006. They also remove the ability of an employer to ask an employee to waive their right to a redundancy payment at the end of the fixed term. They also provide that the 'completion of a task' contract is seen as a dismissal for the purpose of an unfair dismissal claim.

Similarly, the Part-time Workers (Prevention of Less Favourable Treatment) Regulations 2000 are designed to ensure that part-time workers are given the same rights as full-time employees in relation to their terms and conditions of work. The Regulations came into force from 1 July 2000. Before this time an employer was able to treat an employee less favourably just because they were not a full-time employee. Again, the regulations state that less favourable treatment will not be unlawful if an employer can objectively justify their actions. They state that less favourable treatment would be justified if it was necessary and appropriate in order for the employer to achieve a legitimate business objective. These regulations were amended in 2002 by the Part-time Workers (Prevention of Less Favourable Treatment) Regulations 2000 (Amendment) Regulations 2002. These regulations made changes mainly relating to the role of the comparator and on pensions.

If a part-time or fixed-term worker feels that they have been discriminated against they are able to make a complaint to the Employment Tribunal. Such a claim should be made within 3 months of them having encountered 'less favourable treatment'.

MAKING A DISCRIMINATION CLAIM TO THE EMPLOYMENT TRIBUNAL

Any job applicant or employee who feels that he has been discriminated against is able to make a complaint to the Employment Tribunal. The courts do not deal with discrimination cases and claims are made to the tribunal in the manner outlined in Chapter 10.

Complaints of sex, race or disability discrimination must be made within three months of the alleged discriminatory act. This time limit also applies to complaints involving sexual orientation, religion or belief and age discrimination. Where there are a continuing set of discriminatory acts, the three-month time limit begins to run from the date of the most recent act. There is no time limit relating to a claim brought under the Equal Treatment Directive.

Discrimination is not often easy to prove. Evidence of discrimination is not always readily available. It is unlikely that employers will admit to have discriminated in the selection or treatment of their workforce. In some situations employers may not believe that their actions amounted to discrimination. In *Khanna v Ministry of Defence* (1981) it was stated that 'it is highly improbable that a person who has discriminated is going to admit the fact, quite possibly even to himself'.

Burden of proof

The Sex Discrimination (Indirect Discrimination and Burden of Proof) Regulations 2001 and the Race Relations Act 1976 (Amendment) Regulations 2003 outline the way in which the burden of proof operates in sex and race discrimination tribunal claims. Similar rules exist in relation to disability, sexual orientation and religion or belief claims. The claimant (job applicant/employee) must establish the facts of their claim. They may produce any available evidence to support their claim. This could include documents and witness statements from colleagues.

Once the claimant has established the facts the burden then shifts to the employer to show (on the balance of probabilities) that they did not discriminate or that they had some justification for their actions. If the employer is unable to do this the tribunal will find that they have unlawfully discriminated against the claimant. An award will then be made in favour of the claimant.

Questionnaire procedure

This procedure is designed to help the person making the complaint to find out more about the reasoning behind the employer's actions. There are standard questionnaires designed for differing types of discrimination claim. A questionnaire must be sent to the employer within three months of the alleged discriminatory act.

If the complainant has already lodged a tribunal claim, he will then have 21 days from that date to send the questionnaire to the employer. Employers do not have to answer questionnaires. They may not return it at all or may answer some but not all of the questions.

However, any failure to answer, or providing any evasive or inaccurate answers may be taken into account in tribunal proceedings. As the tribunal is able to draw adverse inferences from any failure to assist, it is in an employer's interests to complete the questionnaire as fully as possible.

Remedies and awards

After hearing all of the evidence, the tribunal will make its decision. If it finds in favour of the complainant stating that discrimination did occur, it can then make an award.

The tribunal may:

- make a declaration of the rights of the complainant and the employer;
- make a recommendation that the employer do something, for example provide the complainant with a reference; or
- make an award of compensation with no statutory limit and including an award for injury to feelings.

Declarations

A declaration may be made alongside an award for compensation. The tribunal declares the rights of the complainant and the employer. This remedy is often used to prevent further acts of discrimination.

Recommendations

In issuing a recommendation the tribunal orders the employer to do something.

> ### Example
> *Possible recommendations include:*
> - *the employer making a full written apology to the employee;*
> - *the employer removing discriminatory documents, advertisements;*
> - *the employer removing adverse notes from any employee file and noting that the employee has been discriminated against in the past.*

If an employer refuses to comply with a tribunal recommendation and can show no justification for his inaction, the tribunal may increase any compensatory award. The tribunal cannot recommend that a person who was discriminated against during the recruitment and selection process be offered a job when other vacancies become available. Any such vacancies would still have to be advertised in the normal way.

Compensation

This is the most common award. The tribunal can award damages based on, for example, loss of wages or future wages and injury to feelings. Any expenses such as counselling or medical bills incurred as a result of the discrimination may also be reimbursed.

Until November 1993 there was a ceiling on tribunal awards which meant that often the amounts awarded were relatively low compared to the discrimination suffered. However, following the case of *Marshall v Southampton & South West Area Health Authority (No. 2)* (1993), there is now no limit on the amount of compensation that can be awarded. The ceiling was removed by the Discrimination and Equal Pay (Remedies) Regulations 1993 and the Race Relations (Remedies) Act 1994.

Following this tribunals have made substantial compensatory awards. In *Ministry of Defence v Cannock* (1994) armed service women who were forced to leave the service when they became pregnant were awarded damages of over £300 000. In *Armitage v Johnson* (1997) the EAT awarded a prison officer £28 000, £21 000 of the award being for injury to feelings. It has been said that some awards in relation to injury to feelings have become excessive. The Court of Appeal set down guidelines as to how compensation for injury to feelings should be assessed in *Chief Constable of West Yorkshire v Vento (No. 2)* (2002). Here it was stated that awards of between £15 000 and £25 000 should be given only in the most serious cases, such as where there has been a lengthy campaign of discriminatory harassment. Awards of between £5000 and £15 000 should be given in serious cases, which do not merit an award in the highest band. In less serious cases where the act of discrimination is an isolated or one off occurrence it was said that awards of between £500 and £5000 should be made.

Recent examples of large compensation payouts include the following cases. In *Miles v Gilbank and another* (2006) Ms Miles was awarded £25 000 for injury to feelings after she endured a sustained campaign of bullying at work. Having told her manager that she was pregnant she was subjected to a campaign of serious harassment. In *Browne v Greater London Magistrates Courts Authority* (2005) an Employment Tribunal awarded £206 415 to a disabled employee who resigned after three years of trying to get her employer to make reasonable adjustments to her workplace.

Many high-profile compensation payouts result from claims from those working in large investment banks in the City of London, often referred to as 'London's square mile'. Recently (2006) Deutsche Bank Group was ordered to pay Helen Green, a former employee, over £1 million following her successful claim for sex discrimination. She had suffered a long period of harassment and bullying at work. In 2003 Steven Horkulak, a broker at the firm Cantor Fitzgerald won £1 million damages after bullying and harassment caused him to resign from his job. Allowing discrimination to exist within their work environment can prove to be a very costly mistake for employers.

See also: *Coleman* v *Skyrail Oceanic Limited* (1981), *Orlando* v *Didcot Power Station Sports and Social Club* (1996), *Virdi* v *Commissioner of Police of the Metropolis* (2000).

Indirect discrimination

The rules on indirect discrimination are slightly different. In the case of indirect race discrimination, if it can be shown that the act of indirect discrimination was unintentional, no damages can be awarded. In relation to indirect sex discrimination, a new section was inserted into the Sex Discrimination Act 1975 in 1996. This states that no compensatory award should be made in cases of indirect discrimination where the employer did not intend to discriminate unless the tribunal deems that it would be 'just and equitable' to do so.

THE USE OF EQUAL OPPORTUNITIES POLICIES

All employers should formulate and use an equal opportunities policy. The policy should deal with all forms of equality issues and provide details on complaints procedures, training courses and queries. Often this awareness of equal opportunities issues can prevent acts of discrimination from occurring. All employees should be provided with information on any such policy.

The Equal Opportunities Commission, the Commission for Racial Equality and the Disability Rights Commission publish a vast amount of leaflets and guidance on how to draft and implement such policies. Guidance and a model code are also provided in their codes of practice.

WHAT NEXT FOR DISCRIMINATION LAW? FUTURE REFORM

There have been several recent developments in the field of discrimination law. The Employment Equality (Sexual Orientation) Regulations 2003 and the Employment Equality (Religion or Belief) Regulations 2003 are now well established. Cases alleging unlawful discrimination on the basis of either sexual orientation or religion or belief are now being heard by the Employment Tribunal. The Employment Equality (Age Discrimination) Regulations 2006 came into force on 1 October 2006. It will be interesting to monitor the use of these new Regulations.

Perhaps the most significant change due to take place in 2007 is the launch of the new Commission for Equality and Human Rights. As noted above (see page 28), the CEHR will take over the work of the Equal Opportunities Commission and the Disability Rights Commission in 2007. The CEHR will then take over the work of the Commission for Racial Equality in 2009. There is also debate over whether the future will bring new legislative provision in the form of one single Act of Parliament that will deal with all forms of discrimination. This idea has been debated for some years. Having all of the discrimination rules in one place would definitely aid both practitioners and students of employment law. Whether, given the volume of rules that we have considered in this chapter, this would be practical remains to be seen.

SUMMARY CHECKLIST

- Discrimination on the grounds of sex, race and disability are the most widespread.

- The Equal Opportunities Commission, the Commission for Racial Equality and the Disability Rights Commission play a significant role in the enforcement of anti-discrimination law. The Commission for Equality and Human Rights becomes operational in 2007.

- The main anti-discrimination statutes are the Sex Discrimination Acts of 1975 and 1986, the Race Relations Act 1976 and the Disability Discrimination Act 1995.

- The main anti-discrimination regulations cover sexual orientation, religion/belief and age.

- European law has had a major impact in the area of sex discrimination, mainly through the implementation of the Equal Treatment Directive and the Amsterdam Treaty.

- The law recognises three forms of discrimination: direct, indirect and victimisation.

- Direct discrimination occurs when a person is treated less favourably because of his sex, marital status, race or disability.

- Indirect discrimination occurs where an employer imposes a provision, criterion or practice which on the face of it applies to all people but which actually discriminates against a group of people. In relation to indirect racial discrimination claims based on colour/nationality, this occurs when an employer imposes a requirement or condition.

- Victimisation occurs where a person is treated less favourably because of his current or previous involvement in any complaint.

- Sex discrimination can be based on sex or marital status.

- It is unlawful for a person to discriminate against another on the basis of colour, race, nationality, ethnic or national origin.

- A person is only protected by the Race Relations Act 1976 if he is from a particular racial group.

- The employer's motive is irrelevant.

- Discrimination may take place in the arrangements made for the purpose of deciding who should be employed, on the terms on which a person is offered a job, when refusing to employ a person because of his sex/marital status or race, by refusing access to opportunities at work or when dismissing a person or subjecting him to any other detriment.

- There can be no defence to a claim of direct discrimination.

- In claims of indirect discrimination, an employer may be able to show that his actions were justified – they were a proportionate means of achieving a legitimate aim.

- In relation to recruitment, transfers and training, an employer may be able to favour a person from a particular sex/race because there is a genuine occupational qualification.

- The legislation also recognises other discriminatory acts, such as the use of discriminatory job advertisements.

- Employers may be vicariously liable for the discriminatory actions of their employees.

- It is generally unlawful to positively discriminate.

- Sexual and racial harassment can amount to direct discrimination.

2

Discrimination in employment

- It is unlawful to discriminate on the grounds of sexual orientation.
- Under the Disability Discrimination Act 1995 an employer has a duty to make 'reasonable adjustments' to the work premises.
- The DDA 1995 recognises four forms of discrimination: direct, failure to make reasonable adjustments, disability related discrimination and victimisation.
- The DDA 2005 widened the definition of what will be classed as a disability
- It is unlawful to discriminate on the grounds of religion or belief.
- It is unlawful to discriminate on the grounds of age.
- It is unlawful to discriminate on the grounds of trade-union involvement or non-involvement.
- It is unlawful, subject to certain excepted categories, to discriminate against a person with a criminal conviction if that conviction is 'spent'.
- Regulations prohibit discrimination against part-time employees or those on fixed-term contracts.
- Discrimination claims are made to the Employment Tribunal.
- Claims must be made within three months.
- The tribunal may make a declaration, recommendation or award compensation.

SELF-TEST QUESTIONS

1 What is 'direct' discrimination?

2 What is 'indirect' discrimination'?

3 What is 'victimisation'?

4 What are the stages at which discrimination may take place?

5 In what ways might an employer defend a discrimination claim?

6 What are the rules governing 'genuine occupational qualifications'?

7 What impact have the Equal Treatment Directive and the Amsterdam Treaty made on national discrimination law?

8 Under the Disability Discrimination Act 1995 what is the employer's 'duty to make reasonable adjustments'?

9 What is the role of the Disability Rights Commission?

10 Summarise the content of the Employment Equality (Age) Regulations 2006.

11 What remedies/awards may be made by the Employment Tribunal?

CASE SCENARIOS

A

Helen, Annie and Danny work at a local school. Helen teaches maths, Annie teaches music and Danny is the deputy headmaster. Helen has been teaching for ten years and is keen to be promoted. She recently attended a promotion interview but the job was given to her colleague Adrian. Adrian has fewer qualifications than Helen and he has only been teaching for five years. Helen asked her line manager why she did not get the job and he said that the interview panel had thought it 'better to put a man into a top job'.

Annie recently gave evidence in the Employment Tribunal for her colleague Susan. Susan was bringing a claim under the Employment Equality (Sexual Orientation) Regulations 2003 because she felt that she had been discriminated against because she is a lesbian. Annie recently applied to go on a training course but her line manger refused her request. He told her that it was 'pay-back time' for her involvement in Susan's claim.

Danny is 54 years old. He is aware that a vacancy is due to arise for a headmaster at a neighbouring school. Yesterday he telephoned the school to ask about the vacancy. The current headmaster told him that he was too old to apply and that they were 'really looking for someone a bit younger, someone around 40 years old', and 'definitely not someone over the hill'.

Advise Helen, Annie and Danny on any claims that they may have using anti-discrimination law. Would their employer/prospective employer have any defence to any claim made?

B

John manages a large community theatre group. He is staging a performance of Othello and has placed an advertisement in his local newspaper asking for applications for the lead role from 'black actors only'. He also advertises for 'strong and healthy stage-hands'. Adam is a white actor with over ten years of acting experience. He sees the advertisement asking for an actor to play Othello and attends the casting interview. John refuses to watch him act and asks him to leave, saying, '*Didn't you read the advert, mate?*' Adam claims that he has been discriminated against because he is white.

Karl is interested in the theatre and sees the advert for stagehands. He is disabled but is able to lift and carry light loads. He attends for interview and John tells him that he's sorry but he cannot make any special arrangements for disabled workers.

Advise Adam and Karl of any potential claims that they may have using anti-discrimination law. What would be the position if the group were staging Romeo and Juliet and the advertisement asked for 'white actors only'? Would Adam have any claim if he was rejected only on the basis that he was black?

Would John have any defence to any claims made?

Further reading

Discrimination Law Handbook, Camilla Palmer, Tess Gill, *et al.*, 2nd edn. Legal Action Group, 2006.

'Negotiating the Discrimination Minefield at Work', Lorna Findlay, *New Law Journal*, No. 152, 2002, pp. 506–508.

'Knowledge and the Employer's Duty to Make Reasonable Adjustments', Charles Pigott, *New Law Journal*, No. 152, 2002, pp. 1656–1657.

2

Discrimination in employment

'Discrimination Law: Age Through the Looking Glass', Vanessa Molyneux, *Employment Law Journal*, March 2002, pp. 6–8.

'EC Framework Directive on Equal Treatment in Employment: Towards a Comprehensive Community Anti-Discrimination Policy?', Paul Skidmore, *Industrial Law Journal*, No. 30, 2001, pp. 126–132.

'Sexual Orientation Discrimination: Perceptions, Definitions and Genuine Occupational Requirements', Hazel Oliver, *Industrial Law Journal*, No. 33, 2004, pp. 1–21.

'The Employment Equality (Religion or Belief) Regulations 2003', Lucy Vickers, *Industrial Law Journal*, No. 32, 2003, pp. 188–91.

'Happy Birthday RRA?' Ryan Clement, *New Law Journal*, No. 156, 2006, pp. 875–6.

Blackstone's Guide to the Disability Discrimination Act 1995, Caroline Gooding, Blackstone Press, 1996.

'Disability Discrimination', *IDS Employment Law Handbook*, 3rd edn, May 2002.

'Sex Discrimination and Equal Pay', *IDS Employment Law Handbook*, 3rd edn, December 1998.

'Race and Religion Discrimination', *IDS Employment Law Handbook*, February 2004.

'Sexual Orientation Discrimination', *IDS Employment Law Handbook*, May 2004.

Explanation of the provisions of the Employment Equality (sexual orientation) Regulations 2003 and the Employment Equality (religion or belief) Regulations 2003. Department for Trade and Industry, 2003.

Acas: *Age and the Workplace – Employees' Guide*, April 2006.

Acas: *Age and the Workforce – Employers' guide to putting the Employment Equality (Age) Regulations 2006 into practice*, April 2006.

Acas: *Religion and the Workplace*, 2004.

Acas: *Sexual Orientation and the Workplace*, 2004.

For legal updates on the material in this chapter please go to the Companion Website accompanying this book at **www.mylawchamber.co.uk/nairns**

3 The contract of employment

When a person is offered and accepts a job – he becomes an employee. At this stage he will have entered into a binding agreement with his employer – a contract of employment. After asking the question 'What is the contract of employment?' this chapter goes on to discuss:

- the importance of the employment contract;
- the distinction made between an employee and an independent contractor;
- tests that are used to help the courts/tribunals interpret that distinction;
- the status of special categories of worker;
- contents of the employment contract – incorporation, express and implied terms, terms implied by statute;
- the right to a written statement – s 1 of the Employment Rights Act 1996;
- restraint of trade clauses;
- qualifying for employment rights – continuity;
- changing terms of employment;
- working on a Sunday;
- flexible working arrangements.

WHAT IS THE CONTRACT OF EMPLOYMENT?

The employment contract forms the basis of the relationship between the employer and their employee. This relationship was historically referred to as that between a 'master' and his 'servant'. The employment contract is based on the ordinary law of contract and so the same requirements as to agreement, consideration and intention apply. The consideration in an employment contract is the all-important payment for work! In *Laws v London Chronicle Ltd* (1959) Lord Evershed MR stated that 'a contract of service is but an example of contracts in general, so that the general law of contract is applicable'.

Inequality of bargaining power

The difference between the contract of employment and any other contract is that there is usually no equality in the bargaining position of the parties. In today's economic climate individuals often have very little choice over whether or not they accept a particular job on the conditions offered.

Employees have no right to be given an employment contract. They only have the right to a copy of the main terms and conditions of their agreement. This document is referred to as the 'written statement of terms and conditions' or 'written particulars'. If the employer does not provide this, the penalties are minimal. In reality, many employees are not given either a contract of employment or a copy of their written particulars.

Types of contract

Employees are appointed on either full or part-time employment contracts. In recent years there has been a vast increase in the number of part-time employees. A full or part-time contract can exist between the parties for an indefinite period. If employers only want to hire employees for a set period of time, they may offer them 'fixed-term' contracts. These contain a clause stating that the employment will only continue for a set period of time, for example, for one or two years. Employees then know that they are only going to be employed for the time specified in the contract. Note the recent Regulations adopted to protect fixed-term and part-time employees from being subjected to 'less favourable treatment' than their full-time permanent colleagues (see page 95).

Is it better to have a written contract?

An employment contract can be made orally. However, where the employer does provide a contract it is usually given to the employee in writing. When problems arise it is often the terms of the contract that are in dispute. A well written contract will provide a detailed account of what the employer and employee agreed to at the start of their working relationship. Having something written down may help to negotiate solutions to any problems before resorting to legal action. If they do find themselves in a court or a tribunal, a written contract will provide stronger evidence than oral testimony. For these reasons it is better to have a written employment contract.

WHY IS THE EMPLOYMENT CONTRACT IMPORTANT?

The employment contract is important because it provides employees with information on the terms and conditions of their employment. In essence it should inform them of various things including what tasks they will perform when doing the job, where they will do the work, whether the employer has a pension scheme and perhaps most importantly how much they will be paid.

Having been offered a job, many people are so pleased at the prospect of a new start that they may only consider some of the terms of their new contract and not read the document as a whole. When a dispute arises between the employee and the employer, the contract becomes especially important.

THE DISTINCTION BETWEEN AN EMPLOYEE AND AN INDEPENDENT CONTRACTOR

Courts and tribunals may have to decide whether a worker is an employee or an independent contractor or self-employed person. The terms 'independent contractor' and 'self-employed' mean the same thing and so can be used interchangeably. This distinction between the employee and independent contractor is crucial and the tests used to decide on the status of the worker are generally referred to as the:

- control test
- integration/organisation test
- multiple test.

Here we can begin by asking the question 'Who is an employee?' and then move on to consider why it is important to make a distinction between an employee and an independent contractor. The tests used to make the distinction are then discussed.

Who is an employee?

This may sound like an obvious rhetorical question to which you would reply – 'it's someone who works'. As in many areas of law, things here are not quite so straightforward! In *Broadbent v Crisp* (1974) it was stated that 'all employees are workers but not all workers are employees'. This is often described as a grey area of law where there are no obvious right answers. The distinction to be made is that between an employee and an independent contractor. True they both work for a living, but independent contractors work for themselves and employees for an employer. They also work under different contracts:

- an employee works under a contract of service;
- an independent contractor works under a contract for services.

Consider the following example – a taxi driver and a chauffeur essentially do the same job. They both drive people from A to B and receive money for doing so. Are they employees or independent contractors? When you hire a taxi you do so on a temporary basis, paying the driver when you reach your destination. The driver then drives off to find another passenger. Contrast this with the role of the chauffeur, you would pay him a salary and he would work exclusively for you on a permanent basis. Whereas the taxi driver is more likely to own his own cab and be an independent contractor, the chauffeur is more likely to be your employee.

The distinction between an employee and an independent contractor is important mainly due to the differing tax and National Insurance requirements and because it is only an employee who acquires the majority of statutory employment protection rights. For example, only an employee can bring a claim for unfair dismissal or redundancy pay.

Does statute provide any helpful definitions?

There are no clear statutory definitions of who will be classed as an 'employee' or what will be perceived as being a 'contract of employment'. The existing definitions are as follows:

- Section 296 of the Trade Union & Labour Relations (Consolidation) Act 1992 defines a worker as **'an individual who works or seeks to work . . . under a contract of employment' . . . or under 'any other contract whereby he undertakes to do or perform personally any work or services for another party . . . '**
- Section 295(1) of the 1992 Act and s 230(1) of the Employment Rights Act 1996 define an employee as **'an individual who has entered into or works under (or, where the employment has ceased, worked under) a contract of employment'**.
- Section 230(2) goes on to define a contract of employment as **'a contract of service or apprenticeship, whether express or implied, and (if it is express) whether oral or in writing'**.

The contract of employment

Similar definitions exist in, for example, s 54 of the National Minimum Wage Act 1998, reg 1(2) of the Part-time Workers (Prevention of Less Favourable Treatment) Regulations 2000 and reg 2 of the Working Time Regulations 1998. These definitions are not particularly useful. The common law tests can be used to determine whether or not a worker is an employee.

There has been a growth in the level of self-employed people in recent years. Many of the cases here involve builders and construction workers, but the self-employed can also be found in various fields including catering, training, hairdressing, IT, the media and sales.

What types of case come before the courts/tribunals?

Many of these cases arise where a worker is injured or is dismissed. The worker may want to be regarded as an employee to obtain sickness benefit or to make a claim for unfair dismissal. The employer may try to deny him employee status in order to block this.

Conversely a worker may wish to be classed as an independent contractor, often to gain tax advantages. As Smith and Wood state (*Industrial Law*, Butterworths, 2003) 'an independent contractor may be in a better monetary position while working, but at a grave disadvantage if he falls off a ladder or is sacked'. It may be advantageous for employers to employ people on the basis of them being independent contractors. This may lessen their administrative burden with regards to tax and national insurance payments.

Reasons why it is important to distinguish between an employee and an independent contractor

Tax

Employees pay tax under Schedule E and the PAYE (Pay As You Earn) scheme. This means that an employer is responsible for deducting tax from an employee's pay and transferring it to the Inland Revenue. Independent contractors pay tax under Schedule D. They are allowed to set off tax against expenses and may pay tax in arrears. They may also have to pay VAT on services.

National Insurance

Employees pay Class 1 National Insurance contributions which are assessed on how much they earn. These contributions are deducted by their employer, who also makes a contribution on the employees' behalf. It is the payment of these contributions that entitles the employee to benefits, such as the jobseeker's allowance or statutory sick pay. Independent contractors are responsible for the payment of their own contributions and make Class 2 payments. This gives them very limited rights to welfare benefits and does not entitle them to either the jobseeker's allowance or statutory sick pay.

Employment protection rights

Only employees accrue most of the available statutory protections. Only employees can make claims for unfair dismissal, redundancy pay and statutory maternity pay. Independent contractors have no such rights. Note however, that both employees and independent contractors are protected under the discrimination legislation outlined in Chapter 2 and the equal pay legislation outlined in Chapter 4.

Vicarious liability

Employers can be made to be vicariously liable for the wrongdoing of their employees while they are acting 'in the course of their employment'. This duty does not generally apply to independent contractors. (For a general discussion on vicarious liability, see page 341.)

Health and safety

Employers owe a higher duty towards their employees in relation to safety. This is so both under the Health and Safety at Work Act 1974 and at common law. (See further Chapter 9.)

Implied terms

Certain rights and duties are implied into the employee's contract of service, for instance, the duty of mutual trust and confidence. These terms do not relate at all to independent contractors. (See page 120.)

TESTS USED TO DETERMINE THE STATUS OF THE WORKER

The role of the court or Employment Tribunal is to decide whether the worker is in fact an employee or an independent contractor. With little help from statutory definitions, the courts have developed various tests. Different parts of the tests may be used in different cases.

The development of the tests can be traced back to the use of the control test in the nineteenth century. From the 1950s onwards the test of integration or organisation was in common use. The approach today, however, is the use of the 'multiple test'. This test asks various questions such as whether the worker is in business 'on his own account' and/or whether there was any 'mutuality of obligation' between the parties.

What the court or tribunal does is to play a balancing act with the facts of the case. By deciding on the significance or otherwise of, say, who pays the National Insurance contributions or who provides the tools needed for the job, the scales will tip towards the worker being either employed or self-employed. There is no firm set of criteria to be followed and so as Mr Justice May stated in *Graham* v *Brunswick* (1974) 'any one test in my view may be substantially relevant in one case but largely irrelevant in another'.

Control test

In the nineteenth century the only test in existence was the control test. The test is in essence the 'what', 'when', and 'how' test. The court or tribunal asks who was in control of what the worker did, and who controlled when and how he did it. In *Whittaker* v *Minister of Pensions and National Insurance* (1967) it was said that the more control the employer had over the worker, the more likely it was that the worker was an employee. Early comments on the control test appear in the following cases.

In *Yewens* v *Noakes* (1880) Bramwell LJ stated that:

> **a servant is a person subject to the command of his master as to the manner in which he shall do his work.**

In *Performing Rights Society* v *Mitchell & Booker* (1924) McCardie J stated that:

> **the final test, if there is to be a final test ... the test to be generally applied, lies in the nature and degree of detailed control over the person alleged to be a servant.**

Walker v *Crystal Palace Football Club* (1910)

Was a professional footballer playing for a football club an employee?

Held He was an employee because he was subject to the overall control of the club with regard to his training schedule, discipline, and the method of his play.

The contract of employment

Hitchcock v Post Office (1980)

Mr Hitchcock ran a sub-post office. The Post Office exercised some control over his activities, such as the payments of benefits, sale of stamps etc. but he could delegate his work to others and took the risk of profit or loss.

Held He was an independent contractor. The control that the Post Office did have was due to the need to ensure financial control and security rather than to control his role as a manager.

This test was useful in its time, but as the more recent **Hitchcock** case shows, it declined in popularity as workers became more skilled. Increased technology and the advancement of professional jobs meant that in lots of cases the element of control over the worker was not so important. In *Beloff v Pressdram Ltd* (1973) it was said that the greater the skill required for an employee's work, the less significant is control in determining whether the employee works under a contract of service.

The test was applied with differing outcomes in the following cases.

Hillyer v St Bartholomew's Hospital (1909)

A surgeon performed an operation negligently with severe consequences for the patient. Was the hospital or the surgeon liable? This depended on whether or not he was an employee.

Held The surgeon was an independent contractor and merely using hospital facilities. Consequently, the hospital did not have to compensate the patient for the negligence of the surgeon.

However, by 1951 in **Cassidy** (below) a doctor was held to be an employee even though an employer was not able to 'control' the doctor while he worked.

Cassidy v Minister of Health (1951)

Mr Cassidy had an operation and lost several fingers due to the negligence of the surgeon.

Held Cassidy was successful in his claim against the hospital. It was responsible for the action of the surgeon as he was an employee of the hospital and not an independent contractor.

The problems with the test stemmed from the fact that employers were no longer able to take any real control over the skilled members of their workforce. For example, National Health Service trusts employ managers to organise the daily running of hospitals. While this manager will be able to control when a surgeon takes his holidays, he cannot have any control over what the surgeon does in the operating theatre. The same can be said of most skilled jobs. As workers became more skilled, the control test became less influential. The existence of control is still relevant, but today it is only one of several factors to be considered.

Integration/organisation test

The failings of the control test led to the development of the integration, or organisation, test. This test asks how far the worker is integrated into the daily running of the business. If the worker is integrated into, or 'part and parcel' of the business, the worker is more likely to be an employee. This test was developed by Lord Denning in *Stevenson, Jordan & Harrison Ltd* v *Macdonald & Evans* (1952).

Here he stated that 'under a contract of service a man is employed as part of the business and his work is done as an integral part of the business but under a contract for services his work, although done for the business, is not integrated into it but only accessory to it'.

This test was useful in explaining the status of the professional worker, but it was not widely used. Lord Denning had not explained what was meant by the term 'integration' or 'organisation'. In **Cassidy** the surgeon was held to be an employee because he was 'integrated' into the work of the hospital, but Lord Denning had failed to expand on why this was the case. As a result, this test was soon abandoned. Control and integration were to be taken into account, but only as part of a number of other factors, no one factor being conclusive.

Multiple test

The modern approach sees the courts and tribunals looking at all the facts of the case and weighing up those factors which point towards the worker being an employee or an independent contractor. By doing this balancing act they are able to determine the status of the worker. In *Hall* v *Lorimer* (1994) the process was described as the painting of a picture – in every case you put it together and then stand back to see what it looks like.

The first case to adopt this approach and so widen the role taken by the control and integration tests was one involving a dispute over the status of a group of lorry drivers.

Ready Mixed Concrete (South East) Ltd v *Minister of Pensions & National Insurance* (1968)

Ready Mixed Concrete dismissed its drivers and sold their lorries back to them, re-employing them under a new contract. The contract stated that they had to:

- wear company uniforms
- allow Ready Mixed Concrete to use the lorries when required
- only use the lorries for company business
- obey orders from the foreman.

It also said that at some point in the future the men had to sell the lorries back to Ready Mixed Concrete at market value. These rules made the men appear to be employees of Ready Mixed Concrete.

The contract went on to state that the drivers had to:

- maintain the lorries at their own expense
- pay all running costs
- be able to substitute drivers if they were unable to work.

They paid their own tax and National Insurance contributions, had no set hours of work or set meal breaks. They were responsible for planning routes and schedules of work. This made them appear to be working for themselves.

Held The drivers were independent contractors. Whereas some parts of their contract such as them having to follow orders made them appear to be employees, the court was swayed by the fact that they could use substitute drivers. This is something that you can usually only do if you are self-employed. Here the court did the balancing act and decided that there was more evidence indicating that they were independent contractors.

In this case McKenna J held that a contract of service exists and so a worker is an employee if:

- the worker agrees that in return for payment he will provide his own work and skill when doing the job for the employer;
- that while working the employer will have some degree of control over what he does; and
- that the other terms of the contract are consistent with it being a contract of employment.

There have been several recent cases, which have addressed the issue of employee substitution. They refer back to the case of *Ready Mixed Concrete* and so are considered at this point.

In *Express and Echo Publications Ltd v Tanton* (1999) the Court of Appeal stated that the basic nature of a contract of employment is an obligation on the employee to provide his services personally. It was said that if a worker has the authority to provide a substitute to do his work whilst he is absent then it would be very unlikely that he would be classed as an 'employee'. In this case Mr Tanton was employed as a van driver. Express and Echo provided his van and he wore their uniform. The Inland Revenue had classed him as an employee and he paid tax and national insurance contributions on that basis. However, he was not entitled to sick pay or holiday pay. He did not receive a weekly wage but was paid per van journey. He was also entitled to pay someone else to do his job if he was unable to carry out the duties at any time. It was this freedom to substitute that led the EAT to decide that he was in fact self-employed.

In the later case of *McFarlane v Glasgow City Council* (2001) the EAT held that having a limited or occasional power of delegation would not necessarily mean that a person would be classed as being self-employed. In this case 2 gym instructors who were able to employ substitutes to take over their work if they were absent were held to be employees. The difference in this case was that the substitutes were drawn from a list prepared by their employers and it was the employer who paid the substitute instructor.

In *Staffordshire Sentinel Newspapers Ltd v Potter* (2004) EAT Mr Potter worked as a home delivery agent subject to a 'delivery agency agreement'. This was an agreement for services and so he was an independent contractor. In November 2000 he signed a further agreement which provided that if he was not obliged to carry out his duties himself he could, if he so wished, find an appropriate substitute. In March 2003 Mr Potter was sacked and he brought a claim for unfair dismissal. As a preliminary issue, the Employment Tribunal had to consider whether Mr Potter was an employee (and so able to bring a claim), or an independent contractor.

The EAT, stating that the need for personal service is one of the 'irreducible minima' of a contract of service, held that Mr Potter was an independent contractor. The fact that Mr Potter could ask someone else to carry out his duties was held to be inconsistent with a contract of employment.

See also: *Byrne Brothers Ltd v Baird* (2002), *Redrow Homes (Yorkshire) Ltd v Wright* (2004).

● Use of the multiple approach

In *Market Investigations* (below) Cooke J asked if the workers were 'in business on their own account'.

Market Investigations v Minister of Social Security (1969)

A group of women were employed as part-time market researchers. They were able to choose their hours of work but had to work to a set pattern, were told which questions to ask and where to ask them.

Held They were employees as the employer had control over their work and they were not in business on their own account.

In deciding that they were not in business on their own account the court said that the following factors should be taken into account:

- the degree of control by the employer;
- the degree to which the worker risks loss or stands to profit;
- who owns any tools and equipment;
- the degree to which the worker is integrated into the business;
- how the worker is paid;
- whether any deductions are made for tax and National Insurance;
- whether there is any mutuality of obligation;
- whether the parties refer to their relationship as being one between an employer and an employee or an employer and an independent contractor.

This list shows that the factors of control and integration are still important, but that two additional questions are now asked:

- Was the worker in business on his own account?
- Was there any mutuality of obligation between the parties?

The list from *Market Investigations* was approved in the case of *Lee* (below).

Is the worker in business on his own account?

This is often referred to as the 'economic reality' or 'entrepreneur' test. It looks at whether the worker is running his own business rather than working on behalf of the employer. The court or tribunal asks questions such as:

- Who ran the risk of losing money if the business was not successful?
- Had the worker put any capital into the business?
- Was the worker likely to make any profit?
- Did the worker provide his own equipment?
- Could the worker hire his own helpers?
- Was the worker able to profit from the successful management of the business?

Lee v Chung (1990)

Mr Lee, a stonemason, was seriously injured while working on Chung's construction site. He claimed that as an employee he was entitled to damages for the injuries suffered and sick pay. Chung stated that he was not an employee but a casual worker. Chung denied all liability for his injuries. Chung had provided him with the tools and equipment needed to complete the stonework, and had directed him as to which areas of the site he should complete the work. He was then left to do the work without supervision. Lee was paid according to the amount of work that he did but was expected to be on site every day when work was available. He was allowed to work for other employers and, although he did this on a regular basis, he always gave priority to Chung.

Held Lee was an employee. The court balanced the facts and held that 'taking all the foregoing considerations into account the picture emerges of a skilled artisan earning his living by working for more than one employer as an employee and not as a small businessman venturing into business on his own account as an independent contractor with all its attendant risks'.

If the answers to these questions pointed towards the worker being in business for himself, he is classed as being an independent contractor. The livelihood of a self-employed person usually depends on his business making a profit. Whether a business makes a profit is not the everyday concern of the average employee.

Is there any mutuality of obligation?

This second question asks whether there is a mutual commitment between the parties. This is the commitment by the employer to provide work and the commitment by the employee to do any work that is provided. The more evidence there is of mutual commitment, the more likely the worker is an employee. In *Wilson* v *Circular Distributors Ltd* (2006) the EAT held that the requirement for 'mutuality of obligation' can be satisfied if an employer is only bound to offer work if it is available, provided that the employee is bound to accept that work when it is offered.

Employees usually have to work within set rules and guidelines, whereas independent contractors can choose when and where they want to work.

Atypical workers

The workforce now includes 'atypical' workers. These are those who work from home or who work only on a casual basis as 'temps'. It is often difficult to determine the status of such workers because they have flexible working patterns. They are the 'flexible' workforce because they do not work the set 9–5 routine of many employees.

The following cases highlight how the multiple test has been used in such cases. They concern whether or not atypical workers are employees and ask whether the workers are in business on their own account or whether there is any mutual commitment and obligation. There are no set principles, no obvious right answers, only guidelines provided from cases such as *Market Investigations*. Each case is to be decided on its own particular facts.

Casual workers

The following cases highlight the approach of both the tribunals and courts in relation to the 'status' of the casual worker.

O'Kelly v *Trusthouse Forte plc* (1983)

A group of workers waited tables on a 'regular casual' basis. They claimed that they had been unfairly dismissed. The hotel said that they were not employees and so could not make such a claim. The tribunal noted amongst other things that the workers had tax and National Insurance contributions deducted from their wages. They were also given holiday pay. This made them appear to be employees. However, the court was swayed by the fact that the workers did not receive regular wages, sick pay or pension entitlement.

Held There was no single feature to be taken into account, but on balance the facts showed that the workers were not employees. There was no mutuality of obligation.

Clark v Oxfordshire Health Authority (1998)

Ms Clark worked as a 'bank nurse'. She was part of a pool of extra staff who could be contacted on a daily basis to fill in for absent colleagues. She had been given a document entitled 'Statement of Employment'. Tax and National Insurance payments were deducted from her wages. She was also told that the Authority's disciplinary and grievance procedures applied to her. Conversely, Clark was not entitled to be paid when there was no work for her to do. Neither was she entitled to holiday pay or sick pay. Another significant point was that Clark's role was subject to a Whitley Council (Health Service wage scale) agreement which stated that bank nurses were not regular employees and, as such, were not entitled to guaranteed or continuous work. Clark had been dismissed. She made a claim for unfair dismissal which was disputed by the Authority on the basis that she was not an employee.

Held (CA) Clark was not an employee. This decision was based on the fact that there was no mutuality of obligation between the parties. The Authority was under no obligation to offer Clark work and she was under no obligation to accept any work offered. This meant that no contract of employment could exist and so she could not be an employee.

Carmichael and Leese v National Power plc (2000)

In 1988 the then operators of the Blyth A and B power stations advertised for station guides. The jobs involved conducting tours around the power stations and were to be based on a 'casual as required' basis. The workers were to be paid £3.77 per hour. The tours would normally last for two hours and could take place at any time during the day. Carmichael and Leese applied to be station guides. They were successful and each received a letter stating that they were employed on a 'casual as required basis'. They did not work set hours but conducted tours as and when they were required. The work was not full-time and they were only paid for the hours that they worked. In 1995 the power stations were taken over by National Power. They appointed another two guides. Carmichael and Leese complained to the tribunal that they had never received a section 1 statement of the terms and conditions of their employment. National Power said that they were not entitled to such a statement as they were not employees.

Held (HOL) The guides could not be classed as 'employees' because there was no 'mutuality of obligation' between them and National Power plc. The court stressed that both control and mutuality of obligation are essential features of a contract of service and that there was no such obligation here. It was said that there was no mutuality of obligation because there was no obligation on National Power plc to provide work for the guides. Also, if work was made available the guides could decide whether to accept or decline the opportunity to work on any given day. This showed that there was no obligation on their part to agree to work. Consequently, the court held that the guides were not employees.

Similar cases include: **Amarasinghe v Chase Farm Hospitals NHS Trust** (1997) (bank nurse was held to be an employee because of mutuality of obligation), **City of East London FHS Authority v Durcan** (1996) (dentist employed by hospital for one evening per week was held to be an employee), **Stevedoring & Haulage Services Ltd v Fuller** (2001) (dock workers held not to be employees but to have agreed to work on casual ad hoc contracts) and **Cornwall County Council v Prater** (2006) (CA) (lack of mutuality of obligation before and after the completion

3

The contract of employment

of assignments does not mean that a person must be a casual worker and cannot in law be an employee – teacher who worked on separate assignments as a 'home tutor' was an employee).

Agency workers

The following cases highlight the approach of both the tribunals and courts in relation to the 'status' of the agency worker.

McMeechan v Secretary of State for Employment (1997)

McMeechan had been 'on the books' of Noel Employment Ltd for less than one year when the agency went into liquidation. He had been working for a catering firm for four days. He had worked on a series of temporary contracts which stated that he was self-employed. He did not have to accept work. He was subject to the agency's rules and the agency could tell him to end an assignment at any time. He was paid weekly but did not have to work any set number of hours.

Held (CA) The EAT's decision that McMeechan was an employee was the right one. The agency had the power to dismiss him or make deductions from his pay for problems such as bad timekeeping. This was enough to show that he was employed by the agency.

In **McMeechan** the Court of Appeal restated that there was no single factor that could point towards someone being employed or self-employed, and said that this was an especially difficult task when looking at the role of temporary workers. In an earlier case, **Wickens v Champion Employment** (1984), an agency worker had been found to be self-employed. The following more recent cases also illustrate the differing decisions made in relation to the status of agency workers.

In **Motorola Ltd v Davidson** (2001) it was held that an agency worker was an employee of Motorola Ltd. An employment agency had sent him to work at that firm. It was said that Motorola exercised a sufficient degree of control over him for their relationship to be one of employer and employee. This was the case even though his contract was with the employment agency. It was said that even though Motorola did not have a direct contractual right of control over the worker that he was bound by his contract with the agency to comply with reasonable instructions from them.

A differing approach can be seen in the following two cases.

In **Montgomery v Johnson Underwood Ltd** (2001) Mrs Montgomery had alleged that she was an employee of the Johnson Underwood employment agency. She had worked for another firm and that job had been arranged for her by the agency. However, the Court of Appeal held that she was not an employee of the agency because she was not under their control while she was at work.

In **Hewlett Packard Ltd v O'Murphy** (2002) an agency worker was held not to be an employee of the company that he worked for (via the agency) because there was no 'contractual nexus' between them. He could not be an employee of the company as he had no contract with them. This was held to be the case even though he had worked under their control and supervision and been integrated into the workforce.

The more recent decisions on this point continue to confuse the issue.

Dacas v Brook Street Bureau (2004)

Mrs Dacas worked as a cleaner for Wandsworth Council. She had worked there for six years when her contract was terminated summarily. She was 'on the books' of the Brook Street Bureau employment agency and it was the agency that had placed her into her job with the Council. Brook Street Bureau paid her wages and was entitled to discipline her and/or terminate her contract. She alleged that she was an employee of Brook Street Bureau.

Held (CA) Mrs Dacas was an employee of the Council and not an employee of Brook Street Bureau (the agency). Mummery LJ stated that 'the express contract between the employment agency and Mrs Dacas was not a contract of service. Brook Street were under no obligation to provide Mrs Dacas with work. She was under no obligation to accept any work offered by Brook Street to her. It did not exercise any relevant day-to-day control over her or her work ... That control was exercised by the Council, which supplied her clothing and materials and for whom she did the work ... The role of Brook Street was not that of an employer of Mrs Dacas. Rather it was that of an agency finding suitable work assignments for her and, so far as the Council was concerned, performing the task of staff supplier and administrator of staff services ...'

Here, the Court of Appeal disagreed with the previous Employment Appeal Tribunal decision that Mrs Dacas would be classed as an employee of the agency.

Bunce v Postworth Ltd (t/a Skyblue) (2005)

Mr Bunce worked as a welder. He entered into an agreement with the Skyblue employment agency. The agency arranged various jobs for him with, for example, Carillion Rail. His agreement with the agency required him to accept the supervision and instruction of Carillion Rail (or any other client to whom he was assigned). In 2002, Carillion Rail complained about his work and Skyblue terminated his contract of employment. Mr Bunce brought a claim for unfair dismissal but this was dismissed by the Employment Tribunal on the basis that he was not an employee of either Skyblue or Carillion Rail. The EAT agreed with this decision and so Mr Bunce appealed to the Court of Appeal.

Held (CA) Mr Bunce was not an employee of either Skyblue or Carillion Rail. The agency did not exercise any real control over Mr Bunce and so he could not be said to work under a 'contract of service'.

In *Cable & Wireless Plc v Muscat* (2006) the Court of Appeal confirmed the principles outlined in *Dacas* that an agency worker could be an implied employee of an end-user in a tripartite agency/worker/end-user case.

These decisions, especially that of **Dacas** and **Bunce** reaffirm the principle that each case is decided on its own facts.

See also: *Serco Ltd v Blair & ors* (1998), *Franks v Reuters* (2003) CA.

Agency workers do have some rights under the Working Time Directive and the National Minimum Wage Act 1998. The role of employment agencies is governed by the Employment Agencies Act 1973 and the Conduct of Employment Agencies and Employment Businesses Regulations 2003. The 2003 Regulations came into force on 6 April 2004. The Regulations ensure that the precise contractual position between agency, end-user client and worker must be agreed and set out in a single document before the hiring starts. This will ensure that the parties

3

The contract of employment

agree on employment status at the outset of their working relationship. It remains to be seen, however, whether or not the 2003 Regulations will assist tribunals when they are faced with the question of agency worker status. Many factors may be taken into account by the tribunal, not just the documentation in existence between the parties involved. See: *Royal National Lifeboat Institution* v *Bushaway* (2005).

Aside from the 2003 Regulations there also exists an EC proposal for a Directive on agency work. This Directive is referred to as that on 'Working conditions for temporary workers'. The consultation period on this Directive closed in October 2002 and a revised proposal was published by the EC in December 2002. The proposals required that agency workers should not have less favourable employment conditions than permanent workers in the client company where they are sent to work unless this is objectively justified. Unfortunately, at the time of writing the proposals for this new Directive have been shelved. There is no information on whether or not the Commission will consider the proposals again at some point in the future.

Homeworkers

The following cases highlight the approach of both the tribunals and courts in relation to the 'status' of the 'homeworker'.

Airfix Footwear Ltd v *Cope* (1978)

Homeworkers who made shoe heels for Airfix were provided with work on a regular basis. Airfix argued that there was no obligation on it to provide work and that even if it did, the worker could refuse the work. Airfix had employed the workers for seven years.

Held They were employees. Airfix told the workers what to do and how to do it. They were also given deadlines for completion of the work. This plus the seven-year relationship and regularity of work showed mutuality of obligation between the parties and reinforced the fact that the homeworkers were employees.

Nethermere (St Neots) Ltd v *Taverna (1984)*

Ms Taverna was one of several trouser machinists who worked from home. She had no fixed hours and used a sewing machine provided by Nethermere. The only fixed rule was that she had to do enough work to make it worthwhile for the collection driver to call. The driver collected completed garments and supplied materials for the next batch of work.

Held Taverna was an employee. There was mutuality of obligation between the parties. She could decide how much work she did and when she did it, but her long-standing relationship with Nethermere showed mutual obligation. Nethermere was obliged to provide work and Taverna was obliged to complete work, albeit to her own timescale.

For an interesting account of homeworker status and worker status in general see: *Bridges & ors* v *Industrial Rubber plc* (2004) EAT. In this case nine homeworkers were held not to be employees of the company due to an absence of mutuality of obligations.

What if the parties 'label' their relationship as being one between an employer/employee or an employer/independent contractor?

In *Ferguson* v *John Dawson & Partners Ltd* (1976) it was said that the status of the worker is a question for the court and not the parties. In *Young & Woods* v *West* (1980) it was held that the label that the parties put on their relationship may be taken into account but that it will not be conclusive evidence of status. The court will look at the facts of the case first and will only consider the label if the other facts are inconclusive or ambiguous: *Massey* v *Crown Life Insurance Co* (1978).

This prevents the parties from avoiding liability or tax payments by changing their status to suit the situation. For this reason the court or tribunal cannot be swayed only by what the parties have decided to label their relationship.

See also *Dacas* v *Brook Street Bureau* (2004) CA.

No single test

Cases show that there is no single test. The control and integration tests are still used and may form part of the multiple test. In *Montgomery* v *Johnson Underwood Ltd* (2001) the Court of Appeal stated that in deciding whether a person is technically 'an employee' the traditional tests of control and of mutuality of obligation are 'basic and essential'.

In *Barnett* v *Brabyn (Inspector of Taxes)* (1996) the court restated that in determining whether a worker is an employee it is necessary to weigh up all the facts of the case. The multiple test looks at all the facts of the case and asks whether the worker is in business on his own account or whether there is any mutuality of obligation.

This is a grey area of law with no obvious right answers. Until further guidance is forthcoming either by way of legislation or a decisive case the question of status remains unresolved.

When considering the facts in a particular case questions should not be gone through as a checklist. The court or tribunal has to decide which test to use and which parts of the case to take into account. The answer may depend on why the question is being asked. In *Lane* v *Shire Roofing Co Ltd* (1995) a builder injured himself while doing roof repairs. The Court of Appeal said that in cases involving safety at work there was a real public interest in recognising the worker as an employee. This reasoning cannot be relied upon though and it is best to see each case as depending on its particular facts.

Future developments

It can be seen from the array of cases and conflicting decisions that this is a grey area of law. Each case turns very much on its own facts. This is an area ripe for reform.

In 1999 the DTI published a research paper entitled 'The Employment Status of Individuals in Non-standard Employment'. This outlined the problems faced by atypical workers. Then in July 2002 they issued a discussion document entitled 'On Employment Status: In Relation to Statutory Employment Rights' (02/URN 02/1058). This also dealt with the issue of employee status, in particular that of home and agency workers.

Unfortunately to date there are no firm proposals for change stemming from this discussion and consultation process. In March 2006 the DTI issued a summary of responses to its 2002 discussion document. Access to this summary is available on the DTI website. Legal academics have debated possible changes to this area of law for some time. Such debates range from the extension of statutory rights to atypical workers to legislation in the form of one statute providing definitions of what types of worker would and would not be classed as being an employee. It remains to be seen whether any firm proposals for change are forthcoming.

SPECIAL CATEGORIES OF WORKER

In the following cases the status of special categories of worker has already been established.

Directors

It is possible for executive directors to be employees but non-executive directors are likely to be self-employed. An executive director is one involved in the daily running of the company whereas a non-executive director may only have advisory duties.

Partners

Partners are self-employed workers who receive payment dependent on the profits of their firm. There may also be salaried partners who may be classed as employees.

Office holders

These are workers who have public status, for example, judges, magistrates, trustees or prison officers. They are not employees and do not have contracts of employment. They work under the special terms and conditions attached to their appointment. It is also unlikely that members of the clergy will be held to be employees. This point has been debated in several cases. The 1998 Court of Appeal decision in *Diocese of Southwark v Coker* stated that members of the clergy were not entitled to employee status.

However, the position of members of the clergy is now unclear following the House of Lords ruling in *Percy v Church of Scotland Board of National Mission* (2005). Here, the House of Lords held that the relationship between a minister of religion and his or her church can (and in most normal cases will) be one of employment within the meaning of the Sex Discrimination Act 1975. Their Lordships held that the fact that someone is an office holder does not mean that they cannot be an employee.

Crown employees

This includes those who work for the civil service, national health service or armed forces. They may work under a contract of employment but have selective employment protection rights.

Police

All police officers are office holders but are not given a full range of employment rights; for example, they cannot bring a claim for unfair dismissal. Section 200 of the Employment Rights Act 1996 excludes police officers from all general employment rights except those relating to the right to receive a written statement of terms and conditions, the right to be given minimum notice periods and the right to receive a redundancy payment.

Temporary agency workers

Temporary workers are placed with an employer by an employment agency. The Conduct of Employment Agencies and Employment Business Regulations, 2003 state that when the agency enters into a contract with a worker it must provide him with a written statement outlining whether or not he is to be classed as an employee or a self-employed worker. The cases of **Clark** and **McMeechan** (above) highlight the difficulties that have occurred in dealing with the status of agency workers. They may or may not have employee status.

Probationary workers

Probationary workers are classed as employees even though they are on probation. The only difference here is that often the employer has the right to dismiss the employee at the end of the probationary period if he is not impressed with the employee's work.

CONTENTS OF THE CONTRACT - INCORPORATION, EXPRESS TERMS, IMPLIED TERMS AND TERMS IMPLIED BY STATUTE

Incorporation

Terms appear in the employment contract either because they are expressly written into it or because they are implied by law. They may also be implied by statute. Many employees also have part of their terms and conditions agreed under a collective agreement between management and unions. Terms may also be incorporated from the custom and practice of the business. This means that terms may be implied into the contract relating to the way in which things have been done in the business over a number of years. Terms may also be incorporated into the agreement from rule books or office manuals.

Terms are not incorporated into the contract automatically. If terms are to be incorporated from either collective agreements, rule books or manuals, then an express term in the contract should outline the parts of the documents that are to be incorporated into it.

Types of term

The employment contract is made up of a collection of terms and conditions. Three types of term form the contents of the employment contract:

- express terms
- implied terms
- statutory terms.

Express terms

Express terms are those that have been written into the contract and agreed upon by the parties.

> *Example*
> *You will be paid monthly in arrears. Your annual salary will be £17 500 per year. You will be entitled to 20 days' holiday per year, rising to 25 days after 5 years' service.*

3

The contract of employment

Express terms give the employee information on matters such as pay, holiday entitlement and hours of work.

Standard express terms will contain information on:

- the job title and a description of the tasks that the employee will be required to do;
- the rate of pay and when it will be paid;
- the date on which the employee started work;
- the hours of work;
- the place of work;
- any notice requirements.

There may also be clauses relating to restraint of trade after employment, confidentiality, flexibility or mobility. (See further page 135) Flexibility and mobility clauses relate to the employee being required to do a different job (be flexible), or do it in a different place (be mobile). If the employer is expecting the employee to do any of these things then an express term should be inserted into the contract to this effect.

Express terms form the basis of the contract and essentially contain the same information as that given in the employee's written statement of the terms and conditions of employment. If employers provide a detailed contract giving employees all of the required information, there is no need for them to then provide a separate written statement. If the terms in the written statement are different from the express terms in the contract, the contractual terms override them.

If an employee is in breach of an express term, this will be a ground for dismissal. If an employer breaches an express term, employees have two options. They can remain in the job and make a claim for damages relating to the breach. Alternatively they can leave the job and make a claim for constructive dismissal. (See generally, Chapter 6.)

Figure 3.1 highlights the contents of a basic contract of employment.

Implied terms

Implied terms are not written into the contract but are implied into it either because the parties failed to include some information in the express terms or because their existence is obvious or needed to ensure the smooth running of the contract. Implied terms may impose duties or obligations on both the employer and employee.

> #### Examples
> - *Your employer will pay you a weekly/monthly salary.*
> - *You will not steal from your employer.*

If the employee breaches an implied term, the employer will normally be justified in dismissing him. The employer could also ask the court for an injunction to stop the employee from continuing any wrongdoing. If the employer breaches a term, the employee has the option of resigning and making a claim for constructive dismissal or remaining in the job and making a claim for damages. The action taken will depend on the circumstances in each case.

Contract of Employment

Employer: Computerwizz
Unit 33
Industrial Lane
Easington Way

Employee: Mr David Brown
8 Tree Lane
Easington Way

1   The date on which your employment began was 23 November 2004.

2   You are employed as a software technician and repair specialist.

3   Your duties will include repairing systems onsite, ordering materials, answering colleague and customer queries and developing new systems.

4   You will work mainly at the Unit 33 site but will also be expected to visit customers and clients at their place of work. Computerwizz reserves the right to move your main place of employment to another site. You will be given two months' notice of any change.

5   Your rate of pay is £24 000 per annum. You will be paid at monthly intervals directly into your bank account.

6   Your normal hours of work will be 9.30 am–5.30 pm. You may be expected to work extra hours at any time. Overtime at the standard rate will be paid for any extra hours worked. Computerwizz reserves the right to ask you to work on weekends or at any unsociable hour should there be an emergency or incident which affects Computerwizz's operation.

7   You are entitled to 24 days of holiday per year in addition to the normal statutory holidays. This entitlement rises to 27 days after five years' service. The holiday year runs from 1 April to 31 March.

8   Aside from the normal statutory sickness entitlement, you are entitled to be paid in full during the first two months of any certified illness and then at a rate based on 50 per cent of your salary for a further two months. This right only applies where an employee has been working for Computerwizz for a period of three months.

9   If, for any reason, you are unable to attend work, you should telephone Ms Grundy in personnel on the first day of your absence. This call should be made by 9.30 am.

10   Computerwizz operates a company pension scheme. Details of this are contained in the personnel handbook, copies of which are available from personnel.

11   You are entitled to receive one month's notice of the termination of your contract. You must give Computerwizz one month's notice of your intention to terminate your contract. These periods apply where an employee has worked for the company for one month or more.

12   You are subject to company rules on discipline and grievance. Copies of these disciplinary and grievance rules are available in a handbook, copies of which hang in the company canteen and are available from personnel.

Figure 3.1 An example of a basic contract of employment

3

The contract of employment

If you are willing to accept the terms of this contract, please sign and date this document below. Please retain one copy and return the other to personnel at the address given on the attached letter.

Amelia Grundy, Personnel Officer.

I agree to accept the terms of this offer of employment.

Signed ....   Dated   ....

Mr D Brown

Figure 3.1 continued

Duties of the employer: implied terms

The following duties are implied into all contracts of employment. The employer has a duty to:

- pay the employee;
- provide work;
- treat the employee with mutual trust and confidence;
- take reasonable care for the safety of the employee;
- deal promptly with grievances;
- reimburse the employee for any expenses properly incurred while at work;
- write references.

1 To pay the employee

This is a duty to pay the employee when he is available for, or doing, work. See: *Beveridge* v *KLM (UK) Ltd* (2000). This duty is one of the most fundamental under the contract. Voluntary work aside, none of us would like the idea of working without receiving some form of financial reward. The appropriate rate of pay will normally be found either in the employment contract itself or the written statement of terms and conditions. If no rate is stated, a reasonable amount will be paid taking into account the remuneration of other employees doing the same job.

Unless the express terms of the contract provide otherwise, there is no duty to pay the employee when he is unavailable for work or when there is no work to do. The lack of work may be due to, for example, a lack of orders or a shortage of materials. Where the lack of work is due to circumstances beyond the employer's control, there is no duty on the employer to pay the employee.

Browning v Crumlin Valley Collieries (1926)

A mine was forced to close when parts of it became unsafe due to flooding.

Held There was no duty to pay the employees as the closure was beyond the control of the mine owners.

Miles v *Wakefield MDC* (1987)

Miles worked as a superintendent registrar of births, marriages and deaths. His employer withheld 3/37ths of his wages because he refused, as part of industrial action, to carry out marriages on Saturday mornings.

Held (HL) As Miles had been engaged in industrial action, the deductions were lawful. He had not been available for work.

See, however, the statutory rules on guarantee payments outlined at page 176.

2 To provide work

There is no general duty on the employer to provide work. In *Collier* v *Sunday Referee Publishing Co Ltd* (1940) Asquith J said, 'Provided I pay my cook her wages regularly she cannot complain if I choose to take any or all of my meals out'.

However, there are three exceptions to this rule. There is a duty to provide work where:

- the employee works on a piecework or commission basis, meaning that without work the employee would be unable to earn money;
- the employee needs to work on a regular basis to maintain or improve his skills, for example, surgeons or interpreters;
- where failure to provide work would lead to a loss of reputation or publicity, for example, in the case of television personalities, actors or journalists.

In *William Hill Organisation Ltd* v *Tucker* (1998) the Court of Appeal held that all employees with specific skills are entitled to exercise those skills provided there is work to be done. It was said that society had moved on from the days when only actors and musicians were to be the only people having the type of skill that needed to be practised and updated regularly.

Clayton & Waller v *Oliver* (1930)

Oliver was an actor who had been given a leading role in a musical. The employer later removed him from top billing, but offered him a supporting role which he refused. He sued for non-provision of work on the basis that his reputation would be severely damaged by the employer's actions.

Held He was entitled to damages for the loss of opportunity to enhance his reputation.

3 To treat the employee with mutual trust and confidence

This is the most widely applied duty and can be referred to as that of trusting the employee, treating him with respect or treating him fairly. The essence of the duty is that the employer should not do anything that is likely to destroy or seriously damage the relationship of trust and confidence between employer and employee. In *Woods* v *WM Car Services (Peterborough) Ltd* (1982) Lord Denning described it as 'the duty of the employer to be good and considerate to his workers'.

This duty can be applied to any situation where the employer is being unfair or unkind to the employee. The duty can be breached in various ways, for example, in demoting the employee, accusing him of theft without evidence, verbally or physically abusing the employee, constantly criticising his work or generally making his time at work unbearable.

The contract of employment

If the employee is forced to leave his employment because of unkind or unfair treatment, he may make a claim for constructive dismissal.

See further: *Wilson* v *Racher* (1974), *Arden* v *Bradley* (1994), *Bracebridge Engineering Ltd* v *Darby* (1990) and *White* v *Reflecting Roadstuds Ltd* (1991).

Isle of Wight Tourist Board v Coombes (1976)

A director was overheard talking to another employee. He said that his personal secretary was 'an intolerable bitch on a Monday morning'. She was upset and resigned.

Held The director had breached the duty of trust and confidence.

Lewis v Motorworld Garages Ltd (1986)

An employee was demoted without warning. He lost his office and was told to expect a cut in wages. He continued to work for the garage but his employer subjected him to continuous verbal abuse. His work was criticised on a daily basis and he was threatened with dismissal on more than one occasion.

Held This behaviour amounted to a breach of the implied duty that the employer treat his employee with respect.

An interesting case on the issue of mutual trust and confidence is as follows:

Malik v Bank of Credit and Commerce International (1997)

BCCI went into liquidation after being accused of fraudulent, dishonest and corrupt dealings. Malik was a former employee of the bank. He appealed to the House of Lords against the earlier decision that he was not able to claim compensation for the damage that the bank had done to his professional reputation. He found it almost impossible to find new employment due to the fact that he had worked for BCCI.

Held (HL) His appeal was upheld. BCCI was under an obligation not to conduct a corrupt and dishonest business. In doing so it had damaged Malik's future employment prospects. It had undermined the relationship of trust and confidence that had previously existed between them.

In *Omilaju* v *London Borough of Waltham Forest* (2005) CA the court considered the position where an employee resigns and claims constructive dismissal on the basis that an act by his employer was the 'last straw'. The court held that the important question to ask is whether when looking at the employer's treatment of the employee as a whole he can be said to have breached the implied term of mutual trust and confidence.

See also: *BCCI* v *Ali (No. 2)* (2002), *French* v *Barclays Bank* (1998), *Morrow* v *Safeway Stores plc* (2002), *Stanley Cole (Wainfleet) Ltd* v *Sheridan* (2003).

4 To take reasonable care for the safety of their employees

Employers have a duty to ensure employee safety both at common law and under the Health and Safety at Work Act 1974. This is discussed further in Chapter 9. The duty is one only to take reasonable precautions to ensure employee safety.

5 To deal promptly with grievances

There is a duty on the employer to organise grievance procedures so as to assist the employee as soon as possible and not to cause him extra stress.

> **Goold v McConnel** (1995)
>
> A salesman was unhappy about having to work under a new sales scheme. He approached his employer on several occasions asking for an appointment to discuss this grievance. The employer failed to respond to his requests and he resigned claiming constructive dismissal.
>
> **Held (EAT)** It is an implied term of an employment contract that the employer promptly and reasonably allows his employees to discuss any grievance. Failure to do so was a breach of the implied term to deal promptly with grievances and so in breach of contract.

In *Harlow v General HealthCare Group plc* (2002) it was held that when an employee is off work due to illness it is perfectly reasonable for their employer to wait for them to return to work before dealing with any grievance.

6 To reimburse the employee for any expenses properly incurred in the performance of his work

The employer has a duty to reimburse the employee for any expenses that the employee incurs while doing his job. This would include, for example, the payment of hotel bills or travelling expenses.

7 To write references

Whilst there is no general or statutory obligation on an employer to write references, the duty may be implied if it is normal practice in the type of work concerned for a reference to be given. This is also the case where it would be unreasonable to expect a new employer to employ an individual without a reference. In *Spring v Guardian Insurance plc* (1994) the House of Lords held that employers have a duty towards their employees when writing references. Employers should take care to ensure that references are not misleading and should write them with care and skill. Employers may be liable for any losses suffered by an employee as a result of their inaccurate comments. See: *Kidd v Axa Equity and Law Life Assurance Society* (2000), *TSB v Harris* (2000).

Duties of the employee: implied terms

The following duties are implied into all contracts of employment. Employees have a duty to:

- be ready and willing to work;
- use reasonable care and skill at work;
- obey reasonable and lawful orders;
- take care of their employer's property;
- act in good faith.

1 To be ready and willing to work

This implies that employees will present themselves for work and that once there will be willing to work in return for remuneration.

3

The contract of employment

2 To use reasonable care and skill at work

Employees must not be negligent when carrying out their work and must be reasonably competent at their job. If they are negligent or incompetent, they may be found to be in breach of contract. The following cases highlight breaches of the duty to use reasonable care and skill at work.

Janata Bank v Ahmed (1981)

Mr Ahmed worked as a bank manager. Over several years he had agreed to give bank loans and mortgages to customers who were obviously bad credit risks. The bank alleged that in doing so he had been negligent in carrying out his duties. After dismissing him, Janata sued him for damages amounting to £34 640.

Held (CA) Janata's claim was upheld because Ahmed had failed to exercise the proper care and skill required under his contract of employment.

Lister v Romford Ice & Cold Storage Co Ltd (1957)

Mr Lister drove lorries for Romford Ice. He negligently reversed his lorry injuring another employee who happened to be his father. The employer paid damages to his father but claimed reimbursement from Lister on the basis that he had been negligent in the performance of his work.

Held Lister was liable to pay damages as he had breached the duty of using reasonable care and skill while at work.

3 To obey reasonable and lawful orders

It is implied that employees will obey reasonable orders. If they refuse to obey a reasonable order, they can be dismissed without notice by an employer. In *Laws v London Chronicle* (1959) Lord Evershed MR stated that 'wilful disobedience of a lawful and reasonable order shows a disregard of a condition essential to the contract . . . that the servant must obey the proper orders of the master'. In the more recent case of *Macari v Celtic Football and Athletic Co Ltd* (1999) it was held that 'an employee who refuses to obey a lawful and reasonable order, which was given in good faith and without any ulterior motive, is in repudiatory breach of contract'.

United Kingdom Atomic Energy Authority v Claydon (1974)

An express term in Claydon's contract of employment stated that he could be required to work anywhere within the United Kingdom. When he refused to transfer to another city, he was dismissed.

Held He was in breach of contract because he had failed to obey a lawful and reasonable order.

Pepper v Webb (1969)

A gardener who had a record of arrogance was asked to put some plants into the garden. He was just about to go home and refused, saying, 'I couldn't care less about your bloody greenhouse and your sodding garden'. He was dismissed.

Held His dismissal was justified because he had not obeyed a lawful and reasonable order. His behaviour made it impossible for the employer to continue to employ him.

See also: *O'Brien v Associated Fire Alarms* (1969).

Whilst the orders made have to be within the scope of the employee's employment contract, the employee may also be expected to perform duties which are incidental to his main role. This has included the covering of staff absences and the supervision of lunchbreaks by teachers. See: *Sim v Rotherham Metropolitan Borough Council* (1986) and *Gorse v Durham County Council* (1971).

Employees may also be expected to adapt to new methods for performing a job. The increase in technology has meant that employees are now expected to adapt to change and be willing to train and keep up to date with new developments.

Creswell v Board of Inland Revenue (1984)

Here tax workers had to adapt to the use of computers. Training was given, but some workers refused to stop using the manual system of tax assessment.

Held Provided that the training on offer was adequate to meet the new tasks, the workers had to adapt to new methods and techniques.

Employees cannot, however, be ordered to do anything that falls outside the scope of their employment contract. Nor can they be expected to do anything that is not incidental to it or which would expose them to danger or harm. In *Ottoman Bank v Chakarian* (1930) an employee ran the risk of being murdered if he returned to Turkey. It was held that when he refused to return he was not in breach of the implied term to obey lawful orders.

Walmsley v UDEC Refrigeration Ltd (1972)

Mr Walmsley was dismissed after refusing to work in southern Ireland. He did not want to move there because he had heard that the area was a hotbed of IRA activity. He had no evidence of this.

Held He had refused to obey a reasonable order. Had he been told to go to Northern Ireland, his refusal might have been justified.

There is no duty to obey an order if in doing so you commit a criminal act. In *Morrish v Henleys (Folkestone) Ltd* (1972) an employee was not in breach when he was dismissed for refusing to falsify the company accounts.

4 To take care of the employer's property

This is a general duty not to wilfully damage the employer's property or act in a manner likely to result in it being stolen, lost or damaged. In *Superlux v Plaistead* (1958) an employee was found to be in breach of this duty when vacuum cleaners were stolen from the work van parked outside his house. The court held that he should have taken them into his house and so had not taken proper care of his employer's property.

5 To act in good faith

This is the widest duty and is similar to that of the employer having to treat the employee with trust and respect. In *Wilson v Racher* (1974) Edmund Davies LJ stated that 'We have by now come to realise that a contract of service imposes upon the parties a duty of mutual respect'.

Employees should be loyal to their employer and not do anything that would harm their employer's business. Examples of this implied duty would be the employee disclosing the

The contract of employment

3

wrongdoing of work colleagues or giving the rights to any inventions made to their employer. In particular the employee should not:

(a) disrupt the employer's business interests;

(b) be dishonest;

(c) compete with the employer;

(d) disclose confidential information.

Not to disrupt the employer's business interests

Employees have a duty to co-operate with their employer to ensure that the employer's business runs smoothly. In *Secretary of State for Employment v ASLEF* (1972) Lord Denning stated that if an employee purposefully does something to disrupt his employer's business, he will be in breach of contract.

Ticehurst v British Telecom plc (1992)

Ms Ticehurst was a British Telecom manager and union official. Her union called a number of one-day strikes and ordered a general withdrawal of goodwill. She took part in the strikes and on returning to work refused to sign an agreement stating that she would take no further action. British Telecom had written to all of the staff on strike stating that deductions would be made from their pay and that if they returned to work and refused to work normally then they would be sent home. Ticehurst refused to work normally and was sent home. She then sued for deducted pay.

Held (CA) Ticehurst had shown an intention not to work normally and so had withdrawn her goodwill. She was in breach of the implied term to serve her employer faithfully and not disrupt the employer's business interests.

The duty to co-operate can also be seen in the cases of **Sim** and **Cresswell** above.

Not to be dishonest

This implied term covers things such as an employee not stealing from his employer or, as in *Boston Deep Sea Fishing & Ice Company v Ansell* (1888), not taking bribes to do something that would adversely affect the employer's business. In *Sinclair v Neighbour* (1967) this duty was broken when an employee borrowed money from the shop till. Even though he intended to pay it back and had left an 'IOU' in the till, he knew that such actions were prohibited. In *Denco Ltd v Joinson* (1992) the use of an unauthorised password to gain entry to a computer was held to be a dishonest act and a breach of good faith. In *Neary v Dean of Westminster* (1999) Lord Jauncey stated that 'conduct amounting to gross misconduct justifying dismissal must so undermine the trust and confidence which is inherent in the particular contract of employment that the master should no longer be required to retain the servant in his employment'. See also: *Briscoe v Lubrizol Ltd* (2002).

Not to compete with the employer

An employee can, within limits, do whatever he wishes in his spare time. An employee may take a second job provided this does not disrupt his main job by, for instance, making him too tired to do his work properly. An employee, may not, however, work for a competitor.

Hivac v Park Royal Scientific Instruments Ltd (1946)

Five employees installed valves into hearing aids. They did the same job for a rival firm at weekends.

Held The court granted an injunction preventing the men from continuing to work for the competitor. They were in breach of the implied duty not to work for a rival employer.

Not to disclose confidential information

Whilst in employment the employee should not divulge confidential information obtained during that employment. For this duty to be imposed, the employee has to be aware that the information in question should be treated as confidential. Employers need to be able to protect their business interests. Employees often work with customer lists or formulas which, if passed to a competitor, could harm the employer's business.

In *Bents Brewery v Hogan* (1945) Lynskey J said that 'It is quite clear that an employee is under an obligation to his employers not to disclose confidential information obtained by him in the course of his employment'.

An employee has a duty not to divulge confidential information whilst in employment, but this is not necessarily the case once the employee has left that employment. If the employer wants to restrict the use of confidential information after the employee has left his employment, the most effective method of prevention is the inclusion of an express term in the employment contract. This term should restrain the employee's right to divulge such information or use it to his own advantage. Such terms are referred to as 'confidentiality clauses'. Even if the contract does not contain such a clause, there is still an implied duty not to divulge confidential information during employment.

What is confidential information?

What types of information will constitute 'confidential' information will depend very much on the type of business involved. Confidential information is generally any information that is vital to the smooth running of a business.

Example

The formula for Coca-Cola (which only a few company employees may know), or the names and addresses of clients. If an employee 'leaked' the drinks formula, a rival could then make cola under a different name and compete. In the case of customer lists and information, the rival business could contact those customers and offer cut-price work or deliveries. This may result in the original company losing orders. Over a period of time this could lead to disastrous financial consequences.

The following types of information have been held to be confidential information: manufacturing processes, customer lists, chemical formulas, designs, secret formulas, accounts or business plans.

It is important to distinguish between what is confidential information and what is the 'know-how' that the employee has developed over the years. The following case (with the memorable name) discusses this point.

Here, the Court of Appeal made the distinction between two types of confidential information:

- information so essential to the smooth running of the business that it should be treated as a trade secret – here the employee can be restrained from divulging information even after having left the employment;
- information which is confidential and so should not be divulged during employment – but is not important enough to be confidential after an employee leaves the job.

⚖️

Faccenda Chicken v Fowler [1986]

Mr Fowler had sold fresh chickens from a refrigerated van. He resigned and set up a rival company. He and some colleagues took confidential information from Faccenda Chicken which helped them to attract new customers. The information included customer purchasing requirements. There was no express term in Fowler's employment contract preventing this. Faccenda sued him for damages and sought an injunction alleging that he had misused confidential information.

Held (CA) The claim that the information was so confidential that Fowler could be stopped from using it was dismissed. There was a difference between protecting trade secrets and employee know-how. The information that he had used was based on know-how and so was not confidential information.

For the duty to apply after the employee has left the employment, the information would have to be of a highly confidential nature. The court went on to lay down a four-part test to be used where there is no specific clause in the contract relating to confidential information. In deciding whether the 'secret' warrants protection after employment has ceased, the court will consider:

- the nature of the job;
- the nature of the information requiring protection;
- whether this information can be isolated from other information that the employee can divulge or use;
- whether the employer had stressed the nature of the confidential information to the employee.

For the duty to apply, the information has to be highly confidential and the employer would have had to stress this to the employee. If the employee was able to use other information freely, this would help to highlight that information which the employee should not divulge.

In **Faccenda** the information in question related to the prices paid for chickens, and other sales and customer information. The court was not satisfied that this was confidential enough to warrant an injunction being granted to stop the men trading. The 'know-how', skill and knowledge of the employee cannot be protected.

In *Roger Bullivant Ltd v Ellis* (1987) an employee was found to have breached this duty when he copied out a customer list before he left his employer to set up a rival firm. This was held to be information essential for the smooth running of the company. Similarly, placing in a tender for an employer's future business as an employee leaves has also been held to be a breach: *Adamson v B & L Cleaning Services Ltd* (1995).

See also: *Robb v Green* (1895), *Sanders v Parry* (1967), *Lancashire Fires Ltd v S.A. Lyons & Co Ltd* (1997), *Thomas Marshall (Exports) Ltd v Guinle* (1978), AT Poeton (*Gloucester Plating*) Ltd v *Horton* (2000), *Camelot Group plc v Centaur Communications Ltd* (1999).

Public interest disclosures - 'whistleblowers'

A worker who divulges confidential information may be protected but only in specific circumstances. Under the Public Interest Disclosure Act 1998 a worker is protected where they make what is termed a 'protected disclosure' to a 'specified individual in prescribed circumstances'. This Act inserted new sections into the Employment Rights Act 1996. In order for the Act to apply there must have been a 'qualifying disclosure', that disclosure must be a 'protected disclosure' and the worker must have been either dismissed or have suffered a detriment following the disclosure.

What will amount to a qualifying disclosure is set out in s 43B of the 1996 Act. A 'qualifying disclosure' is any disclosure of information, which the worker reasonably believes highlights one of the following:

- that a criminal offence has been committed, or is being committed or is likely to be committed;
- that a person has failed, is failing or is likely to fail to comply with any legal obligation;
- that a miscarriage of justice has occurred, is occurring or is likely to occur in the future;
- that the health and safety of any individual has been, is being or is likely to be endangered in the future;
- that the environment has been, is being, or is likely to be damaged; or
- that information relating to any of the above has been, is being or is likely to be deliberately concealed.

The worker only has to show that he has a reasonable belief that one of the above incidents has, is, or will take place in the future. In order to be protected the disclosure must be made to either:

(a) an employer or other responsible person;

(b) a legal adviser;

(c) a Minister of the Crown (where the employer is an individual appointed by a Minister of the Crown); or

(d) a prescribed person (persons in this category are defined in the Public Interest Disclosure (Prescribed Persons) Order 1999 (as amended in 2003, 2004 and 2005) and includes local authorities).

If a worker divulges confidential information to someone not listed above then they will still be protected if at the time of divulging the information they believed that they would be subjected to a detriment if they had contacted that person. This will also apply where the worker believed that evidence would be destroyed if he made the disclosure to his employer or if he had previously already made the same disclosure to his employer.

A worker will also be protected where the information and disclosure are so serious that all of the above procedures were ignored. However, this will only apply where the information given was very serious in nature and it is held to have been reasonable for the worker to have made the disclosure in this way.

There is no upper limit to the amount of compensation that may be awarded to a whistleblower who has been dismissed. In July 2005 a prison officer who had made a qualifying disclosure about the poor treatment of inmates was awarded £477 000 in damages.

Remedies available to the employer

If the employee is still working for the employer, breach of this confidentiality duty is a breach of contract and so the employer could terminate the employee's contract. If the breach is not that serious, the employer may opt to discipline the employee emphasising the seriousness of his actions. The employer may also apply to the court for an injunction against the employee to either prevent further leaks, and an injunction against a third party to prevent him from using the information. The employer could also make a claim for damages against either the employee or the party who had used the information. This claim would be based on any loss that the employer has suffered due to the breach.

Statutory terms

Statute implies various terms into the employment contract.

Example

Terms implied by statute might include:

- *the 'equality clause' (relating to equal pay) implied into all contracts by s 1 of the Equal Pay Act 1970;*
- *the right not to be unfairly dismissed implied by s 94 of the Employment Rights Act 1996;*
- *the right to be given a copy of disciplinary and grievance procedures implied by s 30 of the Employment Act 2002.*

The employer cannot avoid these terms and cannot ask the employee to sign away any of his statutory rights. There are various provisions surrounding 'contracting out' which are aimed at the protection of the employee. (See s 203 of the Employment Rights Act 1996.)

THE RIGHT TO A WRITTEN STATEMENT OUTLINING THE TERMS AND CONDITIONS OF EMPLOYMENT

The Employment Act 2002 made several changes to the rules on written statements. The relevant parts of this Act came into force on 1 October 2004 and are incorporated where appropriate in this section.

Section 1(1) of the Employment Rights Act 1996 states that: 'Where an employee begins employment with an employer, the employer shall give to the employee a written statement of particulars of employment.' Subsection (2) goes on to say that 'the statement may be given in instalments and (whether or not given in instalments) shall be given not later than two months after the beginning of the employment'. In *Coales* v *John Wood* (1986) it was held that employees have a right to be given a written statement and not only some vague entitlement to one. This means that employers must provide a written statement whether the employee requests one or not.

The contents of the written statement should match the terms of the contract of employment. In *System Floors (UK) Ltd* v *Daniel* (1982) the Employment Appeal Tribunal held that whilst the written statement provided strong evidence of the terms agreed by the parties, it was not the contract of employment. If the written statement does not accurately reflect the contents of the actual contract, it is the contractual terms which prevail: *Robertson* v *British Gas Corp* (1983).

Remembering, however, that not all employees are given contracts of employment, the written statement can be an invaluable source of information.

The statement of employment should contain details under the following heads:

- the names of employer and employee;
- the date on which the employment began;
- whether any employment with another employer counts towards this employment (important for continuity);
- the rate of salary and when it will be paid;
- the hours to be worked, including any overtime provision;
- holiday entitlement and details on holiday pay;

- sick pay, sickness/injury at work;
- pension schemes;
- how much notice the employee or employer has to give to terminate the contract;
- if the job is not meant to be permanent, how long it is likely to last;
- the place where the employee will be expected to work;
- any collective agreements which directly affect the employment;
- if the employee is required to work outside of the United Kingdom for more than one month, details as to for how long and in which currency he will be paid;

The written statement must also include a note providing:

- details of the employer's disciplinary and grievance procedures;
- whether or not a pensions contracting-out certificate is in force for the employment in question.

The information on the note must cover any disciplinary rules and detail any disciplinary/dismissal procedures which apply to the employee. It should also contain:

- details of the person (name/job title etc.) to whom the employee can apply if he is unhappy with any disciplinary/dismissal decision relating to himself;
- details on how any such application may be made;
- details on how the employee is able to seek redress through grievance proceedings; and
- details on how such an application may be made.

A written statement need not be given to:

- employees who have been given a full contract of employment outlining details of the terms and conditions of that employment (this would serve the dual function of being both a contract of employment and a written statement);
- employees who are to be employed for one month or less;
- Crown employees;
- merchant sailors;
- share fishermen/women (those who share in the profit from the catch);
- employees who work mainly outside the United Kingdom.

An employer may provide a written statement in instalments, provided that all of the instalments are given before the end of the initial two-month period. If the employer does not provide an employment contract, the employee must be given a written statement.

Section 1 of the Employment Rights Act 1996 complies with the European Directive on the Proof of the Employment Relationship which was adopted in 1991. Its aim was to 'provide employees with improved protection against possible infringements of their rights'.

Principal statement

Some of the details listed above have to be given in one document. This is the 'principal statement' and should contain information on the names of the parties, the date the employment began, the date when the employee's period of continuous employment began, what the salary is and when it will be paid, the hours to be worked, holidays and holiday pay, job title and the place at which the employee will be expected to work.

The principal statement need not contain details on pensions or sickness and may refer the employee to another document which contains this information. This document has to be reasonably accessible and could, for example, be a works rule book, company handbook or notice on a staff noticeboard in the canteen.

If there are no particulars on, for example, pensions or sick pay then that fact must be stated. It may be that the employer does not have a company pension scheme. If this is the case, it must be stated in the particulars.

What if the employee signs the written statement thinking that it is his contract of employment?

If the employee signs the written statement thinking that it is an employment contract, it is then treated as such. This was held by the Court of Appeal in the case of *Gascol Conversions Ltd* v *Mercer* (1974). The employee must however, believe that he is signing a contract. Signing a document merely to show that he has received it will not suffice.

Changes to the written statement

Any changes to the written statement must be communicated to the employee within one month of the change. Notification of any changes must contain detailed particulars of the actual change being made. There are, however, a number of exceptions to this. Particulars of changes relating to:

- sick leave, entitlement to sick pay;
- pensions and pension schemes;
- disciplinary rules and disciplinary/dismissal procedures; and
- any steps to be taken following the making of an application under the employer's disciplinary, dismissal or grievance procedures

may be given by reference to another document. This document must be made accessible to the employee within their workplace. Where the change relates only to the name/identity of the employer (but continuity is preserved) the employee need only be informed of the change and need not be given new written particulars. When a change of employer occurs, a new and full written statement of particulars must normally be issued.

What if the employer does not give the employee a written statement?

Section 11 of the Employment Rights Act 1996 states that if the employee is not given a written statement or if the statement is incomplete, he may make a complaint to the Employment Tribunal. Section 11(4) of the 1996 Act states that the employee can complain to the tribunal while in employment or within three months of having left employment.

If the statement is incomplete, the tribunal can specify what ought to have been included; if it is incorrect the tribunal can amend it. However, in *Eagland* v *British Telecommunications plc* (1992) the Court of Appeal held that the tribunal had no power to invent particular terms of employment.

This remedy is weak and as such may not be used by the employee who may be concerned about annoying his new employer. If an employee is dismissed for asking for a written statement, this dismissal is automatically unfair.

Section 38 of the Employment Act 2002 introduced additional penalties for employers who fail to provide a written statement. Under this section the Employment Tribunal will award compensation to an employee who has not received a written statement unless there are exceptional circumstances which would make an award unjust or inequitable. Any award made will be between 2 and 4 weeks' pay. A week's pay is calculated in the same way as for unfair dismissal and redundancy calculations. At the time of writing the figure (as from 1 February 2007) is £310.

However, it should be noted that this is not a free-standing right and can only be applied where the employee is bringing another tribunal claim, e.g. for unfair dismissal or discrimination. This section cannot be used where an employee wishes to complain solely of a failure to provide written particulars.

Failure to provide a written statement does not affect the daily running of the contract, but it is good business practice for the employer to provide one. Apart from ensuring that both the employer and employee are fully aware of their respective responsibilities if a problem does arise, a court or tribunal will not look favourably upon an employer who has not provided his employee with the required information.

RESTRAINT OF TRADE CLAUSES

An employee has a duty not to divulge confidential information belonging to his employer whilst in employment. Employers may also attempt to prevent employees from competing unfairly against them once they have left their employment.

Employers do not want clients to move with employees because this may result in a loss of business. The profits of, for example, a hairdressing salon depend on visits from regular customers. If one of the salon's top stylists leaves and takes his particular customers to his new place of work, the salon would lose some of its regular customers and so suffer financially.

If the employer wishes to protect his business interests in this way, he can attempt to do so by placing an express restraint of trade clause into the employment contract. There are four legitimate interests in respect of which an employer is entitled to limited protection. These are: (a) trade secrets and confidential information, (b) information on existing customers and connections, (c) from an ex-employee working for a competitor, and (d) from an ex-employee enticing away current employees. An employer can only protect trade secrets or business interests. In addition, to be effective any such clause would also have to be shown to be 'reasonable' between the parties and in the public interest.

The employee agrees to a restriction on where and for whom he can work for a set period of time after he leaves his job.

A restraint clause could be drafted much like the example below.

> ### Example
> *After leaving employment with this firm you will not work for a competitor within a ten-mile radius of our office for a period of two years.*

The employer can only protect against unfair competition, not competition in general. Such clauses are often found in the contracts of hairdressers, solicitors and executives but they can be used in any contract where the employer wants to prevent an employee from using confidential information or setting up as a rival in the future. If the employer does use a restraint clause, then in any hearing the burden is on the employer to prove that it is reasonable. The exception to this is where the employee is arguing that the clause is not in the public interest. In this case it is up to the employee to prove this.

3

The contract of employment

The way in which restraint clauses are written is very important. The more complex and wide-ranging the clause, the less likely it is to succeed. To ensure that a clause is effective, an employer should draft it with precision ensuring that he is protecting no more than necessary, stating its aims clearly and concisely. In *Wincanton Ltd v Cranny* (2000) a non-competition clause failed to succeed because it had been worded using the company's 'standard form'. It was held to be too vague, too 'wide' in its approach and it was said that it had been designed to cover as many differing situations as possible. The clause was not precise, clear or concise. In *Commercial Plastics Ltd v Vincent* (1965) Pearson LJ stated that 'It would seem that a good deal of legal know-how is required for the successful drafting of a restraint clause'.

⬤ Are restraint clauses valid?

In general restraint clauses are thought to be void and unenforceable unless they are 'reasonable' between the parties and in the public interest. This means that the court will look at the fairness or otherwise of the clause. In doing so the court will look at what it is that the employer is trying to prevent, and by looking at the facts decide on whether or not it would be in the public interest to allow the employer to do so.

The case that developed this idea of 'reasonableness' is that of *Nordenfelt* below.

Nordenfelt v Maxim Nordenfelt Guns & Ammunition Co (1894)

Nordenfelt had been a manufacturer of arms and ammunition. He sold his company and agreed not to work in the same type of business anywhere in the world for a period of 25 years. He then set up business as a rival company and Maxim Nordenfelt sought to enforce the restraint of trade clause and stop him from doing so.

Held (HL) Most of the restraint was valid because Nordenfelt had benefited financially from the sale and it had brought a lot of foreign investment to the United Kingdom. However, to restrict him from working in a business competing or liable to compete in any way was unreasonable because it went further than was needed to protect the new company's interests. Consequently, he was allowed to continue to work for the new business.

This case established the principle that clauses in restraint of trade are void unless the restraint can be shown to be reasonable in the interests of the parties and in the public interest generally. If the clause is reasonable, it can be enforced and the employee stopped or prevented from working.

⬤ Legitimate interests

The employer can only protect legitimate business interests. This means that there has to be something worth protecting before the law will allow any restraint to stand. The restraint can give no more than adequate protection to business interests. In *Morris Ltd v Saxelby* (1916) it was held that there are two areas capable of being legitimate interests for this purpose:

(a) the potential disclosure of confidential information;

(b) the use of trade connections made whilst working for the employer.

The types of confidential information covered here are the same as those discussed above under the employee's implied duty. It would include client lists, trade secrets or other information such as accounts or business plans. An ex-employee using trade connections would, for instance, be contacting customers, clients or suppliers and trying to get them to do business with him rather than his ex-employer. Trade connections are sometimes referred to as the 'good will' of the business. This good will element forms part of the market value of the business and so is very important.

Foster v *Suggett* (1918)

A restraint clause sought to prevent a glassworks manager from working in any part of the United Kingdom glass industry for five years. He had a wide knowledge of various forms of glassmaking and knew about a secret manufacturing process that was only used by his ex-employer.

Held Because of his knowledge of the secret manufacturing process, the restraint was valid.

●Reasonableness and in the public interest

Here the court looks to see if the clause is reasonable as between the parties and in the public interest. The court will consider what the clause is trying to protect in terms of:

1 time
2 type of business covered
3 area
4 public policy.

Whilst the law respects the right of the employer to protect his business, it also respects the rights and freedoms of the employee to be able to move around the job market working wherever he pleases. The law tries to strike a balance between these two issues. Each case turns on its own facts and there are no set precedents. The idea is not to prevent the employee from working ever again. Anything that goes beyond what would be reasonable in the circumstances is not in the public interest. In ***Esso Petroleum Ltd* v *Harper's Garage (Stourport) Ltd*** (1968) the court emphasised that what is reasonable and in the public interest are equally important things and that both have to be considered in each case.

Fellows & Son v *Fisher* (1976)

Fisher, a conveyancing clerk was employed by Fellows & Son of Walthamstow, London. His contract contained a clause restraining him from working in the legal (or associated) profession, anywhere within the postal districts of Walthamstow and Chingford for five years after leaving Fellows. It also restrained him from trying to get work from any of the clients of the firm that he had met while working there. This was a very restrictive clause.

Held The Court of Appeal held that the clause was void because it was not in the public interest to effectively stop Fisher from working altogether. If the clause had been allowed to stand it would have meant that he could not work in any part of the legal or related professions. It is not in the public interest to stop trained persons from being able to work within their chosen field.

Reasonable as in time

The time element of the clause should be no longer than the life span of the information. The employee may, for instance, have information on the design of a new washing machine. If after a while this design becomes commonplace amongst other manufacturers, there is then no knowledge left to protect.

3

The contract of employment

Reasonable as in type of business covered

The restraint clause has to be trying to stop the employee from working in the same field as the one that he has just left. If the scope of the employer's business is worldwide, the restraint may go that far. In *Turner* v *Commonwealth & British Minerals* (2000) it was held that an employer can only restrain those employees who have the necessary knowledge or connections to do harm to their business. An employer cannot place a restraint on an employee which relates to parts of his business of which the employee has no knowledge.

Reasonable as in area

Clauses restricting work in both the United Kingdom and on a worldwide basis have been held to be valid.

Fitch v *Dewes* (1921)

A clause restricting a solicitor's clerk from working within seven miles of Tamworth town hall was held to be valid because the restricted area was so small, giving him the opportunity to work elsewhere.

Office Angels Ltd v *Rainer-Thomas and O'Connor* (1991)

An employment agency wanted to prevent ex-employees from setting up or working in employment agencies within 1.2 miles of the branch at which they had worked.

Held The restraint clause was void. The work that the employees did was largely done over the telephone and so the actual site of any new office was irrelevant. All the clause did was to prevent competition. It did not protect the legitimate interests of the employer.

Littlewoods Organisation v *Harris* (1976)

Mr Harris held a senior position with Littlewoods and knew all of Littlewoods' business secrets relating to new season fashion designs. These designs were to appear in Littlewoods' home-shopping catalogue. His contract of employment contained a restraint clause preventing him from working for Littlewoods' main competitor, Great Universal Stores, for one year after leaving Littlewoods. The clause restricted work on a worldwide basis. Harris left Littlewoods and immediately began work with Great Universal Stores. Littlewoods sought to enforce the restraint. Harris argued that it was too wide in area.

Held Even though the clause could operate on a worldwide basis, it would only apply to the United Kingdom as this was the country in which they were rivals. The clause was not too wide in area and so was enforceable.

Hollis v *Stocks* (2000) (CA)

Mr Stocks had worked as an assistant solicitor for Hollis & Co. The firm was based in Notting-hamshire. His contract contained a restraint clause stating that for 12 months after he left their employment he could not work within a 10-mile radius of the office. The clause also restrained him from advising or representing clients in the surrounding police stations or Magistrates Courts. When Mr Stocks went to work for another firm of solicitors (based within the 10-mile radius) Hollis & Co. obtained an injunction to prevent him from being able to work there. Mr Stocks appealed against this injunction to the COA.

Held Mr Stocks lost his appeal. It was said that the clause was neither unreasonable in relation to time or area, given that there were several large cities just outside the set 10-mile radius. Mr Stocks would have been able to obtain employment as a solicitor in one such city and thus not put his ex-employer in a position of having to protect his legitimate business interests.

Allan Janes LLP v Johal (2006)

Ms Johal had been employed by Allan Janes as a solicitor. Her contract of employment stated that after she left her employment with the firm she would not practise as a solicitor at any place within a radius of 6 miles of their office, for a period of 12 months. Her contract also contained a clause preventing her from dealing with their clients for a period of 1 year. She left her employment and entered into a partnership with another solicitor. Their office was 1½ miles from those of Allan Janes. Ms Johal also began to solicit her previous employer's clients.

Held The clause relating to the radius of 6 miles for a period of 12 months was invalid. Such clauses would only be enforced if they went no further than reasonably necessary to protect an employer's legitimate interests. In this case the restriction served mainly to prevent competition. It was held, however, that the clause preventing 'client poaching' was valid.

Reasonable as in not against public policy

The restraint must not be against public policy. There are no definite rules here. The clause must not act against good business practice and the principles of fairness. What is or is not against public policy depends on the view of the court and often the views held by society at the time.

Bull v Pitney Bowes (1967)

The Pitney Bowes pension scheme document contained a clause which stated that if a retired employee went on to work for a competitor or set up his own rival firm, his pension entitlement would be severely affected. Pitney Bowes was effectively threatening to deduct money from an employee's pension.

Held The clause was not enforceable. It was against public policy to allow employees to be threatened in this way.

See also: *Rock Refrigeration Ltd v Jones* (1997), *Scully UK Ltd v Lee* (1998), *International Consulting Services (UK) Ltd v Hart* (2000) and *Ward-Evans Financial Services Ltd v Fox* (2002).

● Severing the clause – the 'blue-pencil' test

If part of the restraint clause is found to be unreasonable the court may still be able to class the remainder of the clause as enforceable by severing or cutting out the offending part. This can only be done if the remainder of the clause still makes sense after the severance.

Example

After leaving employment the employee agrees that for 6 months he will not set up or work in the business of being a hairdresser within 10 miles of this salon or anywhere in the same city.

3

The contract of employment

Here, the court could use the 'blue-pencil' test and sever the words 'or anywhere in the same city' which may be thought to make the clause too wide in area and so unenforceable. The restraint of 10 miles would suffice and the offending part of the clause can be removed without changing the intentions of the clause or the scope of the contract: *Attwood v Lamont* (1920).

The court has no power to rewrite the clause. It can only edit it by using the test. What is left of the clause in the above example would remain in the contract and be enforceable.

In *Sadler v Imperial Life Assurance of Canada* (1988) the court laid down three conditions necessary for the use of the blue pencil test. It can be used only if:

(a) the unenforceable part of the clause can be removed without needing to add or change the remaining part;

(b) the remaining terms and conditions continue to make sense;

(c) the removal of the words does not change what the clause set out to do.

A case highlighting the problems surrounding severance is *Marshall v NM Financial Management Ltd* (1997). Here a restraint clause in the contract stated that commission owed to an employee would (if he left employment) only be paid if he did not work in competition with his ex-employer. Because of the complex way in which the restraint clause had been drafted, the court found it very difficult to sever any of it. The court did achieve severance by stating that the agreement was concerned with the right to a commission and that even if this offending part was taken out the basis of the agreement remained the same. This was a novel and complex decision and should not be seen as a licence to make restraint clauses as complicated as possible.

A more recent example of where the court was able to sever part of a restraint clause is *TFS Derivatives Ltd v Morgan* (2005). Mr Morgan was a broker with extensive knowledge of foreign markets. On resigning from his position with TSF he was put on garden leave. His contract of employment contained a restraint clause. The clause in question stated that Mr Morgan could not work 'in either any business which is competitive with or similar to a relevant business within the territory ... for a period of six months' after the termination of his employment. Here, the court held that the restraint clause could remain in force but that a phrase within it was unreasonable and unenforceable. It was held that this particular phrase could be removed without the need to add or modify the remaining words. The words 'similar to' were severed from the clause.

What can the employer do if the employee breaches a valid restraint of trade clause?

If an ex-employee breaches a restraint of trade clause, he is in breach of contract and the employer can sue him for damages. This may not be the best remedy due to the fact that the average employee does not have the financial resources to pay out large amounts of compensation. The employer could also apply for an injunction to prevent any further breach of the clause.

Injunctions

An injunction is a court order which, in this case, would prevent the ex-employee from breaching the clause. The employee would, for example, be prevented from working for a rival business or using confidential information to set up in competition with his original employer.

There are two types of injunction: interlocutory and final. An interlocutory injunction could be granted whilst the employer is in the process of taking action against the ex-employee. A final injunction may be granted after the case has been heard in court.

The interlocutory injunction may be of most use to the employer in the situations noted above. The parties often have to wait for months before their case is heard. An interlocutory injunction would protect the employer until a final decision is made. Injunctions are given at the courts' discretion. The court will consider whether or not to grant the injunction taking into account the 'balance of convenience' as set out in the case of *American Cyanamid Co v Ethicon Ltd* (1975). The court will consider (a) whether there is a serious issue to be tried, (b) whether damages would be an appropriate remedy if the injunction was not granted, and (c) what the likelihood would be of the claimant succeeding at trial. There is no guarantee that the court will order an interlocutory injunction and so stop the ex-employee from working.

Search orders

An alternative but less used remedy is the search order deriving from the case of *Anton Piller KG v Manufacturing Processes Ltd* (1976). This order was previously referred to as an 'Anton Piller' order. If granted a search order would allow the employer to go into the ex-employee's premises and search for or seize documents and other evidence which relate to his own business. This might include customer lists or information stored on a computer. The removal would prevent the ex-employee from using the documents or destroying them and so prejudicing the case.

Because of the intrusive nature of this order, very exceptional circumstances have to exist before it is granted. It must be thought that, for example, the ex-employee is about to break an injunction, or that the employer's business is under a very serious and imminent threat of financial harm.

Garden leave

Employers may also put what have been termed 'garden leave' clauses into contracts of employment. This is another form of protection for the employer and may help to prevent the employee from using company information after leaving his employment. When an employee resigns he usually has to work during the notice period laid down in his contract. In garden leave cases the employee has told his employer that he wants to leave, but the employer does not want him to remain on company premises and work out his notice period. This is because during this time the employee may learn of new trade secrets or new customer information which could then be taken to a new employer.

The employer may still want the employee to have some form of notice period, even though the employee is not at work. During this time the employee still has an implied duty not to divulge confidential information. During, say, a three-month break after leaving work, the knowledge that the employee has may become less significant or useful.

The use of a garden leave clause means that the employee is allowed to stay at home (in the garden!) on full pay but is not allowed to work for anyone else during the life of the notice period. This type of clause is often used in the contracts of executives and those with management roles. If the employee breaches this clause by trying to work for a competitor during this time, the employer can then apply for an injunction to stop this.

The following cases highlight the application of garden leave clauses.

Evening Standard Co Ltd v Henderson (1987)

Mr Henderson was a production manager for the Evening Standard. His notice period was 12 months. He wanted to leave to work for a rival newspaper only giving 2 months' notice. The Evening Standard wanted to put him on garden leave as per his contract, effectively paying him not to work for 12 months. He refused. The court granted an injunction stopping him from working for the rival company and putting him on garden leave.

Eurobrokers Ltd v Rabey (1995)

Rabey worked as a money broker. He resigned and Eurobrokers tried to bind him to an express six-month garden leave clause. He did not observe this and began to work for a rival. An injunction was granted to enforce the period of garden leave. The court noted that the employer had spent a lot of time, money and effort in developing contacts for Rabey. The garden leave period would give him the chance to forge new relationships with these clients and so keep their custom.

In *Credit Suisse Asset Management Ltd v Armstrong* (1996) a restraint of trade clause was added to a garden leave clause to give added protection to the employer. See also *Provident Financial Group plc v Hayward* (1989), *GFI Group Inc v Eaglestone* (1994), *William Hill Organisation ltd v Tucker* (1998) and *TFS Derivatives Ltd v Morgan* (2005).

QUALIFYING FOR EMPLOYMENT RIGHTS - CONTINUITY OF EMPLOYMENT

It is essential to have some record of the date on which the employee starts to work for the employer. In order to gain some employment protection rights, an employee needs to have been employed for a particular period of time. This time starts to run from the date on which he starts work (as specified in the contract of employment or written statement) and ends with the date in which employment ends. This later date differs depending on the particular circumstances of the case and is referred to as the 'effective date of termination' (EDT). In an unfair dismissal case it is the date on which the employee is dismissed.

There are some employment rights that are gained on the first day of employment and others that are only gained when the employee has worked continuously for a set period of time.

Automatic rights

Employees qualify for the following rights on the first day of their employment:

- sex discrimination
- race discrimination
- disability discrimination
- sexual orientation/religion or belief discrimination
- age discrimination (from 1 October 2006)
- discrimination on trade-union issues
- the right to equal pay
- the right to 26 weeks' ordinary maternity leave
- the right to an itemised pay statement
- the right to make a claim for breach of contract
- the right to be paid the national minimum wage.

Rights requiring periods of continuous service

Employees acquire the following rights after a set period of continuous employment:

- one year for an unfair dismissal claim
- one year to be given written reasons for their dismissal
- two years for a claim for a redundancy payment
- six months for unpaid additional maternity leave
- one year for parental leave
- one month for guarantee pay
- one month for written statement of terms and conditions.

Continuity

To have continuity of employment means to have worked continuously for an employer for a period of time. Any breaks in employment may break the continuity. In cases where there is a break in continuity the employee must begin to build up time again when he returns to work.

Sections 210–219 of the Employment Rights Act 1996 and the Employment Protection (Continuity of Employment) Regulations 1996 deal with continuity issues. These rules are complex. In general:

- weeks with a previous employer may count towards continuity;
- continuity is broken if the employee stops work for the employer;
- if a break is due to sickness, injury, pregnancy, lack of work or agreement with the employer (holiday, bereavement leave etc.) then continuity will not be broken;
- weeks when the employee may be on strike do not count towards continuity, but nor do they break continuity.

CHANGING TERMS OF EMPLOYMENT

Employment contracts are subject to ordinary contractual rules. If the parties wish to change a term or terms in the contract, they must both agree to any change. There cannot be a unilateral or one-sided change of a term. If the employer tries to change a main term of the contract, he will be in breach of contract and the employee has the option of resigning and making a claim for constructive dismissal or claiming damages for the breach.

Minor unilateral changes may be allowed as long as they do not have a negative effect on the way in which the employee does his job or change the way in which he has to do it. The most obvious minor change that would not be disputed is an annual wage rise. If the employee is unhappy with any changes that the employer has imposed he should instigate a complaint through the employer's grievance procedure as soon as possible.

This is because in some situations the court may say that if the employee is aware of the change and continues to work under it, he may have impliedly agreed to the change.

WORKING ON A SUNDAY

Today being able to shop on a Sunday is seen as the norm and all of the major supermarkets and do-it-yourself stores operate Sunday opening hours. Sunday opening is regulated under the Sunday Trading Act 1994. The Employment Rights Act 1996 also protects employees who may not wish to work on a Sunday.

The contract of employment

3

Part IV of the Employment Rights Act 1996 (sections 36–43) provides this protection and applies to:

- shop workers
- betting workers.

Shop workers

Section 232 of the Employment Rights Act 1996 defines shop workers as those 'required to do shop work on a day on which the shop is open for the serving of customers'. This definition includes those who actually serve customers, but has also been held to include workers who perform other roles essential to the daily running of the shop. This would cover jobs such as security guards, clerical officers, cleaners, warehouse staff or shop management.

Betting workers

Section 233 of the Employment Rights Act 1996 defines betting workers as those dealing with betting transactions while working for a bookmaker at a race track or those who work in a betting shop.

Right not to work on a Sunday

Part IV of the Employment Rights Act 1996 gives some shop and betting employees the right to refuse to work on a Sunday. This right does not apply to all workers. Employees who are employed only to work on a Sunday are not covered by those provisions of the 1996 Act.

The Act defines two categories of protected employee: those who are 'protected' shop workers and those who have 'opted out' of Sunday working. Such workers also have a general right not to be dismissed or made redundant for refusing to work on a Sunday.

Protected shop workers

These are employees who were employed in shop work on 26 August 1994. This is the date when the Sunday Trading Act 1994 became law. It also covers those who began shop work after this date but whose contracts do not require them to work on a Sunday. These workers have the right to decide whether or not they want to work on a Sunday. They cannot be forced to do so, but can agree to this by informing their employer that they wish to opt in to Sunday working.

Opting out

This relates to employees who were or are employed after the Sunday Trading Act 1994 came into force. If their contracts of employment require them to work on a Sunday, they have the right to opt out of Sunday working.

If an employee is asked or may be asked to work on a Sunday, s 42(1) of the Employment Rights Act 1996 provides that the employer must give the employee a written statement saying this. Section 42 contains precedents detailing the type of statement that the employee should receive.

As with the ordinary written statement, this should be given to the employee within two months of starting work. The statement should inform the employee that he is required, or may be required, to work on a Sunday. It should also give the employee the chance of refusing to do so by opting out. The employee should put any objection to Sunday working in writing and give it to his employer.

After this objection has been given to the employer, the employee has effectively opted out, but a period of three months must pass before the opt-out is confirmed. During these three months the employee can be required to work on a Sunday. After the three months have passed, he cannot.

If an employer fails to give the employee a written statement, after informing the employer of his wish to opt out, he need only wait for one month before the opt-out is confirmed.

Opting in

Employees may also give an employer an opting in notice stating that they would have no objection to working on a Sunday. There is nothing to prevent them from changing their minds at a later date.

FLEXIBLE WORKING ARRANGEMENTS

Here, we consider the situation where an employee asks their employer if they can change their terms and conditions of employment in order to help with their childcare arrangements. As from 6 April 2003 the right to request flexible working arrangements is available to all employees who have been in service with their employer for at least six months. These rules previously only applied to employees who are responsible for the care of a child (see below). Under the Work and Families Act 2006, the right to request flexible working extended to employees with responsibility for caring for adults. This new provision came into force on 6 April 2007.

The rules are set out in s 47 of the Employment Act 2002. The 2002 Act inserted new sections into the Employment Rights Act 1999. The relevant sections of the 1999 Act are 80F–I, 47D and 104C. Detail on the rules can also be found in the Flexible Working (Procedural Requirements) Regulations 2002 (2002/3207) and the Flexible Working (Eligibility, Complaints and Remedies) Regulations 2002 (2002/3236).

The right only applies to employees who care for children under the age of 6 or disabled children under the age of 18. The employee must be the mother, father, adopter, guardian or foster parent of the child and expect to have responsibility for their upbringing. Alternatively, they may be married to or the partner of the child's mother, father, adopter, guardian or foster parent and again expect to have responsibility for their upbringing. Under the 2002 Act employers have a statutory duty to take requests for flexible working seriously and will only be able to refuse requests where they have a clear business reason for doing so.

Employees have the right to request changes to be made to the hours that they work, the times at which they work, or the location at which they are required to work. This would cover requests for home working and job-sharing, for example.

How does the employee apply?

The employee must set out a formal request outlining the desired changes for their employer to consider. The application must be made in writing (either on paper or by email), be dated and specify that it is an application for flexible working under the flexible working provisions in the Employment Rights Act 1999. The employee has to show that they have one of the acceptable relationships with the child, i.e., they are his mother, but they do not have to explain why they are applying for flexible working. The application should also outline the likely impact of any changes on the employer and if possible explain how such changes could be dealt with. An employee may only make one request for flexible working per year.

When considering their request the employer will arrange a meeting with the employee. This should take place within 28 days of the original request being made. This meeting gives both parties the opportunity to discuss the request and any problems or issues that may surround the application. The employee has a right to be accompanied at the hearing. If an employer agrees to the request the employee's terms and conditions of employment are permanently changed. They do not have any right to have their working pattern changed back to its original form without prior agreement from their employer.

●Can an employer refuse the request?

An employer can refuse a request for flexible working on various 'business grounds'. These are set out in s 80G(1)(b) of the 1999 Act and are the:

● burden of additional costs;
● detrimental effect on ability to meet customer demand;
● inability to reorganise work among existing staff;
● detrimental impact on quality;
● detrimental impact on performance;
● insufficiency of work during the periods the employee proposes to work; or due to
● planned structural changes; or
● any other ground that the Secretary of State may specify by regulations at any time.

If an employer does refuse the request then they must set out their reasons for refusal in writing and send this to the employee. An employee may make a claim to the Employment Tribunal where their request is rejected. However, this can only be on the grounds that the employer did not take their request seriously and in doing so did not follow the set procedure. They may also be able to show that their request was denied for some other ground not detailed in the above list. There is a limited right of appeal against a refusal to grant flexible working. Where possible appeals should be heard by a different manager from the one who refused the initial request.

An applicant cannot complain to the Employment Tribunal just because their request is refused. The tribunal will only consider a claim where it can be shown that an employer has not taken an application seriously (no hearing and so on), or declined the request for a reason not contained in the list of 'business grounds'.

If the tribunal finds that the employer unreasonably refused the employee's request for flexible working then they may order the employer to reconsider their decision. The tribunal may also order the employer to pay compensation to the employee. The maximum amount of compensation that may be awarded is 8 weeks' pay. At the time of writing the figure for a 'week's pay' calculation is £310 (as from 1 February 2007).

The DTI have said that 3.8 million employees in the UK will benefit from being able to work flexibly.

SUMMARY CHECKLIST

- There is no right to be given a contract of employment. If one is given, it does not have to be in writing. It can be made orally or be partly oral/written.
- The contract of employment is an important document which details the rights and responsibilities of the employer and employee.
- A distinction is made between employees and independent contractors – employees generally have better employment protection.
- Courts/tribunals use the control, integration and multiple tests to help them decide on the status of the worker.
- Amongst other things, ownership of tools, being able to choose when to work, assuming financial risk over business, working only for short set periods, hiring helpers, the power to substitute workers and working for several people at once may point to the worker being self-employed.
- Things such as regular wage payments, deductions for tax/National Insurance, receipt of holiday/sick pay, membership of an occupational pension scheme, not being able to work for anyone else and being subject to disciplinary procedure may point towards the worker being an employee.
- There is no one single test.
- The 'label' that the parties put on their relationship is only of marginal significance.
- Special rules apply to e.g. agency workers, Crown employees, the police, directors and partners.
- The contract of employment is made up of terms which are either express, implied or statutory.
- Implied terms place duties on the employer and employee, e.g. the employer should treat the employee with mutual trust and respect, the employee should act in good faith.
- Employees have a duty not to divulge confidential information during their employment.
- Employees have the right to receive a written statement outlining the terms and conditions of their employment within two months of starting work.
- If the employer does not provide a written statement, the employee can make a complaint to the Employment Tribunal.
- Employers may try to protect their business interests after the employee leaves by placing a restraint of trade clause into the employee's contract.
- Restraint clauses may be enforceable if they are reasonable between the parties and in the public interest.
- The date on which the employee starts work is important for continuity and qualification for employment rights.
- There can be no unilateral change in the terms of the contract.
- Employees required to work on a Sunday are protected by the Employment Rights Act 1996.
- The right to request flexible working arrangements came into force in April 2003.

3

The contract of employment

SELF-TEST QUESTIONS

1 Why is it important to make the distinction between an employee and an independent contractor?

2 What tests have the courts/tribunals used to help them to make this distinction?

3 What decisions have been made in the cases on 'atypical workers'?

4 What is the difference between an express and an implied term? Give examples of each.

5 How would you define the employer's duty to treat his employees with 'mutual trust and confidence'?

6 What was held in *Faccenda Chicken* v *Fowler*?

7 What is the status of the written statement given under s 1 of the Employment Rights Act 1996?

8 What types of information would you expect the written statement to contain? Does all of the information have to be in one document?

9 When might a restraint of trade clause be enforceable?

10 Can the employer change the terms of the employee's contract without informing the employee of the change?

11 Summarise the law on 'flexible working'.

CASE SCENARIOS

A

Richard and David work for 'Easyspark plc'. They are both electricians who complete contract work for the company. Richard is a senior electrician and has worked for the company for five years. David is currently studying part-time at university and so only works when he is needed. Richard is paid an annual salary of £20 000. David is paid £6.00 per hour, but only for the hours that he actually works. He never works during exam time as he is too busy revising! Easyspark provides all of the tools needed to complete the work. Both Richard and David pay tax and national insurance contributions. On a few occasions David has asked his brother Ben to go to work in his place. Ben gets on well with Richard. They both have to wear company uniforms while at work. Richard also has the use of a company van.

Last Friday Richard and David were working at a local hospital. They were involved in an accident when a scaffold collapsed. Richard broke his arm and David his leg. They will both be off work for some time. Easyspark decided that Richard and David were responsible for the accident. It decides to dismiss them both.

They both begin claims for unfair dismissal. Easyspark prepares to defend Richard's claim but says that David has no claim as he was not an employee.

Advise David of the ways in which a court or tribunal may determine his status as an employee or otherwise.

B

Judith works for 'Happy College'. She is a marketing manager who has been involved in a secret project concerned with the marketing of new courses. Judith knows that the college needs to recruit lots of new students in order to avoid staff redundancies. She knows that a rival college (situated only three miles from Happy College) is interested to find out what information her research has produced. Judith's employment contract contains a clause which states that:

> Upon leaving this employment, the employee is not to work for an educational institution within an area of 30 miles and for a period of five years.

Just before her findings are published, Judith is offered a new job at the rival college. She decides to accept the position and passes on the information on the courses to the rival even before she has resigned from Happy College. The rival college goes on to market the new courses in its own name.

Christopher, Judith's original boss is very angry at the loss of this confidential information and the fact that she is leaving to work for a rival.

Advise Christopher of any possible action that he may take. Judith is presently having to work three months' notice at Happy College. Is there any way that Christopher can arrange for her to be off-site during this time? In relation to the restraint clause in Judith's contract of employment, will the college be able to enforce this clause when she begins her new job?

● Further reading

'Contracts of Employment', *IDS Employment Law Handbook*, 4th edn, August 2001.

'What's in a Name: Defining Employee Status', Adrian Williams, Legal Executive, June 2002, pp. 23–25.

'Post-Termination Covenants in the Spotlight Again', David Cabrelli, *Industrial Law Journal*, No. 33, 2004, pp. 167–79.

'Employee Status – Ongoing Saga', Nigel Baker, 29 CSR 23, 177, March 2006.

'Legal Status of Employees', Nigel Baker, 27 CSR 25, 198, April 2004.

'New Rights for Temporary Workers', Sarah Spooner, *New Law Journal*, 154 NLJ 1811, 3 December 2004.

'A Critical Appraisal of the Criteria Determining Employee Status', Adrian Williams, *Business Law Review* (2003) 24 BLR 239.

'Fitting a Square Peg into a Round Hole – Appraising the Employment Status of Agency Workers', Adrian Williams, *Business Law Review* (2004) 25 BLR 1236.

Producing a Written Statement, ACAS leaflet, January 2005.

Written Statement of Employment Particulars, DTI leaflet (06/543).

Example Form of a Written Statement of Employment Particulars, DTI leaflet (06/534).

Flexible Working – the Right to Request, DTI leaflet (06/545).

For legal updates on the material in this chapter please go to the Companion Website accompanying this book at **www.mylawchamber.co.uk/nairns**

The contract of employment

4

Equal pay, maternity and other individual employment rights

In addition to the rights not to be unfairly dismissed or suffer discrimination, employees are also entitled to various free-standing employment rights. The most significant of these is the right to equal pay between the sexes. The right to equal pay is another anti-discrimination measure akin to the right not to suffer discrimination on the grounds of sex.

The law also provides a variety of rights and benefits relating to maternity provision. All pregnant employees are entitled to the protection of a basic set of maternity rights. They are entitled to take time off work both during their pregnancy and after their baby is born. Special rules also relate to the payment of wages and benefits during pregnancy. Taken together, the package of maternity provision aims to ensure that no woman is disadvantaged or suffers hardship during her pregnancy. Men also have the right to take paternity leave. There is also a general right to take parental leave.

Employees are also entitled to be remunerated at a rate consistent with the national minimum wage. Employees are also entitled to various other individual employment rights. These rights include, for example, the right to an itemised pay statement and the right to take time off work to undertake public duties.

This chapter outlines the law on equal pay, maternity and rights, the national minimum wage and other individual employment rights. It begins by discussing the need for equal pay legislation and goes on to discuss:

- the Equal Pay Act 1970, the 'equality clause';
- the male 'comparator';
- equal pay for 'like work';
- equal pay for 'work rated as equivalent' under a job evaluation scheme;
- equal pay for 'work of equal value', the use of independent experts;
- the employer's defence, 'genuine material difference';
- European law, art 141 and the Equal Pay Directive;
- the Equal Opportunities Commission Code of Practice on Equal Pay;
- making an equal pay claim to the Employment Tribunal, remedies;
- maternity rights, the Employment Rights Act 1996, the Pregnant Workers Directive, and the Social Security Contributions and Benefits Act 1992;
- time off for ante-natal care;
- dismissal or selection for redundancy on grounds of pregnancy or childbirth;
- statutory maternity pay, maternity allowance and the sure start maternity grant;

- the right to ordinary maternity leave and additional maternity leave, compulsory leave;
- the right to return to work;
- notification rules;
- paternity and parental leave, adoption pay and leave;
- health and safety issues relating to pregnancy;
- other individual employment rights, the right to an itemised pay statement;
- the right not to have unlawful deductions made from wages;
- notice periods;
- guarantee payments;
- sick pay;
- time off work to undertake trade-union duties, public duties, or if to be made redundant to look for work or organise training;
- the national minimum wage;
- data protection.

EQUAL PAY

The equal pay legislation aims to ensure that men and women who are doing the same or similar work are paid the same wages. Historically men may have been paid a higher salary based purely on their gender and the fact that they were seen as the family 'breadwinner'. In many cases women are more likely to be found working in the poorly paid section of an organisation. In such cases pay inequality may be hard to prove because there will be few men working in the same or a similar role. In other cases, however, employees may find themselves in the same job but earning a lot less than a colleague of the opposite sex.

Whilst there is still scope for improvement in the provision of equal pay between the sexes, national and European law does provide a forum under which employees can complain of pay inequality.

The national law on equal pay is contained in the Equal Pay Act 1970 and the Equal Pay (Amendment) Regulations 1983. More recently, the Equal Pay Act 1970 has been amended by the Equal Pay Act 1970 (Amendment) Regulations 2003 and the Equal Pay Act 1970 (Amendment) Regulations 2004. The European law on equal pay is found in art 141 (formerly 119) of the Treaty of Rome and the Equal Pay Directive.

An employee or other worker who wishes to make a claim for equal pay may do so in the Employment Tribunal. Claims can be made directly under Art 141 or the Equal Pay Directive. Claims made under the Equal Pay Act 1970 must be interpreted in light of this European law. Tribunals are able to refer difficult cases to the European Court of Justice.

The Equal Opportunities Commission also plays a role in the promotion of equal pay between the sexes. (The role of the EOC was discussed at page 29.)

The Equal Opportunities Commission has also produced a Code of Practice on Equal Pay (further discussed at page 161). This code states that 'tackling the gender pay gap reduces the risk of litigation' and that 'it can also increase efficiency by attracting the best employees, reducing staff turnover, increasing commitment, and reducing absenteeism.' The code goes on to state that by 'helping employers to check the pay gap in their organisation and by encouraging good equal pay practice, the code reinforces the government's commitment to closing the gap between men's and women's pay.'

Overview of an equal pay claim

Figure 4.1 highlights the possible stages involved in the formation of an equal pay claim.

EQUAL PAY ACT 1970

The Equal Pay Act 1970 states that there is a right to equal pay between the sexes. In *Glasgow City Council v Marshall* (2000) the House of Lords reiterated the point that the 1970 Act is not concerned with whether pay is 'fair' but with whether pay is unequal because of discrimination between the sexes. Whilst problems concerning equal pay are usually thought of as involving female employees, the 1970 Act applies equally to men.

The Act applies to all employees, independent contractors and trainees. It deals mainly with equality in pay but is also concerned with the provision of equal benefits such as bonuses, holi-

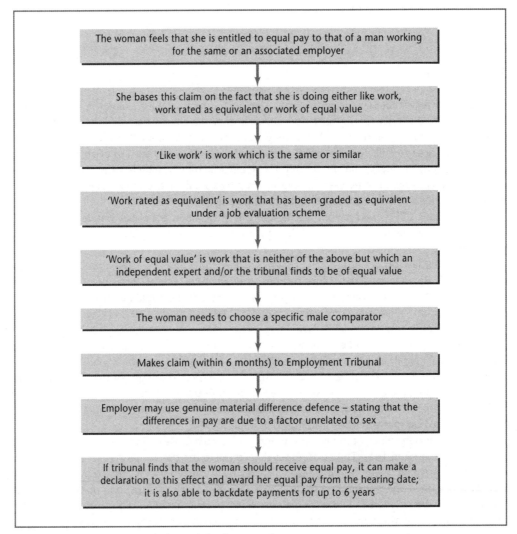

Figure 4.1 Possible stages in a claim for equal pay

days and hours of work. An employer cannot legally contract out of the provisions of the equal-pay legislation. This means that employers cannot ask employees to waive the right to make a claim for equal pay.

The 'equality clause'

Section 1(1) of the Equal Pay Act 1970 states that:

If the terms of a contract under which a woman is employed at an establishment in Great Britain do not include (directly by reference to a collective agreement or otherwise) an equality clause they shall be deemed to include one.

This is what is referred to as the 'equality clause', which is implied into all contracts of employment. This equality clause gives a woman the right to receive equal pay.

Section 1(2) of the 1970 Act goes on to outline the situations in which an equality clause will become effective. It notes three situations in which a woman will be entitled to equal pay. These are where:

- she is employed on **like work** with a man in the same employment;
- she is employed on **work rated as equivalent** with that of a man in the same employment; or
- she is employed on **work of equal value** to that of a man in the same employment.

If a woman can show that her work is comparable with that of a man under one of these heads, she will be entitled to receive pay equal to his.

The male 'comparator'

A woman must be able to compare her work with that of a male comparator.

> **Example**
> *Deborah works as an administrator. She is paid £16 700 per annum. She works with another three female administrators who earn the same salary. The fifth member of their team, Edward, will not reveal his salary details. Deborah believes that he earns up to £4000 per annum more than her and the other three women. In her claim for equal pay Deborah would use Edward as her 'male comparator'.*

Every equal pay claim must be brought on the basis of an actual male comparator. The woman can choose which man to use as her comparator but cannot use a hypothetical male. The male comparator will normally be working for the same employer as the woman at the time of her claim. However, in *Macarthys v Smith* (1979) it was held that a woman can base the claim on the earnings of her predecessor. In *Diocese of Hallam Trustee v Connaughton* (1996) it was held that the woman could also choose a man who takes over her job after she leaves employment.

A woman must choose a male comparator who is employed either by the same employer or an associated employer. Section 1(6) of the 1970 Act states that the comparator must be employed 'in the same employment' as the claimant, for example:

(a) claimant/comparator employed in the same establishment;

(b) claimant/comparator employed by 'associated employers'; or

(c) claimant/comparator employed at establishments in Great Britain at which common terms and conditions are observed.

An associated employer is one where 'one is a company of which the other (directly or indirectly) has control or if both are companies of which a third person (directly or indirectly) has control'. Recent cases have stated that even if an employer is not an 'associated employer' within the above definition a claim may still be made if there is a sufficient connection between the two forms of 'employment'. In *British Coal Corporation v Smith* (1996) it was said that a comparator from another employer could be used if the terms of employment were 'substantially comparable'.

In *Lawrence v Regent Office Care Ltd* (2000) it was said that the question to ask was whether the differences in pay could be attributable to a single source. Where there is no common employer the question is whether there is some common factor that causes the difference in pay and whether there is someone who can remedy that differential. In this case it was said that the applicant and the comparator must be 'in a loose and non-technical sense in the same establishment or service'.

In *South Ayrshire Council v Morton* (2002) the Court of Session held that a teacher employed by one local authority could use a comparator from a different authority because the salary rates for both employees were set by the same national collective agreement.

In *Armstrong v Newcastle-upon-Tyne NHS Hospital Trust* (2006) female workers who worked for one National Health Trust hospital could not use male workers in another NHT hospital as comparators. This was because there was no 'single source' responsible for setting rates of pay. These decisions highlight the fact that each claim will turn on its own facts.

See also: *Allonby v Accrington & Rossendale College* (2004), *Robertson v DEFRA* (2005).

Equal pay for 'like work'

Section 1(2)(a) of the 1970 Act states that where a woman is employed on like work with a man in the same or associated employment she is entitled to equal pay.

Here the woman alleges that she is employed on like work to the male comparator who earns more than she does. The tribunal will look at what their jobs entail and question whether they have the same job title, carry out the same tasks or have the same level of responsibility.

To be employed on like work means that the work must be regarded as being either the same or broadly similar. Any differences between the work must not be of practical importance.

The following cases highlight situations in which a female employee alleged that she was employed on like work to a male comparator.

Shields v E Coomes Holdings Ltd (1978)

Ms Shields worked as a counter assistant at a bookmakers owned by Coomes Holdings Ltd. She was paid 92p per hour. A man was employed in the same shop, doing the same job for £1.06 per hour. They were required to do identical tasks, the one exception being that the man was expected to deal with any troublemakers or rowdy customers. During the three years that Shields had worked there this man had never been called on to deal with any such customers. Nor had he been given any training on how to deal with security issues. Shields brought an equal-pay claim based on the fact that she did like work to her male comparator.

Held (CA) The differences between Ms Shields' and the male comparator's work were not of practical importance. The tasks that they performed were identical; they were employed on like work and Shields was entitled to equal pay.

Capper Pass Ltd v *Lawton* (1976)

Ms Lawton worked as a cook and was responsible for the preparation of meals for company directors and their guests. She prepared lunch for 10–20 people every day. She brought a claim for equal pay based on the fact that two chefs who prepared meals for the main dining room earned more than she did. She claimed that she was working on like work to these men. The men were responsible for the preparation of 350 meals per day, served in three sittings. There were also differences in the types of kitchen duties that they were expected to complete.

Held (EAT) Although there were differences in the work that Ms Lawton and the men did, in the circumstances these were not of practical importance. She was found to be working on like work to the chefs and succeeded in her claim for equal pay.

Noble v *David Gold & Son (Holdings) Ltd* (1980)

Ms Noble brought an equal pay claim using male warehouse workers as her male comparator. The men were employed to load and unload supplies. Noble and her female colleagues were employed on lighter work including sorting, packing and labelling.

Held Noble did not work on like work with the men working in the warehouse. The work was not broadly similar and the differences between their duties were of practical importance. Consequently, she failed in her claim for equal pay.

See also: *Thomas* v *National Coal Board* (1987), *Eaton* v *Nuttall* (1977), *Electrolux* v *Hutchinson* (1976), *Dugdale* v *Kraft Foods* (1977).

Equal pay for 'work rated as equivalent'

Section 1(2)(b) of the 1970 Act states that where a woman is employed on work rated as equivalent to that of a man in the same or associated employment she is entitled to equal pay.

Section 1(5) of the 1970 Act states that 'A woman is to be regarded as employed on work rated as equivalent with that of any man if, but only if, her job and their job have been given an equal value, in terms of the demand made on a worker under various headings (effort, skill, decision making etc.), on a study undertaken with a view to evaluating in those terms the jobs to be done by all or any of the employees in an undertaking or group of undertakings.'

Here, the woman alleges that she is employed on work that has been rated as equivalent to that of her male comparator. This deals with the situation where jobs have been graded and compared under a job evaluation scheme. In such claims the tribunal will question whether the woman's employer has carried out a job evaluation scheme and if so whether the two jobs were rated as equivalent.

Job evaluation schemes

A job evaluation scheme is a scheme or study whereby an evaluation is made of all of the jobs in the workplace. The jobs are graded according to, for example, the levels of effort, skill or decision-making involved.

In *Eaton* v *Nuttall* (1977) it was stated that a job evaluation scheme should be 'thorough in analysis and capable of impartial application'. It should be possible 'to arrive at the position of a particular employee at a particular point in a particular salary grade without taking other matters into account except those unconnected with the nature of the work'.

There are two types of job evaluation scheme, a non-analytical scheme and an analytical scheme. A non-analytical scheme will evaluate jobs by looking at the tasks involved as a whole and ranking them in a level of seniority. An analytical scheme will look at various factors such as the levels of effort, skill and decision-making expected of a person doing the job.

It is generally thought that a job evaluation scheme should take an analytical approach. In *Bromley and others v H & J Quick Ltd* (1988) the Court of Appeal emphasised that a job evaluation scheme must be both non discriminatory and also analytical. Analytical means that the jobs of each worker 'must have been valued in terms of the demand made on the worker under the various headings'.

Not all employers will have implemented a job evaluation scheme. They can, however, begin to implement such a scheme after an employee begins a tribunal equal pay claim. If an employer decides to do this the evaluation must be completed before the date of the tribunal hearing. In *Arnold v Beecham Group Limited* (1982) it was held that a completed job evaluation scheme is one which has been formally accepted by both management and employees even if it has not yet been implemented.

●Equal pay for 'work of equal value'

Section 1(2)(c) of the 1970 Act states that where a woman is employed on work of equal value to that of a man in the same employment she is entitled to equal pay. Equal value claims are made where the woman is unable to bring a claim under either of the first two headings. In looking at what will constitute 'equal value' the tribunal will consider the demands made upon the employee with regard to effort, skill and decision-making.

This section was added to the 1970 Act by the Equal Pay (Amendment) Regulations 1983. This amendment was made following the European Court of Justice decision in *Commission of the European Communities v United Kingdom* (1982). In this case the European Court had said that the 1970 Act did not fully comply with the art 141 principle of equal pay for work of equal value. (See page 161.)

Equal value claims can be extremely complex and can often take many years to resolve. In October 2004 changes were made to tribunal procedures in equal value claims. The aim of these changes was to speed up and streamline such claims. The Employment Tribunals (Constitution and Rules of Procedure) Regulations 2004, Employment Tribunals (Constitution and Procedure) (Amendment) Regulations 2004 and the Equal Pay Act 1970 (Amendment) Regulations 2004 introduced these changes. The Regulations came into force on 1 October 2004.

Equal value claims must now normally be struck out if the work of the woman and that of the male comparator have been given different values on an appropriate study (see above). The Employment Tribunal President is now able to appoint tribunal panels with specialist knowledge of equal value cases.

The new procedural rules are contained in Schedule 6 of the Employment Tribunals (Constitution and Rules of Procedure) Regulations 2004 and are referred to as the 'Employment Tribunals (Equal Value) Rules of Procedure'.

These rules state that:

- no new facts shall be admitted in evidence unless they have been disclosed to all other parties in writing;
- the parties may be required to send copies of documents or other information to the other parties and to the independent experts; and
- the employer may be required to grant the independent experts access to his premises to conduct interviews with relevant persons.

The maximum timescale for an equal value claim is set at 25 weeks where no independent expert has been appointed and at 37 weeks where experts are appointed.

The tribunal hearing will take place in stages. During the Stage 1 hearing the tribunal will decide on whether the claim for equal value should proceed and on whether to deal with the claim itself or appoint independent experts. As noted above, the tribunal will strike out a claim if a job evaluation scheme has taken place which has found that different values have been given to the applicant and her comparator. During the Stage 2 hearing the tribunal will resolve any disputed facts to enable the independent experts to prepare their report. A full hearing will then take place. The outcome of the case will be determined at this hearing.

The Employment Tribunal now has the ability to manage equal value cases more effectively. The role of the independent expert has also been extended.

Use of independent experts

As noted above, the tribunal will have to decide on whether the woman's work is of equal value to that of her male comparator. The tribunal may make this decision based solely on the evidence before them or they may ask an independent expert to prepare a report.

Until 1996 the tribunal had to brief an independent expert in all equal-value claims. Now, under the Sex Discrimination and Equal Pay (Miscellaneous Amendments) Regulations 1996 the tribunal can, but is not obliged to, brief an independent expert.

Independent experts are appointed from an Acas panel. The expert would normally visit the employees' place of work and observe them carrying out their daily duties. They have no direct right to access the employer's premises. Access must be arranged by negotiation with the employer. Note, however, that the tribunal may order the employer to grant the independent expert access to his premises.

The expert is able to interview the employees, managers and other employees who may be able to provide relevant information. The expert should complete his report as soon as is reasonably possible. The tribunal can ask the expert for interim progress reports and can remove him from office if the expert does not co-operate with set deadlines.

The expert's report should conclude by stating whether or not he believes that the woman's work can be said to be of equal value to that of the comparator. The expert's conclusions are merely recommendations. The tribunal can choose to ignore the expert's findings and take further evidence from the employees and managers themselves. The burden of proof is on the woman to show that the comparable jobs are of equal value.

Choice of comparator

An equal-value claim will not be heard if there has been a job evaluation study which has ranked the jobs unequally. However, there may be situations in which an equal value claim can be made even if there are men doing like work or work rated as equivalent. This is where a woman is able to choose a man who is not employed on these terms as her comparator.

This was the case in **Pickstone** (below).

Pickstone v Freemans plc (1988)

Ms Pickstone worked in the warehouse at Freemans. She claimed that her work was of equal value with that of a man employed as a 'checker warehouse operative'. This man received a higher salary than Pickstone. The extra payment amounted to £4.22 per week. The problem here was that there was one man doing exactly the same work as Pickstone. Could she still bring a claim?

Held (HL) She could bring an equal-value claim. Only her comparator should not be doing like work or work rated as equivalent. It did not matter that other employees were working on that basis.

● The employer's defence, genuine material difference

Section 1(3) of the Equal Pay Act 1970 states that an employer may be able to defend an equal-pay claim by showing that any differences in pay are due to there being a genuine material difference between the workers. This genuine material difference must relate to something other than sex. In claims concerning 'like work' and 'work rated as equivalent' the employer must prove that the genuine material difference is the reason for the variation in pay. In equal value claims the employer need only show that this may be a defence.

> ### Example
> *Deborah has succeeded in showing that she is employed on 'like work' to Edward and that he is paid £4000 per annum more than her. On the face of it she will succeed in her claim for equal pay. However, if their employer can show that there is a reason why Edward is paid at the higher rate which does not relate to him being a man and her a woman, the employer will successfully defend the claim.*

In *Bilka-Kaufhaus GmbH* v *Weber von Hartz* (1986) the European Court held that the material difference must relate to a legitimate economic need. In *Rainey* v *Greater Glasgow Health Board* (1988) the House of Lords said that the defence could also relate to administrative needs but that to justify a variation in pay these should be both 'significant and relevant'. In *Davies* v *McCartneys* (1989) the Employment Appeal Tribunal stated that there is no limit on the number of factors which can constitute a material difference.

In *Strathclyde Regional Council* v *Wallace* (1998) a group of female teachers claimed that they were doing like work with male comparators who were employed as principal teachers. The women were doing the same work as the principal teachers but were not being appointed or paid as such. However, the Council was able to show that the differences in pay were not due to sex discrimination but to their statutory promotion structure and financial constraints. They succeeded in using these reasons as evidence of a genuine material difference.

> ### Example
> *Possible genuine material differences include:*
>
> - *qualifications*
> - *levels of experience/service*
> - *degree of skill required*
> - *level of responsibility*
> - *geographical pay differences*
> - *approved pay scales*
> - *market forces, economic considerations*
> - *administrative efficiency*
> - *red circling (see below).*

Many of these differences are self-explanatory. For example, a female employee who has only been employed for six months may reasonably expect a male colleague with 25 years' service to earn more than she does. This difference is based on the fact that the man has gained considerable experience during this time and not because he is a man. Some possible material differences warrant special consideration.

Geographical pay differences

Differences in pay based on geographical differences have been held to be genuine material differences. For example, it is generally thought acceptable for employers to pay higher salaries to employees working in London. This means that a man and woman could be employed on like work but in different cities. Where the man works in London and the woman in Newcastle, an employer may be able to defend any equal-pay claim by raising geographical difference as the genuine material difference.

In this example the reason for the difference in pay would be the fact that the cost of living is higher in London.

Market forces

In some situations economic market forces may force an employer to pay higher wages to some employees to attract them into a particular occupation. This may amount to a genuine material difference.

Rainey v *Greater Glasgow Health Board* (1988)

Glasgow Health Board decided to set up its own prosthetic service. Qualified prosthetists were paid wages equal to that of medical physics technicians. However, the board felt that in order to attract enough applications from prosthetists it was necessary to offer them higher wages. This was because many prosthetists worked in the private sector where higher salaries were paid. Ms Rainey was already employed by the health service. She made a claim for equal pay based on the fact that a prosthetist from the private sector was earning more than her.

Held The difference in pay was due to a genuine material difference that did not relate to sex. In this case market forces had meant that the Board was justified in awarding higher salaries to outside applicants.

Enderby v *Frenchay Health Authority* (1994)

Ms Enderby was one of several female speech therapists working for the health authority who claimed that their work was of equal value with that of male principal pharmacists and male clinical psychologists. She claimed that the men earned up to 60 per cent more in salary than she did, and argued that the reason that speech therapists were paid less was that the jobs were normally done by women. The health authority argued that there was an overall shortage of applicants to the other professions. This in turn meant that higher salaries had to be offered to those workers, both to attract them into the professions and ensure that they remained with the health authority. The higher pay was due to there being a separate collective bargaining machinery and pay negotiations for the two male groups. They asserted that differences in pay were due to reasons not connected to sex and that consequently a genuine material difference existed.

Held The ECJ accepted that such market forces could constitute a genuine material difference, but said that an employer may not necessarily be able to justify the whole of the difference in pay based on market forces.

Ratcliffe v North Yorkshire County Council (1995)

North Yorkshire County Council had established a direct service organisation following the introduction of compulsory competitive tendering for the provision of school meals. The work of school dinner ladies had been rated as equivalent to that of other Council employees including roadsweepers, refuse collectors and leisure attendants. These other jobs were almost exclusively done by men. On the introduction of competitive tendering the Council found that it could not compete for the school meals contract unless it introduced pay cuts. The result of these pay cuts was to reduce the women's pay to below that of their male comparators. The Council tried to argue that the pay cuts represented a genuine material difference unrelated to sex. It said that the cuts had been made for economic reasons to avoid the loss of the school meals contract.

Held This could not be used as a genuine material difference. The material factor which led to the difference in pay was due to the difference of sex and was, therefore, unlawful.

Where an employer has raised economic market forces as a genuine material difference and these forces cease to be an issue, the pay levels of any previously affected employee should be increased.

In *Benveniste v University of Southampton* (1989) the University had successfully used its lack of financial resources as a genuine material difference. It had appointed a female lecturer on a lower pay scale to her male colleagues. Once these financial problems were resolved, the tribunal held that the lecturer should begin to receive equal pay.

See also: *Naafi v Varley* (1977), *Calder v Rowntree Mackintosh Confectionery Limited* (1993), *Barber v NCR (Manufacturing) Ltd* (1993), *Tyldesley v TML Plastics Ltd* (1996), *Angestelltenbetriebsrat v Weiner* (2000).

Red circling

In some situations a man's salary may be higher than that of a woman in the same or similar job because it has been 'red circled'. This means that his salary has been protected because for health or other reasons he has had to take a lower paid job. This can amount to a genuine material difference as long as the decisions to 'red circle' were not made on a discriminatory basis. The following case provides an example of where a 'red circling' defence failed.

Snoxell v Vauxhall Motors (1977)

Vauxhall Motors had always used separate pay grades for men and women. In 1971 Vauxhall changed this policy and introduced an amended structure equalising the pay scales. One exception was made in relation to one previously male-graded position. This post had mistakenly been graded at too high a point on the salary scale. When the changes were made, the job was moved to its accurate place on the scale, but the men who were already doing the job remained on their original salary. This meant that they were protected on this higher grade and 'red circled'. There were no women in this group of 'red circled' workers, as none had been employed on the original purely male pay scale. Vauxhall stated that this 'red circling' amounted to a genuine material difference with regard to paying men more than women who were doing the same job.

Held (EAT) In deciding whether any 'red circling' situation did amount to a genuine material difference, the reasons why the jobs were 'red circled' had to be investigated. Here the original reason to 'red circle' had been discriminatory because women had not been allowed to work at the same protected grade as the men. As such, Vauxhall's defence failed and Snoxell was successful in her claim for equal pay.

See also: *Charles Early and Marriott (Witney) Ltd v Smith & Ball* (1977).

EUROPEAN LAW, ARTICLE 141 (FORMERLY ARTICLE 119) AND THE EQUAL PAY DIRECTIVE

The Equal Pay Act 1970 was enacted to comply with the European principle of equal pay contained in art 141 of the Treaty of Rome. This article is directly applicable in the United Kingdom and so creates a right to equal pay.

Article 141 states that:

Each Member State shall . . . ensure and subsequently maintain the application of the principle that men and women should receive equal pay for equal work.

It goes on to define 'pay' as 'the ordinary basic or minimum wage or salary and any other consideration, whether in cash or in kind, which the worker receives, directly or indirectly, in respect of his employment from his employer'.

The Equal Pay Directive of 1975 expands upon art 141 stating that the principle of equal pay means that:

for the same work or for work to which equal value is attributed, the elimination of all discrimination on grounds of sex with regard to all aspects and conditions of remuneration.

The Directive also states that where a job evaluation scheme is used for determining pay, it must be based on the same criteria for men and women and be drawn up so as to eliminate any discrimination on the grounds of sex. Britain responded to the Equal Pay Directive by amending the Equal Pay Act 1970 to include the principle of equal value. These changes were made under the Equal Pay (Amendment) Regulations 1983.

Individuals are able to make an equal-pay claim under the Equal Pay Act 1970 or under art 141. Tribunals are able to refer cases to the European Court of Justice. Article 141 is directly enforceable and takes precedence over our national law. The Equal Pay Directive is only enforceable against a state employer or an emanation of the state.

This would mean that only employees working for such bodies could claim under the Directive. However, as the Directive repeats the contents of art 141 and does not raise any new issues, it is said to clarify art 119 and as such can be relied upon by all employees. (See further page 9.)

The European Commission has also issued further guidance on equal pay in the form of a 'Memorandum on Equal Pay for Work of Equal Value' in 1994 and a code of practice 'on the implementation of equal pay for work of equal value for women and men' in 1996.

EOC CODE OF PRACTICE ON EQUAL PAY (2003)

The Equal Opportunities Commission Code of Practice on Equal Pay provides guidance on equal pay issues and the implementation of an equal pay policy. Whilst the code is not legally enforceable, it can be used as evidence in any tribunal proceedings.

The code states that: 'It is good equal pay practice to provide employees with a clear statement of the organisation's intentions in respect of equal pay'. It goes on to state that the policy should:

- set objectives;
- identify the action to be taken;
- implement that action in a planned programme in partnership with the workforce;
- assign responsibility and accountability for the policy to a senior manager; and
- commit the organisation to set aside the resources necessary to achieve equal pay.

The code also states that everyone involved in setting the pay of staff should be committed to and, if possible, trained in the identification of sex discrimination in the pay process.

The code also advises employers to adopt a pay review system in order to monitor pay equality in the workplace. All employees should be able to access information on the operation of any such system or policy. The code states that 'the validity of the review and success of subsequent action taken will be enhanced if the pay system is understood and accepted by the managers who operate the system, by the employees and by their unions' and that 'employers should therefore aim to secure the involvement of employees and, where possible, trade union representatives.' The more transparent and accessible a pay system becomes the more likely issues of inequality are able to be addressed.

The code also provides a suggested equal pay policy in s 3. A copy of this policy is reproduced in Figure 4.2.

MAKING AN EQUAL PAY CLAIM TO THE EMPLOYMENT TRIBUNAL

An employee or other worker who wishes to make an equal-pay claim must submit their application to the Employment Tribunal. This is done by completing form ET1 in the same manner as outlined in Chapter 10 (pages 368–370). The claim is for pay arrears and damages.

Claims involving equal pay differ from those relating to unfair dismissal and discrimination in that the applicant has six months to make a claim. The claim can be made whilst the woman is still in employment or within six months of her leaving that employment.

There is no direct right to extend this time limit. Whereas in unfair dismissal and discrimination cases the tribunal may extend the three-month time limit where it is 'just and equitable' to do so, no such direct discretion exists in equal pay cases. However, the Equal Pay (Amendement) Regulations 2003 inserted a new section into the Equal Pay Act 1970 which provides for the calculation of a 'qualifying date'. Under this provision the six-month application period may be extended if it is found that an employer deliberately concealed any fact relevant to the claim, or if the employee is disabled.

The Employment Act 2002 introduced the use of equal pay questionnaires. These are designed to assist a woman in gaining the information needed with which to decide whether or not to make a claim for equal pay. The employer will be asked to provide information on, for example, pay scales. Equal pay questionnaires take the same form as those used in sex, race and disability discrimination claims. (These types of questionnaire are discussed at page 96.)

The rules on the use of the equal pay questionnaire can be found in s 7B of the 1970 Act. This provision came into force on 6 April 2003. An employer has eight weeks within which to reply to the questionnaire. Replies will be admissible as evidence in the tribunal. There is no statutory obligation on an employer to return a questionnaire. However, if an employer does fail to respond or returns the questionnaire showing vague or incomplete answers the tribunal is able to take this into account.

A model equal pay policy

We are committed to the principle of equal pay for all our employees. We aim to eliminate any sex bias in our pay systems.

We understand that equal pay between men and women is a legal right under both domestic and European law.

It is in the interest of the organisation to ensure that we have a fair and just pay system. It is important that employees have confidence in the process of eliminating sex bias and we are therefore committed to working in partnership with the recognised trade unions. As good business practice we are committed to working with trade union/employee representatives to take action to ensure that we provide equal pay.

We believe that in eliminating sex bias in our pay system we are sending a positive message to our staff and customers. It makes good business sense to have a fair, transparent reward system and it helps us to control costs. We recognise that avoiding unfair discrimination will improve morale and enhance efficiency.

Our objectives are to:

● Eliminate any unfair, unjust or unlawful practices that impact on pay
● Take appropriate remedial action.

We will:

● Implement an equal pay review in line with EOC guidance for all current staff and starting pay for new staff (including those on maternity leave, career breaks, or non-standard contracts)
● Plan and implement actions in partnership with trade union/employee representatives
● Provide training and guidance for those involved in determining pay
● Inform employees of how these practices work and how their own pay is determined
● Respond to grievances on equal pay as a priority
● In conjunction with trade union/employee representatives, monitor pay statistics annually.

Figure 4.2 EOC Code of Practice on Equal Pay: Section 3: An equal pay policy
Source: Equal Opportunities Commission

At the tribunal hearing the employee has the burden of proving that her male comparator is doing the same or broadly similar work, work rated as equivalent or work of equal value. She would also have to show that his contract of employment contains a more favourable term or terms. This will normally mean that she will provide evidence showing that the comparator is paid more than she is.

In considering the evidence, the tribunal will look at the employment contracts of both the woman and her male comparator. It will be interested in any job description that has been attached to their roles. The tribunal may also ask an independent investigator to visit their place of work to observe them completing daily duties.

Independent experts are normally used in equal-value claims. Such claims can take a long time to resolve. The case of *Enderby v Frenchay Area Health Authority* (1993) took over ten years to eventually be decided by the European Court of Justice. As noted above, there are now rules in place which are designed to sreamline and speed up such claims.

If, having considered all of the evidence, the tribunal accepts the woman's claim, she will be awarded pay equal to that of the male comparator. However, this will not be the case where an employer can successfully raise the defence of genuine material difference.

Remedies

If the woman succeeds in her claim for equal pay the tribunal will make a declaration stating that she is entitled to equal pay from that day onwards. It will order her employer to increase her pay to that of her male comparator. If the inequalities relate to benefits or bonuses, these will also be increased. Damages may also be awarded.

In *Hayward* v *Cammell Laird Shipbuilders Ltd* (1988) the House of Lords held that the approach is contractual and that where the woman has shown that her contract contains terms which are less favourable to that of the man, she is entitled to have the term changed and the benefit that it gives equalised.

There is no maximum award limit in an equal-pay claim. The tribunal will award the employee the difference between her and her comparator's pay and conditions. This amount will be awarded from the date of the hearing and backdated for a period of up to six years before she made her claim.

This six-year backdating period was extended from two years by the Equal Pay (Amendment) Regulations 2003. This change followed the decision of the ECJ in *Levez* v *TH Jennings (Harlow Pools) Ltd* (1999) and that of the court in *Preston* v *Wolverhampton Healthcare Trust Ltd* (2001). The two-year backdating period had been found to be in contravention of European law.

MATERNITY RIGHTS

Pregnant employees are entitled to various basic statutory maternity rights. These rights allow them to take time off work and to receive some form of payment during their pregnancy. The amount of time that a woman can take off work during pregnancy and the amount of money that she will be entitled to from her employer will differ with her length of service. Women who are not employed when they become pregnant are also entitled to various benefits.

The government has also expanded the rights available as part of their 'family friendly' policy. Until recently the major provisions in this area were those introduced in April 2003. At that time there was an increase in the provision of maternity leave and pay and a new right for fathers to take up to 2 weeks' paid paternity leave. The government also introduced a general right for parents to take up to 13 weeks' parental leave. At the time of writing the Work and Families Act 2006 has recently received Royal Assent (21 June 2006). Many of the provisions in this Act came into force on 1 October 2006. The remainder came into force on 6 April 2007. For this reason the remainder of this section outlines the law as it stands at the time of writing and also provides an outline of the changes that came into force in October 2006/April 2007.

Whilst these rights form a basic entitlement, many employers provide enhanced contractual rights providing for extra leave, childcare provision on return to work or schemes whereby women can return on a part-time basis. If a woman's contract of employment provides her with more favourable rights than the basic statutory rights then she is able to take advantage of those rights and vice versa.

Even though an employee's contract may not outline any enhanced rights, the employee may negotiate extra benefits with her employer. The types of extra allowances and benefits that may be made available will differ with each particular employer. Some employers may make no extra provision at all.

It is often difficult to work out what types of benefit or leave a pregnant woman is entitled to. This is because the law in this area is generally complex. In *Lavery* v *Plessey Telecommunications Ltd* (1983) it was said that the law on maternity was 'of inordinate complexity exceeding the worst excesses of a taxing statute'.

Much depends on the woman's expected date of confinement. This is the date on which she has been told that her baby is likely to be born. The best way to work out the rights available to a particular woman is to take her expected date of confinement and then assess her entitlement by counting backwards in weeks.

In order to assess what leave or benefits a particular woman is entitled to she should be asked the following questions:

- When is the expected date of confinement?
- How long has she worked for her employer?
- Has she paid national Insurance contributions?

Table 4.1 details statutory maternity rights in relation to maternity leave and payments during leave.

Table 4.1 Maternity rights as from 6 April 2003: rates as of 1 April 2007

Right	Who is entitled?	Notification?	When does it start? What does she get?
26 weeks of ordinary maternity leave	all employees (regardless of length of service)	written notice by end of the 15th week before EWC, informing employer of pregnancy, EWC and date on which maternity leave will begin	can begin from the 11th week before the EWC, leave for 26 weeks
26 weeks of additional maternity leave	employees who have completed 26 weeks' continuous service by the beginning of the 14th week before the EWC	do not have to inform employer – should assume taking AML if woman decides to go back earlier give at least 28 days' notice	starts at end of ordinary maternity leave for 26 weeks (total possible leave 52 weeks)
Statutory maternity pay	employees employed in the 15th week before EWC and who have 26 weeks' continuous service into the 15th week and earn at least £87 per week on average up to last pay day before end of 15th week	give employer at least notice of date when ordinary maternity leave, so SMP is to begin	earliest SMP can start is from the 11th week before EWC, 26 weeks of SMP (6 weeks at 90% of salary) then 20 weeks at £112.75 per week or 90% of woman's average weekly earnings if less than £112.75
Maternity allowance	those who cannot claim SMP, employed or self-employed, for 26/66 weeks up to and including the EWC earning on average £30 in any 13 of those 66 weeks	claim made to benefits agency from 26th week of pregnancy	can begin from 11th week before EWC, 26 weeks at £112.75 per week (or 90% of woman's average weekly earnings)

Abbreviations:

EWC = expected week of confinement
SMP = statutory maternity pay
AML = additional maternity leave
MA = maternity allowance

Table 4.2 outlines the changes that came into force under the Work and Families Act 2006 and the Maternity and Parental Leave etc. and the Paternity and Adoption Leave (Amendment) Regulations 2006/2014 relating to babies due to be born or placed for adoption on or after 1 April 2007.

Table 4.2 Changes that came into force 1 October 2006.

- all employed women will be entitled to 52 weeks statutory maternity leave regardless of length of service;
- the payment period for Statutory Maternity Pay/Adoption Pay and Maternity Allowance will be extended to 39 weeks (from April 2007) (with provision to extend to 52 weeks by at latest Spring 2010);
- the notice a woman must give if she is changing her date of return from maternity leave will be increased from 28 days to 8 weeks;
- optional keeping in touch days will be introduced, enabling a woman to work for up to 10 days during her maternity leave period;
- the father (or a partner with parental responsibilities) will be able to take additional paid paternity leave of up to 26 weeks if the mother returns to work without using up her entitlement.

THE PREGNANT WORKERS DIRECTIVE (92/85/EC)

Many of the basic statutory entitlements during pregnancy were improved after the adoption of the European Directive on 'the introduction of measures to encourage improvements in the safety and health of pregnant workers who have recently given birth or are breastfeeding'. This directive is commonly referred to as the Pregnant Workers Directive.

The Directive states that employers should carry out health and safety risk assessment in relation to pregnancy. It also states that there is a general right to a minimum of 14 weeks' maternity leave, time off for ante-natal care, and that pregnant women should not work nights during pregnancy. Article 10 of the Directive states that no pregnant woman should be dismissed on the grounds of her pregnancy.

STATUTORY MATERNITY RIGHTS

The statutory maternity rights afforded to employees are outlined in the Employment Rights Act 1996 (as amended by the Employment Relations Act 1999), the Social Security Contributions and Benefits Act 1992 and the Employment Act 2002. Further provision is contained in the Maternity and Parental Leave Regulations 1999, the Maternity and Parental Leave (Amendment) Regulations 2002, the Social Security, Statutory Maternity Pay and Statutory Sick Pay (Miscellaneous Amendments) Regulations 2002, the Statutory Maternity Pay (General) Regulations 2005, and the Social Security (Maternity Allowance) (Earnings) (Amendment) Regulations 2003. More recent provision is contained in the Work and Families Act 2006, the Maternity and Parental Leave etc. and Paternity and Adoption Leave (Amendment) Regulations 2006, the Statutory Paternity Pay and Statutory Adoption Pay (General) and the Statutory Paternity Pay and Statutory Adoption Pay (Weekly Rates) (Amendment) Regulations 2006. These new provisions came into force on 1 October 2006 and will have full effect by 1 April 2007. These rights fall into four main categories:

- the right to take time off for ante-natal care
- the right not to be dismissed on maternity-related grounds

- the right to maternity benefits
- the right to ordinary and additional maternity leave.

Time off for ante-natal care

Section 55 of the Employment Rights Act 1996 states that all pregnant employees are entitled to take reasonable time off work for ante-natal care. This right applies to all employees regardless of the length of time that they have worked for their employer. Employees must be paid their normal salary during any time taken. Ante-natal care can include hospital or clinic appointments, examinations, or visits to a midwife before the baby is born. It can also include relaxation and parentcraft classes.

The right only extends to taking 'reasonable' time off work. An employer should not unreasonably refuse a woman time off, but, should her absences become frequent, the employer may ask her to attend some appointments in her own time.

On the second occasion that a woman asks to take time off for an ante-natal appointment, an employer can ask her to produce a certificate from either a doctor or midwife confirming that she is pregnant. She should also be able to show the employer an appointment card or some other document stating the time and date of her appointment.

An employee who has been unreasonably refused time off to attend an ante-natal appointment, who is not paid during any time taken, or is dismissed for asking to take time off can make a complaint to the Employment Tribunal.

The right not to be dismissed or selected for redundancy on maternity-related grounds

Section 94 of the Employment Rights Act 1996 states that an employee has the right not to be unfairly dismissed by an employer. Section 99 of the Employment Rights Act 1996 goes on to say that it is automatically unfair for an employer to dismiss a woman on any ground relating to pregnancy and childbirth. Regulation 20(1)(a) of the Maternity and Parental Leave Regulations 1999 expands on this. This regulation states that 'a woman will be deemed to have been unfairly dismissed if the reason for her dismissal was that she was pregnant, gave birth to a child, was suspended from work on maternity grounds, took ordinary maternity leave, additional maternity leave, parental leave, or time off work to look after dependants'.

An employee is entitled to these rights irrespective of the length of time that she has worked for her employer. She has the right not to be dismissed or selected for redundancy on these grounds up until the end of her maternity leave and for up to four weeks afterwards if she has been unable to return to work due to illness. An employer who does dismiss an employee during her pregnancy or maternity absence must provide her with a written statement outlining the reasons for the dismissal.

In *Larson v Dansk Handel & Service* (1997) the European Court of Justice held that a Danish woman dismissed following periods of illness connected to childbirth was not protected by the Equal Treatment Directive. This decision was disputed in the case of *Brown v Rentokil* (1998). Here, the ECJ held that European law prohibits the dismissal of a woman at any time during her pregnancy where her absence is due to a pregnancy-related illness. These decisions were based on claims of sex discrimination in dismissal.

It is also unlawful for an employer to select an employee for redundancy on any ground relating to pregnancy or childbirth. If a redundancy situation has arisen during a woman's absence from work, she must be offered a suitable alternative position on her return. The work that she is offered must be suitable in that it reflects similar duties to those for which she was originally employed. The terms and conditions on which she is offered the job should not be less favourable than those in her original contract.

If a woman is dismissed or selected for redundancy for reasons relating to her pregnancy, she can make a complaint to the Employment Tribunal. She may also complain if she has not been given written reasons outlining why she was dismissed. Any claim must be made within three months of the date when her employment comes to an end.

The right to maternity benefits

All pregnant women are entitled to some form of payment during their maternity leave. This provision has recently been expanded by the Employment Act 2002 and the amendment regulations (outlined at page 166). Note the changes due to be made by the Work and Families Act 2006. The following details a woman's basic entitlement. Any extra benefits provided for by her contract of employment may be added to this basic entitlement.

There are three types of maternity benefit:

1 statutory maternity pay

2 maternity allowance

3 the sure start maternity grant.

Statutory maternity pay

Statutory maternity pay is regulated by Part XII of the Social Security Contributions and Benefits Act 1992 (as amended). A woman is only entitled to statutory maternity pay if:

● she has worked for her employer for 26 weeks at the 15th week before the expected date of confinement; and

● her average earnings in the eight weeks up to the birth are at or above the lower limit applicable for National Insurance contributions.

If a woman is eligible under the above criteria, she is entitled to a payment of 26 weeks' statutory maternity pay. These payments are paid by her employer. The payments are made as follows:

26 weeks

For first 6 weeks	At 90% of her usual salary
For remaining 20 weeks	At £112.75 per week or 90% of the woman's average weekly earnings if less than £112.75.

A woman can choose the date on which she wants to begin to receive statutory maternity pay, but this date cannot be earlier than the 11th week before she is due to give birth. Payments are made even if she does not intend to return to work after she has given birth.

Statutory maternity pay is paid in the same way as a woman's salary and tax and National Insurance payments are payable. Employers are able to recoup some of the statutory maternity pay paid to employees. They are able to recoup 92 per cent of the amount paid each tax year.

If their total National Insurance liability in any tax year is not more than £40 000 they are able to recoup 104.5 per cent of the amount paid. This additional allowance exists to compensate the administrative burden in organising the scheme that is placed on small businesses.

Maternity allowance

Women who are not eligible for statutory maternity pay may be able to claim maternity allowance. This is paid under the Social Security Contributions & Benefits Act 1992 and the Social Security (Maternity Allowance) (Earnings) Regulations 2000 (as amended).

This allowance may also be claimed by women who have recently left work or are self-employed and have paid National Insurance contributions. Women may choose the date on which they would like to begin to claim their allowance, but no payments can be made until 11 weeks before the woman is due to give birth.

A woman is entitled to maternity allowance if:

- she has worked for her employer for 26 of the 66 weeks before the expected date of confinement; and

- she is working for her employer on the 15th week before the expected date of confinement, and she has earned an average of £30 per week in any 13-week period.

A woman who meets these criteria is entitled to 26 weeks of maternity allowance. Maternity allowance is paid as follows:

> **£112.75 per week for 26 weeks or 90% of a woman's average earnings if this is less than £112.75.**

Maternity allowance is payable for up to 26 weeks. It is paid directly from the Benefits Agency. A woman is normally given an order book cashable at the post office or by direct payment into a bank account. If a woman is unable to claim maternity allowance, she may be able to claim incapacity benefit or income support.

The sure start maternity grant

A pregnant woman (or their partner) who is claiming income support, income-based jobseeker's allowance, pension credit, child tax credit (at a higher rate than the family element), or working tax credit (where a disability or severe disability element is included in the award) may be able to obtain a payment from the Social Fund. This payment is referred to as the sure start maternity grant. It is a one-time payment of £500 and is designed to help a woman to buy necessities, such as a crib and nappies. This grant is available where either a woman or her partner are receiving any of the above benefits. Any savings that they have are not taken into account.

Claims can be made at any time from the 29th week before the baby is born and up to three months after the birth. The grant does not have to be repaid.

The right to ordinary and additional maternity leave

The rights to ordinary and additional maternity leave (as amended by the Employment Act 2002) are set out in ss 71–85 of the Employment Rights Act 1996 and the Employment Relations Act 1999. All employees are entitled to a period of maternity leave. Note the changes due to be made by the Work and Families Act 2006.

Ordinary maternity leave

Section 71 of the Employment Rights Act 1996 states that all pregnant employees are entitled to take 26 weeks of ordinary maternity leave. A woman does not have to have worked for her employer for any specific length of time before being eligible for this leave.

A woman is entitled to receive all of her contractual benefits apart from her salary during this time. These benefits would include, for example, holiday entitlement and private healthcare insurance. The earliest that the 26 weeks of leave may begin is the 11th week before the expected week of confinement.

Additional maternity leave

Section 73 of the Employment Rights Act 1996 (as amended) states that employees who have worked for an employer for a period of 26 weeks by the beginning of the 15th week before the expected week of confinement are entitled to an additional period of maternity leave. This additional leave can be for up to a period of 26 weeks and begins at the end of the 26-week period of ordinary maternity leave. This entitles a woman to a total of approximately 52 weeks' maternity leave, as set out in Figure 4.3.

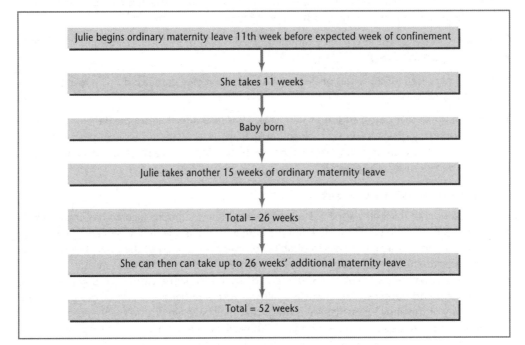

Figure 4.3 The total of ordinary and additional maternity leave

The contractual benefits available to the woman during this time are subject to negotiation with her employer.

THE RIGHT TO RETURN TO WORK AFTER ORDINARY MATERNITY LEAVE OR ADDITIONAL MATERNITY LEAVE

Generally, all employees are supposed to return to work at the end of their maternity leave or absence. An employee who is not allowed to return to work at the end of her leave may make a claim for unfair dismissal. On her return, the woman is entitled to the same terms and conditions of employment that she had before she took her maternity leave.

Compulsory leave

Section 72 of the Employment Rights Act 1996, Article 8(2) of the Pregnant Workers Directive and reg 8 of the Maternity and Parental Leave etc. Regulations 1999 (as amended) state that all employees have to take two weeks of compulsory leave after their baby is born. An employer who does allow a woman to return to work within two weeks of giving birth is liable to be fined up to £500. The Health and Safety Executive enforces this provision. Under Schedule 5 of the Factories Act 1961 it is also an offence to permit a woman to work in a factory within four weeks of giving birth.

NOTIFICATION REQUIREMENTS AS AMENDED BY THE EMPLOYMENT ACT 2002

A woman's right to maternity leave, absence and to return to work after the birth are much dependent on her following the required notification rules. These are outlined in the Maternity and Parental Leave Regulations 1999 (and Amendment Regulations 2002). The regulations state that the woman must keep her employer informed of her intentions to return to work.

An employee should inform her employer of the fact that she is pregnant and of the expected date on which she will give birth. This should normally be confirmed by a medical certificate. She should also notify her employer of the date on which she intends to start to take her ordinary maternity leave and the date on which she would like statutory maternity payments to begin. Such notifications should be made by the end of the 15th week before her expected week of confinement.

Statutory maternity pay cannot begin to be paid until the beginning of the 11th week before the expected date of childbirth.

If the woman gives birth before the date on which she has said that she would like her maternity leave to begin, it begins on that day. The woman should then inform her employer of the birth as soon as reasonably practicable.

If a woman fails to provide her employer with the required notice within the time limits, she may lose her right to maternity leave and statutory maternity pay. The time limits can be extended only where the circumstances show that it was not reasonably practicable for the woman to provide notification.

An employee does not have to give her employer advance notice of the fact that she intends to return to work immediately after the end of her 26 weeks of ordinary maternity leave. If she decides to return before the end of the 26 weeks, she must give her employer 28 days' notice of her return.

There is no longer a requirement for a woman to inform her employer that she intends to take additional maternity leave. The employer should assume that this additional period of leave will be taken unless informed otherwise. If the woman decides to return to work before the end of her additional maternity leave she must give her employer at least 28 days' notice of her return. Note that this notice period is due to be increased to 8 weeks by the Work and Families Act 2006.

PATERNITY AND PARENTAL LEAVE

Paternity leave

As from 6 April 2003 fathers have been entitled to take up to two weeks' paid paternity leave. The Employment Act 2002, the Statutory Paternity Pay and Statutory Adoption Pay (General) Regulations 2002 (as amended) and the Paternity and Adoption Leave Regulations 2002 (as amended) cover this right. The following relates to a basic statutory entitlement. It is worth noting that the father's contract of employment may provide for additional provision. Men are entitled to up to two weeks' paid paternity leave. Paternity leave must be taken within eight weeks of the birth of a child. The leave may be taken in a single two-week block or split into two separate weeks.

In order to qualify for paternity leave a man has to show that he has a specific relationship with the mother of the child in question. Paternity leave is given to allow him time off work to help the new mother with initial childcare. In order to qualify for paternity leave he must have been employed for 26 weeks by the end of the 15th week before the expected week of confinement. He must self-certify this fact to his employer and state that he wishes to take paternity leave. Statutory paternity pay is paid at the same rate as statutory maternity pay. Where the man's earnings are not less than the lower earnings limit for national insurance contributions the rate is £112.75 per week or 90 per cent of his average weekly rate if he earns less than £112.75. Note the changes due to be made by the Work and Families Act 2006.

The right to take paternity leave is additional to the right to take parental leave as discussed below.

Parental leave

The United Kingdom implemented the Parental Leave Directive in the Employment Rights Act 1999. The right to parental leave is contained in ss 76–80 of the 1999 Act. The right is also governed by the Maternity and Parental Leave Regulations 1999 and the Maternity and Parental Leave (Amendment) Regulations 2002. These statutory provisions apply only if there is no workplace agreement already in force.

The right to take parental leave is available to both men and women. It may be taken as an extension of a woman's maternity leave. It is a right to take up to 13 weeks (in total) off work if you have a child under the age of five years. Parents of disabled children are entitled to 18 weeks of parental leave. This leave must be taken prior to their child's eighteenth birthday. Unless an individual's contract of employment provides otherwise, parental leave is normally unpaid leave. Parental leave is given to assist an individual in caring for their child during its formative years. In order to qualify for parental leave a person has to show that they have completed one year of continuous service with their present or previous employers. Time spent in more than one employment can be added together to total one year.

The individual must be able to show that they have responsibility for a child. A person has responsibility if they have parental responsibility within the meaning of s 3(1) of the Children Act 1989. This states that 'parental responsibility means all the rights, duties, powers, responsibilities and authority which by law a parent of a child has in relation to the child and his property'. A man will also have parental responsibility where they are registered as the father of a child. It follows that guardians and adoptive parents will qualify for the right to parental leave but step parents and foster parents do not unless they have acquired parental responsibility.

Any leave amounting to less than a whole week will count as a week for the entitlement. An employee must give their employer 21 days' notice of any date on which they intend to take leave. An employer can postpone parental leave for up to six months but when doing so must agree alternative dates on which it can be taken. Postponement can only take place where the employer can show that there are 'business reasons' preventing him from allowing the employee to take leave at the requested time. The employer cannot postpone parental leave where it is to be taken immediately following the birth of a child.

Regulation 18 of the 2002 amendment regulations states that a person returning to work after four weeks' or less parental leave is entitled to go back to the job that they had before taking leave. This applies where the leave has been isolated and not taken after an earlier block of four weeks' parental leave or additional maternity leave. If the employee has taken this extra time then they are only entitled to go back to their original job if it is reasonable in the circumstances for an employer to allow them to do so. If return to the same job is an unreasonable proposition then the employee is entitled to go back to a job which is both 'suitable' and 'appropriate'. This means that the employee should expect to go back to a job on comparable pay and conditions to the one they had before taking parental leave.

If an employer refuses a request to take parental leave and can show no 'business reason' for this refusal an employee may make a complaint to the Employment Tribunal. If the tribunal finds in favour of the employee they may make a declaration to that effect and may award compensation. The amount of compensation will be 'just and equitable' depending on the employer's behaviour and the actual loss suffered by the employee. An employee has the right not to suffer a detriment because they have asked to take or have taken parental leave. Any dismissal on these grounds will be automatically unfair.

Adoption pay and leave

Similar rights exist for parents who adopt a child. Adoption pay and leave is governed by the Employment Act 2002, the Statutory Paternity Pay and Statutory Adoption Pay (General) Regulations 2002 (as amended), and the Paternity and Adoption Leave Regulations 2002 (as amended).

An employee who adopts a child is entitled to 26 weeks of ordinary adoption leave and 26 weeks of additional adoption leave. During ordinary adoption leave they are entitled to statutory adoption pay. Where a married couple adopt only one of them is entitled to adoption leave. The other parent may be entitled to paternity leave if the conditions outlined above are met. A parent will be entitled to adoption leave if they have been in continuous employment for 26 weeks with the same employer by the week in which an approved match has been made. An employee has to inform their employer of their intention to take leave within seven days of being told by an adoption agency that they have been matched with a child. This is the case unless it is not reasonably practicable for them to do so. They need to give their employer notice of the date on which the child is to be placed with them and the date on which they would like their adoption leave to begin.

Statutory adoption pay is paid in the same way as statutory maternity pay. An employee receives £112.75 per week or 90 per cent of their average weekly earnings if they earn less than £112.75 per week. Adopters who do not have average weekly earnings above the lower earnings limit for National Insurance contributions are not entitled to statutory adoption pay. Additional adoption leave is normally unpaid unless an employee has an arrangement with their employer that provides otherwise. Note the changes due to be made by the Work and Families Act 2006.

If an employee has been absent on ordinary adoption leave they are entitled to return to the same job that they had before taking leave. An employee also has the right not to be subjected to any detriment or dismissed due to the fact that they have taken adoption leave. Any dismissal on such grounds would be automatically unfair.

A male adoptive parent is also able to claim paternity leave. He must expect to have responsibility for the child's upbringing and have continuous employment of 26 weeks ending with the week in which he is told that his family has been matched with a child. The right is to take two weeks' paid paternity leave from work. This can be taken in either one two-week block or two one-week blocks. Only one period of leave is available regardless of the number of children placed with the family. During paternity leave the man will be paid £112.75 for each of the two weeks or 90 per cent of his average weekly earnings if this amounts to less than £112.75.

HEALTH AND SAFETY ISSUES

Employers must pay special attention to the health and safety of pregnant employees. They should conduct a workplace pregnancy risk assessment. This forms part of the general duties under common law and the Health and Safety at Work Act 1974 (see page 330). The assessment should highlight any risks or hazards that could affect the health and safety of pregnant women or their babies.

Employers should take all reasonable steps to remove or reduce the effect of any such hazard or risk. If there are any potential risks to pregnancy which cannot be reduced or eliminated, then employers should ensure that pregnant employees do not come into contact with those risks. In most cases this will mean assigning the employee to a different job during her pregnancy. If alternative work is available and an employer refuses to give it to the pregnant woman, she can complain to the Employment Tribunal.

If alternative work is not available, an employer may suspend the woman from work on maternity grounds. She should be paid her normal wages during any suspension.

When an employer has done a pregnancy risk assessment, he should inform all female employees of his findings. Potential risks may include having to carry heavy items or having to work with radioactive materials or chemicals.

EXCLUSIONS

Not all women are entitled to the range of statutory maternity provisions. The excluded occupations are policewomen, those working on share fishing vessels, and all employees working ordinarily outside of Great Britain. These workers are not entitled to the right to take time off work for ante-natal care, to protection from unfair dismissal or to maternity leave or absence. In most cases their contract of employment will provide comparable protection.

OTHER INDIVIDUAL EMPLOYMENT RIGHTS

Employees are also entitled to various free-standing employment rights. These rights are:

- the right to an itemised pay statement
- the right not to have unlawful deductions made from wages
- notice periods
- guarantee payments
- to receive sick pay
- to take time off work
- the right to receive the national minimum wage.

The right to an itemised pay statement

Section 8 of the Employment Rights Act 1996 states that every employee is entitled to an itemised pay statement. This is normally provided as a pay slip at the end of every week or month.

The statement should show the gross amount earned, any tax or National Insurance deductions made and any fixed deductions. Fixed deductions are those agreed upon by the employee and could include car-parking charges or pension payments. The statement should also detail the amount of net pay that the employee will receive after these deductions are made.

If an employer does not provide an itemised pay statement, an employee can complain to the Employment Tribunal. An employee has three months from the refusal to provide a statement in which to make a complaint. The tribunal can make a declaration awarding the employee any unlawful deductions made from his salary during the 13 weeks before his claim.

Unlawful deductions from wages

The rules on deductions from wages exist to ensure that an employee does not have random deductions made at the end of each week or month of employment. Generally an employer cannot lawfully make deductions from an employee's wages.

Section 13 of the Employment Rights Act 1996 states that employers must not make unlawful deductions from an employee's wages unless:

(a) the deduction is required or authorised to be made by virtue of a statutory provision of the worker's contract; or

(b) the worker has previously signified in writing his agreement or consent to the making of the deduction.

Deductions authorised by statute would include income tax and National Insurance payments. These can lawfully be deducted. Employees may also have expressly agreed for other payments, for example, pension payments, to be deducted from their pay.

There are also specific rules relating to retail workers. Section 19 of the Employment Rights Act 1996 states that agreements may be made between employers and retail workers which enable deductions to be made to recover cash shortages or stock deficiencies.

There are some situations in which an employer can make unauthorised deductions from wages. Section 14 of the Employment Rights Act 1996 states that an employer can make unauthorised deductions from an employee's pay to:

- recover any overpayment of wages;
- recover any overpayment of expenses incurred by the employee during his employment;
- reflect the time an employee spent away from work during strike action; or
- where the deductions are made following a court order.

If none of these exceptions applies and an unauthorised deduction is made, an employee can complain to the Employment Tribunal. The claim must be made within three months of the deduction or, where there have been several, the most recent deduction.

If the tribunal finds that an unauthorised deduction has been made, it can make a declaration ordering the employer to reimburse the employee for his loss.

Notice periods

It is important for both employers and employees to know how much notice has to be given before the contract of employment is terminated. The interim period between notice and the last day of employment will enable an employee to look for another job or the employer to look for a replacement.

In most cases the employee's contract of employment will provide details on how much notice needs to be given. This may be more than the statutory minimum period of notice. This information may be contained in the contract itself or the written statement of terms and conditions of employment (see page 132). If the contract does not set a definite period, the court may imply a reasonable timescale.

If an employer terminates an employee's contract without giving the employee the proper notice, the employee may bring a claim for wrongful dismissal. The claim would be made to recover the wages that he would have received during the balance of the notice period. An employee will not always work during his notice period. In some cases an employer will pay the employee wages in lieu of notice, meaning that the employee will not have to attend work again but will not lose out on any wage entitlement.

Statutory notice periods

Section 86 of the Employment Rights Act 1996 sets out minimum notice periods which differ according to the length of time an employee has worked for an employer.

Time employed	Entitled to notice of
1 month–2 years	1 week
2 years–12 years	1 week for every completed year
12 years +	Maximum of 12 weeks

Section 86 also states that where an employee has been employed for one month or more, he must give at least one week's notice. If an employee has been employed for less than one month then they will be expected to give 'reasonable notice'.

Guarantee payments

Section 28 of the Employment Rights Act 1996 states that employees who have been employed for one month or more have the right to be paid even on days when they are not required to do any work. These payments are referred to as 'guarantee payments' and are paid where an employee has been temporarily 'laid off'.

The employee must have been laid off because:

- there has been a diminution in the requirements of the employer's business for work of the kind that the employee does; or
- where there has been any other occurrence affecting the employer's business in relation to the kind of work which the employee is employed to do.

If this happens, the employer must make a guarantee payment to the employee. The amount paid should not exceed (as of February 2007) £19.60 per day. This payment can be paid for up to five days in any three-month period. The daily rate is reviewed, but not necessarily raised on a regular basis.

An employee is not entitled to a guarantee payment for any day where:

- the reduction in work is due to a strike, lock-out or other industrial action; or where
- the employer has offered the employee suitable alternative work for that day and the employee has unreasonably refused to do that work.

If an employer refuses to make this payment, the employee may complain to the Employment Tribunal. An employee has three months from the date on which the payment should have been made to make a claim. If the employee succeeds in his claim, the tribunal can make a declaration and order the employer to make the guarantee payments.

Sick pay

All employees are entitled to receive a basic amount of sick pay when unable to attend work because of illness. In some cases the employee's contract of employment may provide for enhanced rights during sickness absence. Any such details may be provided as part of the employee's statement of the written terms and conditions of employment (see page 132).

Statutory sick pay

All employees are entitled to receive payments of statutory sick pay for the first 28 weeks of their illness. Statutory sick pay is regulated by the Social Security Contributions and Benefits Act 1992 and the Statutory Sick Pay Act 1994. In order to qualify for statutory sick pay an employee must:

- be suffering from some disease/physical or mental disability which renders him incapable of work; and
- the period of his incapacity must be a period of four or more consecutive days.

The period of incapacity begins with the first day that the employee is absent from work and ends on either the day the employee returns to work or at the end of 28 weeks. The present statutory sick pay payment is (as of April 2007) £72.55 per week.

Statutory sick pay is paid by the employer and replaces the employee's normal salary payment. Employers cannot now recoup any payments of statutory sick pay from the government unless the amount paid in any month exceeds 13 per cent of their liability for National Insurance contributions in the same month. This means that, in the main, employers are responsible for all payments of statutory sick pay.

An employee is normally required to inform his employer that he will not be attending work by 10 a.m. on the first day of the employee's absence. An employee will also be expected to produce a medical certificate detailing the reason for absence after not having attended work for seven days. Up until this time an employee must complete a form to 'certify' that he is absent from work through illness.

If an employer unreasonably refuses to pay statutory sick pay, an employee may ask the employer to provide written reasons for his refusal. The employee may then complain to the Benefits Agency or to an adjudication officer with a right for appeal to the Social Security Appeals Tribunal and the Social Security Commissioner.

● The right to take reasonable time off work

There are some situations in which an employee can ask his employer to be allowed to take either paid or unpaid time off from work. These are where the employee needs time off to:

1 undertake trade-union duties
2 undertake public duties; or
3 look for work or organise training.

If an employer unreasonably refuses to allow the employee to take time off, the employee can make a complaint to the Employment Tribunal. An employee must make this complaint within three months of the refusal.

The tribunal can make a declaration ordering the employer to allow the employee reasonable time off in the future. If an employer has acted very unreasonably, the tribunal may also order the employer to pay compensation. This will reflect the amount of wages that the employee would have earned during the requested time away from work and any consequential loss.

Time off work for trade-union duties

Section 168 of the Trade Union and Labour Relations (Consolidation) Act 1992 states that an employer should allow an employee paid time off from work to undertake trade-union duties.

This section relates to the work of union officials. The employee should continue to be paid his normal remuneration during any time off. Time off should be allowed for duties such as attendance at meetings, negotiation and training.

There is an Acas code which provides guidance on the allocation of time off for trade-union duties. This code is referred to as the Acas Code of Practice: Time off for Trade Union Duties and Activities. This was published in 2003.

Section 170 of the 1992 Act also provides that union members are to be given unpaid time off from work to participate in union activities. This also covers the work of union representatives. Examples of activities would include attendance at meetings or conferences. The 1992 Act expressly states that industrial action is not a union activity for the purposes of the allocation of time off work.

The right is only that the employee be given a reasonable amount of time off work. What will amount to a reasonable amount of time will differ with the circumstances in each case. Employers might consider the reason for the request and how much time off the employee has been given in the recent past. The Acas code recommends that the employer and employee negotiate when the time will be taken. The employer is able to consider the size and resources of his organisation. It would not be unreasonable to refuse time off where, for example, an order date would not be met because of employee absence.

Time off work to undertake public duties

Section 50 of the Employment Rights Act 1996 states that an employer should allow an employee to take reasonable time off from work to undertake public duties. This right will apply to employees who work either as magistrates or for:

- a local authority (e.g. local councillors)
- a statutory tribunal (e.g. Employment/Social Security tribunal)
- a police authority
- a board of prison visitors or a prison visiting committee
- a relevant health body (e.g. a National Health trust)
- a relevant education body (e.g. school governors)
- the Environment Agency or the Scottish Environment Protection Agency.

Employees who are involved in any of these activities should be allowed to take time off to attend meetings or hearings. An employee is only entitled to take reasonable amounts of time off from work. In deciding whether to allow an employee to be absent, the employer is allowed to consider the effect that it will have on his business, how much time is required, and how much time off the employee has been given in the recent past. There is no statutory right to be paid during this time off. This is a matter for negotiation between the employer and employee.

Time off work to look for work or organise training

Section 52 of the Employment Rights Act 1996 states that when an employee has been told that he is going to be made redundant, the employee is entitled to take reasonable time off work to look for a new job or arrange training. The employee should continue to be paid during this time.

The right to receive the national minimum wage

The National Minimum Wage Act 1998, the National Minimum Wage Regulations 1999 (as amended) and the National Minimum Wage Act 1998 (Amendment) Regulations 1999 regulate the law on the minimum wage. The 1998 Act aims to relieve poverty amongst low earners by providing that an employer pays them at least the minimum wage. The right to receive the minimum wage applies from the first day of employment.

The Low Pay Commission is responsible for overseeing the impact of the minimum wage and the review of minimum wage rates. (The role of the Commission is discussed further at page 31). The DTI has produced a guidance handbook and various useful leaflets on this topic. These can be accessed via the DTI website.

Section 1 of the 1998 Act places an obligation on employers to pay workers an amount per hour not less than the set minimum wage. The hourly rate is calculated by working out the total wages paid in what is termed the 'pay reference period'. The hourly rate should be paid for any period when a worker is working at the employer's disposal and carrying out his duties. This includes situations where he is at work and there is no work to do. In *British Nursing Association* v *Inland Revenue* (2002) it was held that nurses providing a telephone helpline and working during the night from home were to be regarded as working through their shifts even though they were free to do as they pleased between calls. They were entitled to the minimum wage during this time.

Who is entitled to the national minimum wage?

The following persons are entitled to the national minimum wage:

- full- and part-time workers;
- casual, agency and temporary workers;
- homeworkers and freelance workers;
- those of retirement age or pensioners who are working; and
- piece workers.

The following workers are not entitled to the national minimum wage:

- the self-employed;
- apprentices and undergraduates who are on sandwich courses;
- members of the armed forces, share fishermen and volunteer workers;
- resident workers in religious communities, prisoners employed during their time in prison;
- au pairs and nannies, companions who are treated as part of an employer's family;
- members of an employer's family who live at home and participate in the running of the family business;
- apprentices under the age of 18 and those who are between 19 and 26 years in the first 12 months of their apprenticeship;
- certain workers on schemes funded by the European Social Fund on government training schemes, work experience or temporary work schemes or schemes to help the unemployed to find work; and
- homeless persons taking part in certain schemes under which they are provided with shelter and other benefits in return for work.

It has also been held that pupil barristers are not covered by the national minimum wage, *Edmunds* v *Lawson* (2000).

One interesting case in this area related to the question of whether tips left by restaurant customers via cheque or credit card payments could be used by an employer to form part of an employee's minimum wage. In *Nerva* v *UK* (2002) the ECHR held that such tips will normally be the property of an employer and so will constitute part of any wages paid by him to his staff when he distributes them.

National minimum wage rates

As from 1 October 2006 the minimum wage rates are as follows:

Main rate (aged 22+):	**£5.35 per hour**
Youth rate (18–21)	**£4.45 per hour**

As from 1 October 2007 the rates will be as follows:

Main rate:	**£5.52 per hour**
Youth rate:	**£4.60 per hour**

The young persons' (aged between 16 and 17 years) rate is currently £3.30 per hour. This is due to increase to £3.40 per hour on 1 October 2007.

Duty of an employer to keep records – s 9 1998 Act

An employer is under a duty to keep detailed records providing salary details that can be used to show that an individual is receiving the minimum wage. Under s 10 of the 1998 Act a worker is entitled to ask an employer for access to these work records. He may do this if he does not believe that he is in receipt of the minimum wage. The worker has the right to be accompanied whilst looking at these records. A worker requests access to such records by issuing the employer with a 'production notice'. The employer must give the worker details of a place and time at which he can view the records. The records must be produced within 14 days of the employer receiving the notice unless the employer and worker agree otherwise.

Under s 11 of the 1998 Act if an employer fails to produce some or all of the records requested or fails to allow the worker to inspect the records/be accompanied then the worker may make a complaint to the Employment Tribunal. The complaint must be made within 14 days of the time allowed for production unless this is not reasonably practicable. If the tribunal finds in favour of the worker they may make a compensatory award of up to 80 times the national minimum wage rate in force at the time of the claim.

What if the employer does not pay/refuses to pay the national minimum wage? ss 19-22 1998 Act

Her Majesty's Revenue and Customs (formerly the Inland Revenue) enforces this part of the Act. If they find that an employer is not paying the minimum wage they can serve them with an enforcement notice. This will instruct them to comply with the law within a set period of time. If an employer fails to comply with this notice HMRC may issue a penalty notice. The penalty notice imposes a financial penalty on the employer of twice the current minimum hourly rate for each day from the time the enforcement notice was issued, and for each worker named in the enforcement notice who has not been paid the money due.

In the case of *Inland Revenue Wales & Midlands* v *Bebb Travel Plc* (2002) the Employment Appeal Tribunal held that an enforcement notice could not be served on an employer in relation to an employee who had left their employment. In this case a worker who remained with the employer succeeded in their claim for backdated pay whereas one who had left did not. This loophole was removed in 2003. Under the National Minimum Wage (Enforcement Notices) Act 2003 an enforcement notice is valid even if the worker's employment has come to an end before the notice was issued. The Act has retrospective effect for up to six years.

An employer can appeal to the Employment Tribunal against an enforcement notice by showing that they are in fact paying their workforce the minimum wage.

Under ss 31–33 of the 1998 Act an employer may also be liable to a criminal fine not exceeding £5000 should they be convicted of the following offences:

- refusing to comply with the national minimum wage regulations;
- failing to keep proper wage records;
- keeping false wage records; or
- obstructing an enforcement officer or failing to give them required information.

HMRC officers also have the power to visit an employer and inspect wage records for themselves. HMRC are able to make a complaint to the Employment Tribunal on behalf of any worker who has not been paid the minimum wage. This claim is based on there having been an unlawful deduction from wages. A worker can make a complaint to the Employment Tribunal on the same basis or make a claim in the courts based on breach of contract.

Right not to be dismissed or suffer a detriment

Section 104A of the Employment Rights Act 1996 states that dismissal of an employee will be automatically unfair if it is due to their entitlement to the national minimum wage or for any reason relating to the enforcement of the 1998 Act. A worker also has the right not to be subjected to any detriment for either of the above reasons.

See also: *Walton* v *Independent Living Organisation* (2003), *Wright* v *Scottbridge Construction Ltd* (2001).

DATA PROTECTION

The Data Protection Act 1998 came into force on 1 March 2000. The 1998 Act repealed and replaced the Data Protection Act 1984. The 1984 Act only applied to computerised records. The 1998 Act applies to personal data recorded manually, in print or computerised records. The Act gives effect to the EC 1995 Directive on Data Protection. The following information summarises the main provisions of the 1998 Act. Further information is available on the government website www.dataprotection.gov.uk.

The Office of the Information Commissioner is discussed above (see page 33; note also the comment on the Data Protection Code of Practice at page 33). This officer is responsible for 'the promotion of good information handling and the encouragement of codes of practice for date controllers'. The Commissioner oversees the operation of the 1998 Act. The Commissioner may serve an enforcement notice or prosecute a defaulting 'data user'.

The Act gives rights to individuals in respect of personal data processed about them by others. Employers will inevitably need to keep records of some data relating to each employee. This information could relate to, for example, their address or other personal details, their sickness record or qualifications. Data may be collected during the recruitment process, whilst the employee is working for their employer or when they resign, are dismissed or made redundant.

The 1998 Act regulates the activities of both data controllers and data processors. A 'data controller' is 'any person who, either alone or jointly with others, determines the purpose for which (and the manner in which it is done) personal data is to be processed'. A 'data processor' is 'any person who processes the data on behalf of the data controller'. A 'data subject' is the person to whom the data relates, that is, the employee. Here, the Act is considered with particular reference to employees but it also applies to other individuals in varying circumstances.

There are eight data protection principles contained in the Act. These are listed in Schedule 1. Data controllers must comply with these principles. The principles may be summarised as follows:

- personal data must be processed fairly and lawfully

In order for the data to be processed both fairly and lawfully the data controller must obtain consent from the employee. There is also a provision whereby data may be processed fairly and lawfully without consent where, for example, the data is processed for the purpose of performing a contract to which the employee is a party, or in the administration of justice. There are also rules on the processing of 'sensitive personal data'. This would include information on, for example, the employee's political beliefs or ethnic origin. Such information may only be processed with the employee's consent or if it is classed as being 'necessary' to process such data. This would be the case where an employer uses the information in relation to the development of an equal opportunities policy.

- personal data must only be obtained for specified and lawful purposes

This means that employers must only obtain personal data as part of their 'relationship' with the employee and only for lawful purposes.

- personal data shall be adequate, relevant and not excessive in relation to the purpose for which it is processed

Employers should take care when collecting employee data. It should be relevant and not excessive having regard to the relationship between them and the employee.

- personal data should be accurate and, where necessary, kept up to date

An employer should ensure that any data held about an employee is accurate. They should also take measures to ensure that the data is kept up to date.

- personal data processed for any purposes shall not be kept longer than is necessary for those purposes

Any data held should not be kept for any longer than is necessary.

- personal data must be processed in accordance with the rights of the data subject under the Act

Employers should process personal data in accordance with the rights provided under the 1998 Act.

- appropriate technical and organisational measures are to be taken against unauthorised or unlawful processing of personal data and of accidental loss, destruction or damage of the data

Employers should ensure that security measures are in place to prevent unauthorised/unlawful processing of personal data. They should also aim to prevent accidental loss, destruction or damage to that data.

- personal data shall not be transferred outside the European Economic Area unless that country is able to ensure adequate levels of protection for the rights and freedoms of data subjects

This provision extends protection in relation to other European countries.

Employees or 'data subjects' have various rights under the 1998 Act. These rights are listed in Schedule 1, part 2 of the 1998 Act. The employee has the right to be informed if any of their personal data is to be processed by their employer. Employees are also entitled to be informed of the nature of such information. The have the right to request in writing that an employer cease or not begin to process data which may cause them damage or distress. Employees also have the right to request that their personal data is not used for direct marketing. If an employer fails to comply with the 1998 Act they may have to compensate any employee who is adversely affected by that failure.

SUMMARY CHECKLIST

- Women and men have the right to equal pay for like work, work rated as equivalent or work of equal value.
- The law on equal pay is contained in the Equal Pay Act 1970, the Equal Pay (Amendment) Regulations 1983, the Equal Pay Act 1970 (Amendment) Regulations 2003, the Equal Pay Act 1970 (Amendment) Regulations 2004, art 141 of the Treaty of Rome and the Equal Pay Directive.
- An employee who wants to make a claim for equal pay can do so to the Employment Tribunal.
- Claims can be made directly under art 141 or the Equal Pay Directive.
- Claims made under the Equal Pay Act 1970 must be interpreted in light of European law.
- The Equal Pay Act 1970 applies equally to men.
- Section 1 of the Equal Pay Act 1970 inserts an equality clause into all contracts of employment.
- The equality clause gives a woman the right to equal pay.
- This right extends to situations in which a woman is employed on like work, work rated as equivalent or work of equal value to that of a man in the same business.
- A woman must be able to compare her work with that of a male comparator.
- Like work means work which is the same or broadly similar.
- Work rated as equivalent is work that has been graded and compared under a job evaluation scheme.
- Job evaluation schemes should be both non-discriminatory and analytical.
- The tribunal may consider whether work is of equal value.
- The tribunal may ask an independent expert to prepare a report and decide whether the job is of equal value.
- The tribunal can choose to accept or reject the expert's report.
- An employer may defend an equal-pay claim by showing that any pay inequalities are due to a genuine material difference which is not related to sex.
- The genuine material difference must relate to either economic or administrative needs.
- The Equal Opportunities Commission Code of Practice on Equal Pay provides guidance on equal pay issues and the implementation of an equal-pay policy.
- The time limit in which equal-pay claims have to be made is generally six months.
- At the hearing, the woman has the burden of proving that her male comparator is doing comparable work.
- The woman must show that her comparator's contract contains more favourable terms in relation to, for example pay, benefits.
- If the tribunal accepts her arguments, she will be entitled to equal pay from the date of the hearing.
- The tribunal will make a declaration ordering her employer to increase her salary and equalise any terms in her contract.

- There is no maximum award limit in an equal-pay claim.
- The tribunal will award the woman the difference in money between their salaries.
- The woman is entitled to backdated equal pay for a period of up to six years.
- All pregnant employees are entitled to various basic maternity rights.
- A woman's contract of employment may provide enhanced maternity rights.
- Many maternity rights are based on the Pregnant Workers Directive.
- Statutory maternity rights are outlined in the Employment Rights Act 1996, the Social Security Contributions and Benefits Act 1992 and the Employment Act 2002.
- New rights are due to be introduced under the Work and Families Act 2006.
- All employees have the right to take reasonable time off for ante-natal care.
- All employees have the right not to be dismissed or selected for redundancy on maternity related grounds.
- There are three types of maternity benefit: statutory maternity pay, maternity allowance and the sure start maternity grant.
- All women have a right to take 26 weeks of ordinary maternity leave.
- Women who have worked for their employer for 26 weeks before the 14th week before their expected week of confinement are entitled to take extra maternity leave referred to as additional maternity leave.
- Employees have a general right to return to work after maternity leave.
- A woman must comply with the notification rules, notifying her employer of the fact that she is pregnant, when she would like maternity leave and payments to begin.
- Employers must pay special attention to the health and safety of pregnant employees.
- All employers must complete a pregnancy risk assessment.
- Fathers are entitled to take two weeks' paid paternity leave.
- Parents are entitled to up to 13 week's parental leave.
- Adoptive parents are entitled to adoption leave and pay.
- All employees are entitled to an itemised pay statement.
- Employers must not make unauthorised deductions from wages except where they relate to the recovery of paid wages or expenses, payments for periods where the employee was on strike or payments authorised by a court order.
- All employees are entitled to minimum periods of notice.
- Employees who are 'laid off' work through no fault of their own are entitled to guarantee payments not exceeding five days in any three-month period.
- All employees are entitled to up to 28 weeks of statutory sick pay.
- Employees are entitled to take reasonable time off work to undertake trade-union duties or public duties.
- Employees who have worked for their employer for two years and have been told that they are to be made redundant are entitled to take reasonable time off work to look for another job or organise training.
- Employees are entitled to the national minimum wage.
- The Data Protection Act 1998 gives rights to individuals in respect of personal data processed about them by others.

SELF-TEST QUESTIONS

1   On what basis might a woman be able to bring a claim for equal pay?

2   Can a woman choose any man as her 'male comparator'?

3   When might the Employment Tribunal use an independent expert to investigate an equal-pay claim?

4   On what basis might an employer defend an equal-pay claim?

5   What has been the impact of European law in relation to equal pay?

6   What types of benefit might be paid during maternity leave?

7   What are the rules relating to how much leave a woman can take during her pregnancy?

8   What are the rules with regards to the taking of paternity and parental leave?

9   When might an employer be able to make unauthorised deductions from employee wages?

10   In what type of situation may an employer be required to pay a 'guarantee payment' to his employees?

11   Outline what is meant by the term 'national minimum wage'.

CASE SCENARIOS

A

Sharon works as a chef in the catering department of a local council. She is responsible for preparing lunch for approximately 35 councillors from Monday to Friday each week. She has become aware that Ian, another chef employed by the council, earns £3000 per annum more than her. Ian works in the staff canteen and is responsible for the supervision of breakfast and lunch from Monday to Friday each week. At any one sitting he and his team cater for up to 1000 council employees.

Sharon does not understand why Ian earns more than she does as she believes that they essentially do the same job. Her friend Sarah has told her that there is a law which states that 'men and women should be paid the same'. Sarah does not have any further information. Sharon decides to pursue the matter further.

Advise Sharon of any possible action she might take to resolve her problem. What might be the basis of any such claim? What would the significance be of the Council responding to Sharon's claim by stating that Ian is paid more because:

● *he previously worked in a top London restaurant;*

● *he was employed for his organisational skill and 12 years of experience; and*

● *it would have been impossible to recruit him on a lesser salary?*

4

Equal pay, maternity and other individual employment rights

B

Jan and her husband William work for the same company, Wistow Tours Plc. Jan has just found out that she is pregnant. They are delighted but Jan is worried about how her employer will react to the news. Jan is a customer services manager and has a very important and demanding job within the organisation. She has worked for the company for five years. William has worked there for two years. Jan is concerned about how much time she will be able to take off work during her pregnancy and after the birth. She is also worried about how much she will earn during this time. She wants to return to her job after giving birth. When she told her employer that she was pregnant he said 'Well, you needn't think that you're getting much time off to go to the doctor or after you have had the baby'. William asked his manager if he would be able to take any time off when the baby was born and was told that he was not entitled to any leave.

Advise Jan as to her rights with regard to:

- *time off for ante-natal care;*

- *ordinary and additional maternity leave;*

- *statutory maternity pay and maternity allowance.*

Advise William as to his rights with regard to:

- *paternity leave and pay.*

Advise both Jan and William as to their rights with regard to:

- *parental leave.*

C

Christopher works for a local publishing company. He is responsible for administrative duties such as photocopying and answering the telephone. His boss, Neil Hunter is renowned for being thrifty and was very annoyed when the government introduced the national minimum wage legislation. Christopher is 25 years old. He earns £4.00 per hour and has been told by his friend Holly that this is less than the national minimum wage. When he approached his boss, Neil told him to 'take a hike' and refused to discuss the matter any further. He has decided to take legal advice on the matter but is hoping that he does not have to raise any salary payments. Holly has advised Christopher to get in touch with Alex Taylor from Her Majesty's Revenue and Customs. She believes that he will be able to help him with his claim for the minimum wage.

Advise Christopher with regard to:

- *whether he is being paid the national minimum wage;*

- *whether he can ask to inspect any wage records that Neil may have and if so how any such request should be made;*

- *whether HMRC will be able to assist him in any way.*

Advise Neil with regards to:

- *his duties under the National Minimum Wage Act 1998;*

- *what penalties he may incur if he insists in continuing to pay salaries at beneath the level of the national minimum wage.*

Further reading

Equal Opportunities Commission: Code of Practice on Equal Pay, 2003.

Sex Discrimination and Equal Pay, IDS Handbook, 3rd edn, December 1998.

'Pressure Builds for Equal Pay', Kate Godwin, *Equal Opportunities Review*, No. 105, 2002, pp. 7–17.

Maternity and Parental Rights: a guide to parents' legal rights at work, Camilla Palmer, Joanna Wade, Alexandra Heron and Katie Wood, Legal Action Group, 2006.

Job Evaluation: An Introduction, ACAS (BO1).

'*Parents at Work*', ACAS Advisory Booklet, (B17), March 2004.

ACAS: Code of Practice – Time off for Trade Union Duties and Activities, April 2003.

'*A detailed guide to the National Minimum Wage*', DTI, October 2004.

'*Maternity Rights*', DTI, 2003.

For legal updates on the material in this chapter please go to the Companion Website accompanying this book at **www.mylawchamber.co.uk/nairns**

4

Equal pay, maternity and other individual employment rights

5

The use of disciplinary and grievance procedures

Employers should adopt and make effective use of both disciplinary and grievance procedures. This can help to maintain good employee relations within the workplace. A workplace without good employee relations encourages absenteeism, low motivation, disloyalty and poor levels of performance and productivity. The Employment Act 2002 and the Employment Act 2002 (Dispute Resolution) Regulations 2004 introduced statutory minimum discipline and grievance procedures. There is no exception for small employers. The relevant provisions came into force on 1 October 2004.

Before these minimum standards were introduced employers were encouraged to have fair discipline and grievance procedures. They were guided by the Acas code of practice on discipline and grievance. The aim of the new framework was to provide a statutory basis for disciplinary and grievance procedures to ensure that employers adopt at least a minimum set of rules. It was hoped that this in turn would reduce the amount of complaints made to the Employment Tribunal. The statutory minimum is a basic statutory duty and employers may choose to develop their own procedures over and above that minimum. Neither employers nor employees are able to exclude these minimum standards from their employment relationship.

All employers should develop a disciplinary code. This code contains a set of rules which inform their employees of what they can and cannot do in the workplace. Disciplinary procedures are those procedures used by an employer to discipline employees who have breached the disciplinary code.

The importance of disciplinary procedures should be noted in relation to unfair dismissal claims. Unless an employer follows the statutory disciplinary procedure the Employment Tribunal will find dismissals to be automatically unfair.

Grievance procedures enable employees to make a complaint about their employer, colleagues or their working environment. They form a structure under which employees can ensure that their complaint is taken seriously.

Used together, disciplinary and grievance procedures ensure that the employer is able to run his workplace efficiently. In a business where set disciplinary and grievance procedures are commonplace, both employers and employees have a recognised and structured mechanism in which to resolve any problems. The Acas handbook *Discipline and Grievances at Work* states that 'in a well-managed organisation disciplinary procedures may not be needed very often' but that 'if a problem does arise then they are vital'. It also states that 'good procedures can help organisations to resolve problems internally – and avoid Employment Tribunal claims'.

By first outlining the importance of the use of disciplinary and grievance procedures this chapter goes on to discuss:

- providing information on disciplinary and grievance procedures;
- the Acas Code of Practice on Disciplinary and Grievance Procedures;

- the Acas handbook, *Discipline and Grievances at Work*;

- disciplinary codes and procedures;

- stages involved in disciplinary proceedings, investigations, counselling/informal action, disciplinary meetings and appeals;

- disciplinary penalties, warnings and dismissal;

- procedural fairness in unfair dismissal cases;

- grievance procedures;

- the stages involved in grievance proceedings;

- the statutory right to be accompanied – Employment Rights Act 1999;

- statutory procedures – Employment Act 2002.

WHY USE DISCIPLINARY AND GRIEVANCE PROCEDURES?

A workplace suffering from poor industrial relations is often staffed by employees with low morale. They may not like going to work and may work slowly and effortlessly because they feel undervalued and unhappy. This in turn will mean that their employer's business will suffer.

Whatever the nature of the business, eventually clients or customers will become affected by the attitude of the workforce. Orders may be processed late and customers given bad service. Eventually profits will fall, and if the management does not try to resolve the situation, industrial action may begin. More employees are likely to be dismissed and a large number of tribunal claims made.

Employers who use effective and fair disciplinary and grievance procedures are more likely to be able to avoid the above scenario and promote positive industrial relations within the workplace. Employees who are able to discuss any problems through an internal grievance procedure are more likely to do this before making any claim to the Employment Tribunal.

If employers can resolve their problems at this level, tribunal cases may be avoided altogether, thus saving all the parties time and money. This may also ensure that an employee continues to work for his employer. In many cases an employer will not want to lose a valued or long-standing employee. It can be counterproductive to lose an experienced employee as a result of a trivial problem in the workplace. The training of new employees can mean further expense and inconvenience for the employer. In today's economic climate even skilled employees may find it very difficult to obtain new employment.

Employers also need to be able to discipline employees when they either make a mistake at work or do something more serious, such as assault or harass a colleague. In cases where the employee has committed only a minor offence, such as being late for work, a simple warning may suffice. An employer must take care when administering disciplinary procedures. In circumstances where the issue of a final written warning/holding of a disciplinary hearing is a wholly disproportionate reaction to a relatively trivial act of misconduct by an employee, this could amount to a fundamental breach of contract. In the case of *Stanley Cole (Wainfleet) Ltd v Sheridan* (2003) it was held that such action could amount to a breach of the implied term of trust and confidence. In such cases the employee could resign and complain constructive dismissal.

The earlier an employer becomes involved in disciplining the employee, the more likely it is that the problem will be quickly resolved. In turn, this could mean that the employee is able to remain in employment. Obviously, where an employee's behaviour amounts to 'gross misconduct', this may not be possible as such an employee will normally be dismissed.

PROVIDING INFORMATION ON DISCIPLINARY AND GRIEVANCE PROCEDURES

Section 3 of the Employment Rights Act 1996 states that employers must provide all employees with details of any workplace disciplinary and grievance procedures and disciplinary rules. This forms part of the employer's duty to provide his employee with a written statement of the terms and conditions of employment under s 1 of the 1996 Act (see page 132).

The statement need not contain full details of the procedures but should provide the employee with information on where he can locate further information. Employees should also be given the names of the staff members whom they ought to contact should they wish to begin grievance proceedings or be dissatisfied with any decision made in disciplinary proceedings.

Communicating information to the employee

Employers must ensure that they communicate details of their disciplinary and grievance procedures to all employees. If employers do not send employees full copies of the procedures with either the contract of employment or written statement of terms and conditions, these should be made available at the workplace. Employers could either refer employees to their personnel department or hang copies of the procedures in communal areas, such as works canteens.

Whilst it may be obvious to employees that there will be specific rules relating to, for example, bad timekeeping, low productivity or violent behaviour, employees cannot be expected to guard against the breach of any unusual disciplinary rule that they are unaware of. The following case highlights a situation in which an employer failed to communicate details of a new disciplinary rule to his employees.

Brooks & Son v Skinner (1984)

Brooks & Son had come to an agreement with the workplace union that any employee who failed to return to work on the day after the company Christmas party would be dismissed. This decision was not communicated to the employees. Mr Skinner was dismissed when he failed to turn up for work on the day following the Christmas party.

Held His dismissal was unfair. He could not be punished for breaking a rule that had not been brought to his attention.

THE ACAS CODE OF PRACTICE: DISCIPLINARY AND GRIEVANCE PROCEDURES (2004)

The Acas code of practice on 'Disciplinary and Grievance Procedures' provides guidance on the use of both disciplinary and grievance procedures. The code guides employers on how to draft effective and workable procedures and how to maintain discipline within their organisation.

Employers do not have to use the code when drafting their own disciplinary/grievance procedures. They could choose to ignore the code altogether. Alternatively, they could choose to adopt some recommendations, formulating specific areas of their procedures to deal with situations likely to occur in the workplace.

In reality, most employers do use the Acas code as guidance on how to implement and use disciplinary/grievance procedures. The code is generally thought to be the best example of good practice in the use of such procedures. An employer who does not adhere to the spirit of the code in disciplinary proceedings would not be looked upon favourably by the Employment Tribunal. Whilst the code has no legal effect, it can be used as evidence in tribunal proceedings.

> **Example**
>
> *Sue's employer has accused her of stealing £33 from the office petty cash. Sue denies the charge. Her employer arranges a disciplinary hearing. Several employees tell their employer that they suspect that another employee, Shabnam, committed the theft. The employer does not carry out any investigation and forgets to send Sue a letter informing her of the date of her disciplinary hearing. The hearing takes place in her absence. On the day following the hearing Sue is dismissed. If Sue makes a claim for unfair dismissal to the Employment Tribunal, the panel will not look favourably on the fact that her employer did not investigate the issues surrounding the theft or allow her to attend a disciplinary hearing.*

It is extremely unlikely that an employer who has obviously ignored the code will successfully defend any unfair dismissal claim. In unfair dismissal claims the tribunal will pay particular attention to the way in which the employee was dismissed. The panel will consider whether an employer implemented his disciplinary procedures fairly. (This is further discussed at page 203.)

ACAS HANDBOOK: *DISCIPLINE AND GRIEVANCES AT WORK*

The Acas handbook *Discipline and Grievances at Work* (2003) provides guidance on all issues surrounding the use of disciplinary procedures. It also contains a copy of the Acas code on 'Disciplinary and Grievance Procedures'. The handbook is aimed primarily at employers, but could also be read by employees who are interested in finding out more about workplace disciplinary procedures.

The handbook provides employers with a checklist on how to deal with a disciplinary issue. Guidance is also given on the best way to deal with disciplinary hearings and appeals. Special rules relating to absence from work and sub-standard work are also discussed. In essence, the handbook pads out the information given in the code and provides further guidance. Copies of both the handbook and the code are available from Acas and are also accessible via their website. The site also provides an interactive guide to discipline and grievance.

Acas: Handling discipline: an overview

The Acas handbook *Discipline and Grievances at Work* contains several very useful flowcharts explaining the various forms of disciplinary and grievance procedures. Figure 5.1 is a reproduction of the chart on 'Handling discipline: an overview'.

The handbook points out that the main purpose of operating a disciplinary procedure is to encourage improvement in an employee whose conduct or performance is below acceptable standards. Note that if the employer is contemplating dismissal or certain action short of dismissal then they must follow the statutory procedure.

DISCIPLINARY CODES AND PROCEDURES

A disciplinary code sets out workplace rules. Disciplinary procedures set out the procedures that employers may use when disciplining an employee. The Acas handbook on discipline and grievances

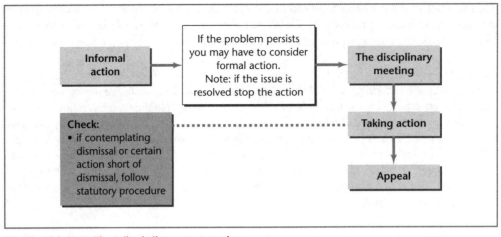

Figure 5.1 Handling discipline: an overview

Source: Acas

at work states that disciplinary procedures 'are an aid to the effective management of people' ... but that they 'should not be viewed primarily as a means of imposing sanctions or as leading to dismissal'.

The Acas handbook states that disciplinary procedures are necessary because they set standards. The handbook goes on to state that 'a good disciplinary procedure helps employees keep the rules, and helps employers deal fairly with those who do not'.

The existence of a disciplinary code can act as a deterrent for those employees who may contemplate causing trouble at work or not doing their job properly. If an employee realises that he may be disciplined and ultimately dismissed for a breach of the code, he may be more likely to remain out of trouble and work to a high standard. Rules will normally cover issues such as absence, timekeeping and holiday arrangements, health and safety, use of an employer's equipment and facilities, misconduct, substandard performance, discrimination, bullying and harassment.

Some employers adopt different codes in relation to issues surrounding the capability of the employee. Here, the issue is not whether the employee has committed any form of misconduct; rather, the employee may just not be very good at his job. Here, an employer would, for example, offer the employee extra training before implementing any disciplinary sanction.

The Acas code outlines what form a disciplinary procedure should take and what types of information it should contain. Paragraph 59 of the code of practice states that when drawing up and applying disciplinary procedures employers should have regard to the requirements of 'natural justice'. This means that before any hearing takes place the worker should be informed of the allegations made against them and the evidence which exists to support such allegations. Employees shoud be given the opportunity of meeting with someone who is not directly involved in the matter. Workers should also be given the opportunity to challenge any allegations before any disciplinary penalty is imposed. Employees should also be provided with a right of appeal against any decision taken.

Paragraph 60 of the code states that disciplinary procedures should:

- be put in writing;
- say to whom they apply;
- be non-discriminatory;
- allow for matters to be dealt with without undue delay;
- allow for information to be kept confidential;

- tell employees what disciplinary action might be taken;
- say what levels of management have the authority to take disciplinary action;
- require employees to be informed of the complaints against them and supporting evidence, before a meeting;
- give employees a chance to have their say before management reaches a decision;
- provide employees with the right to be accompanied;
- provide that no employee is dismissed for a first breach of discipline, expect in cases of gross misconduct;
- require management to investigate fully before any disciplinary action is taken;
- ensure that employees are given an explanation for any sanction; and
- allow employees to appeal against a decision.

The procedure should set out details of what will and will not be regarded as acceptable behaviour in the workplace. The rules should also specify the kinds of offences that will be regarded as 'gross misconduct' and which will normally lead to dismissal without notice.

Standards may be set on, for example:

- bad behaviour, such as fighting or drunkenness;
- unsatisfactory work performance;
- harassment or victimisation;
- misuse of company facilities (for example email and Internet);
- poor timekeeping;
- unauthorised absences; and
- repeated or serious failure to follow instructions.

Serious offences such as assault, major theft or fraud are normally regarded as 'gross misconduct' offences. However, what will amount to 'gross misconduct' may differ with the type of business involved. For example, in a company where some of the workforce know details of a secret formula, disclosing that formula to anyone outside of the business may amount to 'gross misconduct'. The Acas handbook states that any procedure may also include rules on health and safety, discrimination, bullying and harassment.

The rules should also provide information on which staff member the employee should contact if he wants to arrange holiday leave or if he is unable to attend work due to illness. If employees know what procedures they are expected to follow in such situations, they are more likely to comply with them. The disciplinary procedure should outline the possible penalties that can be imposed for various levels of breach. It should also detail some timescale that means that any disciplinary matter is dealt with quickly.

Appendix 2 of the Acas handbook *Discipline and Grievances at Work* contains a model disciplinary procedure. This model procedure is reproduced below.

5

The use of disciplinary and grievance procedures

Disciplinary procedure

1 Purpose and scope

This procedure is designed to help and encourage all employees to achieve and maintain standards of conduct, attendance and job performance. The company rules (a copy of which is displayed in the office) and this procedure apply to all employees. The aim is to ensure consistent and fair treatment for all in the organisation.

2 Principles

(a) Counselling will be offered, where appropriate, to resolve problems.

(b) No disciplinary action will be taken against an employee until the case has been fully investigated.

(c) At every stage in the procedure the employee will have the right to be accompanied by a trade union representative, or work colleague.

(d) No employee will be dismissed for a first breach of discipline except in the case of gross misconduct, when the penalty will be dismissal without notice or payment in lieu of notice.

(e) An employee will have the right to appeal against any discipline imposed.

(f) The procedure may be implemented at any stage if the employee's alleged misconduct warrants such action.

The minimum three-step statutory procedures will be followed if an employee faces dismissal or certain kinds of action short of dismissal.

3 The procedure

Stage 1 – Improvement note: unsatisfactory performance
If performance does not meet acceptable standards the employee will normally be given an improvement note. This will set out the performance problem, the improvement that is required, the timescale and any help that may be given. The individual will be advised that it constitutes the first stage of the formal procedure. A record of the improvement note will be kept for ... months, but will then be considered spent – subject to achievement and sustainment of satisfactory performance.

Stage 1 – first warning: misconduct
If the conduct does not meet acceptable standards the employee will normally be given a written warning. This will set out the nature of the misconduct and the change in behaviour required. The warning should also inform the employee that a final written warning may be considered if there is no sustained satisfactory improvement or change. A record of the warning should be kept, but it should be disregarded for disciplinary purposes after a specified period (e.g. six months).

Stage 2 – final written warning
If the offence is sufficiently serious, or there is a failure to improve during the currency of a prior warning for the same type of offence, a final written warning may be given to the employee. This will give details of the complaint, the improvement required and the timescale. It will also warn that failure to improve may lead to action under Stage 3 (dismissal or some other action short of dismissal), and will refer to the right of appeal. A copy of this written warning will be kept by the supervisor but will be disregarded for disciplinary purposes after ... months subject to achievement and sustainment of satisfactory conduct or performance.

Model disciplinary procedure

Source: Appendix 2 of Acas handbook *Discipline and Grievances at Work*

Stage 3 – dismissal or other sanction
If there is still a failure to improve the final step in the procedure may be dismissal or some other action short of dismissal such as demotion or disciplinary suspension or transfer (as allowed in the contract of employment). Dismissal decisions can only be taken by the appropriate senior manager, and the employee will be provided, as soon as reasonably practicable, with written reasons for dismissal, the date on which the employment will terminate, and the right of appeal. The decision to dismiss will be confirmed in writing.

If some sanction short of dismissal is imposed, the employee will receive details of the complaint, will be warned that dismissal could result if there is no satisfactory improvement, and will be advised of the right of appeal. A copy of the written warning will be kept by the supervisor but will be disregarded for disciplinary purposes after ... months subject to achievement and sustainment of satisfactory conduct or performance.

Statutory discipline and dismissal procedure
If an employee faces dismissal – or certain action short of dismissal such as loss of pay or demotion – the minimum statutory procedure will be followed. This involves:

- step one: a written note to the employee setting out the allegation and the basis for it
- step two: a meeting to consider and discuss the allegation
- step three: a right of appeal including an appeal meeting

The employee will be reminded of their right to be accompanied.

Gross misconduct
The following list provides examples of offences which are normally regarded as gross misconduct:

- theft, fraud, deliberate falsification of records
- fighting, assault on another person
- deliberate damage to organisational property
- serious incapability through alcohol or being under the influence of illegal drugs
- serious negligence which causes unacceptable loss, damage or injury
- serious acts of insubordination
- unauthorised entry to computer records

If you are accused of an act of gross misconduct, you may be suspended from work on full pay, normally for no more than five working days, while the alleged offence is investigated. If, on completion of the investigation and the full disciplinary procedure, the organisation is satisfied that gross misconduct has occurred, the result will normally be summary dismissal without notice or payment in lieu of notice.

Appeals
An employee who wishes to appeal against a disciplinary decision must do so within five working days. The senior manager will hear all appeals and his/her decision is final. At the appeal any disciplinary penalty imposed will be reviewed.

Model disciplinary procedure continued

5

The use of disciplinary and grievance procedures

STAGES INVOLVED IN DISCIPLINARY PROCEEDINGS, INVESTIGATIONS, COUNSELLING/INFORMAL ACTION, DISCIPLINARY MEETINGS AND APPEALS

Disciplinary procedures should set out the possible stages involved in disciplinary proceedings. Depending on the size of the organisation, either the owner of the business, managers or personnel officers will organise and oversee the operation of the disciplinary procedure. In most cases a member of the company's personnel department will be assigned the role of disciplinary officer and will deal with complaints on a regular basis. The Acas handbook states that all members of staff who are to be involved in the conduct of disciplinary proceedings should be trained in the appropriate manner.

The stages involved in disciplinary proceedings are outlined in Figure 5.2.

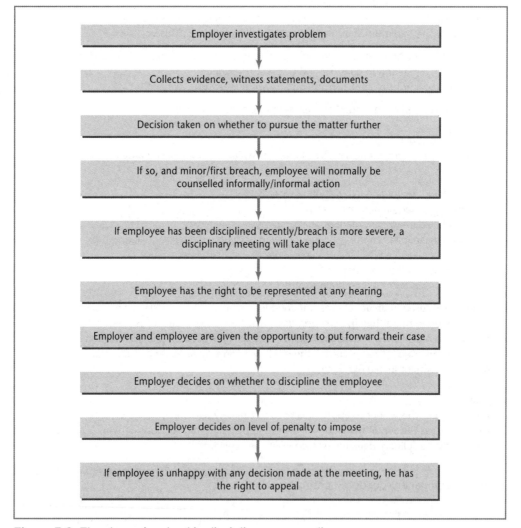

Figure 5.2 The stages involved in disciplinary proceedings

Investigations

Once an employer becomes aware that an employee has breached the disciplinary code, a thorough investigation of all of the issues should be made. This investigation should be completed before any disciplinary proceedings begin. If the breach of discipline is slight, it may be investigated by the employee's line manager. In more serious cases a senior manager may be expected to conduct the investigation. In most cases the size and resources of the particular organisation will dictate who is assigned to the task of completing the investigation.

In cases involving gross misconduct offences, such as theft or fraud, the police will normally conduct their own investigation. Any internal disciplinary proceedings should be halted during the police investigation.

An employer may consider suspending an employee on full pay whilst any investigation takes place and, if necessary, until any disciplinary hearing has taken place. An employer should not generally suspend an employee without pay as this would amount to a breach of the employment contract. In some cases the contract may state that suspension without pay is possible, but this is not common.

When investigating the complaint made against the employee, the line manager or personnel officer should interview and take statements from any potential witnesses. It is important for such statements to be taken as soon as possible. The more time that lapses between an incident and investigation the more likely it is that witnesses will forget what they saw or become confused on what did actually happen. Once the investigation is completed, a decision can then be made as to whether the matter should be taken further. If a thorough investigation does not provide any evidence of employee misconduct, no action should be taken by the employer.

Counselling/informal action

In most cases, and especially where the breach is a first offence, the employer should have an informal chat with the employee. He should discuss what it is that the employee is alleged to have done wrong.

The Acas handbook *Discipline and Grievances at Work* contains a useful flowchart on 'Informal disciplinary action'. This flowchart is reproduced in Figure 5.3.

At this stage the employee may be counselled and asked if he has any particular problems that may have led to the conduct in question. Discussions at this stage may prevent further incidents from occurring and will show the employee that the employer has an interest in his welfare. It may be that the employer is able to help with any problems that are brought to light at this stage. This informal approach may also serve as a warning to an employee that he should not reoffend. An employer may decide to give an employee an 'informal oral warning'. If this informal approach is unsuccessful or if the actions of the employee warrant further investigation, formal disciplinary penalties should be implemented progressively. (These penalties are discussed below at page 200.)

Disciplinary meetings - formal action

Any disciplinary meeting should be conducted fairly. The purpose of the meeting is twofold. The employer is able to outline his case against the employee and the employee is given the chance to defend the allegations or his actions. An employee should be given adequate warning of the date of any proposed meeting. The employee must be given time to consider his position and prepare any defence to the employer's claims.

Employees have the right to be represented at any hearing (see further page 207). The probable stages involved in a disciplinary hearing are outlined in Figure 5.4.

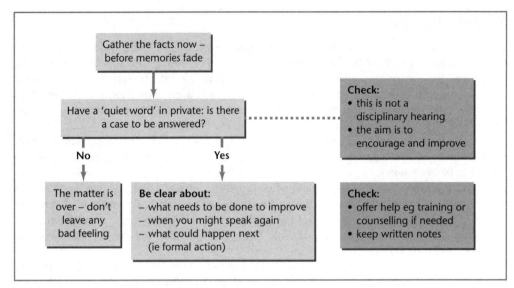

Figure 5.3 Informal disciplinary action

Source: Acas

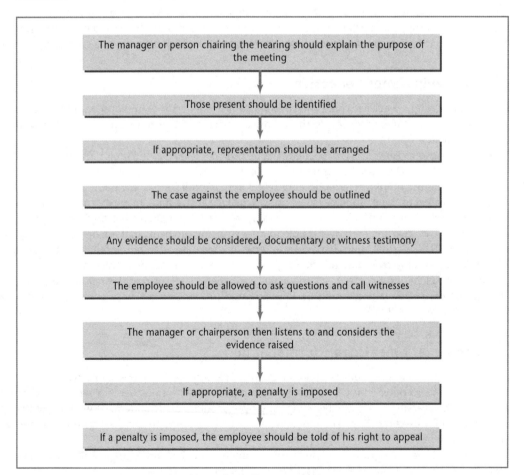

Figure 5.4 The stages involved in a disciplinary meeting

The Acas handbook *Discipline and Grievances at Work* contains a useful flowchart on 'The disciplinary meeting'. This flowchart is reproduced in Figure 5.5.

Appeals

The disciplinary code should also provide a mechanism whereby employees can appeal against any penalties imposed at the disciplinary meeting. The appeal should not be dealt with by any manager or personnel officer who was involved in the initial meeting. Wherever possible the appeal should be heard by a more senior employee or manager than the person who presided over the original meeting. Where in small companies either of these changes is not possible, the person who heard the original case can hear the appeal. This person should then try to be as impartial as possible and not be swayed by his initial decision. An employee should be informed of the results of the appeal and the reasons for the decision as soon as possible. This information should be confirmed in writing.

The Acas handbook *Discipline and Grievances at Work* contains a useful flowchart on 'disciplinary appeals'. This flowchart is reproduced in Figure 5.6.

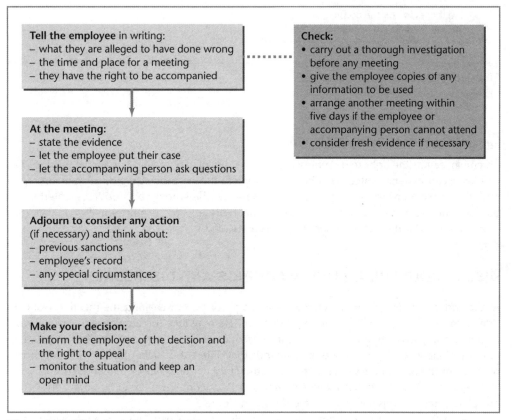

Figure 5.5 The disciplinary meeting

Source: Acas

5

The use of disciplinary and grievance procedures

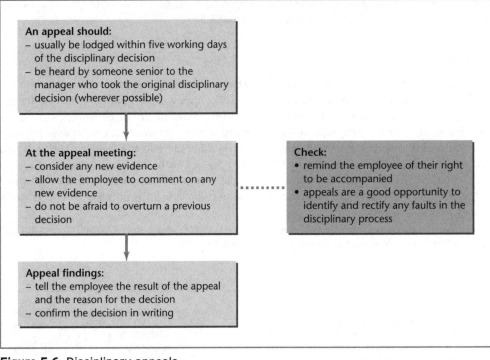

Figure 5.6 Disciplinary appeals
Source: Acas

Representation at hearings

An employee has the right to be represented at any disciplinary meeting or appeal hearing. The employee can be represented by either a staff representative, shop steward, trade-union representative or work colleague. Employers may also allow the employee to be represented by an outsider, such as a friend or family member. Legal representation is not normally allowed. (See further page 207 – the statutory right to be accompanied.)

DISCIPLINARY PENALTIES, WARNINGS AND DISMISSAL

At the end of the disciplinary meeting, the manager or person chairing the meeting will consider all of the evidence before making a decision. He may take the employee's previous work record and any mitigating circumstances into account. If he feels that an employee should be formally disciplined, the Acas code recommends that different penalties be imposed depending on whether the issue in question is one of unsatisfactory performance or misconduct.

The Acas handbook *Discipline and Grievances at Work* contains a useful flowchart on 'Taking disciplinary action'. This flowchart is reproduced in Figure 5.7.

An employer may also consider fining an employee or suspend him without pay in cases involving misconduct. He may also decide to reprimand the employee or demote him to a different job. He may transfer the employee to alternative employment. Whether or not such sanctions are available depend on those stipulated in the employee's contract of employment.

This means that an employee who has not been in trouble before and who has committed a minor breach is likely to be given an improvement note. Where the employee is responsible for

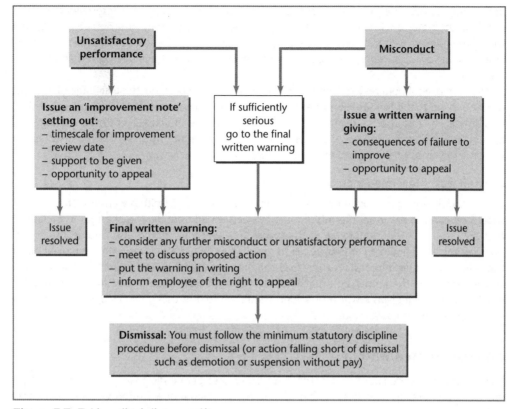

Figure 5.7 Taking disciplinary action

Source: Acas

an act of misconduct then he is likely to be given a written warning. In some situations, however, the employee may have committed a serious breach of the disciplinary code and the employer may enter the disciplinary process at a higher stage.

> **Example**
>
> *Andrew was disciplined after he verbally abused his line manager and threatened him with violence. Although he has worked for the company for three years and has not been in trouble before, his employers decide to give him a final written warning.*

The purpose of any sanction is to 'punish' the employee for his past mistakes, but also to encourage him not to breach any rules in the future. An employee who has committed a gross misconduct offence may be dismissed without being previously disciplined.

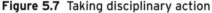 **Unsatisfactory performance – issue an 'improvement note'/Misconduct – issue a written warning**

Improvement note – unsatisfactory performance

An 'improvement note' is the least severe of the disciplinary penalties and is used in cases of unsatisfactory performance. This may be used where the employee has committed a first offence or where his actions constitute a minor breach of discipline. At the end of the disciplinary meeting the employer should inform the employee that they are to be given an

The use of disciplinary and grievance procedures

improvement note. This note should set out the performance problem, the improvement that is required, the timescale for achieving that improvement, a review date and outline any support that the employer will provide to assist the employee. It should also outline the fact that the employee has an opportunity to appeal against the fact that they have been given an improvement note.

The employee should be told that the improvement note represents the first stage of a formal procedure and that if the situation does not improve they may be given a final written warning, or ultimately be dismissed. A record of the improvement note should be kept on the employee's personnel file. This record should be kept for a specified period, normally six months. During this time the employee's performance will be monitored and reviewed.

Written warning - misconduct

In cases involving misconduct employees should be issued with a written warning. This warning should set out the nature of the misconduct in question and outline the changes in behaviour that are required of the employee in the future. The warning should also outline the consequences involved should an employee fail to improve. It should also inform the employee that if they commit further misconduct then they may receive a final written warning. The warning should remain on the employee's personnel file for a specified period, usually for six months. Employees who are given a written warning should be told of their right to appeal against the decision to issue such a warning.

Final written warning

This is the harshest penalty that an employer can impose before dismissing an employee. If an employee has already been given either an improvement note or a written warning and either further misconduct or unsatisfactory performance occurs then they may be given a final written warning.

A final written warning may also be issued in the first instance where either the unsatisfactory performance or misconduct was sufficiently serious to warrant it. An employee who is given a final written warning should be told of their right of appeal against such a decision.

If a final written warning is imposed, the employee will be advised to improve his work or behaviour and not to reoffend.

The employee should be told that he has been given a final written warning and that a record of the warning will be kept on his personnel file. These details may be kept on file for a period between twelve months and two years. An employer may change this timescale to fit in with any particular case. In some situations the offence may have been so serious that the details of the final written warning will never be removed from the employee's personnel file.

The employee should be warned that any further breach of discipline will mean that he will be dismissed. All employees in this position should be sent a letter outlining the above and stating that the employee has been given a final written warning.

Employees who have been given a final written warning should be told that they have the right to appeal against this decision. They should also be given the name of the staff member whom they should contact should they decide to appeal.

Dismissal or other sanction

An employer will normally only dismiss an employee if all of the other disciplinary penalties have been imposed. Dismissal is obviously the most severe form of discipline. Note that where an employer is proposing to dismiss an employee (or take any action short of dismissal such as demotion or suspension without pay) he must follow the minimum statutory discipline procedure. (See further, page 209.)

An employer may choose to discipline an employee in a variety of situations. If an employee has previously been given a final written warning, details of which remain on his personnel file, the employee may be dismissed following a further breach of discipline. If the employee, whether having been disciplined before or not, commits a gross misconduct offence, he is likely to be dismissed. Unless an employee has committed a gross misconduct offence, he should not be dismissed for a first breach of discipline.

An employee who is dismissed should be sent a letter stating that he has been dismissed and outlining the reasons for the dismissal. The employee should also be told that he has the right to appeal against the decision. The letter should also provide details on the name of the staff member that the employee should approach if he decides to appeal.

An employee who has been employed for one year or more can ask an employer to provide full written reasons for the decision to dismiss. This request must be made within three months of the date on which his employment ends. An employer must reply to any such request within 14 days of receipt.

As noted above, if the employer does not want to dismiss the employee, he is able to consider alternative penalties, such as demotion or transfer. In most cases the penalty imposed will very much depend on what it is that the employee has done and the circumstances surrounding each particular case.

⬤ Personnel records

Employers should keep detailed and accurate records of any disciplinary meetings and any penalties imposed. Records should detail any witness statements or other evidence that was used in the hearing. Apart from being good practice, this may also help employers in any future tribunal cases.

> ### Example
> In a claim for unfair dismissal, Karen alleges that she was never given the chance to explain her position in a disciplinary meeting. She states that she was stopped in a corridor and told that she had been dismissed. If her employer can produce details from her personnel file detailing that she did attend a proper hearing, her claim for procedural unfairness will fail.

Personnel records and files should be kept confidential. An employee should always be told that a record of both the disciplinary meeting and any penalty imposed is being made. In most circumstances this record should only remain on file for a specified period. The Data Protection Act 1998 governs the keeping of manual and computer records, and allows the 'data subjects', that is employees, access to their personnel records.

⬤ PROCEDURAL FAIRNESS IN UNFAIR DISMISSAL CASES

The rules on procedural fairness in unfair dismissal cases were changed by section 34 of the Employment Act 2002. The statutory discipline and grievance procedure rules introduced by the 2002 Act are discussed in more detail below (page 209). Section 34 of the 2002 Act introduced a new section 98A(2) into the Employment Rights Act 1996. Prior to these changes the tribunal had considered procedural fairness in relation to unfair dismissal. See further, *Polkey v A E Dayton Services Ltd* (1987).

Section 98A(1) of the Employment Rights Act 1996 states that if an employee is dismissed in a situation where their employer has failed to use the minimum statutory disciplinary procedure then that dismissal will be automatically unfair. Note that an employee has to have at least one year's continuous service with their employer in order to accrue the right to claim unfair dismissal. Where an employer fails to use the minimum statutory disciplinary procedure and the dismissal is rendered automatically unfair, the tribunal may increase any compensatory award by between 10 and 50 per cent. A finding of unfair dismissal in these circumstances will also lead to an award of at least four weeks' pay. At the time of writing, the amount used to calculate a week's pay is £310.

If an employer does comply with the statutory minimum disciplinary procedure, this does not mean that any decision to dismiss is automatically fair. However, provided that the employer has followed the minimum statutory procedure, and the dismissal is otherwise found to be fair, the tribunal will not now consider other procedural shortcomings. The situation now is that whilst employers will always have to follow the minimum statutory procedures, they will no longer be penalised for not following their own additional procedures. This is the case where following any additional procedures would have made no difference to the decision to dismiss. Section 98A(2) reintroduced the 'no difference' rule from the case of *British Labour Pump Co Ltd v Byrne* (1979). In essence this section reversed the previous ruling in **Polkey** under which the tribunal had looked at the reasonableness or otherwise of the employer's behaviour. Under the 'no difference' rule, if the employer has followed the statutory minimum disciplinary procedure but has not followed their own internal procedures, the dismissal may not be found to be unfair on procedural grounds if the employer can satisfy the tribunal that following internal procedures would have made no difference to the decision to dismiss.

This was confirmed in the recent case of *Silman v ICTS (UK) Ltd* (2005) EAT. Here, it was said that the effect of section 98A(2) is to reverse the decision in **Polkey** where there has been no breach of minimum statutory procedures. The reintroduction of the 'no difference' rule has been criticised because it is thought that it will reduce the protection afforded to employees and encourage employers to take a less rigorous approach to dealing with disciplinary matters.

GRIEVANCE PROCEDURES

Guidance on the use of grievance procedures is also contained in the Acas code of practice and the *Discipline and Grievances at Work* handbook. The Employment Act 2002 introduced statutory minimum grievance procedures. These are discussed further below (page 209).

Employers use specific grievance procedures to deal with employees' complaints. An employee may wish to raise a grievance concerning, for example, his employer, a colleague or their working environment. An employee often starts grievance proceedings following a specific event at work which has made him feel unfairly treated or undervalued. Employers should take grievance issues seriously because unresolved problems at this stage may result in tribunal applications later.

Example

Reasons why an employee might instigate grievance procedures:

- *disagreements over appraisals or job evaluation exercises;*
- *allocation of work where the employee feels that he is being overworked or given the work that no one else wants to do;*
- *unfairness in the way that overtime is allocated;*

- *disagreements over having to work with an incompetent or disruptive fellow employee;*
- *disagreements over performance-related pay;*
- *harassment/bullying at work;*
- *discrimination;*
- *health and safety issues.*

Employers should use a set grievance procedure to deal with all complaints. A copy of this procedure should be given to all employees. Often employers will supply this information with details of their disciplinary procedures. Grievance procedures should be made available in writing and should encourage disputes to be settled quickly and effectively. The Acas handbook on *Discipline and Grievances at Work* states that 'it is clearly in management interests to resolve problems before they can develop into major difficulties for all concerned'.

The procedures should provide employees with details of the name of a staff member whom they should contact if they wish to make a complaint. If an employer requires employees to complete a specific form before making any complaint, details of this and the forms should be made readily available.

The Acas handbook *Discipline and Grievances at Work* contains a useful flowchart on 'The grievance procedure'. This flowchart is reproduced in Figure 5.8.

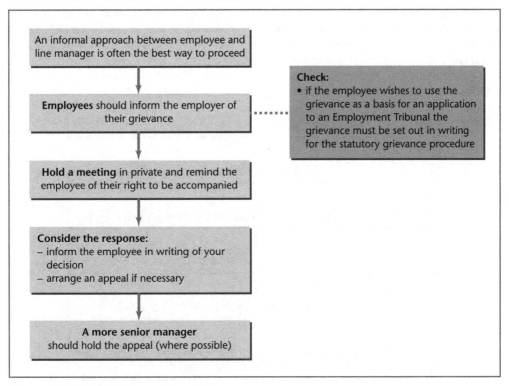

Figure 5.8 The grievance procedure

Source: Acas

● Steps involved in grievance proceedings

Employers may draft grievance procedures to suit their particular organisation but they must adhere to the basic statutory minimum. The procedures should outline the steps through which a complaint may progress. These steps usually reflect the involvement of different levels of manager within the organisational hierarchy. The steps below reflect those used in standard grievance procedures.

Different members of staff and managers will have the responsibility of responding to the grievance at different stages. Each step should also set out a timescale during which the grievance should be considered and resolved. These timescales should allow for a review of any decisions by both the employer and employee at any stage. Details of any appeal procedure should also be provided.

The number of steps included in the procedure is largely dictated by the size and resources of any particular business and the levels of available managerial hierarchy. There are normally three steps through which a grievance may progress. Some larger organisations then incorporate a final step which involves a further appeal being heard by a higher level of management. An example of standard grievance steps appears in Figure 5.9.

Step 1

An employee with a grievance should first raise the problem with his supervisor or immediate line manager. The person in this position will differ according to the organisation and size of the business. Details of the grievance should be given in writing. Employees must complete step 1 of the statutory grievance procedure if they wish to later use the grievance as the basis of a tribunal application. (See further page 209.)

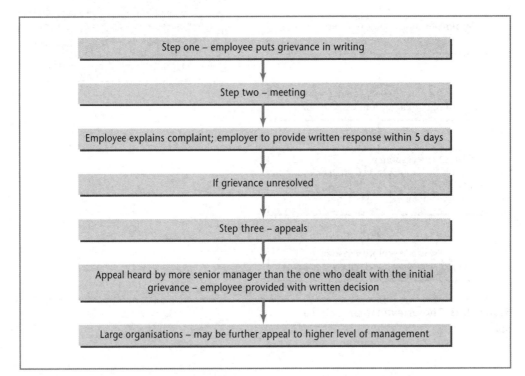

Figure 5.9 The standard steps involved in a grievance procedure

Step 2

After the employee submits their grievance in writing their employer will invite them to a meeting to discuss the grievance further. The employee has a right to be accompanied at that meeting (see below). The Acas code states that the employee should be allowed to explain their complaint and say how they think it should be settled. It also states that if the employer reaches a point in the meeting where they are not sure how to deal with the grievance, or feels that further investigation is necessary, then the meeting should be adjourned to take advice or make further investigation. Employers and employees will normally be expected to go through the statutory grievance procedures (see page 209).

Following the meeting, the employer should provide the employee with a written response to their grievance within a reasonable time, normally five days. The employer should also inform the employee of their right to appeal against any decision made. If it is not possible for an employer to respond within five days then the employee should be provided with an explanation for the delay and be told when they can expect to receive a response from their employer.

Step 3

If an employee informs their employer that they are not happy with the decision taken following the grievance meeting then the employer should arrange an appeal. The appeal should be dealt with by a more senior manager than the one who dealt with the initial grievance. The employer should invite the employee to a further meeting and, following that meeting, the employee should be informed of the final decision taken regarding their grievance.

As the appeal stage is part of the statutory procedure (see page 209), if the employee begins a tribunal claim against their employer any award of compensation may be reduced if the employee has not exercised their right of appeal. The employee has a right to be accompanied at any appeal hearing (see below). The employee should be provided with a written decision following the appeal hearing. In some larger organisations there may be a further appeal to a higher level of management. This is usually not possible in smaller firms. In small firms the first appeal will complete the grievance procedure.

Grievance meetings

Grievance meetings should be conducted fairly. All members of staff who are involved in hearing complaints should receive full training. Employers should ensure that they investigate matters thoroughly before any meeting takes place.

During the meeting the employee should be given every opportunity to outline his complaint. The aim of the meeting is to settle the complaint as quickly as possible. Any decisions made should be communicated to the employee in writing. Should he not agree with the decision, he should be told that he can appeal.

THE STATUTORY RIGHT TO BE ACCOMPANIED AT DISCIPLINARY AND GRIEVANCE MEETINGS

It has been noted elsewhere in this chapter that an employee has the right to be accompanied at disciplinary and grievance meetings. This right was administered on an ad hoc basis until the Employment Relations Act 1999 brought in a new set of statutory rules. These rules can be found in ss 10–15 of the 1999 Act. An employee has the statutory right to be accompanied at disciplinary and grievance meetings. Section 37 of the Employment Relations Act 2004 extended this right. Sections 29–40 of the Employment Act 2002 extended this right to meetings conducted as part of the statutory minimum disciplinary and grievance procedure. The right to be accompanied is further outlined in the Acas code of practice on 'Disciplinary and Grievance Procedures' and in the handbook on *Discipline and Grievances at Work*.

What is the statutory right?

The statutory right is one to be accompanied by one person who is either:

- a fellow worker; or
- a full-time union official or a lay union official who has received training in this area.

The statutory right does not include a right to be accompanied by a lawyer or any other person. However, an employer may decide to allow such persons to accompany the employee.

The right to be accompanied applies to situations where the employee is required or invited by their employer to attend certain disciplinary and grievance meetings. The employee must make what is termed a 'reasonable request' to his employer, asking to be accompanied at the hearing. The right to be accompanied does not apply to informal counselling sessions as long as they do not result in any formal action.

Section 13(4) of the 1999 Act states that the statutory right to be accompanied applies specifically to meetings which could result in:

(a) the administration of a formal warning to a worker by his employer;

(b) the taking of some other action in respect of a worker by his employer (such as suspension without pay, demotion or dismissal); or

(c) the confirmation of a warning issued or some other disciplinary action taken (such as an appeal hearing).

This right also applies to any disciplinary meetings held as part of the statutory disciplinary and grievance procedure. It also includes any meetings held after an employee has left employment. The right to be accompanied in relation to grievance meetings applies only where the problem raised concerns the 'performance of a duty by an employer in relation to a worker'.

It is not reasonable for an employee to request the attendance of someone whose presence would prejudice the hearing or who might have a conflict of interest. Also, it would not be sensible for an employee to request the attendance of someone who works at a distance from their place of work when someone suitably qualified is available on site. There is no duty on an individual to agree to accompany the employee at the hearing. No pressure should be put on an individual who has expressed that they do not want to be involved.

What role does the representative play at the hearing?

The chosen representative has the right to address the hearing. They can ask questions but do not have the right to answer questions on the employee's behalf. The Acas code states that it is 'good practice to allow the companion to participate as fully as possible in the hearing'.

Section 37 of the Employment Relations Act 2004 states that the employer must permit the worker's companion to:

(a) address the hearing in order to do any or all of the following:

    (i) put the worker's case;

    (ii) sum up that case; or

    (iii) respond on the worker's behalf to any view expressed at the hearing

and

(b) confer with the worker during the hearing.

Can the employer refuse to allow a person to be accompanied?

If the worker makes a request to be accompanied, but the chosen companion is not available at the time of the proposed meeting the employer should postpone the meeting to a time proposed by the worker. The alternative time must be reasonable, and within five working days of the date proposed by the employer.

An employer should not refuse an employee's reasonable request to be accompanied at the meeting. If an employer does refuse then the employee is able to make a complaint to the Employment Tribunal. If the tribunal finds against the employer they may order him to pay compensation of up to two weeks' wages. Where the failure leads to a finding of unfair dismissal, greater legal remedies might be involved. The employee and their representative have the right not to suffer any detriment or be dismissed due to them exercising the statutory right to be accompanied.

STATUTORY PROCEDURES - EMPLOYMENT ACT 2002

As noted above, the Employment Act 2002 and the Employment Act 2002 (Dispute Resolution) Regulations 2004 introduced new statutory minimum disciplinary and grievance procedures. The relevant parts of the 2002 Act are Section 29 and Schedule 2. The relevant provisions came into force on 1 October 2004.

All employers should implement at least minimum statutory disciplinary and grievance procedures. There is no exception for small employers. Until the implementation of statutory procedures employers were merely encouraged to have fair disciplinary and grievance procedures. They were guided solely by the Acas code of practice on disciplinary and grievance procedures as discussed earlier in this chapter. The aim of the statutory procedures is to provide a statutory basis for disciplinary and grievance procedures to ensure that employers adopt at least the minimum of rules. It is hoped that this in turn will mean that fewer complaints are made to the Employment Tribunal. The duty is only a basic statutory duty and employers may choose to develop their own procedures over and above those outlined as the statutory minimum. Employers and employees cannot exclude these rules from their employment relationship.

The Acas handbook *Discipline and Grievances at Work* contains a useful flowchart on 'The statutory procedure'. This flowchart is reproduced in Figure 5.10.

Disciplinary and dismissal procedures

The standard statutory discipline and dismissal procedures can be found in Schedule 2 of the Employment Act 2002. The procedures apply to disciplinary action short of dismissal (but not to oral and written warnings and suspension on full pay) based on either conduct or capability. They also apply to those forms of dismissal listed below. The procedure does not apply to constructive dismissal.

The procedure applies to dismissals including those based on:

- conduct;
- capability/absence from work;
- expiry of a fixed-term contract;
- redundancy (unless sudden closure of business or collective consultation obligations apply);
- retirement; and
- some other substantial reason (unless dismissed employees are offered re-engagement on different terms).

The use of disciplinary and grievance procedures

5

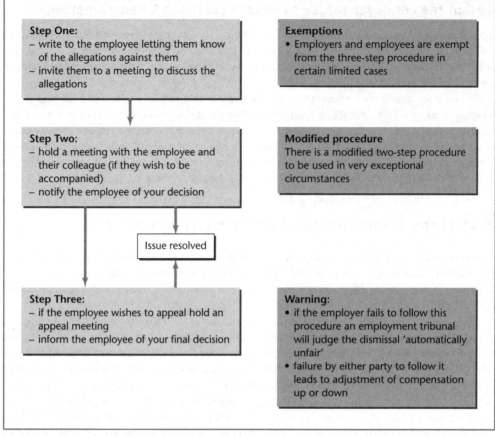

Figure 5.10 The statutory discipline and dismissal procedure
Source: Acas

There are two types of procedure: standard procedure and modified procedure. Standard procedure applies in most situations. The modified procedure applies in cases of gross misconduct where it is reasonable for an employer to dismiss an employee without investigation and without notice or pay in lieu of notice. As noted above, if an employer fails to follow this procedure, any dismissal will be automatically unfair. If an employee fails to follow the statutory grievance procedure (see below) then in most cases they will not be allowed to pursue a claim in the Employment Tribunal. The procedures consist of a three-step process and are summarised below.

Step 1 – statement of grounds for action and invitation to meeting

The employer must set out in writing what it is that the employee is alleged to have done. A copy of this statement must be sent to the employee together with an invitation for him to attend a meeting to discuss the matter further.

Step 2 – meeting

A meeting must take place before an employer can take any action against an employee (except where that action is a precautionary suspension from work). The meeting must not take place unless the employer has informed the employee of the basis of the allegations and the employee has had a reasonable opportunity to consider his response to that information. The employee must take all reasonable steps to attend the arranged meeting. Following the meeting the employer must inform the employee of any decision made and inform him of any right to appeal if he is not satisfied with the decision. The employee has the right to be accompanied at any meeting (see page 207).

Step 3 - appeal

If an employee wishes to appeal against a step 2 decision he must inform his employer. The employer must then invite him to attend a further meeting. The employee must make all reasonable efforts to attend this meeting. The appeal meeting need not take place before the dismissal or disciplinary action takes effect. After the appeal the employer must inform the employee of his final decision. If possible the appeal should be dealt with by a more senior manager than that involved in any earlier meeting. The employee has the right to be accompanied at any meeting (see page 207).

Schedule 2 also contains a modified two-step procedure relating to cases of misconduct.

- Step 1 – statement of grounds for action
- Step 2 – appeal

This applies where an employee has been dismissed for gross misconduct. In such cases the employer must set out the reasons that led to dismissal and send a written copy to the employee. The employee should be informed of the fact that they have the right to appeal against the decision. If an employee wishes to appeal then they must inform their employer. The employer should then invite the employee to attend a meeting. The employee has a right to be accompanied at that meeting (see page 207). The employee must take all reasonable steps to attend the meeting. Following the meeting the employer must then inform the employee of their final decision. Where possible, the appeal should be dealt with by a more senior manager than that involved in any earlier meeting.

Grievance procedures

The standard statutory grievance procedure can be found in Schedule 2 of the 2002 Act and is summarised below.

Step 1 - statement of grievance

The employee must set out the grievance in writing and send the statement to the employer.

Step 2 - meeting

The employer must invite the employee to attend a meeting to discuss the grievance. The meeting must not take place unless the employee has informed the employer of the basis for the grievance and the employer has had a reasonable opportunity to consider his response to this information. The employee must take all reasonable steps to attend the meeting. After the meeting the employer must inform the employee of his decision as to his response to the grievance and notify him of the right to appeal against the decision if he is not satisfied with it. Employees have the right to be accompanied at this or any appeal meeting (see page 207).

Step 3 - appeal

If the employee wishes to appeal he must inform the employer. The employer must then invite him to a further meeting. The employee must take all reasonable steps to attend the meeting. After the appeal meeting the employer must inform the employee of his final decision. If possible the appeal should be dealt with by a more senior manager than that involved in any earlier meeting.

5

The use of disciplinary and grievance procedures

Schedule 2 also contains a modified two-step grievance procedure. This does not involve any meetings. The employee merely sets out their grievance in writing to their employer and the employer responds to them in writing outlining their response.

Failure to follow statutory procedures – ss 31–33

Aside from being able to bring a breach of contract claim an employee (with 1 year's service) who has been dismissed may also bring a claim for unfair dismissal. If an employer has not followed the minimum statutory procedures then any dismissal will be automatically unfair. Where an employer fails to follow the minimum procedures and the dismissal is rendered unfair the tribunal may increase the employee's compensatory award by 10–50 per cent. If, however, the employee has failed to follow part of the procedure or failed to take his right to appeal under it and he is found to have been unfairly dismissed the tribunal may reduce his compensatory award by 10–50 per cent.

If an employee fails to use the minimum statutory grievance procedure they are then disqualified from making a claim to the Employment Tribunal. In order to encourage an informal resolution of the grievance, tribunals are not able to accept claims from employees for a period of 28 days from the date on which they raised their grievance in writing with their employer.

It remains to be seen if these statutory rules will reduce the number of complaints made to the Employment Tribunal. Given that they provide for only basic procedures it is probable that most employers will have more sophisticated procedures already in place.

SUMMARY CHECKLIST

- Employers should adopt and make effective use of both disciplinary and grievance procedures.
- Disciplinary procedures are those used by an employer to discipline any employee who has breached a workplace rule.
- Grievance procedures are those used by an employee who wants to make an official complaint against his employer, a fellow colleague or concerning the workplace environment.
- All employers have a duty to provide employees with details of any workplace disciplinary and grievance procedures.
- Statutory minimum disciplinary and grievance procedures came into force in October 2004.
- Acas has produced guidance on the use of disciplinary procedures in the form of its code of practice on 'Disciplinary and Grievance Procedures'.
- Acas has also produced a handbook, *Discipline and Grievances at Work*, which contains a copy of a model code.
- Employers should investigate all issues thoroughly before beginning any disciplinary procedures.
- An employee who has committed a minor breach and is previously of good character should be dealt with informally or issued with an improvement note.
- More serious issues should be dealt with at a disciplinary meeting.
- An employee has the right to be represented at any meeting by a colleague, a shop steward or a trade-union representative.

- At the end of the hearing the employer may impose penalties, namely a final written warning or dismissal.
- Unless the employee has committed an offence of gross misconduct, he should not be dismissed for a first breach of discipline.
- An employee who is disciplined should be told that he has the right to appeal against this decision.
- Accurate and detailed records should be kept of any disciplinary meetings and any penalties imposed.
- If an employee (with one year's continuous service) is dismissed in a situation where their employer has failed to use the minimum statutory disciplinary procedure then that dismissal will be automatically unfair.
- Employers may have different procedures for dealing with employees' grievances.
- The stages in grievance procedures are organised to fit in with an organisation's managerial hierarchy but must meet at least the minimum statutory standard.
- Employees should submit their grievance in writing, their employer will then invite them to a meeting to discuss the grievance further.
- All grievance meetings should be conducted fairly.
- Employees should be allowed time to explain their side of the case in any grievance meeting.
- At the end of the meeting the employee should be told that he can appeal against any decision which he feels is unsatisfactory.
- Employees have a statutory right to be accompanied at most meetings.
- Schedule 2 of the Employment Act 2002 contains the standard statutory discipline and dismissal procedures.
- There are two types of procedure – standard procedure and modified procedure.

SELF-TEST QUESTIONS

1 Why should employers adopt formal disciplinary and grievance procedures?

2 What types of situation may cause an employer to begin disciplinary proceedings?

3 What types of situation may cause an employee to begin grievance proceedings?

4 What is the legal status of the Acas code of practice on 'Disciplinary and Grievance Procedures'?

5 What can an employee expect to happen in a disciplinary meeting?

6 What range of penalties may be imposed?

7 When might an employee be dismissed for a first breach of discipline?

8 Explain what is meant by the 'no difference' rule.

9 If an employee fails to use the minimum statutory grievance procedure, are they still able to make a claim to the Employment Tribunal?

5

The use of disciplinary and grievance procedures

10 What are the likely steps involved in grievance proceedings?

11 What are the general rules relating to an employee's statutory right to be accompanied at disciplinary and grievance meetings?

12 Outline the standard statutory discipline and dismissal procedures contained in Schedule 2 of the Employment Act 2002.

CASE SCENARIOS

A

Yvonne manages a large chain of Italian restaurants. The owner of the restaurants has asked her to draft new disciplinary and grievance procedures suitable for use with all levels of employee. Yvonne does not know where to start. She lists the types of offence that would warrant instant dismissal but cannot progress further without help.

Advise Yvonne as to how she should draft the new procedures. Your answer should assist her with:

● *where she might be able to find help on the drafting and implementation of disciplinary and grievance procedures;*

● *what types of information the new procedures should contain;*

● *whether or not she has to tell her employees about the procedures;*

● *whether or not she must incorporate statutory minimum procedures into that of the company.*

B

Alison and Darren work for 'Finefoods plc', a company which makes microwave ready meals. Alison works as a packer, packing the completed product into boxes for distribution. Darren works taking orders in the distribution office. Last Monday Shirley, the accounts manager, mistakenly left £200 of petty cash on a table in the distribution office. Seeing this as an easy way to make extra cash, Darren put the money in his pocket. He later asked Alison into the office and shouted at her, stating that her work is 'pathetic', 'useless', and that she is 'fat' and should 'go back to eating ready meals, not packing them!' Alison left in tears. On the following day Shirley realised that the money had gone missing. She asked Darren if he had found it and he said that, as Alison had been in the office at the time, she must have stolen it. Shirley then immediately walked up to Alison, accused her of theft and, without giving her a chance to explain, dismissed her.

Advise Alison as to her right to:

● *bring a grievance against Darren or Shirley;*

● *whether she can be represented and/or accompanied at any grievance meeting;*

● *complain about the fact that she was dismissed by Shirley without being able to attend and be represented at a disciplinary meeting.*

Shirley later looked at the office closed-circuit video tapes. She realises that Darren is responsible for the theft.

What action, if any, might Shirley take against Darren?

Further reading

Acas Code of Practice No. 1 – 'Disciplinary and Grievance Procedures (2004)'.

Acas Advisory Handbook, *Discipline and Grievances at Work*, 2003.

'The A–Z of Work', Acas.

'*Resolving disputes at work: New procedures for discipline and grievances: A guide for employees*', 2004, DTI.

For legal updates on the material in this chapter please go to the Companion Website accompanying this book at **www.mylawchamber.co.uk/nairns**

5

The use of disciplinary and grievance procedures

6 Termination of the employment contract

Most employment disputes arise when the contract of employment is terminated. There are various ways in which this can occur. The most common reasons for termination are where the employee resigns to take up a new position, or where the employer dismisses the employee.

The rules on termination of the employment contract appear in both the common law and statute. A termination of the employment contract at common law is referred to as a '**wrongful dismissal**'. A termination in contravention of a statute is referred to as an '**unfair dismissal**'.

It is important to note from the outset that these two claims are separate types of action. In a claim for wrongful dismissal the employee is alleging that the employer has breached the terms of the employment contract. In unfair dismissal claims the employee is alleging that he was dismissed unfairly.

Whereas in unfair dismissal cases the tribunal considers the fairness or otherwise of the dismissal, in wrongful dismissal cases the court or tribunal is not concerned with fairness, but only with whether what the employer has or has not done amounts to a breach of the employment contract.

This chapter begins by providing an overview of both wrongful and unfair dismissal claims. It then goes on to discuss:

- the definition of wrongful, unfair, summary and constructive dismissal;
- the ways in which an employment contract might be terminated;
- termination of the employment contract at common law, wrongful dismissal, notice periods, non-use of disciplinary procedures;
- summary dismissal;
- making a wrongful dismissal claim to the court or Employment Tribunal;
- termination in contravention of statute, unfair dismissal;
- the effective date of termination;
- constructive dismissal;
- eligibility to make an unfair dismissal claim;
- automatically unfair reasons to dismiss;
- automatically fair reasons to dismiss;
- potentially fair reasons to dismiss;
- the 'reasonable range of responses' and procedural fairness;
- written reasons for dismissal;
- the Acas arbitration scheme;

- making an unfair dismissal claim to the Employment Tribunal, the overlap with wrongful dismissal claims;
- remedies, reinstatement, re-engagement, compensation;
- calculation of awards.

OVERVIEW OF A WRONGFUL DISMISSAL AND UNFAIR DISMISSAL CLAIM

Figure 6.1 highlights the differences between a wrongful dismissal claim and a claim for unfair dismissal.

6

Termination of the employment contract

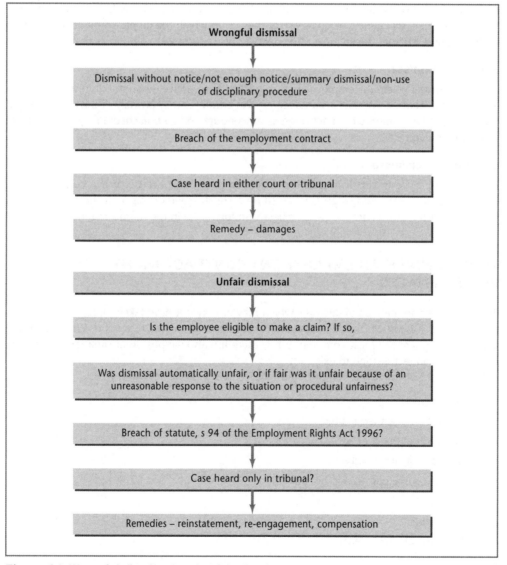

Figure 6.1 Wrongful dismissal and unfair dismissal compared

Defining the various forms of dismissal

It is important to separate the types of dismissal that may result in a claim to either the court or tribunal. The following basic definitions highlight the differences between the four types of dismissal discussed in this chapter.

Wrongful dismissal

Dismissal is in breach of the employment contract because the employer has given no notice, not enough notice or, for example, breached the employment contract by failing to follow set disciplinary procedures.

Unfair dismissal

This is a dismissal in breach of statute; the employer either dismisses the employee for an automatically unfair/fair reason, or for a potentially fair reason. In 'potentially fair reason' cases the tribunal considers the fairness or otherwise of the way in which the employer made the decision to dismiss, and whether the employer's disciplinary procedures were used in a fair manner.

Summary dismissal

This is a dismissal where the employee is dismissed with no notice, wrongful dismissal unless the employer has 'cause' to dismiss instantaneously. An employer may lawfully dismiss in this way if the employee has committed an act of gross misconduct and so breached a major term of the employment contract.

Constructive dismissal

Here the employee is not dismissed but is forced to resign because of the conduct of his employer; employee's resignation is taken to be a constructive dismissal. If the employee has one year's continuous service, he can pursue a statutory claim in the normal manner.

WAYS IN WHICH AN EMPLOYMENT CONTRACT MIGHT BE TERMINATED

Before considering the type of dismissal which may or may not have taken place, it is important to look at the ways in which the employment contract might come to an end. Whilst dismissal and resignation are the most common forms, there are also various other situations which will result in the contract ceasing to exist.

The contract of employment may be terminated in any of the following ways:

- by agreement
- by completion of a specific task
- by frustration of the contract
- by the death of either party
- by dissolution of a partnership or liquidation
- by dismissal
- by resignation
- by the expiry of a fixed term.

Termination by agreement

An employment contract will automatically be terminated where the employer and employee agree to bring their working relationship to an end. The agreement must be unconditional and there must have been no coercion on the part of the employer who may be trying to avoid paying a redundancy and/or an unfair dismissal payment.

If the employee later denies that he agreed to the termination of their contract, the court or tribunal will look carefully into the circumstances surrounding the case. If an employee cannot show that he has been dismissed, then he has no further claim against his employer. Consequently, it is important to check on whether the employer did coerce the agreement, or put the employee under any form of duress.

In *McAlwane* v *Boughton Estates* (1973) Donaldson J stated that: '. . . tribunals should not find an agreement to terminate employment unless it is proved that the employee really did agree, with full knowledge of the implications it had for them'.

In this case an employee had been given notice of dismissal. While working through this notice he asked his employer if he could leave immediately to begin a new job. The employer agreed and he later claimed that he was entitled to both a redundancy payment and unfair dismissal compensation. Boughton Estates argued that, as he had asked to leave his employment, he had agreed to the termination of his contract.

Boughton argued that there had been no dismissal and that, consequently, he was not entitled to any payment. It was held that he had not agreed to the termination of his contract. He had merely varied his notice requirements by looking for work while knowing that he was about to lose his job.

The following case highlights a situation in which it was held that the employees did agree to the termination of their employment contracts.

Humber & Birch v *University of Liverpool* (1985)

Liverpool University sent out 'early retirement' circulars asking for volunteers from its lecturing staff who might want to take early retirement. Volunteers would receive enhanced retirement payments after leaving their employment. Humber and Birch volunteered to take early retirement. They agreed to the dates on which their employment would end, and on which they would receive the enhanced payments. Then, following the termination of their contracts, they alleged that they had not agreed to leave the University, but had in fact been dismissed. They said that the University had terminated their contracts and that they were entitled to a redundancy payment.

Held (CA) The claim was dismissed because the agreements to terminate the lecturers' contracts had been genuine agreements. The lecturers had agreed to take early retirement in order to receive the extra money. Consequently, there had been a mutual agreement to terminate the contracts of employment and no dismissal.

See also: *Igbo* v *Johnson Matthey Chemicals Ltd* (1986), *Logan Salton* v *Durham County Council* (1989).

Termination by completion of a specific task

If an employee is employed to complete a specific task, his contract of employment will end when he has completed that task. For example, a firm may employ a computer specialist to install a software package. The specialist is employed only to complete the installation and his contract terminates when that has been done. When the contract ends the employee has not been dismissed. His contract has merely ceased to exist.

● Termination by frustration

A contract of employment will automatically end where a frustrating event means that the parties are no longer able to perform their obligations under the original terms of the agreement.

The rules on frustration are part of the general rules of contract law. Frustration occurs where an event which is beyond the control of the parties intervenes and prevents the contract from continuing, or allows it to continue but in a radically different way from that intended. Where a contract is frustrated, no dismissal has taken place. The contract has merely ceased to exist. The employee is unable to claim any compensation for losing his job due to a frustrating event.

> ### Example
> *Ursula and Gary contract to appear in a West End musical. On the night before the opening night there is a fire, and the theatre is burnt beyond repair. As there is no theatre, there can be no production. Consequently, they are unable to perform. They have not been dismissed; their contracts have been terminated by frustration. Their contracts could not continue to exist in their original form because there was no way that the parties could do what it was that they had originally agreed to do.*

Two of the more common events which induce frustration are illness and imprisonment. Here, an employee may be unable to continue to perform under the terms of his contract either because the employee is too ill to work, or in prison and so unable to attend work.

Illness

An employee may be unable to attend work due to either a short or long-term illness. In some cases an employee's absence from work will frustrate, and so terminate, his contract. In *Marshall v Harland & Wolff* (1972) the tribunal stated that the question to ask was whether the nature of the employee's illness was such that further performance of his obligations was impossible, or radically different from that originally intended when he entered into the contract.

Poussard v Spiers (1876)

Poussard was an opera singer who had contracted to sing at Spiers' theatre for three months. Just before the opening night she was taken ill and was unable to perform. An understudy was appointed. The understudy performed Poussard's role for two weeks. Poussard then announced that she wanted to return to the role. Spiers was happy with the work of the understudy and told Poussard that her illness had frustrated their contract.

Held As her illness had forced Spiers to continue with the opera in a radically different manner to that intended, it had frustrated their contract. Consequently, Poussard was not entitled to be reinstated in the role or to any compensation.

Condor v Barron Knights (1966)

The Barron Knights' drummer had contracted to play a summer season. The group agreed to do a show every evening. The drummer had been suffering from a nervous illness brought on by the stress of work. Under medical advice he was only able to perform in four shows each week. His contract was terminated and he alleged that he had been wrongfully dismissed.

Held His illness had frustrated the contract; he had not been dismissed. He had contracted to work seven evenings per week. Had he done this, there was evidence to show that his mental and physical health would have suffered. Consequently, it was impossible for him to perform at the level required under the contract.

As time has moved on, the courts have become more reluctant to find that an employee's illness will frustrate the contract of employment and so leave the employee without a job and without compensation. In some ways the rules of frustration act against the ideals behind employee protection.

Guidelines on when an illness may frustrate a contract were first outlined in *Marshall v Harland & Wolff* (1972), and then set out and expanded in *Egg Stores Ltd v Leibovici* (1977). Mr Leibovici had been absent from work for four months. He had been involved in an accident and was too ill to return to work. Egg Stores continued to pay him wages up until January 1975. In April 1975 he asked if he could return to work but was told that he could not. Egg Stores had employed someone else to do his job. Leibovici argued that this refusal constituted a dismissal. Egg Stores argued that his illness had frustrated their contract.

The Employment Appeal Tribunal held that in cases involving illness:

there may be an event, (for example, a crippling accident), so dramatic and shattering that everyone concerned will realise immediately that to all intents and purposes the contract must be regarded as at an end. Or, there may be an event, such as illness or accident, the course and outcome of which is uncertain. It may be a long process before one is able to say whether the event is such as to bring about the frustration of the contract.

Philips J concluded by stating that frustration would occur where:

- even though at the time of the event the outcome was uncertain,
- the time arrives where it can be said that matters had gone on for so long, and the prospects for the future were so low,
- that it was no longer practical to consider that the contract of employment would still exist.

The Employment Appeal Tribunal stated that in considering questions of illness the following factors should be taken into account:

- the length of time that the employee has worked for the employer;
- how long that employment was expected to continue, for example, indefinitely or for a set period;
- the nature of the job;
- the nature, length and effect of the illness/accident;
- the need of the employer to have the work done, and the need for the employer to appoint a replacement to do it;
- the risk to the employer of acquiring obligations in respect of redundancy payments, or compensation for unfair dismissal to the replacement employee;
- whether the employer has continued to pay the employee;

6

Termination of the employment contract

- the acts and comments of the employer, including the manner of any dismissal;
- whether in the circumstances, a reasonable employer could have been expected to allow the contract of employment to exist for any longer.

This list was extended in the case of *Williams* v *Watsons Luxury Coaches Ltd* (1990). Here the court held that the following should also be taken into account, namely:

- whether there is any prospect of the employee recovering;
- whether the employer had paid the employee sick pay during his absence from work.

This shows that in some situations an illness may frustrate the contract of employment. Decisions must be made dependent on the *Egg Stores* and *Watson* guidelines. It will seem that only in very serious cases will the fact that an employee is ill result in his contract of employment being terminated by frustration.

See also: *Harman* v *Flexible Lamps Ltd* (1980), *Notcutt* v *Universal Equipment Company Co Ltd* (1986).

Imprisonment

When an employee has been sentenced to a term of imprisonment he will obviously be unable to attend work during the duration of that sentence. The argument has been made that imprisonment should not frustrate an employment contract because it is not self-induced. This makes the point that it is the judge who prevents the employee from attending work by sending him to prison, and so the employee himself has no control over events.

Looked at another way, however, it is the employee who has committed the crime. If the employee had not done so, he would not then have found himself in court to be sentenced.

Whilst there have been conflicting decisions on this point, the most recent cases show that it is accepted that a sentence of imprisonment can frustrate an employment contract.

Hare v *Murphy Bros* (1974)

Mr Hare had been sentenced to 12 months' imprisonment. He had been charged with unlawful wounding. He had worked for Murphy Bros as a foreman for 25 years. The wounding had taken place outside of work. Murphy terminated his contract of employment while he was in prison. Murphy said that, as he was unable to attend work, the contract had been frustrated. When Hare was released from prison he asked if he could return to work. He was told that another man had been employed to do his job. He claimed that he had been unfairly dismissed.

Held The sentence of imprisonment had frustrated his employment contract. A year was a long time to expect Murphy to cope with the fact that he was unable to attend work. Consequently, Hare had not been dismissed and could make no claim for compensation.

F C Shepherd & Co Ltd v *Jerrom* (1986)

Mr Jerrom had been sentenced to between six months and two years in Borstal. He was an apprentice plumber who was convicted following his involvement in a gang fight. At the time of arrest he was 21 months into his apprenticeship. Shepherd & Co terminated his contract of employment while he was in Borstal. The company refused to allow him to resume his training on his release. He claimed that he had been unfairly dismissed.

> *Held (CA)* Jerrom's contract had been frustrated when he was sentenced to serve at least six months in Borstal. There had been no dismissal and consequently, Jerrom could make no claim for compensation.

Interesting debate on possible frustration of the employment contract prior to imprisonment can be found in the decision in *Four Seasons Healthcare Ltd* v *Maughan* (2005). Here, Mr Maughan had worked for Four Seasons as a registered mental nurse. He was suspended from duty following allegations that he had abused a patient. He was arrested and bailed and remained suspended from work throughout ensuing criminal proceedings. He was later found guilty of a number of offences and sentenced to two years' imprisonment.

Four Seasons argued that Mr Maughan's contract had been frustrated prior to his being imprisoned, namely from the time that he assaulted the patient and when bail conditions were set which prevented him from entering his place of employment. The Employment Tribunal held that Mr Maughan's contract of employment was frustrated when he was imprisoned but not before that time. This meant that the employer had to pay Mr Maughan wages up until the time that he was imprisoned.

Termination by the death of either party

A contract of employment will automatically end on the death of either the employer or employee. In relation to the death of the employer, this rule is only relevant to those cases where the employer also owns the business. In other cases, the remaining partners usually continue to run the business, meaning that the contracts of employment remain unaffected. If this is not the case, the employees will be treated as having been dismissed and will be entitled to redundancy payments.

Termination by dissolution of a partnership or liquidation

At common law where a partnership is dissolved or a business goes into liquidation, contracts of employment automatically terminate. However, under statute employees are treated as having been dismissed and are entitled to redundancy payments. This is the case unless the business continues under new ownership, or if individual contracts of employment are not continued.

Termination by dismissal

Aside from situations in which an employee resigns from a job, dismissal is the most common way in which a contract of employment is terminated. Section 95(1) of the Employment Rights Act 1996 states that an employee is dismissed by his employer if:

(a) the contract under which he is employed is terminated by his employer either with or without notice;

(b) the employee is employed under a limited-term contract and that contract terminates by virtue of the limiting event without being renewed under the same contract; or

(c) the employee terminates his contract with or without notice as a result of his employer's conduct.

Subsection (b) relates to the expiry of a limited term contract; subsection (c) to constructive dismissal. (These forms of dismissal are discussed in more detail at pages 225 and 232 respectively.)

Before an employee can make any claim, he must be able to show that he has been dismissed. In many cases there will be evidence of dismissal, and the employer will not dispute the fact that it took place. However, in some cases an employer may deny having dismissed the employee, and so attempt to block the employee's claim for compensation.

The most common form of dismissal is where an employer tells an employee that he has been dismissed. At common law, if the employer has not given the employee the required notice of dismissal, the employee will be able to make a claim for wrongful dismissal. In unfair dismissal actions the employee needs to show that he has been dismissed before he is able to make a claim. Whether or not words or actions will constitute a dismissal will depend on the particular circumstances of the case.

Futty v D & D Brekkes Ltd (1974)

Mr Futty worked as a fish filleter at Hull Docks. The dock workers often used abusive language during 'bantering' sessions. During one such session the exchange of comments between the workers got more and more abusive. Futty's supervisor shouted at him, saying 'If you don't like the job, f... off.' Futty left the dock and found another job. He later claimed that he had been unfairly dismissed.

Held There had been no dismissal, the comments had formed part of the normal 'industrial language' that was used in the workplace. Futty had terminated his own employment contract by finding another job.

See also, *Tanner v D T Kean Ltd* (1978) in which the words: 'What's my f.....g van doing outside, you're a tight bas...d. I've just lent you £275 to buy a car and you are too tight to put juice in it. That's it; you're finished with me,' were held not to be a dismissal. The comments were said to be words that a reasonable employee would have understood to have been a reprimand!

Here the judge stated that the question to ask is: 'How would a reasonable employee in all the circumstances have understood what the employer intended by what he said and did?'

An employer's actions may also constitute a dismissal. In *Alcan Extrusions v Yates* (1996) a new shift system was imposed in the factory. The workers protested at the changes. Yates and his colleagues told their employer that they would only work the new shift system under protest, and that they would reserve their right to claim unfair dismissal. They then put in a claim for unfair dismissal while still working under protest. The terms and conditions of their employment had been severely affected by the shift changes.

Here, the Employment Appeal Tribunal held that where an employer fails to consult with the workforce before introducing a fundamental change in the terms of employment, this could constitute a dismissal.

● Termination by resignation

An employee may terminate his contract of employment by resigning from his job. An employee can resign at any time but must give his employer notice of his intention to leave. The contract of employment will normally specify how much notice must be given. Section 86 of the Employment Rights Act 1996 states that an employee should give his employer a minimum of one week's notice. (See further page 176.)

If an employee leaves his employment without giving the required notice, he will be in breach of contract. The employee would then be liable to pay damages to his employer. In practice, employers do not pursue a damages claim against an employee unless a large amount of money is involved.

An employee who resigns from his job must do so independently, and without coercion or duress from his employer. The following case highlights a situation in which an employee was coerced into resigning.

Essex County Council v Walker (1972)

Ms Walker had a serious disagreement with her employer. Following the incident she was told that it would be in her best interests to resign. She did so and claimed that she had been made redundant. When she made a claim for a redundancy payment the Council stated that she was unable to claim because she had not been dismissed. It alleged that she had resigned voluntarily.

Held Where an employee is coerced or pressurised into resigning, this is not a valid resignation but a dismissal.

In this case Brightman J stated that: '. . . if an employee is told that they are no longer required in their employment and are expressly invited to resign, a court of law is entitled to come to the conclusion that, as a matter of common sense, the employee was dismissed'.

See *Caledonian Mining Co Ltd v Bassett* (1987), *Hellyer Brothers v Atkinson & Dickinson* (1994).

At common law once an employee has resigned from his job, he can make no claim for wrongful dismissal. This is because no dismissal has taken place. The position is slightly different under statute. There, in cases where an employee is forced to resign due to the conduct of his employer, the employee may be able to make a claim for constructive dismissal. (See further page 232.)

Termination by expiry of a fixed term/limited term

All fixed-term contracts have a set date on which they begin and on which they terminate. A fixed-term contract will automatically terminate on the date on which it is designed to come to an end. Whilst this means that the contract terminates automatically at common law, the end of the contract may still amount to a dismissal for statutory purposes. A limited-term contract is one which is not intended to be permanent. It ends either on the expiry of a fixed term or on the performance of a specific task. A limited-term contract may also end following the occurrence of a specific event or following the non-occurrence of that specific event.

This is the form of dismissal outlined in s 95(1)(b) of the Employment Rights Act 1996 (noted at page 223).

TERMINATION OF THE EMPLOYMENT CONTRACT AT COMMON LAW – WRONGFUL DISMISSAL

At common law an employer can lawfully dismiss an employee by giving him the correct amount of notice, or wages in lieu of that notice. Wrongful dismissal occurs when an employer dismisses an employee and either gives the employee no notice of that dismissal, or insufficient notice. There will also be a wrongful dismissal where an employer terminates a fixed-term or limited-term contract before the date on which it is set to terminate.

This is a common law action based on the fact that the employer has breached the terms of the employment contract. This action is separate to that of unfair dismissal.

Example

Martin is entitled to four weeks' notice under his contract of employment. His employer dismisses him with only four days' notice. His employer has breached the terms of his employment contract and he is entitled to make a claim for wrongful dismissal.

Shove v Downs Surgical plc (1984)

Mr Shove had been employed with companies in the same group as Downs Surgical since 1937. He was appointed chairman and managing director of Downs Surgical in 1981. In July 1982 he became ill and underwent a coronary by-pass. On 7 September 1982 he was dismissed without notice. His contract of employment stated that he was entitled to not less than 30 months' notice of the termination of his employment. He successfully sued for the loss of his salary of £36 000 per annum, the use of the company Daimler, BUPA membership for himself and his wife, and membership of the company health and pension schemes. After tax he was awarded £60 729 in damages.

Where an employee is dismissed with no notice, he is able to make a wrongful dismissal claim unless he has himself committed actions amounting to a serious breach of the employment contract. In such cases an employer may lawfully dismiss an employee without giving him any notice. (This is termed 'summary' dismissal and is discussed further below.)

In all but summary dismissal situations, an employer must give the employee notice of dismissal.

An employee may also make a claim for wrongful dismissal where an employer has failed to follow the correct disciplinary procedures. This failure will amount to a breach of the employment contract.

In wrongful dismissal actions the court or tribunal is not interested in the fairness or otherwise of the dismissal. The only issue in wrongful dismissal actions is whether or not the employer has breached the contract of employment. The employee sues for the wages and/or benefits that he would have received during the notice period. The employee may also seek an injunction or a declaration of their contractual rights.

● Summary dismissal

Summary dismissal is a form of common law dismissal. It is often referred to as 'dismissal for cause' because the employer is said to have cause to dismiss the employee. It occurs where an employer dismisses an employee instantly without giving him any notice.

An employer can lawfully do this where the employee has done something which amounts to gross misconduct. The employee's actions must be so serious as to amount to a breach of the terms of the employment contract. What will amount to gross misconduct may vary with the type of employment involved, and each case must be decided on its own facts.

The employer's disciplinary code should set out the range of actions that will constitute gross misconduct (see page 191). If an employee is summarily dismissed and his actions do not amount to gross misconduct, the employee can make a claim for wrongful dismissal.

In the case below Lord Evershed stated that where an employer argues that a summary dismissal was justified, the question to ask is whether the employee had disregarded the essential conditions of his employment contract. If the employee has done so, the employer is entitled to dismiss him without notice.

Laws v London Chronicle (1959)

Ms Laws was employed as an assistant to an advertising manager, Mr Delderfield. She had only been working for the newspaper for three weeks when she was summarily dismissed. She and Delderfield had been in an editorial meeting. He left and when she began to follow him she was ordered not to leave by the managing director. She disobeyed this order and at that point was dismissed. She argued that this minor act of disobedience did not warrant summary dismissal, and that as she had received no notice of dismissal she had been wrongly dismissed.

Held (CA) Her actions were neither wilful nor particularly serious, and so did not amount to a breach of her employment contract. Consequently, she had been wrongfully dismissed and was able to make a claim for damages.

In *Jupiter General Insurance Co v Sheroff* (1937) the court stated that only in exceptional circumstances should an employer dismiss an employee following an isolated incident. The test to be applied must vary with the nature of the business and the position held by the employee. Consequently, each case must be decided on its own merits.

The following cases highlight situations in which employers have argued that they were able to lawfully dismiss an employee without notice because the employee had committed an act of gross misconduct.

See also: *Wilson v Racher* (1974), *Savage v British India Steam Navigation Co Ltd* (1930), *Neary v Dean of Westminster* (1999).

Denco v Joinson Ltd (1991)

Mr Denco was employed as a temporary supervisor on the nightshift at Joinson Ltd. He was also a shop steward. He was summarily dismissed when his employer realised that he had, without authorisation, accessed the company's computer system. He had gained access to confidential information, including amongst other things, customer lists and salary accounts.

Held His dismissal was lawful; he had deliberately used an unauthorised password in order to gain access to information that he knew was confidential. His actions amounted to gross misconduct and Joinson was entitled to summarily dismiss him.

Pepper v Webb (1969)

A head gardener was asked to plant some flowers. He was just about to leave work and said, 'I couldn't care less about your bloody greenhouse or your sodding garden'. He was summarily dismissed.

Held His dismissal was lawful; he had breached the terms of his employment contract by disobeying lawful orders. This, combined with other incidents of insolence had amounted to a breach of contract. Consequently, he was unable to make a claim for wrongful dismissal.

> **Sinclair v Neighbour** (1967)
>
> A manager took £15 from his employer's till, leaving an IOU. He intended to replace the money but knew that his employer would not have authorised him to take it. He was summarily dismissed and claimed that he had been wrongfully dismissed.
>
> **Held** Even though he had intended to, and in fact did repay the money, he had still acted in a dishonest manner. Consequently, his misconduct meant that his employer could lawfully dismiss him without notice.

MAKING A WRONGFUL DISMISSAL CLAIM TO A COURT OR EMPLOYMENT TRIBUNAL

Where an employee can show that his dismissal was wrongful for any of the reasons outlined above, he is entitled to make a claim for damages. The award of damages is intended to put the employee in the position that he would have been in had his employer not breached the terms of the employment contract.

In other words, the employee should receive an amount which reflects the pay or benefits lost due to not having been given any or adequate notice. This means that aside from pay, the court or tribunal will also take into account things such as private healthcare, pension entitlement and the use of company cars.

The employee may also seek an injunction to restrain an employer from breaching their contract of employment or a declaration outlining their contractual rights. These remedies are 'equitable' in that they are granted at the discretion of the court. They are seldom either sought or awarded. In rare cases an employee may seek a public law remedy by way of a judicial review. However, it should be noted that most cases concern claims for damages only.

Wrongful dismissal claims can be brought in either a court or tribunal. In the courts there is no limit to the amount of damages that can be claimed for a breach of contract. In the tribunal, however the damages are limited to a maximum of £25 000. (For a discussion on the role of the courts and tribunal jurisdiction, see pages 2 and 366–367 respectively.)

Claims must be made to the tribunal within three months of the dismissal. The employee has six years in which to make a claim to the court.

The amount of damages awarded may be reduced if the employee has done nothing to mitigate his loss since being dismissed. The burden of proof is on the employer to show that the employee has failed to take reasonable steps to mitigate their loss. If the employee finds another job before the date of the hearing his earnings can be deducted from the loss suffered. Deductions may also be made for any state benefits paid following the dismissal. This means that the employee may be penalised for not looking for another job. Damages are not normally awarded for loss of future job prospects or for injured feelings. In *Johnson v Unisys Ltd* (2001) it was held that damages cannot be awarded for any distress caused by the manner of the dismissal or the damage caused to the employee's reputation. See also: *Eastwood v Magnox Electric Plc* (2002), *McCabe v Cornwall County Council* (2003). Employees have to pay tax on sums awarded over £30 000.

Possible defences to claims of wrongful dismissal

An employer may be able to defend a claim for wrongful dismissal by either:

- showing that there was no dismissal, for example, that the employee resigned or that the contract was frustrated; or
- by showing that the dismissal was lawful because it followed an act of gross misconduct.

TERMINATION OF THE EMPLOYMENT CONTRACT IN CONTRAVENTION OF A STATUTE: UNFAIR DISMISSAL

At common law an employer can lawfully dismiss an employee by giving him the required notice of dismissal. The sacked employee can only take action against his employer if he can show that he has been wrongfully dismissed. The law on unfair dismissal seeks to remedy this situation by giving the employee the right only to be lawfully dismissed if that dismissal can be shown to be fair.

The right to claim unfair dismissal has existed since February 1972, when it was introduced in the now repealed Industrial Relations Act of 1971. An unfair dismissal claim is a statutory claim. Claims for unfair dismissal can only be made to the Employment Tribunal.

The right not to be unfairly dismissed

Section 94 of the Employment Rights Act 1996 states that:

An employee has the right not to be unfairly dismissed by his employer.

This is a general right which applies to all eligible employees. Here, the tribunal looks at the fairness or otherwise of the employer's reason for dismissing the employee. However, even where the employer has a fair reason to dismiss, it does not follow that the tribunal will find that the dismissal was fair.

The tribunal will also consider the manner in which the dismissal took place, looking at the response of the employer to the situation, and at whether there was any procedural unfairness.

THE EFFECTIVE DATE OF TERMINATION (EDT)

Before considering the fairness or otherwise of a dismissal, it is important to ascertain the date on which the employee's contract of employment was terminated. This date is referred to as the 'effective date of termination'. There are two reasons why an employee needs to be able to pinpoint the effective date of termination (EDT). These are:

- to show that the employee has the required one year continuity of service and so is 'qualified' to make the unfair dismissal claim;
- to show that the employee is making his tribunal claim within the three-month time limit.

> *Example*
> *Ann is dismissed on 1/12/05, she began work for her employer on 9/12/04. Her EDT is 1/12/05, meaning that she does not have one year of continuous service, and cannot make a claim for unfair dismissal.*
>
> *Philip is dismissed on 13/08/05; he began working for his employer on 18/12/03. His EDT is 13/08/05, meaning that he does have the required one year's service. However, he does not submit his tribunal claim until 13/12/05. He has not submitted form ET1 within the three-mo[nth] time limit (expired on 13/11/05) and so cannot make an unfair dismissal claim.*

The date that will stand as the EDT will differ with the circumstances of the dismissal. Section 97(1) of the Employment Rights Act 1996 lists the different circumstances that set the EDT as:

(a) in relation to an employee whose contract of employment is terminated by notice, whether given by his employer or by the employee, means the date on which the notice expires;

(b) in relation to an employee whose contract of employment is terminated without notice, means the date on which the termination takes effect; and

(c) in relation to an employee who is employed under a limited-term contract which terminates by virtue of the limiting event without being renewed under the same contract, means the date on which the termination takes effect.

Section 97(2) expands this to cover the situation where an employee gives the employer a counter-notice which is shorter than the employer's notice. In that case the EDT is the date on which the counter-notice expires. If an employee accepts wages in lieu of notice, then the EDT is the date on which the employee leaves and not the date on which the notice expires. If the employee is given contractual notice which is shorter than the statutory minimum to which he is entitled, the EDT is the date on which that statutory notice expires.

CONSTRUCTIVE DISMISSAL

This is the third form of dismissal outlined in s 95 of the Employment Rights Act 1996. Section 95(1)(c) of the Act states that an employer will be treated as dismissed by his employer if:

> **the employee terminates the contract under which he is employed (with or without notice) in circumstances in which he is entitled to terminate it without notice by reason of the employer's conduct.**

This covers the situation where an employer's conduct makes it impossible for the employee to continue working for him. In *France* v *Westminster City Council* (2002) EAT Mr Justice Wall stated that 'in relation to constructive dismissal, in broad terms, there have to be four elements. There has to be a breach of contract by the employer which can be either an actual breach or an anticipatory breach, and the breach must be sufficiently important to justify the employee resigning; or it can be one of the last of a series of incidents which justifies leaving. The two other conditions normally are that the employee must leave in response to the breach and not for some other unconnected reason, and finally, the employee must not take too long about it.'

When an employee resigns in these circumstances it may still constitute a dismissal for the purpose of statutory protection. However, the right to claim constructive dismissal only applies if the employee has one year's continuous service. It allows an employee who has resigned to make a claim to the tribunal where this would otherwise have been impossible. This is because a claim for ⸱ dismissal can only normally be made where the employee has been dismissed.

⸱e has merely resigned and was not constructively dismissed, the employee has ter-
act. As at common law, this prevents the employee from making any further claim.
he employer must amount to a serious breach of contract. In other words, an
aim constructive dismissal following some minor incident. Each case must be
acts. What might be a major incident in some cases may not be in others. A
of events can entitle an employee to resign and claim constructive dis-
n employee resigns following what he perceives to be the 'final straw'. In
ugh of Waltham Forest (2005) the Court of Appeal held that the 'final
to the employee's resignation must have contributed to the cumulative

breach of contract. The act itself may be relatively insignificant and not unreasonable but it must not be entirely trivial. The leading case on constructive dismissal is:

Western Excavating (EEC) v Sharp (1978)

Mr Sharp had been suspended from work without pay as part of Western Excavating's disciplinary process. He did not have much money and asked his employer for an advance on any wages that he might receive on his return to work. The employer refused and he resigned claiming constructive dismissal. He stated that the refusal had been so unreasonable as to force him to resign.

Held The employer's refusal had not been so serious as to breach the employment contract. Consequently, Sharp was not able to claim that he had been constructively dismissed.

In this case Lord Denning stated that: 'If the employer is guilty of conduct which is a significant breach, going to the root of the contract of employment which shows that the employer no longer intends to be bound by one or more of the essential terms, then the employee is entitled to treat himself as discharged from any further performance.' This had not been the case in *Sharp*. This principle was reaffirmed in the case of *Morrow* v *Safeway Stores Plc* (2002). Here, it was held that where an employer breaches an implied term 'by conduct likely to destroy or seriously damage' the employment relationship then the employee is entitled to resign and claim constructive dismissal.

In *Kerry Foods Ltd* v *Lynch* (2005) it was held that giving an employee notice of dismissal in accordance with the terms of his contract is not a breach of contract. Consequently, if an employee resigns (for no good reason) during that notice period he will not normally be able to claim constructive dismissal.

Courtaulds v Andrew (1979)

Mr Andrew was an experienced supervisor with an unblemished service record. During a heated argument his manager shouted, 'You can't do the bloody job anyway!' His comments were heard by some of Andrew's colleagues. Andrew walked out of the building and claimed that he had been constructively dismissed.

Held He had been constructively dismissed. The manager's words had breached the implied contractual term of mutual trust and confidence and meant that Andrew had acted reasonably in terminating his employment contract.

See also: *Weathersfield (Van and Truck) Rentals* v *Sargent* (1999), *Stanley Cole (Wainfleet) Ltd* v *Sheridan* (2003).

Employee must react quickly

In situations where an employer's actions breach the employment contract, the employee must remove himself from the workplace as soon as possible. If he remains at work for any length of time, he may be taken to have agreed, or acquiesced to the breach.

In **Sharp** (above) the Court of Appeal held that an employee is entitled to resign and claim constructive dismissal if:

- the employer's actions are regarded as a significant breach of contract;
- the employee responds quickly; and
- the employee's resignation obviously relates to his employer's conduct.

The employee has the choice of either acting quickly or accepting what has happened and continuing to work for the employer. The longer the employee delays in submitting his resignation, the more likely it is that it will be assumed that the employee has acquiesced.

Jeffrey v Laurence Scott & Electromotors Ltd (1977)

Mr Jeffrey waited $3\frac{1}{2}$ months after his employer's breach before resigning and claiming constructive dismissal.

Held There had been no constructive dismissal; Jeffrey had resigned. Having waited so long, he was taken to have acquiesced to his employer's actions.

Examples of conduct that will warrant constructive dismissal

There is no definitive list of the types of conduct that may or may not allow an employee to resign and claim constructive dismissal. Much depends on the facts in each case. The following list merely illustrates the types of conduct that have been held to be a significant breach of the employment contract:

- harassment;
- victimisation;
- verbal abuse;
- physical abuse;
- the unilateral changing of an employee's duties or status;
- demanding that an employee transfer or move to a new location;
- falsely accusing an employee of misconduct or incapability.

A constructive dismissal is not necessarily an unfair dismissal

Even if an employee can show that he was constructively dismissed, this does not mean that he is automatically entitled to any compensation. By showing that he was dismissed, the employee has merely jumped through the first hoop! There is no statutory remedy for constructive dismissal. The claim merely forms part of an action for either unfair dismissal or a redundancy payment.

The tribunal must still question whether or not the dismissal was fair. If it was, the employee is not entitled to any compensation. If it was unfair, the employee is entitled to the same compensation for the fact that he was forced to resign as he would have been had he been dismissed. In *Cape Industrial Services Ltd v Ambler* (2002) the EAT set out the issues to be taken into account in deciding whether a resignation amounts to constructive dismissal and if so whether that dismissal can be said to be unfair. The court stated that the following questions should be considered:

(a) What are the relevant term or terms of the contract that are said to have been breached?

(b) Is the party able to show that a breach or breaches of such terms have taken place?

(c) If this is the case, are those breaches/that breach a fundamental breach of the contract?

(d) If there has been a fundamental breach of contract did the employee resign in response to such a breach? If so, then were they constructively dismissed?

(e) If the employee was constructively dismissed as set out above then has the employer shown a potentially fair reason for the constructive dismissal? If they have not then the dismissal is unfair. If they are able to show a potentially fair reason then did the employer act reasonably or unreasonably in treating that reason as a sufficient reason to dismiss?

See also: *Lewis* v *Motorworld Garages Ltd* (1985), *Robinson* v *Crompton Parkinson Ltd* (1978), *Warnes* v *Cheriton Oddfellows Social Club* (1993), *Holland* v *Glendale Industries Ltd* (1998), *Horkulak* v *Cantor Fitzgerald International* (2004).

It should be noted that under the statutory grievance procedures the tribunal will not hear complaints concerning constructive dismissal unless the employee has first followed the appropriate minimum statutory grievance procedure. (See generally page 209.)

ELIGIBILITY TO MAKE AN UNFAIR DISMISSAL CLAIM

Not all employees are able to make a claim for unfair dismissal. Figure 6.2 highlights the stages involved in assessing whether or not an employee is eligible to make a claim. Each employee must be able to show that he meets this eligibility criteria before the tribunal will agree to hear the employee's case.

The applicant must be an employee

An applicant can only make an unfair dismissal claim if he can show that he was an employee at the time of the dismissal. In most cases this will not be in dispute, but note the discussion on employees and independent contractors above (pages 104–107).

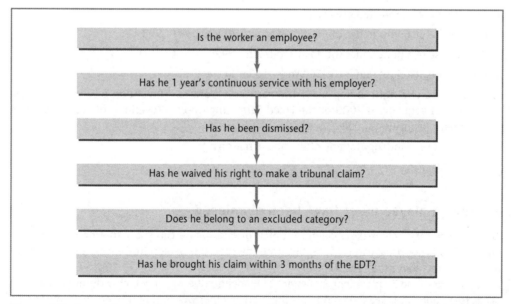

Figure 6.2 Assessing whether a dismissed employee can make a claim for unfair dismissal

6

Termination of the employment contract

● The employee must have at least one year's continuous service with the employer

It used to be the case that an employee had to have at least two years' continuous service with their employer in order to make a claim for unfair dismissal. This rule was changed by the Unfair Dismissal and Statement of Reasons for Dismissal (Variation of Qualifying Period) Order 1999. This order reduced the qualifying period to one year. Consequently, an employee now has to be able to show that they have at least one year's continuous service with their employer in order to be eligible to make an unfair dismissal claim. The reduction in the qualification period was welcomed but the period of one year could still be said to be too onerous. Employers may still dismiss an employee who has worked for less than one year knowing that they are unable to make a claim for unfair dismissal. If the employer gives the employee adequate notice prior to dismissal then they are also able to avoid a claim for wrongful dismissal.

Exceptions to the one-year qualification period

An employee does not have to have worked for his or her employer for one year in order to make an unfair dismissal claim relating to:

- trade union membership, non-membership or activities or where they are dismissed because they took protected industrial action;
- pregnancy, childbirth, maternity, maternity leave, parental leave or dependant care leave;
- health and safety;
- the assertion of a statutory right;
- some retail work where an employee is dismissed for refusing to work on a Sunday;
- a refusal to work hours in excess of the maximum which can be required under the Working Time Regulations;
- the performance of functions as a trustee of a pension scheme;
- the performance of functions as an employee representative;
- the making of a protected disclosure;
- the exercise of a right under the National Minimum Wage Act 1998;
- the exercise of a right under the Tax Credits Act 1999;
- the exercise of a right under the EC Works Council Directive;
- the exercise of a right under either the Part-time Workers (Prevention of Less Favourable Treatment) Regulations 2000 or the Fixed-Term Employees (Prevention of Less Favourable Treatment) Regulations 2002;
- selection for redundancy for any of the above reasons.

(See generally, page 142.)

● The employee must have been dismissed

An employee may only make a claim for unfair dismissal if he can show that he has been dismissed. This is not usually in dispute, but note the special provision in the case of constructive dismissal noted above (page 229).

Section 95 of the Employment Rights Act 1996 defines the way in which a dismissal may take place. (see page 223). See the comments there on whether words of abuse, etc. will constitute a dismissal. There must be an actual dismissal and not merely a threat that it might occur in the future.

In unfair dismissal actions the employer must be able to show that he had a reason to dismiss the employee, and that it was a fair reason. The employer's reason to dismiss must be based on something that he knew at the time, for example, that the employee had stolen money from the employer, and not on something that the employer finds out after the dismissal has taken place.

Retirement age

Note that the law on retirement ages changed on 1 October 2006. The Employment Equality (Age) Regulations came into force on that date. (see generally page 87). Prior to 1 October 2006 the general rule was that an employee dismissed after his 65th birthday was not entitled to bring a claim for unfair dismissal. As from 1 October 2006 there are no age limits attached to the right to claim unfair dismissal.

The employee must not have waived his right to make a tribunal claim

The general rule here is that an employee cannot normally agree to waive their right to make a claim for unfair dismissal. Any agreements that purport to waive this right are void. However, there are exceptions to this general rule. An employee will be unable to make an unfair dismissal claim in the tribunal where they have:

(a) agreed to submit their claim to arbitration under the Acas arbitration scheme (see page 254), or

(b) agreed to settle their claim in full by an agreement promoted by Acas, have

(c) entered into a compromise agreement which states that they will not pursue such a claim, or where they have

(d) excluded their rights under a dismissal procedure agreement.

At the time of writing there are no such dismissal procedure agreements in force.

The employee must not be from an excluded category

There are certain categories of employee which are excluded from the right to make an unfair dismissal claim. The excluded categories are:

- employees who have been employed for less than one month
- certain Crown employees
- members of the police force
- share fishermen/women
- employees working under illegal contracts.

At the present time members of the armed forces are also excluded from the right to claim unfair dismissal. However, provision has been made to extend this and other employment rights to members of the armed forces where they have 'availed themselves of the service redress procedures applicable to them'. This means that they must first have used the internal army procedure to make their complaint. Provision for the extension of this right is contained in s 192 of the Employment Rights Act 1996. However, at the time of writing there is no detail as to when this particular section will come into force.

Note that under the statutory disciplinary/grievance procedure rules employees cannot normally make a claim to the Employment Tribunal until they have participated in at least the minimum standard workplace disciplinary/grievance procedure (see generally page 211).

● Employee must make his claim within three months of the effective date of termination

An employee must make his unfair dismissal claim within three months of his effective date of termination. This time limit is strictly adhered to, and only in exceptional circumstances may it be extended. (For a discussion on making an application to the Employment Tribunal, see pages 368–369).

● REASONS WHY A PERSON MAY HAVE BEEN DISMISSED

After the employee has submitted his unfair dismissal claim, the tribunal will consider the reason why the employer decided to dismiss him. The employer will state the reason for dismissal on form ET3 (see page 383.)

In some cases it is automatically either unfair or fair to dismiss an employee. There is also a set of reasons for which it may potentially be fair to dismiss an employee. In these cases the tribunal must look at the circumstances surrounding the dismissal and decide on whether it was a fair dismissal in those circumstances. The tribunal takes two things into account:

- whether the employer's reaction was a reasonable response to the situation;
- whether the dismissal was carried out in a fair manner.

Figure 6.3 outlines the automatically unfair/fair and potentially fair reasons for dismissal.

This means that if the employee has been dismissed for an automatically unfair reason, he is entitled to compensation. If he was dismissed for one of the two fair reasons, he has no claim. However, in cases where the dismissal is potentially fair, this does not mean that the tribunal will find that it was a fair dismissal. The tribunal will consider both the substantive and procedural fairness of the decision to dismiss.

This chapter continues by outlining the automatically unfair and fair reasons to dismiss. The rules on potentially fair dismissals are then discussed.

● Automatically unfair reasons to dismiss

In the following situations it is automatically unfair for an employer to dismiss an employee:

- on the basis of sex/race/disability discrimination;
- on the grounds of pregnancy, or a reason connected to pregnancy etc.;
- for trade-union membership or refusal to belong to a trade union;
- in connection with the statutory recognition or derecognition of a union;
- following the taking of protected industrial action;
- on the basis that the employee has a spent conviction;
- because of a transfer of undertaking;
- for the assertion of a statutory right;
- for any reason connected to health and safety;

Automatically unfair reasons to dismiss

- on the basis of sex/race/disability discrimination;
- on grounds of pregnancy, or a reason connected to pregnancy including the taking of maternity, parental, adoption or paternity leave, or time off to look after dependants;
- for trade-union membership or refusal to belong to a trade union;
- in connection with the statutory recognition or derecognition of a union;
- following the taking of protected industrial action
- on the basis that the employee has a spent conviction;
- because of a transfer of undertaking;
- for the assertion of a statutory right;
- for any reason connected to health and safety;
- for the refusal to work Sundays by certain shop and betting workers;
- following the exercise of a right under the National Minimum Wage Act 1998;
- following the making of a protected disclosure;
- because an employee performs duties as a trustee of an occupational pension fund or as an employee representative;
- because an employee has acted as a worker's 'companion' at a disciplinary/grievance hearing;
- due to the taking of action in relation to a tax credit;
- on the basis that an employee has acted in connection with their rights under the Part-time Workers (Prevention of Less Favourable Treatment) Regulations 2000 and the Fixed-term Employees (Prevention of Less Favourable Treatment) Regulations 2002;
- following a request for flexible working arrangements;
- on the basis that an employee has acted in connection with their rights under the Transnational Information and Consultation of Employees Regulations 1999;
- following the exercise of a right under the Working Time Regulations.

Automatically fair reasons to dismiss

- national security;
- dismissal during an unofficial strike or industrial action.

Potentially fair reasons to dismiss

- capability/qualifications;
- conduct;
- redundancy;
- statutory illegality;
- some other substantial reason.

Figure 6.3 Automatically unfair, fair and potentially fair reasons for dismissal

- for the refusal to work Sundays by certain shop and betting workers;
- following the exercise of a right under the National Minimum Wage Act 1998;
- following the making of a protected disclosure;

6

Termination of the employment contract

- because an employee performs duties as a trustee of an occupational pension fund or as an employee representative;
- because an employee has acted as a worker's 'companion' at a disciplinary/grievance hearing;
- due to the taking of action in relation to a tax credit;
- on the basis that an employee has acted in connection with their rights under the Part-time Workers (Prevention of Less Favourable Treatment) Regulations 2000 and the Fixed-term Employees (Prevention of Less Favourable Treatment) Regulations 2002;
- following a request for flexible working arrangements;
- on the basis that an employee has acted in connection with their rights under the Information and Consultation of Employees Regulations 2004;
- following the exercise of a right under the Working Time Regulations;
- where an employer dismisses an employee without first going through the required disciplinary procedure.

Discrimination

It is automatically unfair for an employer to dismiss an employee on the basis of gender, race, or the fact that the employee is disabled. Note also, discrimination in relation to sexual orientation, religion or belief and age (as from 1 October 2006).

Pregnancy or a reason connected to pregnancy etc.

It is automatically unfair for an employer to dismiss an employee because she is pregnant, or for any other reason connected to her pregnancy. This is outlined in s 99 of the Employment Rights Act 1996, and discussed further at page 167. This includes the taking of ordinary/additional and compulsory maternity leave, parental leave, paternity leave and adoption leave. This is outlined in the Maternity and Parental Leave Regulations 1999 and the Paternity and Adoption Leave Regulations 2002. Under Section 57A of the Employment Rights Act 1996 it is also automatically unfair to dismiss where an employee has taken time off to look after dependants.

For trade-union membership or refusal to belong to a trade union

Section 152 of the Trade Union and Labour Relations (Consolidation) Act 1992 states that it is automatically unfair for an employer to dismiss an employee if the reason was that the employee:

- **(a)** was, or proposed to become, a member of an independent trade union, or
- **(b)** had taken part, or proposed to take part, in the activities of an independent trade union at an appropriate time, or
- **(c)** was not a member of any trade union, or of a particular trade union, or of one of a number of particular trade unions, or had refused, or proposed to refuse, to become or remain a member.

In connection with the statutory recognition or derecognition of a union

It is automatically unfair to dismiss an employee due to their involvement in a range of actions connected to statutory recognition or derecognition. This is outlined in Schedule 1A of the Trade Union and Labour Relations (Consolidation) Act 1992. 'Involvement' includes supporting or opposing an application for recognition, influencing others to support/not support such an application, voting in recognition ballots or influencing the way in which others vote in such ballots.

Following the taking of protected industrial action

In general terms it is automatically unfair for an employer to dismiss an employee due to the fact that he is taking or has taken protected industrial action. Schedule 5 of the Employment Relations Act 1999 inserted section 238A into the Trade Union and Labour Relations (Consolidation) Act 1992. This has since been amended by the Employment Relations Act 2004. This section states that the dismissal of an employee for taking lawfully organised, official industrial action is automatically unfair if:

- the dismissal takes place within 12 weeks of the employee commencing industrial action; or
- dismissal occurs after this 12-week period but the employee has returned to work before the end of the 12 weeks; or
- dismissal occurs after this period and the employee has not stopped taking protected industrial action before the end of that period, and the employer did not take all reasonable steps to resolve the dispute.

Should s 238A not apply, further protection is contained in s 238 itself. In cases involving official industrial action or a lock-out by the employer, s 238 of the 1992 Act states that the tribunal cannot hear unfair dismissal claims unless it can be shown:

(a) that one or more relevant employees of the same employer have not been dismissed, or

(b) that a relevant employee has, before the expiry of the period of three months beginning with the date of his dismissal, been offered re-engagement and that the complainant has not been offered re-engagement.

This covers the situation in which an employer may decide to dismiss only part of the workforce, or then re-engage certain employees but not others. In such cases the affected employees are able to make a claim to the Employment Tribunal. Relevant employees are those who were either taking industrial action or were directly interested in any dispute.

Spent convictions

It is automatically unfair for an employer to dismiss an employee on the basis that he has a conviction which is 'spent' under the Rehabilitation of Offenders Act 1974 (see further page 94).

Following a transfer of an undertaking

It is automatically unfair for an employer to dismiss an employee for any reason connected with the transfer of an undertaking. The Transfer of Undertakings (Protection of Employment) Regulations 1981 have recently been revoked by the Transfer of Undertakings (Protection of Employment) Regulations 2006. The new Regulations came into force on 6 April 2006. Regulation 7 of the Transfer of Undertakings (Protection of Employment) Regulations 2006 states that a dismissal is automatically unfair if the transfer, or a reason for the transfer, is the reason or principal reason given for the dismissal.

There is an exception under reg. 7(2) which states that a dismissal in such circumstances will not be automatically unfair where it was made for an 'economic, technical or organisational reason entailing changes in the workforce of either the transferor or the transferee before or after a relevant transfer'. Changes must have been made to the workforce of either the transferor or the transferee before or after the relevant transfer. If this is the case, the dismissal will be treated as being potentially fair under the heading of 'some other substantial reason'.

6

Termination of the employment contract

For the assertion of a statutory right

It is automatically unfair for an employer to dismiss an employee if the reason for that dismissal was the fact that the employee had brought proceedings to assert a statutory right, or alleged in good faith that the employer had infringed one of those rights. This is outlined in s 104 of the Employment Rights Act 1996.

Example of relevant statutory rights include:

- any right under the Employment Rights Act 1996 for which the remedy is a complaint to the employment tribunal;
- the right to ask an employer to stop deducting union subscriptions/contributions to a union political fund;
- the minimum notice requirements;
- the right to complain of action short of dismissal on grounds related to union membership or union activities;
- the right to time off for trade-union duties and activities;
- matters connected to the right to be accompanied at disciplinary and grievance hearings;
- rights under the Working Time Regulations;
- the right to be consulted under the terms of the Transfer of Undertakings (Protection of Employment) Regulations 2006.

For health and safety reasons

Section 100 of the Employment Rights Act 1996 states that it is automatically unfair to dismiss an employee for any reason relating to health and safety.

Section 100 of the 1996 Act outlines the situations in which a dismissal will be unfair. This is where the reason for the dismissal is that:

(a) the employee was carrying out, or proposed to carry out, activities in connection with prevention of health and safety risks at work, having been designated to do so by their employer; or

(b) the employee was a health and safety representative and performed, or proposed to perform, any function as such; or

(c) an employee brought to his employer's attention circumstances which he reasonably believed were harmful or potentially harmful to his health and safety; or

(d) where the employee believed that he was in imminent danger and left work refusing to return while the danger continued; or

(e) where an employee, believing that he was in imminent danger, took steps to protect himself or others from that danger.

For the refusal to work on a Sunday by certain shop/betting workers

It is automatically unfair to dismiss certain shop and betting workers who refuse to work on a Sunday (see pages 143–145).

Following the exercise of a right under the National Minimum Wage Act 1998

It is automatically unfair for an employer to dismiss an employee on the basis that they have exercised a right under the National Minimum Wage Act 1998. This is outlined in s 104A of the Employment Rights Act 1996 and covers situations such as where an employee requests that he be paid the national minimum wage, or where the employer has been prosecuted under the Act for failing to pay the national minimum wage. Dismissal due to either of these reasons is automatically unfair (see further pages 178–181).

Following the making of a protected disclosure

Under s 103A of the Employment Rights Act 1996 it is automatically unfair to dismiss an employee if the reason for their dismissal is that they made a protected disclosure. This is commonly known as 'whistleblowing' and is regulated by the Public Interest Disclosure Act 1998 (see further page 130).

Because an employee performs duties as a trustee of an occupational pension fund or as an employee representative

Under s 102 of the Employment Rights Act 1996 it is automatically unfair to dismiss an employee if the reason for that dismissal is that they have performed or proposed to perform any duty in their role as a pension fund trustee. Under s 103 of the 1996 Act it is automatically unfair to dismiss an employee if the reason for that dismissal was that they acted in their capacity as an employee representative. It is also automatically unfair to dismiss an employee because they become a candidate in an election seeking to appoint employee representatives.

Because an employee has acted as a worker's 'companion' at a disciplinary/grievance meeting

It is automatically unfair to dismiss an employee because they have acted as a 'companion' to a worker during a disciplinary or grievance meeting. (see notes above under 'assertion of a statutory right').

Due to the taking of action in relation to a tax credit

It is automatically unfair to dismiss an employee if the reason for that dismissal relates to a claim for tax credit under the Tax Credits Act 1999. This is outlined in s 104B of the Employment Rights Act 1996.

On the basis that an employee has acted in connection with their rights under the Part-time Workers (Prevention of Less Favourable Treatment) Regulations 2000 and the Fixed-term Employees (Prevention of Less Favourable Treatment) Regulations 2002

It is automatically unfair for an employer to dismiss an employee if the reason for that dismissal relates to the fact that an employee has asserted their rights under either of the above Regulations (see further page 95).

Following a request for flexible working arrangements

Under s 104C of the Employment Rights Act 1996 it is automatically unfair to dismiss an employee if the reason for that dismissal is that they have made a request for flexible working arrangements (see further page 145).

On the basis that an employee has acted in connection with their rights under the Information and Consultation of Employees Regulations 2004

These regulations implemented the European Works Council Directive 94/45/EC. It is automatically unfair to dismiss an employee if the reason for that dismissal was that they were a member of a special negotiating body, a member of a European Works Council, an information and consultation representative, or an election candidate aspiring to be a member or representative.

Following the exercise of a right under the Working Time Regulations

It is automatically unfair to dismiss an employee for asserting his rights under the Working Time Regulations (see notes above under 'assertion of a statutory right').

Where an employer dismisses an employee without first going through the required disciplinary procedure

It is automatically unfair to dismiss an employee without first going through the required statutory disciplinary procedure (see generally, Chapter 5).

Automatically fair reasons for dismissal

There are two situations in which it is automatically fair for an employer to dismiss an employee. These are reasons relating to:

- national security
- dismissal during an unofficial strike or industrial action.

National security

A government minister may issue a certificate stating that certain employment will be excluded from unfair dismissal protection. This is done in order to protect national security, and is used in those cases where an employee may breach national security by giving evidence in tribunal proceedings.

Dismissal during an unofficial strike or industrial action

Under s 237 of the Trade Union and Labour Relations (Consolidation) Act 1992 an employee has no right to complain of unfair dismissal if at the time of the dismissal he was taking part in an unofficial strike or industrial action. This means that an employee who is dismissed for taking unauthorised industrial action cannot make any claim following that dismissal.

In relation to the taking of official industrial action Schedule 5 of the Employment Relations Act 1999 inserted a new s 238A into the 1992 Act. This section was outlined above under the heading 'following the taking of protected industrial action.'

Potentially fair reasons for dismissal

There are five potentially fair reasons for dismissal. These are set out in s 98 of the Employment Rights Act 1996 and are:

- capability/qualifications
- conduct
- redundancy
- statutory illegality
- some other substantial reason.

The onus or burden of proof is on the employer to show the reason for the dismissal. If he fails to show that the dismissal took place due to events surrounding one of the above four categories, or for 'some other substantial reason' then the dismissal will be rendered unfair. If he is able to show that the reason to dismiss was in relation to capability/qualifications, conduct, redundancy, statutory illegality or for some other substantial reason then the dismissal will be potentially fair.

It should be noted, however, that just because an employer can show that he had a potentially fair reason to dismiss the employee, this does not mean that the dismissal will be automatically fair. The tribunal will consider the case in two stages. Figure 6.4 highlights these stages.

The employer may rely on more than one reason for the dismissal. The tribunal is only interested in the employer's reason at the time of dismissal. Consequently, any new information that the employer receives following the dismissal is irrelevant.

Stage one – the potentially fair reasons to dismiss

The potentially fair reasons for dismissal are found in s 98(1) and (2) of the Employment Rights Act 1996. In order to pass through stage one the employer must show that he had a potentially fair reason for dismissing the employee.

Capability/qualifications

Section 98(2)(a) states that a dismissal may be fair where it relates to 'the capability or qualifications of the employee for performing work of the kind which he was employed by the employer to do'.

This means that an employer may be able to fairly dismiss an employee because he lacks capability or the right qualifications for the job. Section 98(3) defines capability as being assessed by reference to 'skill, aptitude, health or any other physical or mental quality', and qualifications as meaning any degree, diploma or other academic, technical or professional qualification' relevant to the position which the employee held.

An incapable employee is one who is unable to perform his duties as required under the contract of employment. Examples would include an employee who makes lots of mistakes, is slow to complete his work, or who is unable to work with colleagues or deal with clients. An employee may also be incapable due to illness. Once the employer has shown that capability or qualifications was the reason for dismissal, the tribunal will go on to consider the reasonableness of that decision and the procedures followed.

Conduct

Section 98(2)(b) of the Employment Rights Act 1996 states that a dismissal may be fair if it 'relates to the conduct of the employee'. This may relate to an isolated incident or a series of events which has led to the dismissal. An employer may also dismiss an employee for an offence of gross misconduct. (For an example of the types of conduct that may constitute gross misconduct, see page 193). This is the most commonly used reason for dismissal. Once the employer shows that conduct was the reason for dismissal, the tribunal will go on to look at the reasonableness of the decision to dismiss and at the procedures that were followed.

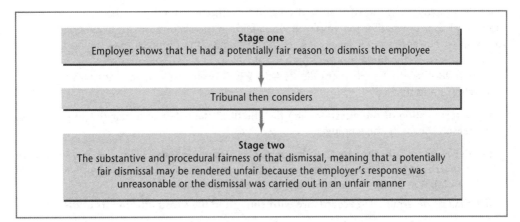

Figure 6.4 The two stages of consideration of a potentially fair reason for dismissal

Redundancy

Section 98(2)(c) of the Employment Rights Act 1996 states that a dismissal may be fair if 'the employee was redundant'. Here, the employer has to show that redundancy was the reason for the dismissal and that that redundancy was conducted fairly. (For a discussion on the definition of redundancy, see page 267). Once the employer shows that the redundancy was the reason for dismissal, the tribunal will go on to look at the reasonableness of the decision to dismiss and at the procedures that were followed.

Statutory illegality

Section 98(2)(d) of the Employment Rights Act 1996 states that a dismissal may be fair if 'the employee could not continue to work in the position in which he held without contravention (either on his part or on that of his employer) of a duty or restriction imposed by or under an enactment'.

This means that an employer may fairly dismiss an employee if by continuing to employ him, either the employee or the employer will be committing an offence.

Examples

- *Continuing to employ someone whose work permit has expired.*
- *Continuing to allow a banned driver to work as a lorry driver.*

Some other substantial reason

Section 98(1)(b) of the Employment Rights Act 1996 states that a dismissal may be fair 'for some other substantial reason'. This is a 'catch all' provision and there is no exhaustive list of the types of situation that may or may not constitute 'some other substantial reason' to dismiss.

Examples

Situations that have been held to be 'some other substantial reason' to dismiss are:

- *a refusal to accept a change in the terms of an employment contract relating to hours, pay, or duties;*
- *a business reorganisation where the workload remains the same, but certain employees are deemed to be unsuitable for the new requirements of the business;*
- *the pressure from a third party to dismiss.*

Stage two - the fairness of the dismissal - reasonable range of responses and procedural fairness

Once the employer has shown that he dismissed the employee for a potentially fair reason, the tribunal will look at whether the employer acted fairly in the circumstances. Consequently, even where an employer has a potentially fair reason to dismiss, the dismissal may still be held to be unfair. At this stage the burden of proof is neutral.

Section 98(4) of the Employment Rights Act 1996 sets out the general principles of fairness. This section states that:

the determination of the question whether the dismissal is fair or unfair (having regard to the reason shown by the employer):

(a) depends on whether in the circumstances (including the size and administrative resources of the employer's business) the employer acted reasonably or unreasonably in treating it as a sufficient reason for dismissing the employee, and

(b) shall be determined in accordance with equity and the substantial merits of the case.

The questions asked by the tribunal are:

- Did the employer's decision to dismiss fall within the range of responses that would have been made by a reasonable employer?
- Were procedures followed fairly?

The range of reasonable responses

In *Iceland Frozen Foods* v *Jones* (1982) the Employment Appeal Tribunal laid down general principles on what is and is not a 'reasonable response'.

Jones worked as a night-shift foreman. He was dismissed when he forgot to lock up the premises at the end of his shift. He claimed that he had been unfairly dismissed. The tribunal of first instance did not consider the test for unfairness from s 98(4) and so on appeal the EAT held that Jones's dismissal had been unfair.

The EAT went on to state that the correct approach for tribunals to adopt when dealing with the question of fair dismissal under s 98(4) is as follows:

(a) the tribunal should begin by looking at the wording of s 98(4);

(b) in applying this section, the tribunal must consider the reasonableness of the employer's conduct, not simply whether the tribunal considers the dismissal to be fair;

(c) in judging the reasonableness or otherwise of the employer's conduct, the tribunal must not substitute its own decision as to what was the right course of action for the employer to take;

(d) in many cases there is a band of reasonable responses to the employee's conduct, within which one employer might reasonably take one view, another quite reasonably take another;

(e) the function of the tribunal is to determine whether in the particular circumstances of each case the decision to dismiss the employee fell within the band of reasonable responses which a reasonable employer might have adopted.

This approach was questioned in the cases of *Haddon* v *Van den Bergh Foods Ltd* (1999) and *Wilson* v *Ethicon Ltd* (2000). However the approach from *Iceland Frozen Foods* was reaffirmed in the joint appeal hearings in the cases of *Post Office* v *Foley* (2000) and *HSBC (formerly Midland) Bank Plc* v *Madden* (2000). Here it was held that the tribunal must not substitute its own view as to whether the employer had acted reasonably, but rather must decide whether the view taken by the employers at the time of dismissal was reasonable.

In the recent case of *J Sainsbury Plc* v *Hitt* (2003) the court held that the range of reasonable response test also applies to determine whether any investigations carried out by the employer prior to dismissal were reasonable in all the circumstances.

There are no set 'reasonable responses'. What may be reasonable in one set of circumstances may not be in another. The employer should consider the particular employee involved looking at his past service record and how he has dealt with similar cases in the past. If their dismissal falls within the band of reasonable responses, it is fair; if the dismissal falls outside the band, it is unfair. The ultimate test is whether, by the standard of a reasonable employer, the employer acted reasonably in treating the reason shown as a sufficient reason to dismiss.

Procedural unfairness

Even where the employer can show that he has a potentially fair reason to dismiss and that the decision to dismiss was reasonable in the circumstances, the employer will have to show that he implemented at least statutory minimum disciplinary procedures.

For a general discussion on the use of disciplinary procedures, see Chapter 5. Note also that as from 1 October 2004 employers have been required to implement at least minimum statutory disciplinary procedures. If an employer fails to do this prior to dismissal, that dismissal will normally be rendered automatically unfair.

The employer should ensure that, before dismissing an employee, he has:

- set out the issues involved in writing;
- held a fair disciplinary meeting;
- allowed the employee to appeal against any decision to dismiss.

Employees under threat of disciplinary action should be given the chance to defend any allegations at the disciplinary meeting. In *Clark v Civil Aviation Authority* (1991) the EAT stated that a hearing should be conducted in the following way. The employer should:

- explain the purpose of the meeting;
- identify those present;
- if appropriate arrange representation;
- inform the employee of the allegations;
- indicate the evidence against the employee;
- give the employee the chance to defend the allegations.

Note that there is both a standard and a modified procedure. Note also that employees have a statutory right to be accompanied at disciplinary and grievance meetings (see further page 207).

The rules on procedural unfairness in unfair dismissal cases were changed by s 34 of the Employment Act 2002. (The statutory discipline and grievance procedure rules introduced by the 2002 Act are discussed in more detail at page 209). Section 34 of the 2002 Act introduced a new Section 98A(2) into the Employment Rights Act 1996. Prior to these changes the tribunal had considered procedural fairness in relation to unfair dismissal. See further, *Polkey v A E Dayton Services Ltd* (1987).

Prior to the introduction of the minimum statutory discipline and grievance procedures in 2004 the tribunal considered whether the employer had implemented their disciplinary procedures fairly prior to dismissal. Under the new statutory procedures only a failure to adhere to at least the minimum standard of disciplinary procedure will render a dismissal automatically unfair.

Section 98A(1) of the Employment Rights Act 1996 states that if an employee is dismissed in a situation where their employer has failed to use the minimum statutory disciplinary procedure then that dismissal will be automatically unfair '*if the non-compliance of the procedure is wholly or mainly attributable to failure by the employer to comply with its requirements*'.

However, provided that the employer has followed the minimum statutory procedure, and the dismissal is otherwise found to be fair, the tribunal will not now consider other procedural shortcomings. The situation now is that whilst employers will always have to follow the minimum statutory procedures they will no longer be penalised for not following their own additional procedures. This is the case where following any additional procedures would have made no difference to the decision to dismiss. Section 98A(2) of the 1996 Act states that failure by an employer to follow a procedure in relation to the dismissal of an employee shall not be regarded for the purposes of s 98(4) as by itself making the employer's action unreasonable if 'he shows that he would have decided to dismiss the employee if he had followed the procedure'.

Section 98A(2) reintroduced the 'no difference' rule from the case of *British Labour Pump Co Ltd v Byrne* (1979). In essence this section reversed the previous ruling in *Polkey* under which the tribunal had looked at the reasonableness or otherwise of the employer's behaviour. Under the 'no difference' rule, if the employer has followed the statutory minimum disciplinary procedure but has not followed their own internal procedures the dismissal may not be found to be unfair on procedural grounds if the employer can satisfy the tribunal that following internal procedures would have made no difference to the decision to dismiss. As this is a relatively recent development it remains to be seen what impact the new statutory procedures and the move away from the decision in **Polkey** has on future tribunal reasoning and decisions. (See generally, Chapter 5.)

FAIRNESS IN RELATION TO THE FIVE POTENTIALLY FAIR REASONS

Having set out the fact that the tribunal will be looking for a reasonable response to the situation and the use of at least statutory minimum disciplinary procedures, it is useful to look again at the five potentially fair reasons for dismissal. This section considers the particular issues that the tribunal may have to deal with in relation to each potentially fair reason.

Capability/qualifications

In cases of capability the employer should consider taking other less severe action before either disciplining or dismissing an employee. For example, the employer could implement an appraisal system and training to give the employee the opportunity to improve his skills. In doing so, the employee should be told that if his work does not improve, he will be disciplined.

In *James* v *Waltham Holy Cross UDC* (1973) it was held that an employer should not dismiss an employee on the basis that he is incapable of doing his job without first telling him what he is doing wrong and giving him the opportunity to improve.

If the employer dismisses the employee, he must be able to show that the employee's incompetence was the reason for the dismissal. In most cases there will have been a series of events which led the employer to dismiss. In some cases, however, one serious incident may warrant instant dismissal.

Alidair v Taylor (1978)

An airline dismissed a pilot after he endangered lives by landing a plane in a dangerous manner.

Held His subsequent dismissal was fair. His employer had clearly lost all confidence in his capability as a pilot.

Davison v Kent Meters Ltd (1975)

An employee was dismissed for wrongly assembling 500 components. She said that she had merely been following instructions from her supervisor. He gave evidence stating that he had never shown her how to assemble the components. Her employer alleged that she was incapable of doing her job properly.

Held Her dismissal was unfair; she could not be expected to be able to assemble the components in a specific way if she had not received any instructions.

Where the employer dismisses an employee because of a lack of qualifications, those qualifications must relate to the job that the employee does. For example, whilst it may be fair to dismiss a driver who loses his driving licence, it would not be fair to dismiss a secretary for the same reason.

Blackman v Post Office (1974)

Mr Blackman, a telegraph officer was required to pass an aptitude test. He sat and failed the test three times. This was the maximum number of attempts permitted. He was dismissed.

Held His dismissal was fair; he had to have passed the aptitude test to be allowed to continue in his present position.

Where an employer dismisses an employee who is ill on the grounds of capability, he should have conducted a thorough investigation into the circumstances of the illness before making the decision to dismiss. He should consult with the employee and consider alternatives such as the issue of a warning before considering dismissal.

General guidelines on dealing with sickness dismissals have been laid down in the cases of *Spencer* v *Paragon Wallpapers Ltd* (1977), and *East Lindsey Council* v *Daubney* (1977).

Spencer v Paragon Wallpapers Ltd (1977)

Mr Spencer suffered from back pain. He had been off work for two months. Paragon Wallpapers Ltd asked his doctor (with his permission) how long it would be before he could return to work. The doctor said that he would be unable to return for at least 4–6 weeks. Spencer was dismissed.

Held The dismissal was fair; the length of time that Spencer would be away from work meant that his employers would be forced to find another worker.

In this case the EAT held that in cases where an employee is dismissed for ill health, the tribunal should question whether, in the circumstances, the employer should have been expected to wait any longer for the return of the employee. If the employer should have given the employee more time to recover, the dismissal will be unfair.

The EAT went on to list those factors that should be taken into account in cases of ill health. Note that these resemble the factors from *Egg Stores* discussed above (page 221).

The tribunal should take into account:

- the nature of the illness;
- the length of time that the employee is likely to be absent from work;
- the need for the employer to have the work done;
- the type of work that the employee was employed to do;
- the circumstances of the case.

In *Hart* v *AR Marshall & Sons Ltd* (1978) it was held that the question to ask was: 'Had the time arrived when the employer could no longer reasonably be expected to keep the absent employee's post open for him?'

East Lindsey District Council v Daubney (1977)

Mr Daubney was dismissed on grounds of ill health. The council had decided to dismiss him after reading a report drafted by the District community physician. The physician had been asked to give an opinion on whether or not Daubney should take early retirement. The report had stated that he should.

Held (EAT) Daubney's dismissal was unfair. The Council had decided to dismiss him on the basis of a report written by its own medical adviser. Daubney was given no opportunity to look at the report, or to provide the Council with a medical opinion from another doctor. He had been given no chance to speak out on the fact that he was to be dismissed. He should have been consulted prior to any decision being made.

The EAT went on to state that it is very important to discuss the situation with the employee, consulting him on what may or may not happen in the future. Only in wholly exceptional circumstances will a failure to consult be justified.

The employer should try to help the employee, and if possible work out a timescale after which he can return to work. Only if this is impossible should the employer consider dismissal.

If the employer is dealing with an employee who is absent from work frequently, but only for a few days at a time, the employer needs to make the employee aware of the fact that he is expected to attend work on a regular basis. The employee should then be given a reasonable opportunity to improve his attendance before any disciplinary action is taken.

International Sport Ltd v *Thompson* (1980)

Ms Thompson was absent from work for approximately one week in every month. All of her absences were medically certified. She suffered from various illnesses including dizzy spells, anxiety, bronchitis, a viral infection, cystitis, arthritis of the left knee, dyspepsia and flatulence. Her employer gave her a series of warnings and explained that if her attendance did not improve she would be dismissed. She was eventually given a final warning and when the situation did not improve she was dismissed.

Held There was no point in asking Thompson to be examined by the company's medical adviser or to consult her further. The employer had done all that he could to warn her that her attendance had to improve. Consequently, her dismissal was held to be fair.

See also: *Eclipse Blinds Ltd* v *Wright* (1992), *Links & Co Ltd* v *Rose* (1991), *Mitchell* v *Arkwood Plastics (Engineering) Ltd* (1993).

Conduct

In dealing with cases of misconduct the employer must show that he honestly believed that the employee was guilty of an offence. The employer must also be able to show that he had reasonable grounds for believing this to be the case and that the decision to dismiss was made after a thorough investigation of allegations made against the employee. Cases on 'misconduct' have included issues such as dishonesty, theft, fighting at work, drug-taking, refusing to obey lawful orders, drinking alcohol while at work and the personal use of workplace telephones or the Internet.

Guidelines on how to deal with misconduct dismissals were set down in the case of *British Homes Stores Ltd* below.

The EAT went on to state that in order for a conduct dismissal to be fair, the employer must establish that:

- he genuinely believed that the employee had committed an act of misconduct;
- he had reasonable grounds for that belief; and
- he had carried out an investigation which was reasonable in the circumstances before making any decision to dismiss.

6

Termination of the employment contract

British Home Stores Ltd v Burchell (1980)

Ms Burchell was dismissed for allegedly being involved with a group of fellow employees who were making dishonest staff purchases. BHS had begun an investigation into the thefts and Burchell had been implicated during the investigation by one of her colleagues. The tribunal held that her dismissal was fair. Burchell appealed arguing that BHS had not been able to prove that she was in any way linked to the offences, meaning that her dismissal was unfair.

Held (EAT) Her dismissal was fair. BHS only had to show that it had a reasonable suspicion for believing that she was involved in the thefts.

In *ASDA Stores v Malyn* (2001) the EAT stated that if an employer's disciplinary code states that a particular action will amount to gross misconduct and thus render the employee liable to dismissal then that dismissal will be potentially fair. This is the case if:

(a) it would be thought to be reasonable in the particular industry concerned to specify the act or omission in question as gross misconduct, and

(b) the employer has taken proper steps to bring the code to the employee's attention, ensuring that the employee had access to the code, and

(c) that it could be said that the employee knew that his actions were against the policy outlined in the code.

In *Wade v AHH Pharmaceuticals Ltd* (2002) the dismissal of a driver was held to be fair. His employer had dismissed him for gross misconduct when he left a van containing controlled drugs unsecured while making a delivery. He had been given express instructions not to do this and was aware that to do so would be gross misconduct.

An employer must be able to show that he reasonably believed that the employee was guilty of a misconduct offence. The employer must also have conducted proper disciplinary procedures. The employer should be consistent in his treatment of misconduct dismissals.

John Lewis Plc v Coyne (2001)

Mrs Coyne had worked for John Lewis Plc for almost 14 years. Up until the time she was dismissed she had an unblemished work record. She was dismissed because it was found that she had made 111 personal telephone calls from the company's telephone over a one-year period. During this time she had suffered a personal crisis and often had to call home. In total it was found that the calls had cost the company £37.76. Mrs Coyne had offered to repay this money. The John Lewis disciplinary code had stated that employees were not allowed to use work telephones for personal calls. Before any real investigation of the complaint took place Mrs Coyne was dismissed.

Held (EAT) Her dismissal was unfair. John Lewis had breached the Acas code of practice on discipline; they had not thoroughly investigated the issues surrounding the making of the calls or held meetings in the appropriate manner.

See also: *Conlin v United Distillers* (1994), *Connely v Liverpool Corporation* (1974), *Singh v London County Bus Services Ltd* (1976), *O'Flynn v Airlinks The Airport Coach Company Ltd* (2002), *London Borough of Hillingdon v Thomas* (2002), *Johnson v Scottish & Newcastle Plc* (2002), *Tesco Stores Ltd v Pryke* (2005) EAT.

Redundancy

In some cases an employer's decision to make an employee redundant will be automatically unfair. This is where the decision is discriminatory, relates to a health and safety, pregnancy or the assertion of a statutory right. These reasons mirror those making it automatically unfair to dismiss an employee.

Where an employer decides to make some of his employees redundant, he must select those employees in a fair manner. In order to show that the dismissal was fair the employer must be able to show that:

- the selection criteria were objectively justified and applied fairly;
- a proper individual and collective consultation was conducted before making any employee redundant;
- he tried to find suitable alternative work for any employee who was to be made redundant.

The leading case on redundancy fairness is *Williams v Compair Maxam Ltd*, outlined below.

Williams v Compair Maxam Ltd (1982)

Compair Maxam was in financial trouble. The company decided that, for the business to survive, it would have to make some employees redundant. It told the workplace trade union that redundancies would be necessary but failed to enter into any consultation with either the union or the individuals likely to be affected. The employees were given no warning of their dismissal.

Held (EAT) As no consultation had taken place, the dismissals were unfair.

The EAT went on to state that the question to ask was whether a reasonable employer would have adopted those tactics in the circumstances. The EAT concluded by setting down guidelines to be followed by employers in redundancy situations stating that:

It is a generally accepted view in industrial relations that, in cases where employees are represented by an independent recognised trade union, that reasonable employers will seek to act in accordance with the following principles.

1 The employer will seek to give as much warning as possible of impending redundancies so as to enable the union and employees who may be affected to take early steps to inform themselves of the relevant facts, consider possible alternative solutions and, if necessary, find alternative employment in the business or elsewhere.

2 The employer will consult with the union as to the best means by which the desired management result can be achieved fairly, and with as little hardship to the employees as possible. In particular, the employer will seek to agree with the union the criteria to be applied in selecting the employees to be made redundant and ensure that selection has been made in accordance with that criteria.

3 Whether or not an agreement as to the criteria to be adopted has been agreed with the union, the employer will seek to establish criteria for selection ... that can be objectively checked against such things as an employee's attendance record, their efficiency, experience, and length of service.

4 The employer will seek to ensure that the selection is made fairly in accordance with the established criteria. He will consider any representations the union may make as to such

selection and will seek to see whether, instead of dismissing an employee, he is able to offer them suitable alternative employment.

See also: *Polkey* v *A E Dayton Services* (1987), *Ferguson and others* v *Prestwick Circuits Ltd* (1992), *Heron* v *Citylink-Nottingham* (1993), *Mugford* v *Midland Bank plc* (1997), *Alstom Traction Ltd* v *Stephen Birkenhead & ors* (2002).

● Statutory illegality

When considering whether a dismissal on the ground of statutory illegality is fair, the tribunal should consider whether the employer could have avoided dismissal by finding alternative work for the employee. Whether this would be a reasonable response to the situation will differ with the circumstances of the case, and whether the 'illegality' is a temporary or permanent reason not to continue to employ.

Appleyard v *Smith (Hull) Ltd* (1972)

Mr Appleyard, a mechanic who worked in a small garage, was banned from driving. He spent most of his time road-testing vehicles. Following the ban, his employer was unable to find sufficient work for him to do that would not involve driving. His employer dismissed him, stating that to continue to employ him in his normal capacity would be illegal.

Held His dismissal was fair; the garage owner should not be expected to continue to employ Appleyard where to do so would cause him to break the law.

In this case it was stated that an employer must show that the prohibited part of the employee's job forms a significant part of his daily duties.

● Some other substantial reason

When considering whether an employee has been dismissed fairly for some other substantial reason, the tribunal should first consider the employer's reason for dismissal. The employer must then be able to show that their decision to dismiss was a reasonable response to the situation and that the dismissal was conducted in a fair manner.

Many of the acceptable reasons relate to the business needs of the employer. An employer may dismiss an employee who refuses to accept organisational change. In many cases the needs of the business will be the most important consideration. The employer merely has to show that there is a good business reason for the reorganisation and that it will result in a strengthening of the business.

Hollister v *National Farmers' Union* (1979)

The National Farmers' Union (NFU) reorganised its insurance business, changing the terms of its contracts of employment. The main changes made affected those employees who sold insurance. One such employee refused to accept the changes and was dismissed. The NFU stated that it had dismissed the employee because he had failed to agree to changes which would benefit the running of the business.

Held The dismissal was fair; all that was required was a 'good business reason' to dismiss.

In this case the Court of Appeal stated that in deciding whether such dismissals were fair, the tribunal only had to ask 'whether the reorganisation was such that the only sensible thing to do was terminate the employee's contract unless they would agree to a new arrangement'.

In *Ellis* v *Brighton Co-op* (1976) it was said that the test to be used was whether, if the changes were not implemented, the 'whole business would come to a standstill'.

In *McGibbon and McCoy* v *OIL* (1995) the EAT stated that it was fair for the tribunal to carry out a balancing exercise, whereby the disadvantages to the employee and the advantages to the employer in the new offer of contracts have to be weighed up.

St John of God (Care Services) Ltd v Brook (1992)

A charity-run hospital was facing a financial crisis and was faced with possible closure. The management offered new contracts of employment to the staff. However, the new contractual terms were inferior to those in their original contracts. Out of 170 employees, 30 refused to accept the new terms and were dismissed.

Held (EAT) The dismissals were fair. The hospital had behaved reasonably in offering the new contracts and had showed a business need for the changes.

A dismissal arising from a change in terms is more likely to be fair if:

- many or all of the other employees have agreed to the change;
- the union has agreed to the change; or
- the change is of a trivial nature.

An employer may dismiss for 'some other substantial reason' where pressure is put upon the employer to do so by a third party. In some cases this may be the remainder of the workforce who find it unbearable to work with a certain colleague. The pressure to dismiss may also come from a customer or client who feels that he cannot deal with a particular employee. In such cases it may be fair for an employer to dismiss an employee even though the employee has done nothing wrong.

Dobie v Burns International Security Services (UK) Ltd (1995)

Mr Dobie was employed by a security company which provided the security services at Liverpool airport. He was based at the airport as a security officer. Two separate security incidents took place at the airport. He was not to blame for either of them. Following these incidents the airport refused to have him working there. The airport told Burns to remove him from the site. Burns offered Dobie alternative work but at a lower rate of pay. He refused this work and was dismissed.

Held (CA) His dismissal was fair. His employers had been pressurised into moving him from his original job by a third party. The employers had done all they could to resolve the situation by offering him alternative work.

In *Treganowan* v *Robert Knee & Co Ltd* (1975) an employee was fairly dismissed for some other substantial reason following the refusal of her colleagues to work with her because of her insistent boasting about her sexual antics with her 'toy-boy'.

See also: *Copsey* v *WWB Devon Clays Ltd* (2005), *Willow Oak Developments Ltd T/A Windsor Recruitment* v *Silverwood* (2006).

WRITTEN REASONS FOR DISMISSAL

Under s 92 of the Employment Rights Act 1996 where an employee has one year's continuous service with his employer, he can demand written reasons outlining why he was dismissed. The employee must request these reasons. The employer must provide the written reasons within 14 days of that request. If an employer unreasonably refuses to provide written reasons or where the employer provides incomplete or false reasons, the employee may make a complaint to the Employment Tribunal.

THE ACAS ARBITRATION SCHEME

The Acas arbitration scheme initially applied only to claims involving allegations of unfair dismissal. In April 2003 the scheme was extended to cover cases involving claims for flexible working arrangements. Here, however, we are concerned with the scheme only as it relates to claims of unfair dismissal. Section 212A of the Trade Union and Labour Relations (Consolidation) Act 1992 enabled Acas to set up the scheme. It was set up under ss 7 and 8 of the Employment Rights (Dispute Resolution) Act 1998 and is regulated by the Acas Arbitration Scheme (Great Britain) Order 2004. The scheme became operational on 21 May 2001.

The scheme is a means by which ex-employees who believe that they have been unfairly dismissed may voluntarily submit their case to arbitration rather than to an employment tribunal. The scheme was set up in an attempt to reduce the number of unfair dismissal claims made to the tribunal. It was thought that there was a need for an alternative to the tribunal, a forum that was less legalistic and which meant that claims could be dealt with quickly.

Types of claim covered by the scheme

The scheme is designed for straightforward cases of alleged unfair dismissal. The arbitrator is not able to deal with jurisdictional issues such as, for example, whether or not the person bringing the claim was an employee, whether there has been a dismissal, or whether the person has the requisite period of continuous employment. The scheme is not designed to deal with cases involving questions concerning European law. Acas recruit arbitrators to hear cases. These people are chosen for their knowledge and experience of industrial relations but are not employed directly by Acas. They are employed on a case by case basis.

Agreeing to go to arbitration

An ex-employee or their previous employer cannot be forced to have their case dealt with at arbitration. Both parties must agree to use arbitration. They must sign a written agreement stating that they are willing for the dispute to be settled at an arbitration hearing. Once they agree to submit the case to arbitration it can no longer be dealt with by the Employment Tribunal. It is important that both parties realise this before deciding to opt for arbitration. The agreement must be reached with the assistance of an Acas conciliator or through a compromise agreement.

Both parties must sign a waiver stating that they agree to waive certain rights that they would have had had the case gone to a tribunal. These include the right to a public hearing or to cross-examine witnesses. The ex-employee can withdraw from the procedure at any time but will then be unable to take their claim to the employment tribunal. Once an employer has agreed to go to arbitration they cannot change their minds and ask for the case to be dealt with in the tribunal. The parties are, however, able to settle their case prior to any arbitration hearing.

The arbitration hearing

Once the parties have informed Acas that they wish the case to be dealt with by arbitration a hearing date is set. The hearing is normally held at a convenient location for both parties and usually at a neutral venue. This could be, for example, at an Acas office or local hotel. The hearing can take place at the employee's former workplace with both his and his ex-employer's agreement. At the hearing both the ex-employee and his employer are able to put their case to the arbitrator. Either side may take representation with them to the hearing but no special treatment is given to legal representatives. Having heard the evidence and questioned any witnesses, the arbitrator will decide whether the dismissal was fair or unfair. In making that decision the arbitrator will take the Acas code on '*Disciplinary and Grievance Procedures*' into account along with the Acas advisory handbook on *Discipline and Grievances at Work*. Whether the requirements of the minimum standard of disciplinary procedures have been followed will also be addressed. They will have regard to the general principles of fairness and good conduct in employment.

Awards

The arbitrator is able to make orders for reinstatement, re-engagement or compensation in the same way as the employment tribunal. The amount of compensation awarded will depend on what is 'just and equitable' in the circumstances. The arbitrator must take into account the award limits set in the tribunal. The decision of the arbitrator is binding. There is no right to appeal unless there has been a serious irregularity. There is also a very narrow avenue of appeal relating to European law and matters under the Human Rights Act 1998.

Both the details of arbitration hearings and awards are private and confidential. For this reason there has been little written on the success or otherwise of the scheme to date. Given that it is still a relatively new concept it will be some time before its effectiveness or otherwise can be properly assessed. However, statistics contained in the Acas annual report relating to 2005/6 state that only 6 cases had been dealt with under the scheme.

MAKING AN UNFAIR DISMISSAL CLAIM TO THE EMPLOYMENT TRIBUNAL

An employee who thinks that he has been unfairly dismissed may make a complaint to the Employment Tribunal. The claim must be made within three months of his effective date of termination, or within six months for cases involving industrial action dismissals.

The three-month time limit may also be extended to six months if an employee has reasonable grounds (when the normal three-month period expires) for believing that a statutory or contractual disciplinary procedure was still ongoing. Secondly, it may be extended to six months in constructive unfair dismissal cases. In such situations the employee must comply with statutory grievance procedures and in doing so benefits from an automatic extension to the normal three-month time limit. These procedural extensions are outlined in the Employment Act 2002 (Dispute Resolution) Regulations 2004 and came into force on 1 October 2004.

Overlap with wrongful dismissal claims

In some cases the employee may allege that he has been both wrongly and unfairly dismissed. In such situations the dismissed employee must decide on whether it will be more advantageous to bring a claim in a court or in a tribunal. In *Shove* v *Downs Surgical plc* (see page 226), as Shove was a high-earning employee, it was in his best interests to bring a claim for wrongful dismissal in the courts.

Similarly, in *Hopkins v Norcros* (1992) Mr Hopkins' contract gave him the right to remain in work until he was 60. He was dismissed without notice two years early and sued in a claim for wrongful dismissal. He was awarded £99 604 in lost earnings. Neither of these employees would have received anything resembling these amounts in tribunal compensation.

Where an employee brings a claim for both wrongful and unfair dismissal, he is not able to receive two amounts of money. Any payments which are made for wrongful dismissal should be accounted for and deducted from any unfair dismissal compensation.

Burden of proof

There are three stages in an unfair dismissal action. The burden of proving the case is different at each stage. To begin with, the employee must show that he has been dismissed. This is not often brought into question. Secondly, the employer must show that he either had a fair or potentially fair reason to dismiss. At the final stage, the burden of proving the fairness or otherwise of the dismissal is neutral.

REMEDIES

When the ex-employee completes form ET1, he is asked to tick a box stating what remedy he would like the tribunal to award. The available remedies are set out in ss 112–118 of the Employment Rights Act 1996. All section numbers noted relate to the 1996 Act. The available remedies are:

- reinstatement
- re-engagement
- compensation.

Awards for reinstatement and re-engagement normally also include an award of compensation. Most applicants request compensation. In most cases employees do not want to return to work for the employer for fear of victimisation, or because of the manner in which they were dismissed.

If at the end of the hearing the tribunal finds that the dismissal was unfair then they must explain to the employee that they have the power to award reinstatement and re-engagement. In certain circumstances the employee is also able to apply for what is termed 'interim relief'. This is the case where, for example, they allege that dismissal took place following the making of a protected disclosure or participation in trade-union membership or activities. Claims for interim relief must be made within seven days of the effective date of termination. Following such a claim a hearing date is set and if, following the hearing the tribunal feels that they will ultimately find the dismissal to have been unfair then they may ask the employer to either reinstate or re-engage the employee.

Reinstatement - s 114

If the tribunal makes an award for reinstatement, the employee is reinstated into the job that he did before being dismissed. The employee is entitled to be reinstated on the same terms and conditions that he had previously. This includes the reinstatement of any benefits such as health insurance or a company car. The applicant should also be compensated for the losses incurred from the date of dismissal up until the date of reinstatement.

Where the applicant requests reinstatement, s 116 of the Employment Rights Act 1996 states that the tribunal must consider:

(a) whether the complainant wishes to be reinstated;

(b) whether it is practicable for the employer to comply with an order for reinstatement; and

(c) where the complainant caused or contributed to some extent to the dismissal, whether it would be just to order his reinstatement.

The tribunal should then consider whether it would be just to make a reinstatement order. A reinstatement order should never be made against the wishes of the dismissed employee. If the tribunal decides not to make a reinstatement award, it should consider the possibility of making an award for re-engagement. If the tribunal decides to make neither award, it must make an award for compensation.

If a tribunal makes a reinstatement award, the employer can only refuse to reinstate the employee where it would be reasonable to do so. It may be reasonable for an employer to refuse to reinstate where the relationship between the employer and former employee has irretrievably broken down.

Where an employer unreasonably refuses to reinstate the employee, the tribunal may make an additional award of compensation. This is added to the employee's main compensatory award.

Re-engagement – s 115

If a tribunal makes an award for re-engagement, the employee returns to work either with his original or an associated employer. However, the employee does not return to his original job. He is given a comparable job within the organisation.

When considering whether to make a re-engagement award, the tribunal must again take into account the wishes of the applicant, whether re-engagement is practicable in the circumstances and whether the applicant caused or contributed to his dismissal. The same rules (as outlined above) on refusal to agree to the award and additional compensation apply to re-engagement awards.

Compensation – s 118

Where the tribunal makes an award of compensation, two main elements make up the final award. These elements are referred to as the:

- basic award
- compensatory award.

The basic award reflects the employee's loss from the date of dismissal up until the award is made. It is designed to compensate the employee for the loss of their job. The compensatory award also takes any future losses into account.

The basic award – s 119

The employee's basic award is easily calculated. The tribunal arrives at the awarded figure using a fixed formula. The formula reflects the employee's age and his previous length of service, and multiplies this by his weekly earnings.

Age × Service × Week's Pay

> **Example**
>
> *At the time of writing the maximum amount of weekly pay that can be used is £310. This figure is revised annually. If the employee earns less than £310 per week, the figure that he actually earns is used in the calculation. If he earns more, the £310 figure is used.*
>
> *The multipliers to be used in the age section of the basic award calculation are as follows:*
>
> - *For any service where the employee was 41 or over the factor is 1.5.*
> - *For any service between the ages of 22 and 41 the factor is 1.*
> - *For any service below the age of 22 the factor is 0.5.*
>
> *These figures reflect the amount payable for each year of service. For example, for every year that the employee has worked for the employer while he was between the ages of 22 and 41, he is entitled to one week's pay. The service calculation can only be made for up to a maximum of 20 years.*
>
> *The maximum basic award payable is therefore:*
>
> $$\text{20 years} \times 1.5 \times £310 = £9300$$
>
> *Prior to 1 October 2006, where the employee's effective date of termination is after his 64th birthday, the basic award is reduced by one-twelfth for every completed calendar month after that brithday. The basic award ceases to be payable when the employee reaches 65. Note, however, that this reduction was to be abolished by the Employment Equality (Age) Regulations 2006.*
>
> *The regulations came into force on 1 October 2006 and apply to dismissals which occur on or after that date.*

In some situations the basic award can be reduced. This is where:

- the employer has made an offer to reinstate the employee and the employee has unreasonably refused that offer;
- the employee's conduct before the dismissal was such that it would be 'just and equitable' to reduce the basic award; and
- where the employee was dismissed due to redundancy and has already received a redundancy payment. In this case the amount of that payment would be deducted from the total basic award.

Minimum basic award

In some cases there is a right to receive a minimum basic award. At the time of writing this award is set at £4200 but is increased annually as with the amount set to be used in relation to 'week's pay' calculations. An employee who has been unfairly dismissed for any of the reasons outlined below is entitled to at least the minimum basic award. This applies to cases where the employee has been dismissed because:

- of their trade-union membership or activities, or because
- they carried out duties as a health and safety representative or trustee of an occupational pension scheme, or because
- they carried out functions or activities as an employee representative.

A minimum cash compensation of four weeks' pay is also payable if one of the reasons that the dismissal was unfair was that the employer failed to complete the minimum statutory disciplinary or grievance procedure.

Calculation of the compensatory award – s 123

The compensatory award is not calculated to a fixed formula. The tribunal has a wide discretion over the amount of compensation to award but this is subject to a maximum limit. The tribunal must consider what is 'just and equitable' compensation for the losses incurred by the employee following his dismissal. Since 1999 the maximum award has been inflation linked and is adjusted annually. At the time of writing the maximum compensatory award is £60600.

In cases where a person has been dismissed because they acted as a health and safety representative, made a protected disclosure or were selected for redundancy for either of these reasons there is no limit on the amount of compensation that can be awarded.

Guidelines as to how to calculate the compensatory award were set out in *Norton Tool Co Ltd v Tewson* (1973).

In assessing the compensatory award, the tribunal should take the following into account:

- **Immediate loss of earnings** – this will reflect the amount of earnings that the employee has lost since the time of dismissal and up to the date on which the award is made.

- **Future loss of earnings** – calculating how long the applicant is likely to be unemployed and how likely he is to be able to find another job. This is a discretionary award and if the employee has found a better job, there will be no payment made under this heading. The tribunal may also take into account the future loss of fringe benefits, such as health insurance or the use of a company car.

- **Loss of statutory rights** – after being dismissed the employee will have lost his accumulated statutory right to claim for unfair dismissal and redundancy. The tribunal may take this into account and award a nominal figure, normally between £200 and £500.

- **Loss of pension rights** – these are often difficult to calculate and the tribunal may ask an independent pensions expert to calculate the loss.

- **Expenses** – this will reflect any expenses that the employee has incurred in looking for a new job and could include things such as travelling expenses and relocation expenses if they have been forced to move to a new area.

The tribunal cannot make an award relating to non-economic loss, such as injury to feelings. Compensation can be awarded for financial losses only. In *Dunnachie* v *Kingston upon Hull City Council* (2004) the House of Lords held that when assessing the compensatory award only financial losses can be taken into account.

The tribunal adds any compensatory award to the basic award. Deductions may be made from either the basic or the compensatory awards. These are made at the discretion of the tribunal. Deductions may be made for things such as the conduct of the employee before dismissal, the recoupment of benefits already paid, where the employee has not tried to mitigate his loss by looking for work, or where he contributed to his own dismissal.

The basic and compensatory awards added together are referred to as the 'prescribed element'. At the end of the tribunal hearing the chairman provides the employer with details of how much must be paid to the employee. Where the employee has been receiving state benefits, such as the jobseeker's allowance, the prescribed element must not be paid until the employer has received an account from the Benefits Agency. This will detail the amount of benefit that needs to be recouped from the total award.

The additional award – s 117

Where an employer has unreasonably refused to comply with an order for reinstatement or re-engagement, the tribunal will make an additional award. Where an employer has unreasonably refused to re-employ the employee an additional award of 26–52 weeks' pay can be made. This means that, taking a week's pay to be £310, the additional award will be made in the region of £8060–£16120.

SUMMARY CHECKLIST

- Most employment disputes arise when the contract of employment is terminated.
- A contract of employment may be terminated by agreement, by completion of a specific task, by frustration of the contract, by the death of either party, by dissolution of a partnership or liquidation, by dismissal, by resignation, or by the expiry of a fixed term.
- If an employee agrees to the termination of his employment contract, he must do so freely and without coercion or duress.
- A contract of employment will automatically be terminated where a frustrating event means that the parties are no longer able to perform their obligations under the original terms of the agreement.
- Two of the more common events which induce frustration are illness and imprisonment.
- In cases involving possible frustration due to illness, consideration is given to, for example, the length of time that the employee has worked for the employer, the nature of the job, the nature, length and effect of the illness/accident, and whether there is any prospect of the employee recovering.
- Section 95(1) of the Employment Rights Act 1996 states that an employee is dismissed where his contract is terminated by the employer either with or without notice, where the employee's limited-term contract is not renewed, or where he is forced to resign and so terminate his contract as a result of the conduct of his employer.
- At common law an employer can lawfully dismiss an employee by giving him the correct amount of notice, or earnings in lieu of notice.
- Wrongful dismissal occurs where an employer dismisses an employee giving him no or insufficient notice.
- In all but summary dismissal situations, an employer must give employees notice of their dismissal.
- In wrongful dismissal actions the court or tribunal is not interested in the fairness or otherwise of the dismissal.
- In wrongful dismissal actions the employee sues for the earnings and/or benefits that he would have received during the notice period.
- An employer may lawfully dismiss an employee without notice where he has committed an act of gross misconduct; this is referred to as 'summary dismissal'.
- What will amount to an offence of gross misconduct will normally be set out in the company's disciplinary code.
- Wrongful dismissal claims can brought in either a court or (within limits) an Employment Tribunal.
- There is no limit on the amount of damages that can be claimed in the court; for a breach of contract claim in the tribunal the maximum payable is £25 000.
- Claims to the tribunal must be made within three months of the dismissal, claims to a court within six years.
- An employer may be able to defend a wrongful dismissal claim by either showing that there was no dismissal, or that the dismissal was lawful because it followed an act of gross misconduct.
- An unfair dismissal claim is a statutory claim.

- Claims for unfair dismissal can only be brought in the Employment Tribunal.
- Section 94 of the Employment Rights Act 1996 states that an employee has the right not to be unfairly dismissed by his employer.
- In unfair dismissal cases the tribunal looks at the fairness or otherwise of the employer's reason for dismissal.
- It does not follow that just because an employer has a fair reason to dismiss that the tribunal will decide that the employee was dismissed fairly.
- The employee's effective date of termination (EDT) is the date on which his contract of employment is said to terminate.
- It is important to ascertain the EDT in order to show that the employee has the required continuity of service and that he has made his claim within the three-month time limit.
- Section 97 of the Employment Rights Act 1996 lists the different circumstances that will determine the EDT.
- An employee may resign and claim constructive dismissal on the basis that his employer's conduct made it impossible for him to continue working for that employer.
- In constructive dismissal situations the employee can only make a claim if the employer's conduct amounts to a significant breach of contract, the employee responds quickly, and if the employee's resignation obviously relates to that conduct.
- Even where an employee can show that he was constructively dismissed, this does not automatically mean that that dismissal was unfair.
- Not all employees are eligible to make a claim for unfair dismissal.
- An employee must show that he has passed the 'eligibility' test before the tribunal will hear his claim.
- The person making the claim must have been working as an employee and at the time of making the claim have one year's continuous service.
- The employee must be able to show that he was dismissed.
- The employee must not have waived his right to make an unfair dismissal claim.
- Certain Crown employees, members of the police and armed forces, share fishermen/women and employees working under illegal contracts are excluded from making an unfair dismissal claim.
- An employee must make his claim to the tribunal within three months of his EDT.
- After the employee has submitted his unfair dismissal claim, the tribunal will consider the employer's reason for dismissal.
- In some cases it is automatically unfair to dismiss an employee, for example, on the grounds of pregnancy or a reason connected to pregnancy.
- It is automatically fair to dismiss an employee in cases of national security and during an unofficial strike or industrial action.
- The five potentially fair reasons to dismiss are: capability/qualifications, conduct, redundancy, statutory illegality and for 'some other substantial reason'.
- Capability/qualification dismissals may relate to an employee's lack of qualifications, or the fact that he is too ill to work, lacks aptitude or skill.
- Conduct is the most commonly used reason for dismissal.
- Examples of dismissals for statutory illegality include continuing to employ someone whose work permit has expired, or continuing to employ a banned driver to work as a lorry driver.

6

Termination of the employment contract

- Examples of 'some other substantial reason' include a refusal to accept a change in the terms of employment, pressure from a third party to dismiss, or a business re-organisation.
- The tribunal considers the dismissal situation in two stages – has the employer shown a potentially fair reason to dismiss and, if so, was the employer's response reasonable, and did he follow the statutory minimum disciplinary procedure?
- The general principles of fairness are set out in s 98(4) of the Employment Rights Act 1996.
- Section 94 states that in considering fairness this depends on whether in the circumstances (including the size and administrative resources of the business) the employer acted reasonably or unreasonably in treating the issue as a sufficient reason to dismiss the employee, to be determined in accordance with the equity and the substantial merits of the case.
- General guidelines on fairness were set out in the case of *Iceland Frozen Foods v Jones* (1982).
- Employers must use disciplinary procedures fairly. Where an employer has failed to use the statutory minimum disciplinary procedure prior to dismissal, that dismissal will be automatically unfair.
- Employers should follow the guidance in the Acas code on discipline.
- Employers should conduct a thorough investigation and hold a fair disciplinary meeting before taking the decision to dismiss.
- Employees should be given the opportunity to appeal against any decision to dismiss.
- In incapacity dismissals the employer should consider alternative forms of action, such as appraisal and training, before disciplining an employee.
- Where an employer decides to dismiss an employee on the ground of illness, he must first conduct a thorough investigation into the issues surrounding the illness.
- In illness dismissals, the tribunal should take into account the nature of the illness, the length of time that the employee is likely to be absent from work, the need for the employer to have the work done, the type of work that the employee was employed to do, and the circumstances of the case.
- Employers should consult with employees before any decision is taken to dismiss on the ground of illness.
- In conduct dismissals the employer must show that he honestly believed that the employee was guilty of misconduct, that he had reasonable grounds for this belief, and that he had carried out a reasonable investigation prior to any dismissal.
- In redundancy dismissals the employer must adopt fair selection procedures, consult with unions and the individual employees likely to be affected, and try to find suitable alternative work for any employee about to be made redundant.
- In statutory illegality dismissals the tribunal should consider whether the employer could have avoided dismissal by finding alternative work for the employee.
- In 'some other substantial reason' dismissals where the reason for dismissal is a business reason, the tribunal should check that the changes will result in some benefit to the business.
- An employee with one year's continuous service can demand that his employer supply him with written reasons outlining why he was dismissed.
- The Acas arbitration scheme provides an informal alternative to bringing an unfair dismissal claim in the tribunal.

- The remedies available in the employment tribunal are reinstatement, re-engagement and compensation.
- Reinstatement means that the employee returns to his original job receiving the same pay and benefits to those previously received.
- Re-engagement means that the employee returns to work for his old or a related employer, but he returns to a different job.
- Awards for reinstatement and re-engagement usually include an award of compensation.
- The compensatory award is made up of two elements: the basic award and the compensatory award.
- The basic award is calculated on a fixed formula: Age × Service × Week's Pay.
- The compensatory award can reflect payments for loss of earnings, loss of future wages, loss of statutory rights, loss of pension rights, and expenses.
- Where an employer unreasonably refuses to comply with an order to reinstate or re-engage, the tribunal will make an additional award.

SELF-TEST QUESTIONS

1 Under what circumstances might the employment contract be terminated?

2 How is dismissal defined in s 95(1) of the Employment Rights Act 1996?

3 Define the terms 'wrongful dismissal' and 'unfair dismissal'.

4 What is the significance of the effective date of termination?

5 How can an employee show that he is eligible to make an unfair dismissal claim?

6 What are the automatically unfair and fair reasons for dismissal?

7 What are the five potentially fair reasons for dismissal?

8 What is the general principle of fairness contained in s 94 of the Employment Rights Act 1996?

9 What do you understand to be meant by the term 'procedural fairness'?

10 What is the function of the Acas arbitration scheme in relation to unfair dismissal claims?

11 What remedies are available in the Employment Tribunal?

CASE SCENARIOS

A

'Mirage', a world famous pop band is due to begin its world tour next week. The first concert is due to take place in Chicago and the band is due to fly to the United States on Thursday. The band is rehearsing in London on the Monday before it is due to leave. Charlotte works for the band as a sound engineer. She is looking forward to going to America as she has heard that

Chicago is famous for its night life. On Monday afternoon, the band's manager, Chuck Rich, dismisses Charlotte, telling her that she is not needed on the tour. Her contract of employment states that she is entitled to six weeks' notice of dismissal. She is not given any notice.

As Charlotte storms out of the rehearsal Chuck Rich walks up to Sam, a backing singer and shouts, 'You're fired, mate, take your stuff and get out'. Sam's contract of employment states that he is entitled to four weeks' notice of dismissal. He is not given any notice. Chuck tells him that he has been dismissed because he has found out that he has been stealing concert tickets and selling them to ticket-touts.

On the night before the band is due to leave for Chicago, Liam the drummer announces that he is unable to go on the tour. He has been suffering from severe hand and elbow pain and his doctor has advised him not to drum for at least six months. He has only been a member of the band for nine months. At the last moment Chuck Rich employs a new drummer.

Advise Charlotte and Sam as to whether they are able to make a claim for wrongful dismissal. Will Liam be able to demand that the band take him back as a drummer when the band returns from its tour?

B

Robert Brown worked as a sales representative and marketing consultant for Gerald plc. He began work for Gerald plc on 13 August 2004. He has recently been told that his work was unsatisfactory. Robert alleges that he had been promoted against his wishes and that he was given no training to help him get used to his new duties.

He asked if he could go on a training course but was told that he could not. On 15 September 2005 Mr Smith, Gerald's personnel manager invited Robert into his office and dismissed him. He was given no notice of this dismissal. Gerald plc states that its reason to dismiss was capability. Robert alleges that he asked if he could appeal against the decision to dismiss but that Mr Smith said that he could not.

Advise Robert as to:

● *the likely factors to be taken into account by the tribunal when considering capability dismissals;*

● *the likelihood of him being able to make a successful claim for unfair dismissal;*

● *the remedies that may be available in the tribunal.*

● **Further reading**

Unfair dismissal, IDS Employment Law Handbook, 2005.

Dismissal – Fair and Unfair: A Guide for Employers, Department of Trade and Industry, Advisory Booklet, 06/1400, 2006.

Unfairly Dismissed? Department of Trade and Industry, Advisory Booklet, 06/1401, 2006.

'The Shifting Importance of Procedural Fairness in Unfair Dismissal Proceedings', Adrian Williams, Business Law Review, October 2002, pp. 233–8.

'Arbitration in Employment Disputes', Jessica Learmond-Criqui and Justin Costley, *Business Law Review*, October 2001, pp. 222–4.

'Discipline, Grievances and Dismissal', Acas, November 2003.

'Fair dealing and the dismissal process', Douglas Brodie, *Industrial Law Journal*, 2002 (31), pp. 294–7.

For legal updates on the material in this chapter please go to the Companion Website accompanying this book at **www.mylawchamber.co.uk/nairns**

7 Redundancy and the transfer of undertakings

The law on redundancy and the transfer of undertakings aims to deal effectively with situations in which a business is exposed to change. In the case of redundancy situations an employer may, for instance, have to make some employees redundant because there is no longer enough work for the entire workforce.

Alternatively, an employer in serious financial difficulty may have to resort to closing down the business and making all of the employees redundant.

In the case of a transfer of an undertaking, the business may, for example, have been bought by a competitor wanting to expand its market share in a particular industry.

Redundancy and transfer situations result in worrying times for the workforce. When an employer makes only selected employees redundant they will, no doubt, want to know why they were selected for dismissal. When a new owner buys an existing business the workforce will be anxious to learn of any changes that the new owner intends to make, and whether in fact they are to keep their jobs.

Whilst the law recognises that there is an economic necessity for change, and that in some cases employers must use redundancy or a transfer to enable the business to remain solvent, it does not allow any such changes to be made lightly. The common theme in both redundancy and transfer situations is consultation. Employers must discuss their proposals and decisions with their workplace union and those employees likely to be affected by such proposals.

The law seeks to ensure that any employee affected by either redundancy or a transfer is treated fairly, within strict guidelines, and in the case of the redundant employee, is paid compensation for the fact that he has lost his job.

This chapter begins by outlining the right to a redundancy payment, the types of situation that may force an employer to make employees redundant, and provides an overview of a claim for a redundancy payment. It goes on to discuss:

- the definition of 'redundancy', s 139(1) of the Employment Rights Act 1996;
- employer's business ceases to exist;
- employer closes particular place of work;
- job that employee is employed to do ceases to exist, or ceases to exist at his place of work due to falling demand;
- eligibility to make a redundancy claim;
- the role of the employer in redundancy situations;
- selection of those employees to be made redundant;
- consultation with representatives – the Collective Redundancies and Transfer of Undertakings (Protection of Employment) (Amendment) Regulations 1999, the Collective Redundancies (Amendment) Regulations 2006;

- informing the Department of Trade and Industry;
- individual consultation with employees;
- the offer of suitable alternative work, reasonable refusal, trial periods;
- unfair dismissal arising from redundancy;
- 'bumped' redundancies;
- lay-off and short-time working;
- the redundancy payments scheme, calculations;
- definition of a transfer of an undertaking;
- sources of law on the transfer of an undertaking, the Transfer of Undertakings (Protection of Employment) Regulations 2006, the Acquired Rights Directive 77/187/EEC;
- the definition of a 'relevant transfer', 'contracting out';
- the definition of an 'undertaking';
- the effect of a transfer of an undertaking on the contract of employment;
- the Collective Redundancies and Transfer of Undertakings (Protection of Employment) (Amendment) Regulations 1999 (in relation to transfers).

THE RIGHT TO A REDUNDANCY PAYMENT - S 135 OF THE EMPLOYMENT RIGHTS ACT 1996

Section 135(1) of the Employment Rights Act 1996 sets out the general right to a redundancy payment. It states that:

An employer shall pay a redundancy payment to any employee of his if the employee –

(a) is dismissed by the employer by reason of redundancy, or

(b) is eligible for a redundancy payment by reason of being laid off or kept on short-time.

There is a statutory redundancy scheme which ensures that all redundant employees receive compensation. At the time of writing, the maximum redundancy payment payable under this scheme is £9300. However, some employees may receive in excess of this amount from an in-house redundancy scheme. Many employers offer enhanced payments to reflect long service.

SITUATIONS THAT MAY FORCE AN EMPLOYER TO MAKE EMPLOYEES REDUNDANT

An employer may be forced to consider the possibility of making some or all of their employees redundant for various reasons, the most obvious being that the business is experiencing financial difficulties. By reducing the number of employees the employer is then able to recoup their earnings as capital and attempt to solve any short-term financial problems.

A business may experience financial difficulties due to, for example, falling sales, high interest rates or a recession. The advancement of technology has also been hailed as a prime reason why some employees find that their employer no longer has any need for them to do the job that they have done for many years.

For instance, the introduction of computers into the workplace rationalised many office-based industries, resulting in job losses. Also, in the automotive and engineering industries, whereas in the past many workers were needed to man an assembly line, today the line can be worked by a robot with one employee overseeing the operation. In such cases the workplace management would have had to restructure the workforce so as to cope with the change.

The most drastic redundancy situation lies where an employer is forced to close down the business, thus making all the employees redundant. This occurs where, for example, the business is in dire financial trouble and is eventually rendered insolvent.

There have been many examples of mass redundancy situations over the last decade. The mining and steel industries have seen their workforces shrink to a fraction of their former numbers. The ideal of a 'job for life' is no longer a reality.

The introduction section of the Acas advisory booklet on handling redundancy states that:

> **The growth of British industry requires constant review of products and methods of work, and the successful application of new technology. Our availability to maintain competitiveness in world markets depends on this. It is inevitable, however, that redeployment of labour and redundancies will sometimes be necessary. A poorly thought out approach to change can result in a level of uncertainty which damages company performance and, should redundancies be unavoidable, may lead to financial and emotional costs to the individuals affected.**

The law seeks to ensure that employers take any redundancy situation very seriously, and that the financial and emotional cost to the individual employee is kept to the very minimum. Before an employer makes the decision to make employees redundant, he should first consider other possibilities, such as a reduction in overtime, restrictions on recruitment, or the early retirement of employees. This should help to reduce the number of employees who will need to be made redundant, or may result in there being no need for redundancies at all.

Employers must clearly identify their reasons for making employees redundant. In due course the reason may have to be disclosed to employee representatives and to the Department of Trade and Industry.

⬤ Overview of a claim for a redundancy payment

Figure 7.1 highlights the possible questions to be asked where an employee purports to make a claim for a redundancy payment. In all cases the tribunal will be interested in whether the employer complied with the correct redundancy handling procedures, and whether the employer offered the employee suitable alternative employment.

THE DEFINITION OF REDUNDANCY – S 139(1) OF THE EMPLOYMENT RIGHTS ACT 1996

A dismissed employee can only claim a redundancy payment if he can show that he was dismissed 'for reason of redundancy'. Section 139(1) of the Employment Rights Act 1996 states that a person may be dismissed 'by reason of redundancy' where the dismissal is attributable either wholly or mainly due to:

(a) the fact that his employer has ceased or intends to cease –

   (i) *to carry on the business* for the purposes of which the employee was employed by him; or

   (ii) *to carry on that business in the place* where the employee was so employed; or

(b) the fact that the requirements of that business –

   (i) for employees to carry out work of a particular kind; or

   (ii) for employees to carry out work of a particular kind in the place where the employee was employed by the employer *have ceased or diminished* or are expected to cease or diminish.

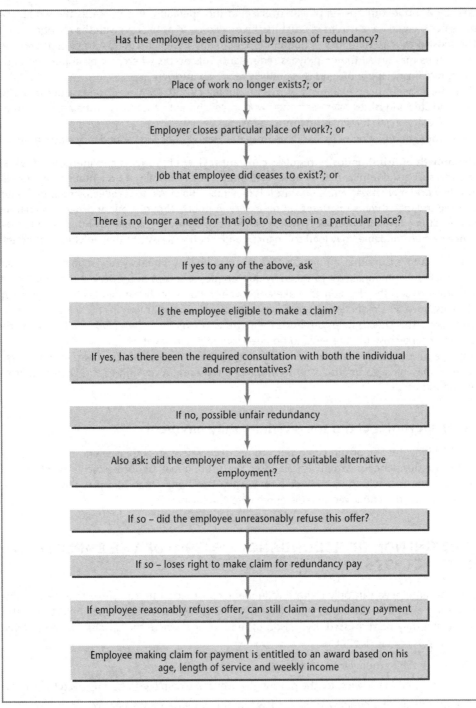

Figure 7.1 Determining whether there is a valid claim for redundancy

This shows that an employer may make an employee redundant where either:

- the business where the employee works/worked has ceased or is going to cease to exist;
- the particular site or section where the employee works/worked has or is going to cease to exist; or
- there is no longer a need for the work that the employee does/did, either generally or at a particular site.

> **Example**
>
> *Gordon works as a packer in a fruit warehouse. He spends his days loading blueberries into boxes and passing them down a conveyor line to be checked and labelled. Due to the falling price of fruit, his employer decides to streamline the operation by ceasing to sell blueberries. As from the date of this change there will be nothing for Gordon to do. Consequently, his employer may make him redundant – there is no longer a need for the work that he does and, after the reorganisation, his particular section will cease to exist.*
>
> *Geraldine is a wine buyer for a famous restaurant chain. The owner of the chain is in severe financial difficulties and feels that she must sell her business and 'cut her losses'. She cannot find a buyer and after a few weeks is forced to close the business down. In this case the place at which Geraldine did her work has ceased to exist. Consequently, she and her colleagues have been made redundant.*

● Employer only has to show that there is a reason for the redundancy

Before considering the s 139(1) definition more closely it is useful to note that an employer only has to show that an employee was dismissed due to redundancy. In doing so the employer must show that there was a need to make employees redundant. The employer does not have to provide evidence or go into any detail of that need.

In other words, at any tribunal hearing the panel is only concerned with whether or not there has been a redundancy, not with the sense or reasoning behind the employer's decision to dismiss.

> **Moon v Homeworthy Furniture (Northern) Ltd** (1977)
>
> Homeworthy decided to close down one of its factories. The company made the entire workforce redundant. The employees claimed that the company had no need to make them redundant, and that the decision to dismiss them had been taken due to poor industrial relations at the site. Homeworthy stated that the workers had been made redundant because the factory was no longer economically viable.
>
> *Held (EAT)* All that they should be interested in was the employer's reason for making the workforce redundant. It was not for the tribunal to become involved in whether or not the redundancies were justified.

Employer's business ceases to exist

When an employer is forced to close a business and make the entire workforce redundant, there is rarely any question that the ending of the workers' employment amounted to a redundancy. The only difficulty that may arise is where the business is taken over by another company/firm or individual. In that case there is no dismissal and no redundancies. The workers' employment contracts are automatically taken over by their new employer.

Employer closes a particular place of work

In this situation an employee may lose his job because his employer has closed down part of the business, for example, closing down two sites of a four-site factory. In doing so the employer is able to concentrate efforts on the remaining sites, and so is more likely to be able to either increase profit, or keep the factory open. Where an employee who works in one of the closing sites is dismissed, he is dismissed for redundancy under the s 139 definition.

It may be that an employer closes down part of an operation in a certain area to develop those in another. For example, a company may decide to close down part of its operation in London and concentrate on employing more staff at its Newcastle site. The dismissed London employees are dismissed for redundancy.

Mobility clauses

In some cases an employee may have a mobility clause inserted into his contract of employment stating that he can be required to work at a different site, or sites from the one at which he is normally employed. Where an employer closes down part of an operation, the question to ask is – could the employee be required to move to the remaining site and continue his work there? In the above example, would a London-based employee be required to move to Newcastle?

This depends on whether or not a mobility clause exists in the contract of employment, and on what definition is given to the s 139 words 'where the employee was employed'.

In *United Kingdom Atomic Energy Authority* v *Claydon* (1974) it was held that the 'place where the employee was employed' means the place that he can be required to work under his contract of employment. This means that if a mobility clause exists, an employee who is asked to move and work elsewhere has not been made redundant. If he refuses to move, he effectively terminates his own employment contract.

Rank Xerox Ltd v *Churchill* (1988)

Ms Churchill worked in the London headquarters of Rank Xerox Ltd. A term in her contract of employment stated that 'the company may require you to transfer to another location'. When Rank Xerox decided to move its headquarters away from London, Churchill refused to move. She claimed that as her place of work no longer existed she had effectively been made redundant.

Held (EAT) The words 'the place where the employee was so employed' in s 139(1) are not to be taken to mean the place where the employee actually works but where, under their contract, he can be required to work. Consequently, Churchill had not been made redundant; Rank Xerox had only moved her place of work, which still existed.

O'Brien v Associated Fire Alarms Ltd (1968)

O'Brien and his colleagues were employed by Associated Fire Alarms to work in and around the Liverpool area. There was a shortage of work in Liverpool and they were told that they would have to go to work in Barrow, some 150 miles away. This would have made it difficult for them to return home to their families each evening. There was no mobility clause in their contracts of employment. The question asked was whether a term could be implied into their contracts, stating that they may be required to work anywhere within the North West. If this was possible, when they resigned they were not redundant; if it was not possible, they were redundant.

Held It would be wrong to imply a mobility clause to this effect; the men had worked in Liverpool for many years. There had never been any previous mention of a possible relocation to Barrow. Consequently, they had been made redundant.

This contractual approach has been frowned upon in later cases (see **Bass** below).

Bass Leisure Ltd v Thomas (1994)

Ms Thomas worked in a depot in Coventry. Her contract contained a mobility clause. Bass Leisure asked her to go and work in a depot only 20 miles away from her original job. She refused to move and claimed that she had been made redundant.

Held (EAT) She had been made redundant. Instead of a contractual test, looking at the mobility clause, one should consider a geographical test, by asking the question, 'Where does the employee work?' The EAT decided that this could not include a site some 20 miles away. It concluded by saying that although looking at the employee's contract of employment was a useful exercise, it was no longer the decisive way of deciding if an employee had been made redundant or not.

This was reaffirmed in the case of **High Table Ltd v Horst** (1998). Here, it was stated that the existence of a mobility clause in an employment contract does not prevent a dismissal being 'by reason of redundancy'.

See also: **Provincial Insurance plc v Loxley** (1990), **United Bank v Akhtar** (1989).

Job that employee is employed to do ceases to exist, or ceases to exist in the place that he works due to falling demand

Here, the job that the employee has been employed to do ceases to exist, or his employer's requirements have ceased, or diminished. This form of redundancy takes place where there has been a fall in the demand for the type of work that the employee does. It is the work that is considered and not the person.

The question to ask is – does the employer still need the same number of employees to do the work? If the need for the work is increasing, but the employer requires fewer employees to do the job due to new technology, there is a redundancy situation.

If, however, the employer has reorganised the business and so needs the same number of employees to run it effectively, there can be no redundancies.

The following cases highlight situations in which employees have argued that they have been dismissed due to redundancy.

Vaux & Associated Breweries Ltd v Ward (1969)

Ms Ward had worked in Vaux pubs for some years. When the brewery decided to update some of its pubs, she was found to be surplus to requirements and dismissed. The brewery was trying to turn the particular bar in which she worked into a 'young persons' bar and wanted to employ more glamorous staff. Ward was replaced by a 17-year-old bunny girl who took over her duties of preparing and serving drinks.

Held Ward had not been made redundant; there had been no drop in the need for the work that she had been doing. Her duties remained necessary; they were just being done by someone else. The requirements for the work of that kind had not changed.

North Riding Garages v Butterwick (1967)

Mr Butterwick had worked for North Riding Garages for 30 years. He was their workshop manager. The garage was sold and after a few months the new owner dismissed Butterwick, alleging that he was inefficient. They said that he was unable to adapt to new methods of work that required him to do administration. Butterwick argued that the changing nature of the work that he was required to do meant that the requirements for work of a particular kind had diminished, and so he had been made redundant.

Held He had not been made redundant; the reason for his dismissal was his inability to adapt to change and not redundancy.

In this case Widgery J stated that 'an employee who remains in the same kind of work is expected to adapt himself to new methods and techniques and cannot complain if his employer insists on higher standards of efficiency than those previously required'.

Johnson v Peabody Trust (1996)

Mr Johnson was a roofer. Unfortunately, however, the Trust did not always have enough work of that nature for him to do. His contract of employment stated that he should be flexible, and able to carry out multi-trade operations where necessary. When he was selected for redundancy, he claimed that his selection was unfair because at the time he had been doing more multi-trade operations than roofing. He argued that his dismissal was unfair because the Trust had tried to justify it by stating that there was not enough roofing work available.

Held (EAT) Where an employee is employed to carry out a particular trade, it is that basic contractual obligation which should be considered. He had been contracted to work as a roofer. There was a fall in demand for his work, consequently he had been made redundant.

Hindle v Percival Boats (1960)

Mr Hindle had been employed for some years as a boat builder. He was skilled in the art of making wooden boats. As time progressed there was a fall in the demand for wooden vessels, customers wanted fibreglass boats. Hindle was found to be very slow at assembling the modern boats. He was dismissed for being 'too good and too slow'. Someone else had to carry on his work after he had left.

> *Held* Hindle had not been made redundant; the requirements of the boatyard has not altered. There was still a pressing need for the type of work that he did.

Nelson v British Broadcasting Corporation (1977)

Mr Nelson was employed as a BBC producer. A term in his employment contract stated that he could be required to work 'when, how, and where' his employers directed him to. He had worked in the Caribbean Service for some time. The BBC decided to close that service due to its increasing costs. Nelson was offered a job with the Home Service. He turned down this offer and claimed that he had been made redundant.

Held (CA) He had not been made redundant. 'Work of a particular kind' meant work that Nelson could be ordered to perform, rather than work which he actually did perform.

Johnson v Nottinghamshire Combined Police Authority (1974)

Two women had been employed by the Police Authority as clerks. They had worked shifts from 9.30 a.m. until 5.30 p.m. The Authority wanted them to work a new shift pattern, from 8 a.m. to 3 p.m., and 1 a.m. to 8 a.m. They refused to work the new pattern and were dismissed. They made a claim for a redundancy payment.

Held (CA) There had been no redundancy. The Authority still needed two clerks to do the same amount of work, albeit at different times. The women had been replaced; there could not have been any redundancy.

There has been much debate as to whether the tribunal should use either the 'job function test' or the 'contract test' in determining whether a redundancy situation has arisen due to a cessation in work. The 'job function test' considers the work that the employee actually did and questions whether there is still a need for that work to be completed. The 'contract test' considers what the employee may have been required to do under the terms of their contract of employment and questions whether there is still a need for any of that work to be completed. Both tests are evidenced in the cases outlined above.

The use of the tests was considered in the case of *Safeway Stores Plc v Burrell* (1997). Here the EAT stated that there is a three-stage process in deciding whether an employee had been dismissed for redundancy. The stages are listed as follows:

(a) Was the employee dismissed?

(b) If so, had the requirements of the employer's business for employees to carry out work of a particular kind ceased or diminished, or were they expected to cease or diminish?

(c) If so, was the dismissal of the employee caused wholly or mainly by the cessation or diminution?

This was affirmed in the case of *Murray v Foyle Meats Ltd* (1999). Here, the House of Lords held that the questions to ask are whether one or other of various states of economic affairs exists, for example, whether the requirements of the business for employees to carry out work of a particular kind have diminished. Once this is established the tribunal should go on to consider whether the dismissal is attributable, wholly or mainly, to that state of affairs.

7

Redundancy and the transfer of undertakings

In this case Lord Irvine stated that 'both the contract test and the function test miss the point' He went on to state that 'the key word in the statute is "attributable" and there is no reason in law why the dismissal of an employee should not be attributable to a diminution in the employer's need for employees irrespective of the terms of the contract or the function he performed.'

In *Shawkat* v *Nottingham City Hospital NHS Trust (No. 2)* (2001) a thoracic surgeon was dismissed for refusing to carry out cardiac surgery in place of the thoracic surgery that he had previously performed. Here it was held that redundancy was not the reason for his dismissal because there had been no reduction in the amount of thoracic surgery that the hospital required. The hospital had merely decided to reorganise and expand by taking on more cardiac work.

See also, *Corus & Regal Hotels plc* v *Wilkinson* (2004) in which it was held that the general manager of a group of hotels had not been made redundant. He had been replaced following a business reorganisation but his work continued to be done by other employees, namely a senior manager and a junior resident manager. The need for the work that he did had not diminished or ceased; it was merely being done by someone else.

ELIGIBILITY TO MAKE A REDUNDANCY CLAIM

Not all employees are eligible to make a claim for a redundancy payment. The worker must be an employee (see further pages 104 and 107). Following that, the rules that exclude an employee from making a claim are akin to those preventing a claim for unfair dismissal. (See page 233 for a more detailed discussion on the various exceptions).

An employee is only eligible to make a claim for a redundancy payment if he:

- has two years of continuous service with his employer;
- has not contracted out of his right to make a claim under a fixed-term contract (only applies to agreements made before 1/10/02);
- is not a Crown employee;
- is not a share fisherman;
- is not employed as a domestic servant by a relative;
- does not belong to the excluded class of employees ordered by the Secretary of State to apply where a collective agreement covers the issue of redundancy;
- is not dismissed for misconduct/industrial action; or
- on being told that he was to be made redundant, has not unreasonably refused a suitable offer of employment.

WAS THE EMPLOYEE DISMISSED?

An employee must be able to show that he was dismissed by his employer before making a claim for a redundancy payment (see pages 223 to 224). The definition of a 'dismissal by way of redundancy' is found in s 136 of the Employment Rights Act 1996. It mirrors the definition of dismissal found in s 95(1) of the 1996 Act, but in this case the dismissal must be for redundancy.

Section 136 states that an employee is dismissed by reason of redundancy if:

(a) the contract under which he is employed by the employer is terminated by the employer (whether with or without notice);

(b) he is employed under a limited-term contract and that contract terminates by virtue of the limiting event without being renewed under the same contract; or

(c) the employee terminates the contract under which he is employed (with or without notice) in circumstances in which he is entitled to terminate it without notice by reason of the employer's conduct.

Morton Sundour Fabrics v *Shaw* (1967)

Morton Sundour told Mr Shaw that it would inevitably have to close the department in which he worked 'at some time in the future'. It did not give him a precise date, but did help Shaw to find a new job. He gave Morton Sundour notice and left to begin the new job. He claimed that he was entitled to a redundancy payment.

Held As he was not actually under notice of dismissal at the time he left, he did not qualify for a redundancy payment.

In most cases the fact that an employee has been dismissed will not be in issue. However, in redundancy situations the employee must have been given a specific date on which his employment is to cease.

There is an exception whereby an employee can leave his employment early without jeopardising his entitlement to a redundancy payment.

Section 142 of the Employment Rights Act 1996 states that an employee can leave his employment before his redundancy becomes effective, provided that during the statutory notice period he serves his employer with a 'counter-notice' stating that he intends to leave early. If the employer accepts this notice, the employee continues to be entitled to his redundancy payment. If the employer refuses the employee's request, the employer must then serve a counter-notice to it. This counter-notice should state that the employee is required to work out his notice.

If the employee then decides to leave his employment before working his notice, it is left to the Employment Tribunal to decide whether it is 'just and equitable' for him still to receive all or part of his redundancy payment.

THE ROLE OF THE EMPLOYER IN REDUNDANCY SITUATIONS

Employers must ensure that they follow correct redundancy handling procedures. They must be able to show that:

- their selection criteria were objectively justified and applied fairly;
- they conducted proper individual and consultative consultation before making any employee redundant;
- they tried to find suitable alternative work for any employee who was to be made redundant.

The leading case on redundancy handling is *Williams* v *Compair Maxam Ltd* (1982). The facts of this case are outlined in relation to fairness at page 251).

Redundancy and the transfer of undertakings

In *Williams* the EAT laid down general guidelines for employers. These guidelines are listed above (page 251) and in summary are that:

- employers should give as much warning as possible of impending redundancies, so as to enable the union and affected employees to consider alternative solutions, and if possible to find alternative employment;

- employers should consult with the workplace union as to the best means by which the redundancies can be implemented fairly, and with as little hardship to employees as possible;

- an agreement should be made with the union as to which selection criteria will be used to isolate the 'pool' of employees to be made redundant;

- employers will consider whether, instead of dismissing particular employees, they should offer them suitable alternative employment.

This chapter continues by looking at the ways in which an employer selects those employees to be made redundant, the rules on consultation with the workplace union and those individuals who are likely to be affected by the redundancies, and the guidelines on offering those employees suitable alternative employment.

Selection of those employees to be made redundant

In situations where an employer only intends to make part of the workforce redundant, the employer must select those employees to be dismissed very carefully. Many employers begin by asking their workforce if any of them would like to take voluntary redundancy. Employees close to retirement or confident of finding new employment may agree to be made redundant.

Often, their employer will offer them an enhanced redundancy payment, or extra pension entitlement for agreeing to the redundancy. Where an employee voluntarily agrees to be made redundant, he is no longer entitled to any statutory redundancy payment. Any payment is paid as an enhancement by his employer.

The way in which an employer chooses to select those employees to be made redundant must be fair and reasonable. Whilst an employee may not be able to dispute the fact that he was made redundant, any deficiencies in either his employer's selection or consultation process could render his dismissal unfair. (See page 245: Procedural unfairness).

Employers must have an organised approach to redundancy. Having made the decision to reduce the workforce, the employer must draft suitable selection criteria. By using these criteria, a 'pool' of employees can be selected from which redundancies will be made. The Acas advisory handbook on *Redundancy Handling* contains a useful section on the use of selection criteria. It states that the employer should:

- agree the selection criteria with employee representatives;
- be objective, fair and consistent; and
- establish an appeals procedure.

The handbook goes on to state that 'as far as possible, objective criteria, precisely defined and capable of being applied in an independent way, should be used when determining which employees are to be selected for redundancy'. It is stressed that 'the purpose of having objective criteria is to ensure that employees are not unfairly selected for redundancy'.

In drafting the selection criteria, the employer should consider such issues as:

- an employee's skill and capability in his job;
- his length of service;

- the types of work that will still need to be done once the workforce is reduced;
- the suitability of employees to take on the remaining tasks;
- an employee's sickness and competence record;
- the possibility of implementing a last-in-first-out selection.

It is generally thought that employees and unions prefer employers to use last-in-first-out selection, meaning that the most recent additions to the workforce lose their jobs, whilst long-standing employees remain employed. This shows some level of fairness and is widely accepted as being a reasonable approach.

However, the last-in-first-out system may not be the best option for the employer. The employer may have recently appointed employees who have particular skills needed to ensure the future success of the business. In this case, it may not be economically viable for an employer to dismiss new employees who may prove to be an asset after workplace reductions are made.

The question then is, how does an employer adopt a fair method of selection? At best the methods of selection are quite crude and an employee may find their profile analysed on a table of boxes with ticks or crosses next to particular issues such as 'skill in information technology'.

The most common method of selection is where an employer drafts a table outlining those skills required by the remaining workforce, and allocates marks for each skill. Every employee is then assessed using the same criteria.

In assessing each employee an employer may use those headings noted above, such as length of service and capability. He may also add particular skills relevant to the business operation.

Figure 7.2 highlights the way in which such criteria may be used to select employees for redundancy.

Name of employee	Length of service (1 mark for each year up to 15 years)	Computer skills (5 marks)	Sickness/ absence record (10 marks)	Capability for remaining jobs (20 marks)
Sam Smith	10	5	7	16
Megan Brown	2	2	8	9
Thomas White	10	4	10	18
Gary Black	6	1	1	5
Nicola Green	4	3	10	11

Name of employee	Total mark/50	Selected?	Not selected
Sam Smith	38		✓
Megan Brown	21	✓	
Thomas White	42		✓
Gary Black	13	✓	
Nicola Green	28	✓	

Figure 7.2 The application of selection criteria in a redundancy situation

Here, the first table shows the marks allocated to each employee in relation to the selection criteria. The employer has made 50 marks available under the criteria which are eventually going to be used on 100 employees. The employer needs to make at least half of the employees redundant.

The employer has decided to select those employees for redundancy who score 35 or less on the selection criteria. Using the sample of five employees noted above, the employer has selected three employees for redundancy. The employer has given credit to length of service and those skills that will be needed when the workforce is reduced.

In deciding whether or not an employer has breached the procedural requirement to select fairly, the tribunal will first consider the fairness of the selection criteria used, and then question whether that procedure was fairly applied. The question to ask is whether the selection for redundancy was one which a reasonable employer could have made. See further *Blatchfords Solicitors* v *Berger & ors* (2001). An employer should keep detailed records of the selection procedures, outlining the marks obtained by each employee, and the reasons why a particular employee was selected for redundancy. The employer should be able to show that the selection criteria were applied objectively and reasonably.

See further: *John Brown Engineering Ltd* v *Brown* (1997), *British Aerospace* v *Green* (1995), *Lloyd* v *Taylor Woodrow Construction* (1999), *Dixon* v *The Automobile Association Ltd* (2003), *Lionel Leventhal Ltd* v *North* (2004), *Bansi* v *Alpha Flight Services* (2004), *Hendy Banks City Print Ltd* v *Fairbrother* (2005).

Automatically unfair selection for redundancy

It should be noted that in some situations it is automatically unfair to select an employee for redundancy. This is where, for example, they are selected because they are pregnant, for a reason concerned with health and safety, due to them being involved in trade union activities or for being a member of a union. This list is not exhaustive. Decisions to make an employee redundant should be capable of being justified following the use of a fair selection procedure. The decision to make someone redundant should not be made for any other discriminatory reason.

Consultation with appropriate representatives

The rules on consultation are outlined in ss 188–198 of the Trade Union and Labour Relations (Consolidation) Act 1992, as amended by the Collective Redundancies and Transfer of Undertakings (Protection of Employment) (Amendment) Regulations 1999.

Where an employer is proposing to make 20 or more employees redundant he has a statutory duty to consult with the workplace union or other 'appropriate representatives'. Under the 1999 Regulations if there is a recognised workplace union then the employer must consult with representatives from that union.

Section 188(1) of the 1992 Act states that:

Where an employer is proposing to dismiss as redundant 20 or more employees at one establishment within a period of 90 days or less, the employer shall consult about the dismissals all the persons who are appropriate representatives of any of the employees who may be affected by the proposed dismissals or may be affected by measures taken in connection with those dismissals.

When should consultation begin?

The European Collective Redundancies Directive (1975/129) (as amended 98/59) states that consultation must begin when the employer is 'contemplating redundancies'. In *APAC* v *Kirvin Ltd* (1978) it was held that the word 'proposing' (in s 188(1) above) meant that consultation need only begin when the employer has formed a definite view that redundancies are needed.

However, in *R* v *British Coal Corporation, ex parte Vardy* (1993) it was thought that consultation should begin at the earliest possible stage, when the employer first thinks that they may need to make some of their workforce redundant.

This consultation should begin in 'good time', and in any event s 188(1A) of the 1992 Act states that:

- where the employer is proposing to dismiss 100 or more employees within 90 days or less at least 90 days before the first of the dismissals are to take effect; and

- where the employer is proposing to dismiss 20–99 employees within 90 days or less at least 30 days before the first of the dismissals are to take effect.

There has been much debate as to what is meant by 'in good time'. In *MSF Union* v *Refuge Assurance Plc & anor* (2002) the EAT held that to be 'in good time' an employer should consider the probable date of redundancies and how long they will need in order to carry out an effective consultation. The date arrived at will then be taken to be the date at which consultation should begin.

In *Burns & ors* v *Scotch Premier Meat Ltd* (2000) it was held that mere 'consideration' of the possibility of redundancy does not mean that an employer should begin the consultation process. However, once an employer makes a definite decision that they will either sell their business as a 'going concern' or make workers redundant then the consultation process should begin. In *Middlesbrough Borough Council* v *TGWU* (2002) it was reaffirmed that consultation must take place before a final decision to make any employees redundant is taken. In *Junk* v *Wolfgang Kuhnel* (2005) the European Court of Justice held that where collective consultation is required by Directive 98/50/EC prior to a redundancy situation, that consultation must be completed before notice of dismissal is given to any employee. Under European law, therefore, an employer proposing to dismiss 20 or more employees at one establishment must complete the 90- or 30-day consultation period prior to giving notice of redundancy. The Department of Trade and Industry has recently stated that it will enter into consultation following this decision.

See also: *Re Hartlebury Printers Ltd* (1992), *GMB* v *Man Truck & Bus UK Ltd* (2000), *Leicestershire County Council* v *Unison* (2005) IRLR 920.

What should the consultation try to achieve?

There are several reasons why it is very important for an employer to consult with employee representatives. At the outset, it may be possible to avoid redundancies by implementing other schemes, such as a ban on overtime, or a freeze on pay increases.

If the dismissals cannot be avoided the parties are still able to negotiate on how best to select for redundancy. Discussions may also take place on how best to help employees who are to be affected by the changes. The employer consults 'with a view to reaching an agreement with the proposed representatives'.

Any failure to consult will normally make a dismissal for redundancy unfair.

What is 'one establishment'?

An employer has an obligation to consult where 20 or more people are likely to be made redundant at 'one establishment'. There is no definition of what will amount to 'one establishment' in the 1992 Act. However, the term has been the subject of debate in several cases. In *Clarks of Hove Ltd* v *Baker's Union* (1978) a bakery and 28 shops were held to be 'one establishment'. In *Rockfon A/S* v *Specialarbejderforbundet i Danmark* (1996) it was held that 'establishment means the unit in which the workers who are to be made redundant carry out their duties'.

Who are appropriate representatives?

Section 188(1B) of the Trade Union and Labour Relations (Consolidation) Act 1992 defines appropriate representatives as:

(a) if there is a recognised trade union, representatives of that trade union; or in any other case

(b) whichever of the following employee representatives the employer may choose from:

    (i) representatives who have been elected by the employees (but not for the purpose of consultation in a possible redundancy situation) who have the authority to receive information and be consulted about the proposed redundancies on their behalf, or

    (ii) representatives elected by the 'affected employees' to act on their behalf for the purpose of consultation in a possible redundancy situation. Here the representatives must have been elected in accordance with s 188A of the 1992 Act.

Section 188A is concerned with the 'election of employee representatives'. The section places various requirements upon an employer who is involved in the election of such representatives. These include making arrangements to ensure that the election is fair and ensuring that enough representatives are elected to represent their workforce. They should also ensure that no affected employee is excluded from standing for election.

What information should the employer disclose during consultation?

Section 188(4) of the 1992 Act states that during consultation the employer shall disclose in writing to the appropriate representatives:

- the reasons for his proposals;
- the numbers and descriptions of employees whom it is proposed to dismiss as redundant;
- the total number of employees of any such description employed by the employer at the establishment in question;
- the proposed method of selecting the employees who may be dismissed;
- the proposed method of carrying out the dismissals, with due regard to any agreed procedure, including the period over which the dismissals are to take effect;
- the proposed method of calculating the amount of any redundancy payments to be made (otherwise than in compliance with an obligation imposed by or by virtue of any enactment) to employees who may be dismissed.

This information should be given to the appropriate representatives by being delivered to them, or being sent by post to an address provided by them. Both before and during any consultation, the employer must allow the representatives access to those workers who may be affected by any redundancies. The employer should also ensure that the representatives are given other assistance, such as rooms in which to meet, and the use of telephones. Representatives normally call large-scale meetings to inform the workforce of any developments.

Complaints to the Employment Tribunal – the protective award

In situations where an employer has failed to consult with the workforce before announcing planned redundancies a complaint may be made to the Employment Tribunal. Where the failure relates to the election of employee representatives the complaint may be brought by any of the affected employees or by any of the employees who have been made redundant. In cases where the failure relates to the role of employee representatives the complaint can be made by any of those representatives. If the failure relates to trade union representatives then the union may bring a complaint. In any other case a complaint may be brought by any of the affected employees or any of the employees who have been dismissed as redundant.

It is left to an employer to show that it was not reasonably practicable for him to comply with the consultation rules and that he took all reasonable steps in the circumstances. If the tribunal finds that no consultation took place and does not accept the employer's defence to inaction then they must make a declaration to this effect. They may also make what is termed a 'protective award'. The objective of this award is to compensate employees for the lack of consultation. The award is made to those who have already been or are about to be made redundant.

The award is made for a 'protected period' which can be up to a maximum of 90 days. The tribunal will decide on the duration of the award on the basis of what is 'just and equitable' and having regard to the 'seriousness of the employer's default'. When the award is made the employee is entitled to one week's pay for each week of the 'protected period'. A week's pay is set in the same manner as for unfair dismissal/redundancy calculations and at the time of writing is £310. No statutory limit applies to a protective award. If an employer fails to pay the award the employee may make a complaint to the Employment Tribunal.

Special circumstances – s 189(6) 1992 Act

In some situations an employer may be able to defend the fact that he did not consult with appropriate representatives. This is where he is able to show that there were 'special circumstances' which prevented him from engaging in any consultation. He would have to be able to show that it was not reasonably practicable for him to comply with the consultation rules and that he took all reasonable steps to comply in the circumstances. If the tribunal accepts this defence then he may avoid liability. There is no statutory definition of what will amount to 'special circumstances'.

In *Clarks of Hove Ltd* v *Bakers' Union* (1978) the Court of Appeal held that a special circumstance must be something 'exceptional', 'out of the ordinary', or 'uncommon'.

An example of a special circumstance would be where the employer had genuinely thought that he would be able to find a buyer for the business. In that case it may not have been reasonably practicable for him to enter into consultation.

In *APAC* v *Kirvin Ltd* (1978) the Employment Appeal Tribunal held that a line had to be drawn between what could be considered a reasonable hope that the business would survive, and a foreseeable insolvency. Where it is obvious that the business will be rendered insolvent there are no special circumstances.

USDAW v *Leancut Bacon Ltd* (1981)

Leancut Bacon was heading for insolvency. Its directors entered into talks with a third party who had shown an interest in buying their shares. Unfortunately these talks broke down. Leancut had no option but to make its employees redundant. Leancut had thought that it had secured a rescue operation, but had had its hopes dashed at the last moment. The false hope had been the reason why it did not engage in any consultation.

Held Special circumstances existed.

Clarks of Hove Ltd v *Bakers' Union* (1978)

Clarks were in severe financial difficulties. They had reached the point where they were no longer able to pay staff wages. They had been aware of the severity of the situation for some time but did not enter into any consultation. They did not announce their imminent closure to the workforce until two hours before the closure took place.

Held No special circumstances existed; Clarks should have consulted with the appropriate representatives as soon as they had realised that closure was inevitable.

There is one situation, outlined by statute, which will not amount to a special circumstance. Section 188(7) of the Trade Union Reform and Employment Rights Act 1993 amended the 1992 Act to exclude one type of situation. This is where the decision leading to the proposed dismissals is made by someone controlling the employer, and that person fails to provide the employer with adequate information on the proposed redundancies. The employer cannot rely on that failure as a special circumstance.

Informing the Department of Trade and Industry

Section 193 of the Trade Union and Labour Relations (Consolidation) Act 1992 imposes an obligation on employers to inform the Department of Trade and Industry (DTI) of any planned redundancies.

An employer who is proposing to dismiss as redundant 100 or more employees must notify the DTI of those dismissals at least 90 days before the first one is due to take effect. Where the employer is proposing to dismiss 20 or more employees, he must notify the DTI of those dismissals at least 30 days before the first of those dismissals takes effect. The Collective Redundancies (Amendment) Regulations 2006 came into force on 1 October 2006. These Regulations amend s 193 of the 1992 Act and state that where 20 or more employees are to be made redundant, notice to the DTI must be given at least 30 days before notice is given to terminate their contracts of employment.

The employer notifies the DTI on form HR1. A copy of the completed form should also be given to the appropriate representatives. Such notification may help the DTI to act where there are to be mass redundancies affecting, for example, one town or particular industry. In such cases the DTI may be able to introduce training schemes or support to help redundant workers obtain new employment.

An employer that fails to notify the DTI of the proposed redundancies commits an offence. This is outlined in s 194 of the Trade Union and Labour Relations (Consolidation) Act 1992. The offence is punishable by way of a fine.

Individual consultation with employees

Once the employer has completed the selection procedure, he will have decided which employees are to keep their jobs and which are to be made redundant. The next step in the redundancy handling procedure is to inform the selected employees that they are to be made redundant. The duty to consult on an individual basis applies even where an employer decides to make only one employee redundant.

Individual consultation should take place before the employee is issued with a dismissal notice. The leading case on personal consultation is *Polkey v A E Dayton Services* (1987). In *Polkey* the employee was found to have been unfairly dismissed when his employer had failed to consult with him about his impending redundancy.

In this case Lord Bridge stated that '. . . the employer will normally not act reasonably unless he warns and consults any employees affected or their representatives . . .'

In *Herron v Citylink–Nottingham* (1993) it was held that where an employer does not consult on an individual basis, he must be able to provide justification for his inaction. Where an employer cannot justify his inaction, any dismissals are likely to be rendered unfair.

The process of consultation with appropriate representatives should not be seen as an alternative to individual consultation. However extensive the consultation with representatives becomes, an employer should still consult on an individual basis: *Rolls-Royce Motors v Price* (1993).

Mugford v Midland Bank plc (1997)

Mr Mugford was made redundant. Midland Bank had consulted with the banking union before his dismissal took place, but it did not consult Mugford on his own selection.

Held (EAT) Consulting with a union does not necessarily absolve an employer from consulting with employees on an individual basis.

In *Alstom Traction Limited* v *Stephen Birkenhead & ors* (2002) the EAT considered the question of individual consultation. In this case former employees of Alstom Traction Limited complained that prior to their redundancy there had been no individual consultation concerning the decision to dismiss. The EAT upheld their claim for unfair dismissal because even though Alstom had consulted with the workplace union there had been no individual consultation. Similarly in *Oakley* v *Merseyside Magistrates' Court Committee* (2003) the EAT held that a courtroom resource manager had been unfairly dismissed where he had received no individual consultation on his impending redundancy.

Time off to look for work or arrange training

Once an employee has been told that he is to be made redundant, he is entitled to time off work to look for a new job or arrange training (see page 178).

Directive on information and consultation

The National Information and Consultation Directive 2002/14/EC was formally adopted in March 2002. The Directive provided new rights for employees on both information and consultation and applies to organisations with 50+ employees. It gives employees the right to be informed about the economic state of an employer's business, to be informed and consulted about employment prospects and about decisions that may lead to substantial changes in the organisation of their workplace. Such changes would include possible redundancies or transfers of the undertaking. This Directive was implemented by the Information and Consultation of Employees Regulations 2004. The 2004 Regulations came into force on 6 April 2005. Under the Regulations employees who work for large organisations have the right to request their employer to inform them of, and consult with them about, business matters which affect their employment. The Regulations apply to companies with 150+ employees. From April 2007 they will apply to companies with more than 100 employees, and from April 2008 to companies with more than 50 employees.

The offer of suitable alternative employment - s 141 ERA 1996

As part of the fair redundancy-handling procedure, an employer should consider whether it will be possible to offer the redundant employee suitable alternative employment. If the employee accepts such an offer, the employer will not have to pay him a redundancy payment. This is because he will continue to be employed by that employer, albeit in a different capacity. This rule applies only where there is a gap of four weeks or less between the contracts.

If an employee unreasonably refuses to accept suitable alternative employment, he loses his right to make a claim for a redundancy payment. The questions to ask are:

- Does the offer relate to suitable alternative employment?
- If the employment was suitable, did the employee unreasonably refuse to accept it?

Suitable alternative employment/reasonable refusal?

An employee is only expected to consider moving on to suitable new employment. An employer has a duty to try to provide suitable alternative employment either within his own, or in an associated organisation. In all cases, what will or will not amount to a suitable offer will depend on the circumstances of the particular employee involved and the type of work that the employee has been offered.

Employers should pursue all possibilities with employees. Even where the job on offer is so obviously inferior to that presently held, it should still be considered. At the end of the day it is left to the employee to decide on whether he would like to take up the new appointment.

An employee can refuse to accept alternative work that is not suitable. The employee is then able to claim a redundancy payment in the normal way. Problems arise where an employer argues that the job on offer is suitable, and the employee argues that it is not.

> **Example**
> *The employee may argue that the new job is unsuitable because by taking it he will experience problems in his personal life. For instance, it may be unacceptable to expect a parent to take up a new position in a location which makes it impossible for the employee to collect their children from school.*

In some cases the employer may be able to offer alternative work which is identical to that which the employee is about to lose. In such cases the work on offer will be classed as suitable alternative employment. However, in other cases where the job on offer is very different from the original job, the employee may argue that it is not suitable work.

Where disputes arise the question of whether an offer amounts to a suitable offer of alternative work is left to the tribunal. The tribunal takes into account both the original and new job considering:

● what each job entails, including any status attached to each;
● the level of earnings, including fringe benefits;
● the hours of work;
● the location/type of workplace and any differences in job prospects.

Where, in the new job, any of the above are less advantageous than those already obtained by the employee, it may be reasonable for the employee to refuse to take the job. If an employee unreasonably refuses to accept a new job, he loses his right to a redundancy payment.

The following cases highlight situations in which the tribunal had to consider whether the employer had offered an employee suitable alternative employment.

> ### *Taylor v Kent County Council* (1969)
>
> Mr Taylor was a school headmaster. He had been made redundant and was offered alternative work in a teaching 'pool'. This meant that he would be called on to do supply teaching when schools were short staffed. His salary and other benefits including his pension entitlement were to remain the same. Taylor refused this offer and made a claim for a redundancy payment. The school argued that he had lost his right to any such claim when he unreasonably refused the offer of alternative work.
>
> *Held* The offer was not a suitable offer. This was due to the fact that, if he took the job, he would lose his status as a school headmaster. Consequently, he was classed as being redundant and was entitled to a redundancy payment.

In this case Lord Chief Justice Parker stated that:

> . . . 'suitable' in relation to that employee means conditions of employment which are reasonably equivalent to those under the previous employment . . . it does not seem to me that by 'suitable employment' is meant employment of an entirely different nature.

In *Rawe* v *Power Gas Corporation* (1966) it was held that it was reasonable for an employee to refuse a new job which entailed a move from the South of England to Teesside. He had argued that the move would result in his wife leaving him and the break up of his family.

In *Souter* v *Harry Balfour & Co Ltd* (1966), Mr Souter had turned down a suitable alternative job because he would not be working in the field for which he had trained. This was held to be a reasonable refusal.

Paton, Calvert & Co v Waterside (1979)

Mr Waterside had been told that due to financial cuts he was going to be made redundant. He found another job while working his notice. Then, his employers received a temporary employment subsidy from the government. This meant that Waterside could continue to employ him for a short time. It offered him his job back and he stated that he was not interested in returning to the company. He claimed that he had been made redundant and his employer argued that by refusing to return he had lost all rights to a redundancy payment.

Held His refusal to return was reasonable and he was entitled to a redundancy payment. He was 61 years of age and the likelihood of him obtaining new permanent employment seemed unlikely. When he did get a new job he had reasonably refused to go back to his uncertain future with his original employer.

Fuller v Stephanie Bowman Ltd (1977)

Stephanie Bowman Ltd moved its premises from Mayfair to Soho. Fuller refused to move to the new site because it was above a sex shop!

Held The refusal to move was based on undue sensitivity and so was unreasonable in the circumstances.

Cambridge & District Co-operative Society Ltd v Ruse (1993)

A redundant manager of a butcher's shop turned down alternative employment as a manager of the butchery department of a supermarket.

Held Given that he felt that the move to the new position would involve a considerable loss of status he had acted reasonably in the circumstances.

See also: *Tocher* v *General Motors Scotland Ltd* (1981), *Thomas Wragg & Sons Ltd* v *Wood* (1976), *Hinchcliffe* v *John L Brierley Ltd* (2001), *Rice* v *Walker (t/a Kitchen Shop)* (2005) EAT.

The four-week rule

For an offer of alternative work to be effective in denying an employee redundancy pay, the new job must begin no later than four weeks after the old job ends. This is outlined in s 141(1) of the Employment Rights Act 1996.

7

Redundancy and the transfer of undertakings

The trial period

It would be unfair to expect an employee to take on a new job without first giving him some sort of trial period. Given that by accepting a new position an employee is giving up any right to a redundancy payment, few employees would risk the chance of beginning a new job without knowing whether or not they would enjoy it, or be competent at it.

For this reason, employees who accept a new position should be given a four-week trial period before being asked to decide on whether they wish to remain in it. If, after the four-week period expires, they decide not to stay, they are entitled to their ordinary redundancy payment. This entitlement is set out in s 138 of the Employment Rights Act 1996.

If an employee is dismissed during the trial period, he is treated as having been dismissed for redundancy under the employee's first contract. This four-week time period is strictly adhered to, but the parties may extend it in order to take into account any training that the employee needs to do before assessing the new job. Any such extension should be documented in writing stating the new date on which the trial period will end.

An employer cannot refuse to allow the first four weeks of employment to be classed as a trial period. In *Elliot v Richard Stump* (1987) the employer offered Mr Elliot suitable alternative employment but denied him a trial period. He then rejected the new job offer and his dismissal was held to be unfair.

UNFAIR DISMISSAL ARISING FROM REDUNDANCY

As redundancy is merely a form of dismissal, it may be either unfair or fair. Redundancy is one of the potentially fair reasons for dismissal outlined in s 98 of the Employment Rights Act 1996. In order for a dismissal to be fair, the employer has to show that redundancy was the reason for the dismissal, and that that redundancy was handled in a fair manner. (See page 251: Redundancy.)

A tribunal is more likely to render a redundancy dismissal unfair where there has been unfair selection, no consultation, or no offer of suitable alternative employment. In such cases the redundant employee would be able to make a claim for both unfair dismissal and a redundancy payment.

Aside from the usual dismissal fairness test, s 105 of the Employment Rights Act 1996 states that a redundant employee will be taken to have been unfairly dismissed if:

> **it is shown that the circumstances constituting the redundancy applied equally to one or more other employees in the same undertaking who held positions similar to that held by the employee and who have not been dismissed by the employer.**

Employee dismissed for misconduct

Section 140(1) of the Employment Rights Act 1996 states that an employee will not be entitled to a redundancy payment where he has been dismissed for misconduct.

'BUMPED' REDUNDANCIES

There has recently been some discussion on whether a 'bumped' redundancy is in fact a redundancy at all.

A bumped redundancy occurs where one employee who was to be made redundant is moved to do the work of another who was not. If the second employee is dismissed, is he redundant?

> **Example**
>
> Kate and Ken work for the same employer. The department in which Ken works is being closed down. His employer decides to employ Ken in the same section as Kate. The employer wants Ken to join Kate's team, but the team already employs its quota of 12 workers. If the employer decides to dismiss Kate to make way for Ken, has Kate been made redundant?

It was thought that in such situations there was a possibility that the second employee had been dismissed by redundancy. This has been deliberated in the cases of *Safeway Stores* v *Burrell* (1997) and *Church* v *West Lancashire NHS Trust* (1998).

In *Burrell* the EAT held that the second person could be classed as redundant as the test for redundancy was whether the requirements of the business for work done by that employee had ceased or diminished. In *Church* it was held that a 'bumped' employee cannot be said to have been dismissed for redundancy under the s 139(1) definition. However, in *Murray* v *Foyle Meats Ltd* (1999) it was held that a bumped redundancy was 'dismissal by reason of redundancy'. This case approved what had been said in *Burrell* but was not directly concerned with 'bumped' redundancies and did not refer to the *Church* decision. At the time of writing this area remains unclear.

LAY-OFF AND SHORT-TIME WORKING

This covers the situation where an employer may try to avoid having to pay redundancy payments by laying off employees on a long-term basis, or placing them on short-time work. Whilst the employer may do either of the above for very genuine financial reasons, employees are left with less money and the uncertainty of when the situation might improve.

Section 147 of the Employment Rights Act 1996 defines a lay-off situation as one where an employer does not provide any work for the employee to do, meaning that the employee does not receive any wages.

The section goes on to define a short-time work situation as being one where there is not enough work for the employee to do. Consequently, the employer only allows the employee to work for part of the week and he is entitled to wages of less than half a week's pay.

Section 148 of the 1996 Act states that where either of the above situations occurs for more than four consecutive weeks, or six weeks in any 13-week period, the employee can give his employer notice of the fact that he intends to claim a redundancy payment.

This notice must be given in writing. The employee effectively terminates his employment contract, claiming that he has been made redundant. An employer may be able to defend such a claim if he can show that there is a reasonable chance of him being able to provide his employee with full-time work for the following 13 weeks.

The employer must raise this 'defence' in a written counter-notice. This should be served within seven days of the receipt of the employee's intention to claim a redundancy payment.

REDUNDANCY PAYMENTS

The redundancy payments scheme was first set up under the Redundancy Payments Act 1965. It is now outlined in Part XI of the Employment Rights Act 1996.

When an employer makes an employee redundant, he must pay the employee a redundancy payment. The payment is meant to compensate the employee for the fact that he has lost his job. In *Wynes* v *Southrepps Hall Broiler Farm Ltd* (1968) it was said that the purpose of the

Redundancy and the transfer of undertakings — 7

scheme was to 'compensate for the loss of security, and to encourage workers to accept redundancy without damaging industrial relations'.

There is a statutory redundancy scheme which sets out basic payment entitlements. Often employers will provide an enhanced scheme, details of which will appear in an employee's contract of employment. In most cases employers will not dispute the fact that redundancy was the reason for dismissal. However, in some situations an employer may refuse to make a redundancy payment.

An employee who believes that he has been dismissed for redundancy must make a written claim to his employer asking for a redundancy payment. If the employer then refuses to pay him the amount owed, the employee is able to make a complaint to the Employment Tribunal. Claims must be made within six months of their dismissal.

The redundancy payment is paid directly by the employer to the employee. An eligible employee is still entitled to the same redundancy payment whether he has secured new employment or not.

Calculating the statutory redundancy payment

A redundancy payment is calculated in the same way as an unfair dismissal basic award. The scheme is set out in s 162 of the Employment Rights Act 1996. An employee is only entitled to a redundancy payment if he has two years of continuous service with his employer.

Qualifying employees are entitled to an award based on their age, service and the amount they earn each week. As with unfair dismissal calculations, the maximum week's pay to be used in the calculation is £310. This figure is revised annually.

If the employee earns less than £310 per week, his actual earnings are inserted in place of the maximum allowance. If the employee earns more, one is still only able to use £310 as the weekly amount.

The statutory redundancy award is calculated as follows:

Age × Service × Week's Pay

The multipliers to be used in the age section of the calculation are as follows:

- for any service where the employee was 41 or over, the factor is 1.5;
- for any service between the ages of 22 and 41, the factor is 1;
- for any service between the ages of 18 and 22, the factor is 0.5.

These figures reflect the amount payable for each year of service. For example, for every year that the employee has worked for the employer while the employee was between the ages of 22 and 41, he is entitled to one week's pay in the form of a redundancy payment.

The service calculation can only be made up to a maximum of 20 years. The maximum statutory redundancy pay available is therefore:

20 years × 1.5 × £310 = £9300

Where an employee successfully claims for unfair dismissal and a redundancy payment, the redundancy payment is set off against the basic unfair dismissal award. Any redundancy payment in excess of the basic award is then offset against the unfair dismissal compensatory award.

Employers must provide employees with a written statement outlining how their redundancy award was calculated. Failure to do so may result in the employer being fined.

What if the employer cannot pay?

As one of the main reasons why an employer may be forced to make some or all of the work-force redundant is financial hardship, it is not unusual to find the situation where an employer does not have enough money to pay redundancy payments. In such cases the government has recognised that employees must still receive payment.

Consequently, where making redundancy payments would force the employer into further hardship or put the remainder of the employer's business at risk the state will pay the employee's redundancy payments on the employer's behalf. Payment is made directly from the National Insurance Fund.

In order to seek assistance from the state, an employer must be able to show that there are no further lines of credit open to him. Where the state pays the redundant employees, the employer must repay the money to the National Insurance fund as soon as possible. These payments can be made in instalments.

In cases of insolvency, redundant employees are able to make a claim for payment to the Department of Trade and Industry (redundancy payments directorate). The employee ranks as a preferential creditor in his employer's insolvency. However, in many cases this will not mean that the employee will get any money, the likelihood being that the employer has no, or few, assets. In such cases the DTI can pay the employee direct from the National Insurance Fund. In order to receive a payment from the NI fund the employee must have either requested a redundancy payment (in writing) from their employer within 6 months of the date that they were dismissed or have applied successfully to an Employment Tribunal within the following six months.

The following payments can be made from the National Insurance Fund:

- up to 8 weeks' wages;
- minimum pay during notice;
- up to six weeks' holiday pay accumulated in the previous 12 months;
- a basic award issued by a tribunal;
- reimbursement of any fees paid for apprenticeship.

WHAT IS A TRANSFER OF AN UNDERTAKING?

A transfer of an undertaking occurs when a business or part of a business is sold or otherwise given to another. As the term states, an 'undertaking' (the business) is transferred (sold or otherwise given) to someone else. This effectively means that once the business is sold, the employees of the original owner become the employees of the new owner.

As stated in the introduction to this chapter, there are usually very sound financial reasons for selling or transferring a business. An employer may just want to make money out of the sale, or the sale may save the business from closure. Whilst the law recognises that such situations are inevitable and necessary, it seeks to protect the employee during the transfer period.

Examples

A transfer of an undertaking might occur in any of the following situations:

- *a company or part of it is bought or otherwise transferred as a going concern by another company;*
- *where all or part of a sole trader's business or partnership is sold or otherwise transferred;*
- *where two companies cease to exist and combine to form a third;*
- *where a contract to provide goods and services is transferred in circumstances which amount to a transfer to the new employer (contracting out);*
- *where there is a transfer of a lease, licence or franchise agreement;*
- *where there is a transfer of a contract for service from one independent contractor to another.*

Sources of law on the transfer of an undertaking

The law on the transfer of undertakings can be found in the Transfer of Undertakings (Protection of Employment) Regulations 2006. The 2006 Regulations came into force on 6 April 2006. The 2006 Regulations revoked the original 1981 Regulations. These Regulations were drafted in order to comply with the European Directive 77/187 'on the approximation of the laws of the Member States relating to the safeguarding of employees' rights in the event of transfers of undertakings, businesses or parts of undertakings or businesses'. This is commonly referred to as the 'Acquired Rights' Directive. This Directive was amended in 1998. In 2001 both the 1977 and 1998 Directives were repealed and replaced by a new consolidating Directive. This is the Acquired Rights Directive 2001 (2001/23/EC). It came into force on 11 April 2001 and changed the numbering of part of the contents of the previous Directives. Other than that it made no major changes to the law.

The Acquired Rights Directive aims to preserve continuity of employment when a business is sold on to a new employer.

The 1981 regulations were amended by the Trade Union Reform and Employment Rights Act 1993, and most significantly by the Collective Redundancies and Transfer of Undertakings (Protection of Employment) (Amendment) Regulations 1995–1999.

The 2006 Regulations build upon the 1981 Regulations. In the main the 2006 Regulations do not make any major changes to the 1981 Regulations. The DTI has published an excellent guide to the 2006 Regulations. *A guide to the 2006 TUPE Regulations for employees, employers and representatives* was published in August 2006 and is available via the DTI website.

THE TRANSFER OF UNDERTAKINGS (PROTECTION OF EMPLOYMENT) REGULATIONS 2006

The 2006 Regulations outline the general rules on the transfer of an undertaking. They apply equally to public and private sector undertakings. The particular Regulations which warrant further consideration are:

- reg 3 – relevant transfers;
- reg 4 – the effect of transfers on contracts of employment;
- reg 5 – the effect of relevant transfers on collective agreements;

- reg 6 – the effect of relevant transfers on trade union recognition;
- reg 7 – the dismissal of an employee because of a relevant transfer;
- reg 10 – occupational pension schemes;
- reg 11 – the duty to provide notification of employee liability information;
- reg 13 – the duty to inform and consult with representatives.

Any attempt by an employer to exclude or limit the application of the Regulations is void. The Regulations apply regardless of the size of the business, or the number of employees involved. The employees of the original owner of the business become employees of the new owner following an effective transfer.

The person who transfers or sells the business is referred to as the *transferor*. The person who buys or acquires the business is referred to as the *transferee*.

The 2006 Regulations do not apply:

- where the undertaking concerned is not in the United Kingdom;
- when the transfer involves only a transfer of company shares, the only change being in the identity of the shareholders; or
- where the transfer is a transfer of assets only.

Regulation 3 - a relevant transfer

An employee's continuity and terms and conditions of employment are only maintained if the sale of the business can be termed a 'relevant transfer'. Regulation 3(1) states that:

These Regulations apply to –

(a) a transfer of an undertaking, business or part of an undertaking or business situated immediately before the transfer in the United Kingdom to another person where there is a transfer of an economic entity which retains its identity;

(b) a service provision change, that is a situation in which –

(i)   activities cease to be carried out by a person ('a client') on his own behalf and are carried out instead by another person on the client's behalf ('a contractor');

(ii) activities cease to be carried out by a contractor on a client's behalf (whether or not those activities had previously been carried out by the client on his own behalf) and are carried out instead by another person ('a subsequent contractor') on the client's behalf; or

(iii) activities cease to be carried out by a contractor or a subsequent contractor on a client's behalf (whether or not those activities had previously been carried out by the client on his own behalf) and are carried out instead by the client on his own behalf, and in which the conditions set out in paragraph (3) are satisfied.

Paragraph (3) sets out the following conditions:

(a) immediately before the service provision change –

(i)   there is an organised grouping of employees situated in Great Britain which has as its principal purpose the carrying out of the activities concerned on behalf of the client;

(ii) the client intends that the activities will, following the service provision change, be carried out by the transferee other than in connection with a single specific event or task of short-term duration; and

(b) the activities concerned do not consist wholly or mainly of the supply of goods for the client's use.

Regulation 2(1) defines a 'relevant transfer' as 'a transfer or a service provision change to which these Regulations apply'.

In order for a transfer to be a relevant transfer, some business activity must pass from one person to the other. The thing transferred between the parties must be either a business or an identifiable part of a business.

Non-commercial ventures

Before the amendments made by the Trade Union Reform and Employment Rights Act 1993, the definition of a 'transfer' did not include undertakings that were not of a commercial nature. This meant that undertakings which operated under charitable status did not fall within the regulations. This position was changed by the decision in the following case.

Dr Sophie Redmond Stitchting v Bartol (1992)

The Redmond Foundation was a non-commercial charitable organisation. It provided help for drug addicts and was funded by an authority grant. This grant was later taken from it and given to another organisation, Sigma. Sigma took over the work that the Redmond Foundation had previously done. Sigma began to look after Redmond's clients and used what had been its premises. Sigma decided to continue to employ some of Redmond's staff. The question was whether the transfer was a relevant transfer under the Regulations.

Held Even though the businesses involved were non-commercial, the Directive and Regulations could still apply.

In *Dr Sophie Redmond* the European Court of Justice stated that the Directive was applicable wherever, 'in the context of contractual relations, there is a change in the legal or natural person who is responsible for carrying on the business and who incurs the obligations of an employer towards employees of the undertaking'.

This case resulted in the amendment of the 1981 Regulations by the Trade Union and Employment Rights Act 1993. Section 33(2) of this Act removed the section of the Regulations which had said that they did not apply to non-commercial ventures.

Transfer must be of an existing economic entity

Article 1(1) (b) of the 2001 Directive states that '... there is a transfer within the meaning of this Directive where there is a transfer of an economic entity which retains its identity, meaning an organised grouping of resources which has the object of pursuing an economic activity, whether or not that activity is central or ancillary'.

It is necessary to ascertain whether what has been sold is still an existing economic entity. This questions whether or not a business retains its identity on transfer. There must be some identifiable economic entity remaining on transfer. In other words, there must be evidence that the business is likely to continue in a similar manner to that previously adopted.

Spijkers v Gebroeders Benedik Abattoir CV (1986)

Spijkers had worked at the abattoir as an assistant manager. It was owned by Colaris. Colaris sold the land, abattoir and premises to another company, Benedik. When the sale took place Colaris had been forced to cease trading. There was no longer any 'goodwill' in the business. When Benedik reopened the abattoir, it employed all but two of the original owner's employees. Spijkers was one of these employees. Colaris did not take on any of the original customers. The question was whether the Directive could apply to the situation where there was no economic entity.

Held The words 'transfer of an undertaking, business or part of a business to another employer' in Article 1(1) of the Directive were to be interpreted as envisaging the case in which the business in issue retained its identity. In order to determine whether or not such a transfer has occurred, it was necessary to consider whether, having regard to all the facts characterising the transaction, the business was disposed of as a going concern, as would be indicated, amongst other things, by the fact that its operation was actually continued or resumed by the new employer with the same or similar activities.

In the case of **Rask v Christensen ISS Kantineservice** (1993) the European Court of Justice listed the factors that would be considered when considering whether a business has retained its identity. These are:

- the type of business/undertaking involved;
- whether or not the tangible assets of the business were transferred;
- the value of the intangible assets at the time of the transfer;
- whether or not the majority of employees were taken over;
- whether or not customers were transferred;
- the degree of similarity between the activities carried out before and after the transfer, and the period, if any, for which those activities were suspended.

In **Securicor Guarding Ltd v Fraser Security Services Ltd** (1996) it was said that the decisive criterion for establishing whether there has been a relevant transfer was whether the business had retained its identity, as would be indicated, in particular, by the fact that its operation was either continued or resumed.

In **Isles of Scilly Council v Brintel Helicopters Ltd** (1995) the EAT stated that examination should be made of 'the similarity between the work done before and after the relevant events, and the identity of those carrying out the work'.

See also: **Wren v Eastbourne Borough Council and UK Waste Control Ltd** (1993).

No contractual link

The lack of a direct contractual link between the transferor and transferee does not automatically mean that the transfer will not be a relevant transfer under the regulations. This means that, for example, where there has been a change in the owner of a franchise there will still be a relevant transfer.

In **Daddy's Dance Hall** (1988) it was held that a change in the leaseholder of a restaurant and bar amounted to a relevant transfer. In **P Bork International v Foreningen** (1989) it was held that where a factory lease was given up, and then the factory was sold freehold to a new employer, that there had been an effective transfer.

Service provision change - contracting out

This is the situation in which an organisation decides to buy in labour to, for example, run its security services, cleaning services, or canteen. In such situations the organisation 'contracts out' this work to a contractor who then employs his own employees to carry out the work. Prior to the introduction of the 2006 Regulations, whether or not the transfer rules applied to 'contracting out' situations remained a grey area of law. In **OCS Cleaning Scotland Ltd v Rudden** (1999) the court stated that 'there is no doubt that the position in law in relation to transfers of undertakings is a mess'. The 2006 Regulations clarify the law in this area by introducing a definition of 'service provision change' within Regulation 3. As noted above, a service provision change is a situation in which:

- activities cease to be carried out by a person (a client) on his own behalf and are carried out instead by another person on the client's behalf (a contractor);
- activities cease to be carried out by a contractor on a client's behalf and are carried out instead by another person (a subsequent contractor) on the client's behalf; or
- activities cease to be carried out by a contractor or a subsequent contractor on a client's behalf and are carried out instead by the client on his own behalf.

The following conditions must also be met. Immediately before the service provision change there must be an organised grouping of employees situated in Great Britain which has as its principal purpose the carrying out of the activities concerned on behalf of the client. The client must intend that the activities will, following the service provision change, be carried out by the transferee other than in connection with a single specific event or task of short-term duration. Finally, the activities concerned must not consist wholly or mainly of the supply of goods for the client's use. If these conditions are met then the transfer will be a relevant transfer under the Regulation 3 definition.

At the time of writing little has been written on the interpretation of this new definition. Suffice to say, however, that the introduction of the service provision change definition will hopefully eliminate the uncertainty that arose in previous cases concerned with 'outsourcing' or 'contracting out.' The new Regulations make it clear that TUPE applies to service provision changes.

For a consideration of the law as it was applied under the old transfer Regulations see the following cases: **Dines v Initial Health Care Services** (1994), **Suzen v Zehnacker Gebauserinigung** (1997), **Betts v Brintel Helicopters** (1997), **RCO Support Services Ltd v UNISON** (2002), **ADI (UK) Ltd v Willer** (2001), **Oy Liikenne Ab Liskojarvi** (2001), **P & O Trans European Ltd v Initial Transport Services Ltd** (2003).

● Regulation 4 – the effect of transfers on contracts of employment

Under the common law rule in **Noakes v Doncaster Amalgamated Collieries Ltd** (1940), when a business was sold, none of the employee's contracts of employment were transferable to the new owner.

This effectively meant that when a business was transferred, the employees ceased to be employed by anyone. They had no right to continue to be employed by the new owner, and depending on whether that owner was interested in employing them, they may have found themselves out of work. This rule was changed by the Acquired Rights Directive and the 1981 regulations and is now outlined in Regulation 4 of the 2006 Regulations.

Regulation 4 states that when a relevant transfer has taken place, the employees of the original owner of the business automatically become the employees of the new owner. Their terms and conditions of employment do not change, and there is no break in their continuity of employment.

Regulation 4(1) states:

a relevant transfer shall not operate so as to terminate the contract of employment of any person employed by the transferor and assigned to the organised grouping of resources or employees that is subject to the relevant transfer, which would otherwise be terminated by the transfer, but any such contract shall have effect after the transfer as if originally made between the person so employed and the transferee.

Regulation 4(2) states:

> on the completion of a relevant transfer –
>
> **(a) all the transferor's rights, powers, duties and liabilities under or in connection with any such contract shall be transferred by virtue of this regulation to the transferee; and**
>
> **(b) any act or omission before the transfer is completed, of or in relation to the transferor in respect of that contract or a person assigned to that organised grouping of resources or employees, shall be deemed to have been an act or omission of or in relation to the transferee.**

This means that the transferee becomes the new employer of all of the employees employed by the transferor at the time of the transfer. The transferee cannot agree to the transfer of some employment contracts and not others. Any rights and/or liabilities which existed under the original contract continue post transfer. Such rights or liabilities are only transferred in respect of those persons employed immediately prior to the transfer.

Exception where employee does not want to work for new employer

An exception to the general rules on the transfer of contracts of employment lies where an employee whose contract is about to be taken over by the new employer states that he does not wish this to happen. This is outlined in reg 4(7). In order to stop the transfer of his particular contract of employment, the employee must notify either the transferor or transferee of the fact that he does not wish to be included in the transfer.

If an employee makes this statement, he effectively terminates his employment contract. However, he is not taken to have been dismissed. This means that he will not be entitled to any compensation.

The exception to this is where the employee terminates his employment because he believes that the transfer will result in a significant detrimental change to his terms and conditions of employment. In such situations the employee may be able to resign and claim constructive wrongful dismissal. This is only on the basis of there being a detrimental change to his situation and not just because he does not wish to have a 'new' employer. This is outlined in reg 4(9) and was discussed in the case of *University of Oxford* v *Humphreys* (2000).

Was the employee employed immediately before the transfer?

In order for an employee's contract of employment to be taken over by the new owner of the business, the employee must have been employed by the original employer immediately before the transfer.

In *Secretary of State for Employment* v *Spence* (1987) it was held that only employees who were employed at the very moment of the transfer had their contracts transferred to the new owner. In this case an employee who had been dismissed by the original employer four hours before the transfer took place was held not to be employed at the time of the transfer, and so not covered by the Regulations.

In *Litster* v *Forth Dry Dock & Engineering Co* (1990) the court confirmed **Spence**, but stated that where an employee had been dismissed 'for a reason connected to the transfer' the employee would be covered by the Regulations when the transfer took place. Here, the employees had been dismissed only one hour before the transfer took place.

See also: *Longden* v *Ferrari* (1994), *Ibex Training* v *Walton* (1994).

Regulation 5 - the effect of relevant transfers on collective agreements

Regulation 5 states that:

> where at the time of a relevant transfer there exists a collective agreement made by or on behalf or the transferor with a trade union recognised by the transferor in respect of any employee whose contract of employment is preserved by Regulation 4(1), then...

> (a) ...that agreement, in its application in relation to the employee, shall, after the transfer, have effect as if made by or on behalf of the transferee with that trade union, and accordingly anything done under or in connection with it, in its application in relation to the employee, by or in relation to the transferor before the transfer, shall, after the transfer, be deemed to have been done by or in relation to the transferee; and

> (b) any order made in respect of that agreement, in its application in relation to the employee, shall, after the transfer, have effect as if the transferee were a party to the agreement.

This means that if there is a collective agreement in existence at the time of the transfer, the transferee takes on that agreement.

Regulation 6 - the effect of relevant transfers on trade union recognition

If an independent trade union has been recognised by the transferor prior to the transfer then following that transfer the transferee will be deemed to have recognised that trade union.

Regulation 7 - the dismissal of an employee because of a relevant transfer

Regulation 7 states that:

> Where either before or after a relevant transfer, any employee of the transferor or transferee is dismissed, that employee shall be treated ... as unfairly dismissed if the sole or principal reason for his dismissal is –

> (a) the transfer itself; or

> (b) a reason connected with the transfer that is not an economic, technical or organisational reason entailing changes in the workforce.

An employee who has one year's continuous service with his employer (either the transferor or transferee) and who is dismissed as a result of a transfer is able to make a claim for unfair dismissal. Dismissal resulting from the transfer of an undertaking is one of the automatically unfair reasons to dismiss (discussed at paage 239). If, however, an employee finds that working for his new employer results in a drastic decline in his original working conditions, he may terminate his employment contract, stating that he has been forced to resign, and make a claim for unfair dismissal.

Economical, technical or organisational reason - Regulation 7(2)(3)

The exception to the rule that an employee will automatically have been unfairly dismissed lies where the employer can show that the employee was dismissed for an economical, technical or organisational reason. The onus is on the employer to show that such a reason existed and that this reason resulted in the dismissal. This Regulation only provides that the dismissal will be potentially fair. It is then left to the tribunal to decide on whether the dismissal was fair or unfair.

There is no statutory definition of what will amount to an 'economic, technical or organisational reason'. The DTI guidance on TUPE 2006 (*A guide to the 2006 TUPE Regulations for employees, employers and representatives*) states that the term is likely to include:

(a) a reason relating to the profitability or market performance of the transferee's business (i.e. an economic reason);

(b) a reason relating to the nature of the equipment or production processes which the transferee operates (i.e. a technical reason); or

(c) a reason relating to the management or organisational structure of the transferee's business (i.e. an organisational reason).

In *Meikle* v *McPhail* (1983) it was said that economic reasons must relate to the conduct of the business. Here, an economic, technical or organisational reason was established when, soon after the transfer took place, the new employer realised that it was not economically viable to run the business with the original number of employees. 'Redundancy' is the most common 'eto' reason.

See also: *Gateway Hotels Ltd* v *Stewart* (1988), *Jules Dether Equipment SA* v *Dassy* (1998).

Regulation 10 – occupational pension schemes

One exception to the fact that a transferee takes on all of the rights and obligations of the transferor is that the transferee does not have to recognise employee occupational pension schemes. This is outlined in reg 10 of the 2006 Regulations. However, s 257 of the Pensions Act 2004 provides that where an employee is a member of an occupational pension scheme prior to a transfer, the transferee must ensure that they are eligible to join their pension scheme or operate a stakeholder arrangement. See further: Transfer of Undertakings (Pension Protection) Regulations 2005.

Regulation 11 – the duty to provide notification of employee liability information

Regulation 11(1) states that:

> **The transferor shall notify to the transferee the employee liability information of any person employed by him who is assigned to the organised grouping of resources or employees that is the subject of a relevant transfer –**
>
> **(a) in writing; or**
>
> **(b) by making it available to him in a readily accessible form.**

This information will assist the transferee in understanding the rights, obligations and duties applicable to those employees who are to be transferred. The transferor must provide the following information:

(a) the identity of the employees who will transfer;

(b) the age of the employees who will transfer;

(c) the contents of their statement of particulars of employment;

(d) on any collective agreements which apply to those employees;

(e) on any instances of disciplinary/grievance action within the preceding two years taken by the transferor in respect of those employees in circumstances where the statutory dispute resolution procedures apply; and

(f) on any instances of legal actions taken by those employees against the transferor in the previous two years, and instances of potential legal actions which may be brought by those employees where the transferor has reasonable grounds to believe such actions might occur.

The information may be given in several instalments but must be given at least two weeks before the completion of the transfer. If special circumstances make this impossible then the information must be given as soon as is 'reasonably practicable'. It may not, for example, be reasonably practical to provide the information in time if the transferor is unaware of the identity of the transferee until very late in the proceedings.

Regulation 13 – the duty to inform and consult with representatives

The consultation provision in reg 13 stems from the Collective Redundancy and Transfer of Undertakings (Protection of Employment) (Amendment) Regulations 1995 and 1999. These Regulations apply to transfer situations in the same way as they do to redundancy situations. They apply to any employee who is likely to be affected by the transfer.

Regulation13(2) states that:

Long enough before a relevant transfer to enable the employer of any affected employees to consult the appropriate representatives of any affected employees, the employer shall inform those representatives of –

(a) the fact that the transfer is to take place, the date or proposed date of the transfer and the reasons for it;

(b) the legal, economic and social implications of the transfer for any affected employees;

(c) the measures which he envisages he will, in connection with the transfer, take in relation to any affected employees or, if he envisages that no measures will be so taken, that fact; and

(d) if the employer is the transferor, the measures, in connection with the transfer, which he envisages the transferee will take in relation to any affected employees who will become employees of the transferee after the transfer … or if he envisages that no measures will be so taken, that fact.

This information should be given to appropriate representatives. These are normally persons from a recognised trade union. If there is no recognised trade union then the information may be given to elected employee representatives. The information must be provided well before any transfer is to take place, and at the very least at a time which gives the representatives the chance to consult with their members. An employer may be able to defend the fact that he did not consult with appropriate representatives by showing that special circumstances existed at the time. This exception also relates to redundancy consultation and is discussed further above (page 281).

During the consultation period appropriate representatives must be given access to the workforce, and other facilities such as the use of telephones and meeting rooms. If an employer fails to consult with appropriate representatives, and has no justification for his inaction, the union may make a complaint to the Employment Tribunal. The complaint must be made within three months of the failure to consult. The tribunal may make a declaration and award appropriate compensation of up to 13 weeks' pay. The tribunal makes this award on the basis of what is 'just and equitable' having regard to the seriousness of the failure of the employer to consult with employees.

SUMMARY CHECKLIST

- The common theme in both redundancy and transfer situations is consultation.
- There is a general right to a redundancy payment under s 135(1) of the Employment Rights Act 1996.
- All eligible redundant employees are entitled to a payment under the statutory redundancy scheme; often employers have enhanced in-house schemes.
- An employer should pursue other possibilities, such as a restriction on overtime, before taking the decision to make employees redundant.
- Employers must clearly identify their reasons for deciding to make employees redundant.
- A dismissed employee can only claim a redundancy payment if he can show that he was dismissed for one of the reasons listed in s 139(1) of the Employment Rights Act 1996.
- This states that an employer may make an employee redundant where either, the business where the employee works/worked has ceased or is going to cease to exist, the particular site or section where the employee works/worked has or is going to cease to exist, or, there is no longer a need for the work that the employee does/did, either generally or at a particular site.
- The employer only has to show that he had a reason for making employees redundant; the tribunal will not question the validity or otherwise of his decision.
- Where an employer is forced to close the business and make the entire workforce redundant, there is rarely any question that the ending of the workers' employment amounted to a redundancy.
- An employee may have a mobility clause inserted into his contract of employment, stating that he can be required to work at a particular site or sites.
- The tribunals have considered both contractual and geographical tests.
- Where an employee's job ceases to exist, the employee is redundant; if he is replaced by a new worker, he is not redundant.
- Not all employees are eligible to make a claim for a redundancy payment.
- In order to be eligible, the worker must be an employee and, amongst other things, have at least two years of continuous service with his employer and not have unreasonably refused an offer of suitable alternative employment.
- In order to qualify as redundant, the employee must have been dismissed, or have been given a specific date on which his contract will terminate.
- Employers must follow correct redundancy handling procedures.
- Employers must be able to show that their selection criteria were objectively justified and applied fairly, that they conducted proper individual and collective consultation before making any employee redundant, and that they tried to find suitable alternative work for any redundant employee.
- Guidelines on redundancy handling were set out in the case of *Williams* v *Compair Maxam* (1982).
- Employers may begin the selection process by asking if any employees wish to volunteer for redundancy.

- The selection process must be fair and reasonable; the criteria should allow the employer to select a 'pool' of employees from which redundancies will be made.
- In drafting selection criteria the employer should consider such things as an employee's skill and capability in his job, his length of service, and whether a last-in-first-out selection policy should be adopted.
- Employers must consult with both appropriate representatives and individuals who are likely to be affected by the redundancies.
- This consultation must take place 'in good time' before the first of the redundancies is to take effect and, where 100 or more employees are to be made redundant, at least 90 days before the first redundancy; where 20–99 are to be made redundant, at least 30 days before any redundancy.
- The purpose of consultation is to discuss the proposed changes with representatives, considering any ways in which the redundancies can be avoided, and if that is not possible, how best to implement the changes.
- Appropriate representatives are those either elected by the employees or those belonging to a recognised trade union.
- During consultation the employer should disclose the reasons for the proposed redundancies, his proposed selection criteria, and the methods by which redundancy payments will be calculated.
- An employer may be able to defend the fact that he did not consult with appropriate representatives by showing 'special circumstances'.
- An employer has an obligation to inform the DTI of any impending redundancies.
- Individual consultation should take place before the employee is issued with a dismissal notice.
- An employer should consider the possibility of offering the redundant employee suitable alternative employment.
- If the employee accepts suitable alternative employment, he loses his right to claim a redundancy payment.
- If the employee unreasonably refuses to accept suitable alternative employment, he loses his right to claim a redundancy payment.
- Employees should be given a four-week trial period in their new job.
- An employee is not entitled to a redundancy payment where he has been dismissed for gross misconduct.
- Redundancy payments are calculated in the same way as unfair dismissal basic awards.
- Where an employer cannot afford to make redundancy payments or is insolvent, the state may make the payments on the employer's behalf.
- A transfer of an undertaking occurs when a business is sold or transferred to another person.
- The law seeks to protect those employees likely to be affected by the transfer by preserving their employment conditions and continuity of employment.
- The 2006 Transfer Regulations apply regardless of the size of the business, or how many employees work there.
- The person selling the business is referred to as the transferor, the buyer as the transferee.

- The 2006 regulations apply only where there has been a relevant transfer or a service provision change.
- The transfer must be of an existing economic entity.
- The contracts of employment of those employees affected by the transfer pass with it, meaning that the employees are entitled to the same terms and conditions when working for the new owner.
- An employee can opt out of a transfer by notifying either the transferor or transferee of his disinterest.
- Any dismissal which is made due to a reason connected to a transfer is automatically unfair.
- An employer may be able to justify such a decision if he had an economic, technical or organisational reason for making it.
- Transferors have a duty to consult with appropriate representatives before any transfer takes place.

SELF-TEST QUESTIONS

1 How does s 139(1) of the Employment Rights Act 1996 define the ways in which an employee may be dismissed 'by reason of redundancy'?

2 Why might an employee not be eligible to make a redundancy payment claim?

3 What types of issue might an employer consider relevant when drafting a redundancy selection criteria?

4 What are the timescales for consultation set out in s 188(1) of the Trade Union and Labour Relations (Consolidation) Act 1992?

5 What types of situation may amount to 'special circumstances'?

6 When might an employee refuse to accept suitable alternative employment?

7 From where might an employee receive a redundancy payment if his previous employer is either insolvent or has little money?

8 What is a transfer of an undertaking?

9 Do the 2006 Transfer Regulations apply to contracting-out situations?

10 Does a transferor have a duty to consult with appropriate representatives prior to any transfer taking place?

CASE SCENARIOS

A

Conrad and Alan work for a large insurance company. They receive a memo from their employer stating that the company is in serious financial difficulties and that some employees will have to be made redundant. This memo arrives on 23 October. On the following Monday they are called into their manager's office and told that they are to be made redundant from the end of that week. The company has decided to close down the section in which they work.

Conrad asks why their union has not been consulted on the redundancies. Their manager states that she has just left a meeting with the union. He shouts, 'Four days before you sack us – great!' She apologises, stating that the company had thought that it was about to be bought by an American company. She asks Conrad to leave and then tells Alan that he is to be offered another job with the company. At present he works as a data manager. The new job involves answering telephone queries. He tells her to 'get real', stating that he could have done that work when he'd just left school! Conrad is not that bothered about the situation; he is close to retirement and is more interested in how much redundancy money he is likely to get. He has always wanted to go to the Grand Canyon and plans to spend it on a holiday.

Advise both men as to:

- *whether they have lawfully been made redundant;*
- *whether there has been enough consultation.*

Advise Alan as to whether his redundancy payment will be affected if he rejects the telephone job.

Advise Conrad as to the level of his likely statutory redundancy payment. He is 61 years old and has worked for the company for ten years.

B

Lawrence and Valerie work for an electricity company, 'Sparks'. Valerie is a union representative and has heard rumours that the company is about to be bought by a competitor. Michelle, their sister, works for 'Brightlights', a cleaning company. Brightlights recently obtained a six-month contract to clean Sparks' offices. On Monday 3 January, Valerie is called to a meeting where the rumours of a sale are confirmed. Sparks arrange to meet with the representatives, telling them that the transfer will not occur for eight months. Consultation takes place during this time.

One month before the sale takes place Sparks readvertise for tenders for the cleaning contract. Brightlights fail to renew their contract; it is given to another firm, 'Shiney-Shiney'.

On the day before the main sale is to take place, Lawrence decides that he does not want to work for Sparks, and Valerie is dismissed.

Advise Michelle as to whether the transfer regulations will apply to Shiney-Shiney.

Advise Valerie as to whether she has been lawfully dismissed.

Advise Lawrence:

- *as to whether he can opt out of the transfer;*
- *what the likely consequences of any opt-out will be.*

● Further reading

Redundancy, IDS Employment Handbook, August 2000.

Redundancy Handling, ACAS Advisory Booklet, November 2002.

Redundancy, consultation and notification – Guidance, DTI, 2006/1965.

An Analysis of the Transfer of Undertakings (Protection of Employment) Regulations 2006', John McMullen, *Industrial Law Journal*, June 2006, 35, pp. 113–139.

A guide to the 2006 TUPE Regulations for employees, employers and representatives, DTI, August 2006.

For legal updates on the material in this chapter please go to the Companion Website accompanying this book at **www.mylawchamber.co.uk/nairns**

7

Redundancy and the transfer of undertakings

8 Trade unions, collective bargaining and industrial action

It can generally be said that trade unions do not have as much influence in the workplace today as they have enjoyed during past decades. However, the role of the union remains important in the organisation of workplace relations and in the instigation of industrial action. Even though union membership is on the decrease, the workplace union remains the first port of call for many employees faced with queries on matters of employment law, or when faced with disciplinary action. In addition, whilst strikes are not as commonplace as they were, say, in the 1970s or 1980s, the rules on strike action and other forms of industrial action are still of importance.

The main statute that should be considered in relation to unions and industrial action is the:

● Trade Union and Labour Relations (Consolidation) Act 1992 (TULR(C)A 1992) (as amended).

The Trade Union Reform and Employment Rights Act 1993 was also of major influence in this area. However, whilst this Act is still referred to where appropriate it has mainly been absorbed into other legislation, namely the 1992 Act noted above and the Employment Rights Act 1996. The 1996 Act repealed and consolidated the 1993 Act.

This chapter outlines the law on trade unions, collective bargaining and the rules surrounding industrial action. It begins by outlining the constitution, role and definition of a *trade union* as opposed to an *employers' association* and goes on to discuss:

● the legal status of trade unions;
● the closed shop;
● listing, certification;
● union independence;
● voluntary and statutory recognition;
● the Bridlington principles;
● the use of the 'political fund';
● union rules, the right not to be 'unjustifiably disciplined';
● union ballots;
● collective bargaining;
● industrial action – the 'industrial torts';
● immunity from liability for industrial action;
● loss of statutory immunity;
● secondary action, picketing and criminal liability;
● enforcement.

TRADE UNIONS

A trade union is an organisation set up primarily to assist and represent its workplace members in matters such as collective bargaining and disciplinary hearings. The larger unions will often offer legal helplines and 'perks' for membership, such as low-cost motor insurance. Union activity is usually reported either when trade-union officials are lobbying for pay increases on behalf of their members, when industrial action takes place, or when they appear at the Trades Union Congress (TUC) conference, or political party annual conferences. There are over 300 workplace unions. Whilst some have only a handful of members, UNISON has over 1.3 million members. UNISON was formed on 1 July 1993 following the merger of three public service unions, COHSE, NALGO and NUPE. It is the largest union in the United Kingdom and represents members working in local government, healthcare, higher education, the electricity, gas and water industries, public transport and the voluntary sector.

In general, all workers have the right to belong or not belong to a trade union. However, members of the police force and the armed forces do not have this right. In the case of the police service, the Police Federation acts on behalf of its members.

It is illegal to discriminate against an individual on the grounds of trade-union involvement or non-involvement (see pages 93–94) and automatically unfair to dismiss an individual on the grounds of union involvement/non-involvement (see page 238).

What is a trade union?

Section 1 of the Trade Union and Labour Relations (Consolidation) Act 1992 defines a trade union as:

> **an organisation (whether temporary or permanent):**
>
> **(a) which consists wholly or mainly of workers of one or more descriptions and is an organisation whose principal purposes include the regulation of relations between workers of that description or those descriptions and employers or employers' associations, or**
>
> **(b) consists wholly or mainly of:**
>
> **(i) constituent or affiliated organisations which have those purposes; or**
>
> **(ii) representatives of such constituent or affiliated organisations, and in either case whose principal purposes include the regulation of relations between workers and employers or workers' and employers' associations, or include the regulation of relations between the constituent or affiliated organisations.**

Employers' associations

In some workplaces organisations form in the shape of employers' associations. Section 122 of the Trade Union and Labour Relations (Consolidation) Act 1992 defines an employers' association as an organisation which either:

> **consists wholly or mainly of employers or individual proprietors, and whose principal purposes include the regulation of relations between employers and workers or trade unions.**

The legal status of trade unions

There has been much debate as to whether trade unions can be said to have 'legal personality'. This is important in relation to their powers to be able to sue other individuals/organisations, or be sued themselves. The general rule is that trade unions do not have any legal personality, but are able to sue and be sued in their own name.

Unions may also be prosecuted using their own name and are able to enter into legally binding contracts. In *EEPTU v Times Newspapers* (1980) O'Connor J stated that a union is not to be treated as a body corporate, and that as such it had no legal personality which must be protected through the law of defamation.

The rules on legal personality are set out in s 10 of the Trade Union and Labour Relations (Consolidation) Act 1992. As unions have no legal existence, their property must be 'held' or looked after by trustees. This means that a union's bank account will not be controlled by any one individual. The union executive will appoint a number of trustees to administer the operation of the account. In turn, if a union is sued and the court orders it to pay an amount to another party, the awarded amount will be taken from union funds.

The 'closed shop'

There are two forms of 'closed shop': a 'pre-entry' closed shop and a 'post-entry' closed shop. A workplace with a closed shop in operation is one where belonging to a particular trade union is a condition of either being offered (pre-entry) or keeping (post-entry) a job. The ethics of such a scheme have long been debated, mainly because they removed a worker's freedom to freely join any union. Several governments have acted to bring an end to the operation of the closed shop.

In *Young, James and Webster* v *UK* (1981) the court ruled that the legislation which allowed the closed shop to operate infringed art 11 of the European Convention on Human Rights. However, despite this ruling it remained possible to enforce a legal post-entry closed shop until 1988. The relevant conditions of the then 1988 Employment Act are now contained in s 152 of the Trade Union and Labour Relations (Consolidation) Act 1992. This section states that it is automatically unfair to dismiss an employee on the basis of union membership or non-membership. An employee who is dismissed for either reason is able to make a claim for compensation to the Employment Tribunal.

This means that post-entry closed shops can theoretically exist, but that today no one can be compelled to join, or be penalised for refusing to join a particular trade union. The Employment Act 1990 took away the protection needed for the operation of the pre-entry closed shop. This provision is now set out in s 137 of the 1992 Act which states that it is unlawful to refuse a person employment because he is, or is not a member of a particular union. Again, a person in this situation is able to make a complaint to the Employment Tribunal.

Who can join a union?

Generally all workers have the right to join a trade union. This right is part of the general freedom of association protected under treaties on human rights such as the Universal Declaration of Human Rights (1948), and the European Convention on Human Rights.

In *Cheall* v *APEX* (1983) Lord Diplock said that freedom of association could only be mutual. He argued that there could be no right of an individual to associate with others who are not willing to associate with them. The position is now set out in s 174 of the Trade Union and Labour Relations (Consolidation) Act 1992. This section states that a union may only refuse to admit a person or expel a member if:

- his application does not satisfy an enforceable membership requirement;
- he does not work in the geographical area covered by the union;
- he no longer works for a relevant employer in the case of a company-specific union; or
- because of misconduct.

Enforceable membership requirements are those which stipulate criteria such as employment in a particular trade or occupational group, or having particular qualifications. The effect of s 174 has been to virtually abolish a union's right to define its own identity.

Other than for one of the above reasons it is illegal for a union to exclude or expel an individual from membership. If a person is either refused membership or expelled in this way then they are able to make a complaint to the Employment Tribunal. This is outlined in s 176 of the 1992 Act. The aggrieved person applies (in the first instance) to the tribunal for a declaration. If the tribunal finds that they have a genuine complaint then it will make a declaration to that effect. The tribunal will then give the complainant and the union a minimum of four weeks to settle matters between themselves. It may be that the union 'backs down' and decides to admit or re-admit the member. However, at any point between four weeks and six months the complainant is able to then make a claim to the tribunal for a compensatory award.

This award is designed to compensate them for the fact that they were either refused membership or expelled illegally from the union. The maximum compensation available is set at 30 × a 'week's pay' plus an amount equal to the maximum award available for unfair dismissal. As from 1 February 2007 a 'week's pay' is set at £310. This means that the maximum award available is £69 900. This reflects the payment of 30 × £310 plus the maximum unfair dismissal award (at the time of writing) of £60 600. The tribunal sets the award on the basis of what is 'just and equitable' taking into account any contributing conduct by the individual. If the parties are able to resolve the matter within four weeks then the complainant makes any compensation application to the Employment Tribunal. If, however, the matter is not resolved within that period then the application must be made direct to the Employment Appeal Tribunal. The EAT is able to make an extra compensatory award. At the time of writing this is set at 'not less' than £6700. Considering the figures outlined above the failure of an employer to adhere to s 174 may prove to be a very costly exercise.

Listing – s 2, TULR(C)A 1992

A system operates whereby lists are kept detailing all independent trade unions. There have been provisions in place for the listing of trade unions since the enactment of the Trade Union Act of 1871.

The Certification Officer is responsible for the maintenance of these lists (see page 32). In order for its name to be included on the list, a trade union must set out an application to the Certification Officer. In order to apply, the union must provide details of its rules, a list of its officials, the address of its head office, its name and a small fee. The Certification Officer will then decide whether or not the information provided is sufficient to warrant listing.

If the Certification Officer refuses to list a union, the union is able to appeal to the Employment Appeal Tribunal. The main reasons why a union seeks to be listed is that only a listed union can apply for a certificate of independence (see page 308) and listing carries with it tax advantages.

The Certification Officer may remove a name from the list at any time if she or he believes that the association has failed to fall within the statutory definition of a trade union.

Again, there is a right to appeal against refusal to the Employment Appeal Tribunal. Copies of the list are available for public inspection.

● Certificate of independence – s 6, TULR(C)A 1992

It is important for a trade union to obtain a certificate stating that it is an independent organisation. It is only members of an independent trade union who are entitled to benefits, such as:

- the receipt of information for collective bargaining purposes;
- the right to appoint safety representatives;
- protection against dismissal and action short of dismissal on the grounds of their union activities;
- the right to time off work to carry out trade union duties;
- consultation prior to redundancy;
- consultation prior to a transfer of an undertaking;
- the right to apply for financial assistance in order to conduct a secret ballot.

Section 6 of the TULR(C)A 1992 states that unions are able to obtain such certificates of independence from the Certification Officer. The union will have to meet certain conditions before such a certificate will be granted. Section 5 of the Act sets out these conditions describing an independent trade union as follows.

In order to be classed as being independent the union must not be:

(a) under the domination or control of an employer or group of employers or of one or more employers' associations; or

(b) liable to interference by an employer or any such group, or association (arising out of the provision of financial or material support or by any other means whatsoever) tending towards such control.

If, having looked at the way in which the union operates, the Certification Officer (CO) believes it to be independent, a certificate will be issued. If the certificate is refused, the CO must give the reasons for the refusal.

The leading case on this point, *Blue Circle Staff Association* v *Certification Officer* (1979), is outlined below.

Blue Circle Staff Association v *Certification Officer* (1979)

In 1971 the managers of Blue Circle instigated the setting up of a staff association to act on behalf of their employees. After operating as a staff association for six months the association's committee decided to change the way in which it operated and to run it as a trade union. The committee made an application for a certificate of independence. This application was refused because the Certification Officer did not believe that the association had ceased to be influenced by Blue Circle management. An appeal was made to the Employment Appeal Tribunal.

Held (EAT) The Certification Officer had been right to refuse to grant a certificate. The reasoning behind the original decision is detailed in the guidelines set out below.

In *Blue Circle* the following heads were identified as being relevant when considering whether or not a union is in fact independent.

(a) *History*: Any past links that the union may have had with the relevant employer should be taken into account. The more recent the link, the less likely that the union will achieve independence.

(b) *Finance*: If the employer is still responsible for financing the operation of the union, there can be little case for arguing independence.

(c) *Use of employer's facilities*: If an employer provides the union with facilities, such as the use of stationery, a telephone or photocopier, independence is likely to be doubted.

(d) *Membership*: If the union has drawn its members solely from one company, this may point towards dependence on a particular employer.

(e) *Negotiation record*: The Certification Officer will consider whether there has been strong or 'robust' negotiations between the union and the employer. If the union has shown that the employer can easily coerce the union into backing down on any issue, its independence will be questioned.

(f) *Organisation*: The Certification Officer will also look at the way in which the union is organised.

In **Squibb Staff Association v Certification Officer** (1979) the Court of Appeal held that the test for independence was whether the union was exposed to, or vulnerable to the risk of, interference, regardless as to whether interference had actually taken place.

In **Government Communications Staff Federation v Certification Officer** (1993) GCHQ set up a 'staff association' to assist their workforce. This was a reaction to the fact that the government had withdrawn recognition from trade unions and effectively banned any GCHQ employee from being a member of a union. Here, the Certification Officer refused to issue a certificate of independence to the staff association. This decision was upheld by the Employment Appeal Tribunal on the basis that the association was vulnerable to interference and depended upon the approval of GCHQ management.

Voluntary and statutory recognition

Recognition of a union by an employer can be either achieved on a voluntary or statutory basis. Only a trade union classed as a 'recognised' trade union can engage in collective bargaining with an employer. Section 178(3) of the Trade Union and Labour Relations (Consolidation) Act 1992 defines this situation as 'recognition of the union by an employer, or two or more associated employers, to any extent for the purpose of collective bargaining'.

Recognition is also required in order to obtain rights to benefits such as the disclosure of information for collective bargaining purposes and to be consulted before impending redundancies.

An employer will only negotiate with a union which it 'recognises' for collective bargaining purposes. As the term suggests voluntary recognition occurs when an employer agrees to recognise a trade union for collective bargaining purposes. There are no formal steps to be taken with regards to voluntary recognition. If an employer negotiates with a union by way of collective bargaining then they are said to have automatically 'recognised' that trade union. Until June 2000 this was the only way in which a union could achieve recognition. On 6 June 2000 a new set of rules on 'statutory recognition' were introduced. Schedule 1.1 of the Employment Relations Act 1999 introduced a new Schedule A1 into the Trade Union and Labour Relations (Consolidation) Act 1992. The rules on statutory recognition are set out in Schedule A1.

These rules are generally perceived to be both lengthy and complicated. However, by using the statutory recognition system a union can ensure that an employer recognises their bargaining unit for collective bargaining purposes. In the first instance the union must approach the employer and request recognition. Requests for recognition may only be made where an employer employs more than 21 workers. Such requests should be made in writing, identify the union(s) involved and the 'bargaining unit' and state that the application is being made under Schedule A1 of the 1992 Act. In some cases the employer may voluntarily agree to recognise the union at this stage. The parties have an initial period of ten days during which they are able to negotiate on the issue of recognition. If these negotiations are unsuccessful then the parties have a further 20 days in which to agree on the 'bargaining unit' and the question of recognition. The parties are able to request the assistance of Acas during their negotiations.

If negotiations fail and the parties are unable to come to any agreement then the union may apply for recognition to the Central Arbitration Committee (CAC) (see further page 27). The CAC supervises applications for recognition and in the early stages also takes on the role of assisting the parties with negotiations. The CAC is able to make a declaration requiring an employer to recognise a trade union for collective bargaining purposes. Generally the role of the CAC is to decide whether the union has the support of the majority of the workforce. It must decide whether the union has 'reasonable support' within the unit. This is defined as meaning that at least 10 per cent of the proposed unit must be members of the union. If there is less than 10 per cent of the workers in support of recognition then the CAC will not proceed. There needs to be some evidence of basic support for the union.

If there are already 50 per cent of union members in the bargaining unit then the automatic recognition rules apply and the CAC will make a declaration without first conducting a ballot. However, in some cases the CAC must conduct a secret ballot of union members. Such a ballot will take place where it is thought that:

- it would be in the interests of good industrial relations, where
- a significant number of union members within the unit inform the CAC that they do not want the union to conduct collective bargaining on their behalf, or where
- there is evidence relating to union membership which leads the CAC to conclude that there are doubts as to whether a significant number of the union members within the unit want the union to conduct collective bargaining.

Ballots must be conducted by a suitably qualified independent person and can either take place within the workplace or be conducted by post. Those conducting the ballot must comply with the Department of Trade and Industry Code of Practice on 'Access and Unfair Practices during ballots for trade union recognition or derecognition'. This was introduced in June 2005 and is available on the DTI website. If the result of the ballot is that the union is supported by a majority and at least 40 per cent of the bargaining unit then the CAC will make a declaration stating that the union is to be 'recognised.'

Once recognition is obtained it remains effective for three years and cannot be ended even after that time without the use of the derecognition process. This process allows for derecognition where the employer can show that their circumstances have changed and that they employ less than 21 workers or where the employer or workers believe that there is less than a majority of support for collective bargaining. Such an application can also be made where the original declaration of recognition was made automatically on the basis of majority union membership and the employer believes that membership within the bargaining unit is now less than 50 per cent.

A DTI review document on the Employment Relations Act 1999 (published on 27 February 2003) stated that the new statutory procedure had been very effective.

● The Bridlington principles

The Bridlington principles are so called because they were first adopted in Bridlington in 1939. They are operated by the Trades Union Congress (TUC) to regulate inter-union conflict. The rules are designed to prevent disputes of union membership and competition for the same membership or recognition rights.

> **Example**
>
> *The members of ABCD union may wish to recruit new members from a local factory. EFGH union already operates within the factory, the workforce making up 50 per cent of its membership. If ABCD attempts to recruit at the factory, and then succeeds in taking members away from EFGH union, it will be in breach of the Bridlington principles.*

If such a breach of the rules does occur, the matter is referred to the Disputes Committee of the TUC. If it is found that the rules were breached, the committee will normally order the offending union to terminate the membership of any member obtained in this way.

The use of the 'political fund'

All unions have what is referred to as a 'political fund'. This money is derived from part of the subscriptions that members pay for union membership. The concept of the political fund was set up following the decision in *Amalgamated Society of Railway Servants v Osborne* (1910). In this case the promotion of political aims was declared to be illegal under the Trade Union Act of 1871. Some years later the Trade Union Act of 1913 was passed allowing unions to pursue any of their aims through political objectives, but stating that any financial support for such assistance should be contained in a political fund.

A union may only use its political fund for 'political purposes'. If the money is to be used for political purposes, the majority of members must agree to such a use. A member of a trade union can complain to the Certification Officer if he believes that his union has used money to 'pursue political objectives' which has not come from the political fund.

A union should ballot its members asking if they wish to have a political fund. The ballot must be fully postal, meaning that the members receive voting slips in the post, and are asked to return their vote by post. In order to set up a political fund, there only has to be consensus from a majority of those who vote.

The political fund ballot should be repeated every ten years and any authorisation by a member in relation to pay deductions to the fund is only valid for three years. This is what is commonly referred to as the 'check-off' provision. A union member does not have to contribute to the political fund.

If union members are concerned about the validity of any ballot, they may make an application to have the conduct of the ballot reviewed by the High Court. If the High Court finds that there has been some discrepancy in the way in which the ballot was conducted, it may make an enforcement order requiring the union either to remedy the defect or hold another appropriate ballot.

A union can only spend its political fund on specified expenses. These are set out in s 72 of the TULR(C)A 1992 and are:

- contribution to the funds, or payment of expenses incurred by, a political party;
- provision of any service or property for use by a political party;
- the registration of electors or the selection of candidates for political office;
- the maintenance of any holder of a political office;
- the holding of any conference or meeting by or on behalf of a political party or any other meeting at which business of a political party is transacted;
- the production, publication, or distribution of political literature, film or advertisements which seek to persuade a person to vote for, or not vote for, a political party or candidate.

In *Paul* v *NALGO* (1987) a NALGO member complained that a union campaign against cuts in public services should be paid for out of the political fund. His claim succeeded. The crucial point was the closeness of the election. Even though there was no endorsement of the Labour candidates, it was held by the court that its main purpose was to dissuade candidates from voting Conservative.

Union rules

On becoming a member of a trade union, an employee enters into a contract with that union and so becomes bound by its rules and regulations. If a member then breaches one of these rules, the union may instigate disciplinary proceedings against him or her.

The right not to be unjustifiably disciplined

Section 64(1) of the Trade Union and Labour Relations (Consolidation) Act 1992 provides members of trade unions with the right not to be unjustifiably disciplined by their union.

Section 64(2) lists such discipline as including:

- being expelled from the union;
- having to pay a fine to the union;
- being deprived of access to any benefits, services, or facilities that would otherwise have been made available to them;
- the union encouraging or advising another union or branch not to accept the individual concerned as a member;
- the individual being subject to 'some other detriment'.

Section 65 of the TULR(C)A 1992 defines discipline as being unjustified when it relates to actions such as:

- failing to participate in or support a strike or other industrial action;
- making or intending to make a true complaint that the union has acted contrary to its rules;
- seeking or proposing to seek assistance from the Certification Officer or any other person consulted or asked to provide advice or assistance where the member alleges that there has been a breach of union rules.

The Trade Union Reform and Employment Rights Act 1993 added the following categories to the above list:

- failing to agree or withdrawing agreement to the payment of union subscriptions via check-off;
- becoming or proposing to become a member of another union;
- working, or proposing to work with people who are not union members.

The complete list is now set out in section 65(2) of the 1992 Act.

In other words, the law recognises that there may be some situations in which a union may legitimately discipline its members. However, s 65 outlaws discipline for some types of action.

If a union can lawfully discipline a member, any disciplinary action should be taken in accordance with the rules of natural justice. This means that each member facing disciplinary action is entitled to a fair hearing before any penalties are imposed. The hearing should be conducted before an impartial panel of members. The union member should be given advance notice of the charge set against them and anyone who may have been involved in the investigation of the 'offence' should not then be allowed to sit on the disciplinary panel.

In *Annamunthodo v Oilfield Workers Trade Union* (1961) a member's expulsion from the union was held to be void because he had no knowledge of the precise charge on which it was based.

See also, *Leigh v NUR* (1970); *Taylor v NUM* (Derbyshire Area) (No. 1) (1984); *Bradley v NALGO* (1991).

Roebuck v NUM (No. 2) (1978)

The president of the National Union of Mineworkers (Arthur Scargill) had successfully sued a newspaper for libel on behalf of the NUM. Roebuck was a union member who had given evidence in that action on behalf of the newspaper. Following this, Scargill reported that Roebuck had contradicted himself in a court statement that he had given to union solicitors, and that he had shown confidential union correspondence to the newspaper's solicitors. Scargill argued that this was detrimental to the union's interests and instigated disciplinary proceedings against Roebuck. Scargill then chaired a meeting at which this issue was raised. The matter was then referred to the union's area executive committee. This committee recommended that Roebuck and a colleague be suspended from office. Roebuck complained that he had been unjustifiably disciplined.

Held There had been unjustifiable discipline in that the matter had not been dealt with fairly. Any decision should not have been taken by (in this case Arthur Scargill) the person who first instigated the allegations. It was said that there had been a breach of natural justice in that Scargill had been the 'complainant, the pleader, the prosecutor, the advocate and the chairman in the union proceedings'.

If a union member believes that he has been unjustifiably disciplined, he is able to make a complaint to the Employment Tribunal. The complaint must be made within three months of the unjustifiable disciplinary actions taking place. If the tribunal finds that the discipline was unjustified, it will make a declaration to that effect giving the union a set period within which to remedy its actions.

This period is normally set at four weeks. It may be that the union 'backs down' during this time and decides to revoke the effects of any unjustifiable disciplinary action against the member and refund any money paid in fines. If this does occur the member is still able to make a claim for compensation to the tribunal. Such a claim may be made at any time between four weeks and six months of the declaration being made. The award from the tribunal is designed to compensate the individual for the fact that they have been unjustifiably disciplined. The tribunal will make an award on the basis of what is 'just and equitable'. The maximum compensation available is set at 30 × a 'week's pay' plus an amount equal to the maximum award available for unfair dismissal. As from 1 February 2007 a 'week's pay' is set at £310. This means that the maximum award available is £69 900. This reflects the payment of 30 × £310 plus the maximum unfair dismissal award (at the time of writing) of £60 600. If the parties resolve the matter within four weeks then the complainant makes any compensation claim to the Employment Tribunal. If, however the matter is not resolved within this time a complaint must be made direct to the Employment Appeal Tribunal. The EAT is able to make an extra compensatory award. At the time of writing this is set at 'not less' than £6700.

Union ballots

A ballot is the system by which union members vote for, for example, industrial action. There are various situations in which a union must hold a ballot. There are also strict rules on how a ballot should be administered. In the main, ballots are 'secret' or postal, meaning that members are free to vote without influence or coercion.

Appointment of union officials

Under Section 46 of the Trade Union and Labour Relations (Consolidation) Act 1992 a trade union has a duty to ensure that every member holding an official position must have been selected by a secret ballot of all members. These elections must take place every five years. Those positions that must be filled by way of a secret ballot are:

- members of the executive;
- the president;
- anyone entitled to speak at executive meetings;
- the general secretary.

The use of the independent scrutineer – s 49, TULR(C)A 1992

The union must use an independent scrutineer to oversee the operation of any ballot. The only exception to this is where there is to be a ballot on the holding of industrial action and the number of members entitled to vote does not exceed 50. The use of the independent scrutineer ensures, as far as is humanly possible, that the ballot is conducted in a fair and accountable manner.

Before the ballot takes place, the union must provide the scrutineer with a copy of the register of members. The name of the independent scrutineer must also be sent to every balloted member. The scrutineer must supervise the production and distribution of all voting papers.

All voting papers are returned directly to the scrutineer. They are then retained by him or his officers for a period of one year following the ballot. This ensures that evidence of the number of votes cast and the outcome of the ballot are available in the event of any challenge.

Following a ballot, the independent scrutineer must also draft a report for the union. This report should detail:

- how many voting papers were distributed;
- the number of voting papers later returned;
- the number of valid votes cast in the election for each candidate, or in a ballot, for each position;
- the number of invalid or spoiled votes returned;
- the name of the person (if any) appointed as an independent person to count the votes.

The report should also state that the scrutineer was satisfied that the ballot was held without any unfairness or malpractice and that he was able to carry out his function without anyone calling his independence into question. The rules on the counting of votes and report drafting are set out in ss 51A and 52 of the 1992 Act.

Union accounts and returns

Under s 28 of the Trade Union and Labour Relations (Consolidation) Act 1992 there is a duty on trade unions to keep their accounting records available for inspection for six years. During this time any member is able to inspect the records for any period. The union must allow inspection within 28 days of the request.

Unions must also send annual returns of their accounts to the Certification Officer. These documents must include details on the salary and other benefits paid to each member of their executive, their president and general secretary. Unions are also under an obligation to provide each member with an annual financial statement. This statement should include details on the total income and expenditure incurred during the previous financial year.

These rules are designed to encourage accountability, ensuring that all of the dealings of the union are open to inspection and comment.

COLLECTIVE BARGAINING

Collective bargaining is the process by which a union negotiates with an employer (on behalf of its members) on matters concerning terms and conditions of employment. Collective bargaining is defined in s 178(1) of the Trade Union and Labour Relations (Consolidation) Act 1992 as:

negotiations relating to or connected with one or more of those matters.

This section goes on to list those 'matters' as including:

- terms and conditions of employment;
- the physical conditions in which any workers are required to work;
- engagement or non-engagement, or termination or suspension of employment or the duties of employment, of one or more workers;
- allocation of work or the duties of employment between workers or groups of workers;
- matters of discipline;
- workers' membership or non-membership of a trade union.

Prior to 1972 there was no obligation on employers to allow employees to join a trade union, and thus no obligation on them to recognise trade unions for purposes of collective bargaining. Collective bargaining can take place at a national level or company level. National agreements, those for example which regulate the pay of nurses and teachers, provide the basis upon which local agreements are based. The matters agreed upon at a national level filter down and affect members at the local level.

Collective bargaining is the main tool with which employers and employees (through their union) are able to negotiate on matters affecting the workplace. A workplace where there is no negotiation is unlikely to have good industrial relations.

The collective agreement

Following collective bargaining, the collective agreement is incorporated into the contract of employment of affected employees. Section 178(1) of the TULR(C)A 1992 defines a collective agreement as 'any agreement or arrangement made by or on behalf of one or more trade unions and one or more employers or employers' associations'.

Duty to disclose information for collective bargaining

An employer has a duty to disclose (to the representatives of any independent trade union) all such information as may be relevant to collective bargaining. There is an Acas code of practice entitled the 'Disclosure of Information to Trade Unions for Collective Bargaining Purposes'.

An employer is entitled to withhold relevant information only where:

- it is within the interests of national security;
- the information relates specifically to one employee (unless he has consented to the disclosure);

- the information, if given, would cause substantial injury to the employer's business for reasons other than to effect collective bargaining;
- he could not disclose the information without breaking the law;
- he received the information in confidence; or
- the information was obtained by the employer for the purpose of either bringing or defending legal proceedings.

The right to disclosure of information is set out in ss 181–185 of the Trade Union and Labour Relations Act 1992. The general right is outlined in s 181(1) which states:

> **An employer who recognises an independent trade union shall, for the purposes of all stages of collective bargaining, about matters, and in relation to descriptions of workers, in respect of which the union is recognised by him, disclose to representatives of the union, on request, the information.**

Paragraph 11 of the Acas code of practice provides examples of the types of information which may be relevant in collective bargaining. The types of information that are normally requested relate to:

- pay and benefits;
- conditions of service;
- analysis of staff make-up, including staffing and investment plans;
- data on performance such as productivity;
- the company order book;
- financial cost structures;
- recent gross and net profits;
- assets and liabilities.

Section 182(2) of the 1992 Act states that an employer is not required to produce any document:

- unless it has been prepared for the purposes of conveying or confirming the information; or
- where to compile or assemble the information would involve an amount of work or expenditure which is out of proportion to the value of the information to the conduct of collective bargaining.

Failure to disclose information – ss 183–184 TULR(C)A 1992

If an employer, not covered by one of the exceptions listed above, fails to disclose relevant information for collective bargaining purposes, a union may complain to the Central Arbitration Committee (CAC).

The CAC may in turn deal with the problem itself or refer the matter to the Advisory, Conciliation and Arbitration Service (Acas). If an employer has failed to disclose relevant information, the CAC or Acas will issue a declaration giving the employer a set period of time within which to disclose the information. Normally the timescale is one week. If the employer fails to meet this deadline, a further complaint can be made to the CAC.

INDUSTRIAL ACTION

Industrial action does not make headline news in the way that it did during the 1970s and 1980s. Until fairly recently the last large-scale episodes of industrial action were the disputes over the transfer of journalists in Wapping and the miners' strike in the early 1980s. However, during recent years there has been a resurgence in the taking of industrial action, albeit not on such a large scale. Industrial action is the method by which employees are most able to voice their dissatisfaction with their employers and/or working environment.

An employer's business can be severely affected by industrial action. In order to avoid such financial losses, an employer may be more inclined to enter into negotiations with the workforce, solving underlying problems and so preventing or ending the industrial action.

Workers take industrial action for various reasons. In some cases it arises from a dissatisfaction with pay and other benefits; in others it follows the dismissal of one or several employees.

Whilst all-out strike action is the most dramatic form of industrial action, workers may also:

- work to a go-slow policy (refusing to work overtime or act to increase profit); or
- picket their workplace, or that of another employer, thus preventing colleagues or suppliers from entering.

It used to be the case that when a strike occurred the organisers and participants would be criminally liable for their actions. This, however, takes away the basic freedom of allowing employees to protest against their unjust treatment at the hands of their employer. In *Crofter Hand Woven Harris Tweed* v *Veitch* (1942) Lord Wright stated that '. . . the right of workmen to strike is an essential element in the principle of collective bargaining . . .'

The history of industrial action stems back to case of *Taff Vale* v *ASRS* (1901), the Trades Disputes Act of 1906 and the Industrial Relations Act 1971. The Trade Union and Labour Relations Act 1974 established the concept of statutory immunity. The present position is now outlined in the Trade Union and Labour Relations (Consolidation) Act 1992.

The law on industrial action has been modified, and so weakened over the years. The most severe attack was instigated by the Conservative government under Mrs Thatcher. The present position is that as long as the industrial action takes place free of violence, the organisers/participants are not open to prosecution.

This does not mean, however, that there is a *right* to take industrial action. A trade union instigating industrial action must still adhere to a very complex set of rules in order to achieve statutory immunity from a penalty for organising/taking industrial action.

The 'industrial torts'

There are several forms of industrial tort. This section begins by considering liability for breach of contract and goes on to look at:

- inducement
- intimidation
- conspiracy.

Whilst an employee may not encounter prosecution, he will, on taking strike action, be in breach of his contract of employment. In theory an employee could then be dismissed for this breach. All employees have a duty to be ready and willing to perform their part of the employment contract, namely to work in return for remuneration. Industrial action may also result in a breach of other contracts, such as those for the sale and supply of goods.

Inducing breach of contract

There are two ways in which an employee can be induced to breach his contract of employment. These are referred to as direct and indirect inducement.

Direct inducement occurs where one party induces a third party to break an existing contract that he has with the claimant, usually the employer. In such cases the affected party (the employer) can sue the person who induces the breach of contract. This can only happen if the inducer intended a breach to occur, and knew of the existence of the contract that would be breached.

Lumley v Gye (1853)

A singer was contracted to sing at the claimant's theatre. The defendant persuaded the singer not to sing in the claimant's theatre but to appear for him instead.

Held The defendant was liable for inducing a breach of contract between the claimant and the singer. The scope of this tort has been extended to include any intentional users of unlawful means aimed at interfering with the trade or business of the claimant.

Falconer v NUR & ASLEF (1986)

Mr Falconer was prevented from travelling from Sheffield to London because of a rail strike caused by the action of two trade unions. A secret ballot had not been held. He successfully obtained damages for two nights' hotel accommodation and other incidental expenses incurred. He had had to travel a day earlier in order to fulfil business appointments.

Indirect inducement occurs where one party induces a third party to do an unlawful act, thereby making that party breach a contract and thus causing loss to another party, usually the employer. The inducement must take place by unlawful means.

Torquay Hotel Ltd v Cousins (1969)

Torquay Hotel had refused to acknowledge the Transport and General Workers' union. The union retaliated by cutting official supplies to the hotel and by picketing, taking strike action. The union was held liable for inducing ESSO (which had a contract with the hotel to provide it with oil) into breaching that contract. A union official had telephoned ESSO stating that through industrial action the union would prevent the drivers from entering the hotel grounds and thus stop them from delivering the oil.

See also: *Hadmore Productions Ltd v Hamilton* (1983); *D.C. Thomson & Co Ltd v Deakin* (1952); *Merkur Island Shipping Co Ltd v Laughton* (1983).

Intimidation

The tort of intimidation was defined in the case of *News Group Newspapers Ltd v SOGAT 82* (1986). Here it was stated that:

> **the tort of intimidation is committed when A delivers a threat to B that he will commit an act or use means unlawful against B, as a result of which B does or refrains from doing some act which he is entitled to do, thereby causing damage either to himself or another . . . the tort**

is one of intention and the claimant, whether it be B or the other party must be a person whom A intended to injure.

Intimidation, therefore, is to threaten someone into doing an act which then results in injury (whether financial or otherwise) to a third party.

Rookes v Barnard (1964)

Here, union officials told their employer that they would take strike action unless Rookes (an employee) was dismissed from employment. They wanted to see Rookes dismissed because he had recently resigned from the union. Rookes was dismissed with proper notice. He complained, stating that he had only been dismissed on the ground of the threat of industrial action.

Held (HL) He had in fact suffered loss as a result of the union's unlawful threat. The union was liable, having committed the tort of intimidation.

In order for a successful intimidation claim to be made, the following requirements must be settled:

- there must be an unlawful threat;
- the threat must be intended to harm the claimant;
- the threat must have caused the damaging action; and
- the claimant must have suffered loss.

Conspiracy

It has long been established that liability exists for conspiring with another to cause harm or loss. A conspiracy is an agreement between two or more persons to commit an unlawful act, or to commit a lawful act by unlawful means.

Quinn v Leathem (1901)

The defendants were members of the Belfast Journeyman Butchers and Assistants Association. They wanted to enforce a closed shop in the meat and poultry trade. The claimant (another butcher) continued to employ workers who were not members of the above union. The union reacted to this by coercing other suppliers to boycott his shop.

Held This was a conspiracy. The union had intentionally set out to cause loss.

See also: *Lonrho v Fayed* (1991).

● Immunity from liability for industrial action

In order for a union and the organisers of industrial action to be immune from liability, they must be able to show that their actions attract statutory immunity. Where immunity does not apply employers and, for example, their customers and suppliers who are 'damaged' by the industrial action may bring a civil claim against the union or the organisers of the action. Figure 8.1 highlights the stage through which statutory immunity may appear.

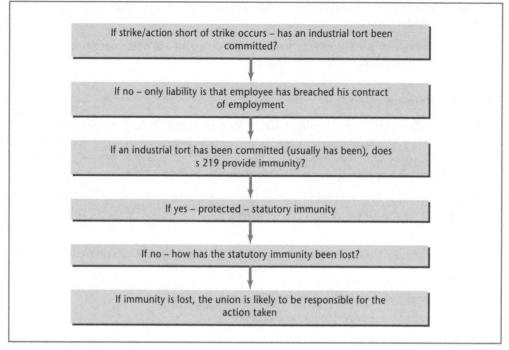

Figure 8.1 Statutory immunity for participants in industrial action

Definition of statutory immunity – s 219, TULR(C)A 1992

Sections 219(1) and (2) of the TULR(C)A 1992 state that:

1 An act done by a person in contemplation or furtherance of a trade dispute is not actionable in tort on the grounds only –

  (a) that it induces another person to break a contract or interferes or induces another person to interfere with its performance; or

  (b) that it consists in his threatening that a contract (whether one to which he is a party or not) will be broken or its performance interfered with, or that he will induce another person to break a contract or interfere with its performance.

2 An agreement or combination by two or more persons to do or procure the doing of an act in contemplation or furtherance of a trade dispute is not actionable in tort if the act is one which if done without any such agreement or combination would not be actionable in tort.

'In contemplation or furtherance of a trade dispute'

There can only be immunity from liability if an action was taken in contemplation or furtherance of a trade dispute. This phrase is sometimes referred to as the 'golden formula'. If a dispute fits within the category of the golden formula, then immunity exists. Section 244(1) of the TULR(C)A 1992 defines a trade dispute as:

> . . . a dispute between workers and their employers which relates wholly or mainly to one of the following –
>
> **(a)** terms and conditions of employment, or the physical conditions in which any workers are required to work;

(b) engagement or non-engagement, or termination or suspension of employment or the duties of employment, of one or more workers;

(c) allocation of work or the duties of employment between workers or groups of workers;

(d) matters of discipline;

(e) a worker's membership or non-membership of a trade union;

(f) facilities for officials of trade unions; and

(g) machinery for negotiation or consultation, and other procedures, relating to any of the above matters, including recognition by employers or employers' associations of the right of a trade union to represent workers in such negotiation or consultation or in the carrying out of such procedures.

If the action taken by the union does not relate to any of the above, there will be no immunity.

To contemplate a trade dispute does not mean that it is a mere possibility. In *Bents Brewery Co Ltd* v *Hogan* (1945) a union was held not to have immunity after it was sued for inducing a breach of contract. It had asked its members for confidential information in order to make a claim for a pay increase. The union's actions had not been in the furtherance of a trade dispute. The act must not be one of mere 'coercive interference', but must be directed towards something which is impending or likely to occur.

See also: *London Borough of Wandsworth* v *National Association of Schoolmasters and Union of Women Teachers* (1993), *TGWU* v *Associated British Ports* (2002), *P* v *NSA/UWT* (2001).

Ballot for industrial action

Section 226 of the TULR(C)A 1992 (as amended by the ERA 2004) states that actions taken by a union to induce a person to take part in industrial action are not protected unless the industrial action is called with the support of a ballot. The authorisation of the industrial action must take place within four weeks of the ballot being held. There is also a Code of Practice on 'Industrial Action Ballots and Notice to Employers' (2005). This provides guidance on the conduct of ballots. The four-week limitation period may be extended to up to eight weeks if this is agreed between the employer and the trade union.

A union only has to obtain a 50+1 per cent majority vote in favour of industrial action. It is under a duty to give an employer at least seven days' notice of any intended industrial action. This notice must be given in writing and must provide enough information to enable the employer to identify those individuals who are likely to take part in the industrial action. There is no longer a duty to actually list the names of those employees.

The ballot should be fully postal. In ballots for strike action, the wording on the voting paper should contain a question asking the voter if he is prepared to take part in a strike or other industrial action. The wording should also inform the voter that if he takes part in a strike or other industrial action, he may be in breach of his contract of employment. It should also inform him that if he is dismissed for taking part in an official strike or other form of industrial action that his dismissal will be unfair. This is the case if the dismissal takes place within twelve weeks of the member taking the industrial action. In some circumstances this period may be extended.

● Loss of statutory immunity

There are several situations in which the immunity from liability will be lost. These are where there has been an infringement of the law regarding ballots, where there has been unlawful secondary action, where there has been pressure to impose union membership, enforce the closed shop, or action taken to persuade an employer to reinstate dismissed unofficial strikers.

An infringement of the law relating to ballots

As noted above, a union can only retain immunity if there has been a properly conducted ballot. If there has been any infringement of the rules on the conduct of the ballot, immunity is lost. Under s 62 of the TULR(C)A 1992 all union members have a right to apply for a court order to prevent or stop industrial action where there has been either no ballot, or one that was not conducted in the required manner. If their claim succeeds, the court will award an injunction effectively preventing the industrial action from either beginning or continuing.

Where there is unlawful secondary action

Immunity will also be lost where there is unlawful secondary action. Section 224(2) of the TULR(C)A 1992 defines secondary action as occurring when a person:

(a) induces another to break a contract of employment or interferes or induces another to interfere with its performance; or

(b) threatens that a contract of employment under which he or another is employed will be broken or its performance interfered with, or that he will induce another to break a contract of employment or to interfere with its performance,

and the employer under the contract of employment is not the employer party to the dispute.

This covers the situation where some workers may decide to picket the place of work of other workers, and thus prevent those workers from crossing the picket line and attending work. Following the mass incidence of the 'flying pickets' in the 1980s, the courts became less sympathetic towards such action.

Express Newspapers v *McShane* (1980)

Some journalists who had worked for a selection of local newspapers were dismissed. A national strike was called to protest at their dismissal. The aim of the union was to stop their members from working, and thus prevent any stories from being prepared for the press. This action was unsuccessful because the Press Association made stories available to the national press. Journalists working on national newspapers were asked to boycott press association copy.

Held (HL) Even though the action had been taken 'in furtherance of a trade dispute', there was no immunity for secondary action.

There is still one form of lawful secondary action: lawful peaceful picketing outside the employee's own workplace which has incidental secondary effect. For example, it may interfere with commercial contracts unrelated to the main dispute.

Where there is pressure to impose union membership, recognition requirements, or to maintain the closed shop

There is no immunity for industrial action which is aimed at persuading an employer to enter into contracts which require the other party to recognise a union or maintain a closed shop. This rule is set out in ss 222 and 225 of the TULR(C)A 1992.

Where action is taken to persuade an employer to reinstate dismissed unofficial strikers

Section 223 of the TULR(C) Act 1992 removes statutory immunity from cases where there is industrial action following the dismissal of unofficial strikers. The protection from immunity is removed if 'one of the reasons' for the organisation of industrial action is the 'fact or belief' that an employer has dismissed one or more employees who are engaged in unofficial industrial action.

Criminal liability

A union may encounter criminal liability as a result of industrial action. Likely offences may be obstruction of the highway, the obstruction of a police officer in the execution of his duty, public nuisance and breach of the peace.

Enforcement

If an industrial tort has been committed (i.e. an unofficial strike) and there is no statutory immunity, the union may be sued by those affected by the action.

The object of the claim will be to put those claimants back into the position they would have been in had the tort not been committed. It is also possible to claim damages for losses suffered. When a trade union is sued successfully, the union will be ordered to pay an amount of damages commensurate with the level of the union's membership. The amounts listed in Table 8.1 are taken from s 22 of the TULR(C)A 1992.

Table 8.1 Amount of damages based on union membership (TULR(C)A 1992, s 22)

Union membership	Limit on damages
Less than 5000	£ 10 000
5000–25 000	£ 50 000
25 000–100 000	£125 000
over 100 000	£250 000

In some situations a person or organisation affected by unlawful industrial action may make an application to the court asking for an injunction.

If the court grants an injunction, the action will either be stopped or prevented from starting. If a trade union fails to follow the order of an injunction, it will be held to be in contempt of court. There is no limit on the amount that a trade union can be fined for such a contempt. The court has the power to order the imprisonment of union officials or the sequestration of union funds if the fine remains unpaid.

SUMMARY CHECKLIST

- Unions represent employees on such matters as collective bargaining, negotiations on wage increases, and on disciplinary matters and hearings.
- Although a trade union has no legal personality as such, it can sue and be sued in its own name.
- Union funds/property is looked after by trustees.
- No one can be compelled to join, or be penalised for refusing to join, a particular trade union.

- A union may only refuse to admit a person or expel a member if his application does not satisfy an enforceable membership requirement, he does not work in the geographical area covered by the union, he no longer works for a relevant employer in the case of a company-specific union, or because of misconduct.
- The Certification Officer is responsible for the maintenance of the list of trade unions.
- A union can appeal to the Employment Appeal Tribunal against a refusal to list.
- Only members of an independent trade union are entitled to benefits such as consultation prior to redundancy or a transfer of an undertaking.
- In order to be classed as independent, a union must not be under the dominition/control of an employer or liable to interference by the employer.
- Only a trade union classed as 'recognised' can engage in collective bargaining with an employer. Recognition may be achieved on either a voluntary or statutory basis.
- The Bridlington principles are designed to prevent inter-union poaching.
- A union may only use its political fund for 'political purposes'.
- Political fund ballots should be repeated every ten years.
- Union members have the right not to be unjustifiably disciplined by their union.
- Members who are justifiably disciplined should be so disciplined under the rules of natural justice.
- Union members who feel that they have been unjustifiably disciplined can complain to the Employment Tribunal.
- A union must appoint an independent scrutineer to oversee the operation of any ballot.
- There is a duty on trade unions to keep their accounting records available for inspection for a period of six years.
- Collective bargaining is the process by which a union negotiates with an employer on matters concerning the terms and conditions of employment.
- An employer has a duty to disclose information to a trade union that may be relevant to collective bargaining.
- Types of relevant information include that on pay and benefits, performance, assets and liabilities.
- Industrial action is the most effective means of protest.
- A trade union must adhere to a very complex set of rules in order to achieve statutory immunity from a penalty for organising/taking industrial action.
- Industrial torts may take the form of inducement, intimidation and conspiracy.
- The actions of a union will attract statutory immunity where they are done in contemplation or furtherance of a trade dispute.
- Statutory immunity will be lost if there is an infringement of the law relating to ballots, there is unlawful secondary action, there is a pressure to impose union membership or recognition requirements or to maintain the closed shop, or where action is taken to persuade an employer to reinstate dismissed unofficial strikers.
- A union may be ordered to pay damages for the harm caused by unlawful industrial action.
- A court may order an injunction to stop/prevent industrial action.
- A union may also be fined, non-payment making the executive liable to imprisonment, and resulting in the sequestration of union assets.

SELF-TEST QUESTIONS

1 What is a trade union?

2 What is meant by the term 'statutory recognition'?

3 To what do the terms 'pre-entry' and 'post-entry' closed shop refer?

4 What might the Certification Officer take into account when having to decide on the independence or otherwise of a trade union?

5 Explain the role of the 'independent scrutineer'.

6 What are the 'Bridlington principles'?

7 What are the 'industrial torts'?

8 What is the concept of 'statutory immunity'?

9 When might statutory immunity be lost?

10 What remedies might a person have against a union which takes industrial action and does not have statutory immunity?

CASE SCENARIOS

A

Russell and Gavin work for a firm of lawyers. The firm employs over 2500 people at different levels. Russell is an advice worker and Gavin helps out in the conveyancing department. There is no workplace union and, unhappy with their present working conditions, the men decide to set up their own union. They intend to call the union 'Helpers at Law Firms' (HALF) and ask their employer's advice. Their employer, Ms Rich, says that they can do as they please as long as they do not coerce other colleagues into joining the union. She even offers to provide them with a room, telephone and photocopier once the union is established. Russell thinks that they should be ready to enter into pay negotiations within six months. Gavin tells him that his friend at the TUC said that Rich has no obligation to enter into negotiations with them because they are not recognised, are not listed and have no certificate of independence.

Advise Russell and Gavin as to:

- *how they may apply to have 'HALF' listed and how they might obtain a certificate of independence;*

- *the likelihood of them obtaining such a certificate;*

- *how their union might achieve 'recognition' from their employer and on any benefits that such recognition would bring.*

B

Most of the employees at 'Marketing Mayhem' belong to the 'PLUS' workplace union. Their employer has recently changed their working patterns and placed a ban on payment for overtime. Most of the workers are forced to do overtime on a weekly basis. Often their advertising clients are unable to wait to receive work on the next day, meaning that the workers often work late into the night to meet deadlines. The union has recently returned from negotiations with the owners of the business. The owners have refused to change this new policy. The union has decided to call for strike action. Two employees, Kate and Kurt, are unsure about whether or not they want to take industrial action. They are afraid that they may lose their jobs.

Advise:

- *the union executive as to how it can lawfully organise a strike;*

- *Kate and Kurt as to the effect of them taking strike action.*

Your answer should take into account the reasons why statutory immunity from strike action may be lost.

 ## Further reading

Trade Unions, IDS Employment Law Handbook, December 2000.

Industrial Action, IDS Employment Law Handbook, August 1999.

Industrial Action and the Law – A Guide for Employees, Trade Union Members and Others, Department of Trade and Industry, 06/551.

Union Membership – Rights of Members and Non-members, Department of Trade and Industry, 06/558.

Department of Trade and Industry Code of Practice: 'Industrial Action Ballots and Notice to Employers', 2005.

For legal updates on the material in this chapter please go to the Companion Website accompanying this book at **www.mylawchamber.co.uk/nairns**

9 Health and safety at work

The provision and maintenance of health and safety standards in the workplace is an important issue for both employers and employees. Thousands of employees are injured at work each year. In 2005/6 there were 212 reported fatal workplace accidents. This is the lowest reported figure in recent years. During the same period 28 605 employees were reported as having major injuries due to workplace incidents. It is estimated that during 2005/6, 30 million working days were lost due to work-related illness (source: *Health and Safety Statistics 2005/2006*, HSC). Work-related accidents and ill health cost employers millions each year.

The roles of the Health and Safety Executive (HSE) and the Health and Safety Commission (HSC) are discussed in Chapter 1 (pages 32 and 33). These paragraphs should be read as an introduction to this chapter.

The law seeks to encourage high standards of health and safety at work. It aims to ensure that both employers and employees do all that is reasonable in the circumstances to ensure that they operate, or are working in, a safe environment. Employers are not lawfully able to dismiss, select for redundancy or subject employees to any other detriment for carrying out designated health and safety duties. Employees should not be penalised for alerting their employers to any health and safety issue or for taking steps to protect themselves from serious and imminent danger.

By first outlining the possible actions resulting from a workplace injury, this chapter goes on to discuss:

- sources of health and safety law (legislation, common law, regulations), approved codes of practice and guidance notes;
- employer's liability at common law, the provision of competent fellow employees, a safe system of work, safe equipment and safe premises;
- breach of statutory duty;
- defences to a common law claim, that the employer was not negligent, contributory negligence, *volenti non fit injuria*;
- vicarious liability;
- statutory control, the Health and Safety at Work Act 1974;
- European health and safety law, the Framework Directive;
- the 'six-pack';
- other major regulations;
- the Working Time Directive.

POSSIBLE ACTIONS RESULTING FROM A WORKPLACE INJURY

When an accident occurs in the workplace the law has two aims:

● to punish the employer who did not provide enough health and safety protection to prevent the accident from occurring;

● to allow the injured employee to make a claim for damages to compensate for his injury.

This involves the use of both the criminal and civil law. An employer may be punished under criminal law, and the employee may sue for compensation using civil law.

In health and safety cases, the common law and legislation work alongside each other. Following an accident, the injured employee may allege that there has been both a breach of contract and a breach of statutory duty. In the same situation his employer may be prosecuted by the HSE for breaching the duties under the Health and Safety at Work Act 1974 or any of the health and safety regulations.

Figure 9.1 and the example below highlight the overlap between civil law and criminal law.

> **Example**
> *Holly slips on the factory floor, breaking her leg. Her employer knew that there was oil on the floor but did nothing to have it removed. Possible claims:*
>
> ● *a civil claim by Holly for damages against her employer;*
> ● *a prosecution by the HSE of the employer for breach of the Health and Safety at Work Act 1974.*

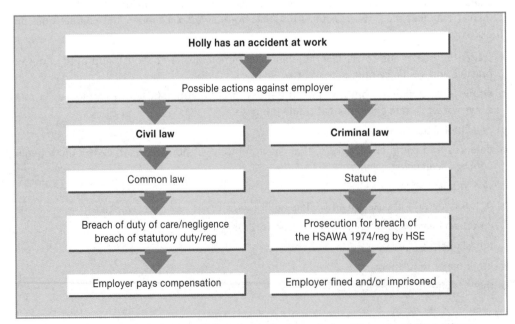

Figure 9.1 The overlap between civil and criminal law in health and safety actions

SOURCES OF HEALTH AND SAFETY LAW

The law on health and safety at work is found in the following forms:

- common law
- legislation
- regulations
- approved codes of practice
- guidance notes.

Common law

Employers have a common law duty to take reasonable care of each employee, and are expected to safeguard employees from any hazard that is reasonably foreseeable. The standard of care required is that of the 'prudent' or reasonable employer. This duty stems from the law of negligence and the implied contractual duty to take care of employee safety.

Legislation

The main statute in this area is the Health and Safety at Work Act 1974. This Act sets out the general duties owed by employers to their employees. It is an 'enabling' Act which means that regulations affecting particular types of industries or occupations can be made under it.

Regulations

Health and safety regulations are made by the Secretary of State acting on proposals made by the Health and Safety Commission. They are made under the provisions set out in the Health and Safety at Work Act 1974, and relate to specific types of workplace problem or industry. Breach of a regulation is a criminal offence and may lead to prosecution. Such a breach may also give rise to a civil claim for breach of statutory duty. This applies unless the particular regulation states that it is not possible to make such a claim.

Examples of regulations include the Workplace (Health, Safety and Welfare) Regulations 1992 and the Reporting of Injuries, Diseases and Dangerous Occurrences Regulations 1995 (RIDDOR). (These are discussed further at pages 351 and 353.)

Approved codes of practice

Approved codes of practice supplement Acts and regulations. They are guides to good practice and help employers to keep up to date with safety developments in their field. If an employer complies with the provisions of a code, he will be said to have met the legal requirement to provide a safe working environment.

Failure to comply with a code is not an offence in itself, but will be taken into account in any legal proceedings. A court or tribunal will not look favourably upon an employer who has failed to meet the standards set in an approved code.

Guidance notes

Guidance notes are issued by the Health and Safety Commission and the Executive. They provide guidance on what is or is not good health and safety practice. They are often produced with approved codes. Guidance notes can be produced on any area of workplace safety.

Failing to follow the advice given in a guidance note is not an offence in itself, but will be taken into account in any legal proceedings. Again, a court or tribunal will not look favourably upon an employer who has failed to meet the standards set in a guidance note.

EMPLOYERS' LIABILITY AT COMMON LAW

Employers have a duty to take reasonable care for the safety of their employees. They must do all that they can to ensure that employees are not injured at work. The duty is only one to take 'reasonable' care, and employers are only expected to do what would be considered to be reasonable in each case. In *Paris* v *Stepney Borough Council* (1951) Lord Oaksey defined 'reasonable care' as 'the care which an ordinary prudent employer would take in all the circumstances'. If an employer breaches this duty and has no defence, he will be liable to pay damages to his injured employee.

The balance of risk, cost and inconvenience

Many workplaces are hazardous environments, even when they are well equipped with accident-prevention measures. Employers are not expected to provide levels of absolute safety in the workplace. The law does not demand the impossible. It allows employers to balance the risk of accidents occurring, with the cost and inconvenience of preventing or reducing the likelihood of such risk.

In *Morris* v *W Hartlepool SN* (1956) the House of Lords held that:

it is the duty of an employer in considering whether some precaution should be taken against a foreseeable risk, to weigh on the one hand the magnitude of the risk, the likelihood of an accident happening and the possible seriousness of the consequences . . . and on the other hand the difficulty and expense and any other disadvantage of taking the precaution.

If employers can show that they have taken reasonable care, they will not be in breach of their common law duty.

Latimer v AEC (1953)

AEC's factory floor was flooded during a heavy rainstorm. The management asked the workforce to return to work but made the workers aware of the dangerous floor. AEC placed as much sawdust as it could find on to the floor. Unfortunately some areas remained uncovered. Mr Latimer slipped on one such area and was injured. He made a claim for damages stating that AEC had not taken care for his safety.

Held AEC had done all that was reasonable in the circumstances. The only alternative would have been for AEC to close the factory. It was not reasonable to expect AEC to do this. The possibility of risk did not outweigh the inconvenience of taking further precautions; consequently AEC was not liable for his injuries.

Employers are only expected to prevent injuries that were foreseeable at the time they occurred. For example, if an employee's hearing is impaired due to excessive noise levels, his employer is only liable for the injuries if the employer knew that the noise was capable of causing harm.

> ### *Down* v *Dudley Coles Long* (1969)
>
> An employee suffered from partial deafness following prolonged use of a hammer-assisted drill. His employer did not provide ear-defenders because at the time medical knowledge was such that it was not known that use of such drills could cause deafness.
>
> *Held* The employer was not in breach of duty as he had done all that was reasonably necessary in the circumstances.

If, however, the danger of the method of doing work becomes apparent, employers have a duty to minimise the risk of harm as soon as possible: *Baxter* v *Harland & Wolff plc* (1990). For example, in the *Down* case (above), if the employers suddenly became aware that prolonged use of the drills could cause deafness, they would be under a duty to provide ear protection as soon as possible. If they did not take action to protect employees from the noise levels, they would then be liable for any future injuries.

Compulsory insurance

The Employer's Liability (Compulsory Insurance) Act 1969 states that all employers must have insurance to cover them against injuries or fatalities occurring in their workplace. The Employer's Liability (Compulsory Insurance) Regulations 1998 increased the amount of insurance cover from £2 million to a minimum of £5 million. The insurance covers any personal injury or fatal accident claims from employees or their estate. Employers should display a copy of their insurance certificate in the workplace. They may be fined if they fail to do this. The Act does not provide a right to compensation but ensures that funds are available to pay for any successful claim. The Health and Safety Executive enforces the 1969 Act.

Claims for breach of duty of care or the implied term in the employment contract

Injured employees may make a claim for compensation based on either a breach of the duty of care outlined in *Donoghue* v *Stevenson* (1932), or a breach of an implied term in their employment contract. This is the duty on employers to take care for the safety of their employees. In essence these claims are based on the same duty to take care. In a negligence claim the employee would have to show that:

1 his employer owed him a duty to take care of his safety;

2 the employer breached this duty;

3 this breach resulted in the accident that caused his injury.

A breach of contract claim is based on the breach of the implied duty to take reasonable care for employee safety. In either case the employee is alleging that his employer's negligence has resulted in him being injured at work.

9

Health and safety at work

The employer's duty at common law is outlined in the case of **Wilsons and Clyde Coal Co Ltd v English** (1938). Here, the House of Lords held that an employer owes a duty to his employees to provide 'the provision of a competent staff of men, adequate material, a proper system of work and effective supervision'.

This forms the basis of the common law duty to provide:

- competent fellow employees
- a safe system of work
- safe work equipment
- safe work premises.

Provision of competent fellow employees

Employers have a duty to employ competent employees. If an incompetent employee injures a colleague, their employer has failed to meet this duty. The employer would then be liable to pay damages to the injured employee.

Employers should provide adequate training and supervision of employees. An employee may do something that results in injury to another without realising that his actions may cause harm. However, in some cases the 'practical joker' employee may realise that he is putting others at risk, but continue to create hazardous situations in the workplace. If an employer becomes aware of such a 'problem' employee, he should remove the problem employee from the workplace as soon as possible.

Hudson v Ridge Manufacturing Co Ltd (1957)

Mr Hudson was injured when a colleague wrestled him to the ground, breaking his wrist. The colleague was a known practical joker and had a reputation for playing pranks. Their employer had been aware of this for four years but had done nothing to prevent him from committing further pranks.

Held The employer was liable for the injury caused to Hudson. The employer had breached the duty to take care of Hudson's safety. It had not provided him with competent fellow employees, and had failed to remove the practical joker when it became obvious that he was likely to cause harm to others.

In **Hudson** Streatfield J stated that 'if . . . a fellow workman is not merely incompetent but, by his habitual conduct is likely to prove a source of danger to his fellow employees, a duty lies fairly and squarely on the employers to remove that source of danger'.

In the similar case of **Ryan v Cambrian Dairies** (1957) the employer was liable for the injuries caused by an employee who was a known bully.

The duty of employing suitably qualified people extends to the provision of staff development, training and the supervision of employees.

Employers are only responsible for employee actions that were predictable in the circumstances. In **Smith v Crossley Bros** (1951) two motor mechanics caused injury to a third by inserting a hose into his anus, filling him with compressed gas. It was held that the employer was not liable in this instance. The childish behaviour of the mechanics was not predictable or preventable. See also: **Coddington v International Harvester Co. of Great Britain Ltd** (1969).

Hawkins v Ross Castings Ltd (1970)

Mr Hawkins was injured after molten metal spilled on to his legs. His injury was partly due to the fact that he was working with an untrained boy who had very little understanding of English. The boy had not been trained in the carrying and pouring of molten metal.

Held The employer was liable for Hawkins' injuries; the employer had failed to employ a competent fellow employee, and had not provided adequate training or supervision.

● Provision of a safe system of work

This duty relates to the way in which the workplace is organised. It is a very wide duty and covers all aspects of safety provision. Employers have a duty to provide employees with safe conditions in which to carry out their work. The giving of hazard warnings, training, supervision and the provision of safety equipment form part of this duty.

Bux v Slough Metals (1973)

Bux was provided with safety goggles but chose not to use them. He was injured and sued his employer, alleging that the employer had failed to provide a safe system of work.

Held The employer had provided suitable safety equipment but had failed to provide a safe system of work. As the employer had failed to point out the dangers of working without safety goggles, the employer had breached the duty to provide adequate supervision and training.

Employees should be instructed to adopt safe methods of doing their work. Employers should point out any likely hazards or risks. Employees should be trained accordingly to deal with any such hazards and risks. If an employer does this, he will have done all that is reasonable to provide a safe system of work. What is reasonable will differ and depends on the type of work and workplace involved in each case.

Even if an employer provides safety instructions, employees may choose not to follow them. They may also refuse to wear safety equipment. In such cases, by providing the instructions and equipment, the employer has done all that is necessary in the circumstances. An employer is not liable for any injuries caused due to non-compliance by his employees.

If the employee's own common sense should have told him how to do the job safely, he will have no claim against his employer if he is injured by doing the job in another way.

Employers are not expected to point out minor hazards to employees. In *Lazarus v Firestone Tyre & Rubber Co Ltd* (1963) the employer had not informed employees that there was a rush to get to the canteen at mealtimes. When one employee was injured in such a rush, the employer was not liable for his injuries.

Employees must also take some responsibility for their own safety. If equipment is provided, they should use it, and employers are not expected to have to remind them on a daily basis of the risks involved in doing their jobs. In *Withers v Perry Chain* (1961) the court held that the relationship between an employer and employee was not the same as that between a 'schoolmaster and pupil'.

Qualcast v Haynes (1959)

An employee was injured when his legs were splashed with molten metal. His employer had provided him with protective spats but he had chosen not to wear them.

Held The employer was not liable for his injuries. The risk of injury would have been obvious to the employee as he was an experienced workman. By providing the spats, the employer had done all that was reasonable in the circumstances.

O'Reilly v National Rail (1966)

A group of scrapyard employees found an unexploded bomb in their workplace. Several men challenged O'Reilly to hit the bomb with a hammer to see what would happen! He hit the bomb and they were injured when it exploded. They sued their employer, saying that the existence of the bomb meant that the employer had failed to provide a safe system of work.

Held The employer was not liable for failing to instruct employees not to hit an unexploded bomb, and was entitled to assume that common sense would have told them not to hit the bomb with a hammer.

Smith v Scott Bowyers Ltd (1986)

Mr Smith was injured when he slipped on an oily floor. His employer knew that the floor was dangerous and had provided all employees with wellington boots. The boots had special gripping soles. Smith had been given a pair of wellingtons, but when the grip had worn from the soles, he had not asked for replacements.

Held The employer was not liable for his injury, and was entitled to assume that he would have taken responsibility for his own safety by asking for a replacement pair of boots.

Baker v Clarke (1992)

An experienced electrician was injured when he did not lock the wheels of mobile scaffolding. He claimed that his employer had not taken care for his safety.

Held The employer was not liable; the employer did not have to provide constant reminders of the risks involved in putting up scaffolding, or the likelihood of harm if it was not accurately assembled.

See also: *Withers* v *Perry Chain Co Ltd* (1961), *Pape* v *Cumbria County Council* (1991), *King* v *Sussex Ambulance Service NHS Trust* (2002).

● Duty extends to protection from psychological harm

The duty to provide a safe system of work extends to protecting the psychological well-being of employees as well as their physical well-being. The following case was the first decision highlighting the effects of stress in the workplace.

Walker v Northumberland County Council (1995)

Mr Walker was employed as a manager for the social services department at NCC. He suffered two nervous breakdowns due to overwork and stress. After the first breakdown he told his employer that he was suffering from stress. NCC said that it would provide help and reduce his workload. When he returned to work, nothing was done to alleviate his stress. He had another nervous breakdown and sued NCC for breach of its duty to take care of his safety.

Held The second breakdown was entirely foreseeable in the circumstances. NCC was liable for his psychiatric injuries. It had failed in its duty to provide a safe system of work.

It has been debated as to whether this duty extends to cases involving post-traumatic stress disorder. In *Frost v Chief Constable of South Yorkshire* (1997) (otherwise known as *White v Chief Constable of South Yorkshire Police* (1999)), the Court of Appeal held that an employer's duty did extend to psychiatric as well as physical injury. However, in the (1999) hearing of this case the House of Lords held that the policemen were not entitled to recover damages for psychiatric illness. This case resulted from the 1989 Hillsborough football stadium disaster. Police officers sued their employer, claiming that they suffered from post-traumatic stress disorder as a result of being on duty at the time of the disaster.

In *Duncan v British Coal* (1997) a mine deputy suffered from a psychiatric illness after going to the assistance of a colleague who had been crushed to death at the coal face. The Court of Appeal dismissed his claim for damages because he did not see the accident happen and was not directly involved in the freeing of the body. However, in *Young v Charles Church (Southern) Ltd* (1997) Mr Young successfully sued his employer for damages. He worked as a labourer and suffered severe psychiatric illness and stress after seeing a work colleague next to whom he was working electrocuted.

Another interesting case concerning a breach of the duty to provide a safe system of work is that of **Johnstone** (below). In this case the duty was breached when an employer expected an employee to work a ridiculous amount of hours each week, which had an effect on both his psychological and physical well-being.

Johnstone v Bloomsbury Health Authority (1991)

Johnstone, a junior doctor, was employed by the Authority to work 40 hours per week. His contract also stated that he would make himself available to work a further 48 hours each week. He sued the Authority, alleging that by requiring him to work an unrealistic number of hours, it was not providing him with a safe system of work.

Held The Authority was liable for not taking care for his health, safety and well-being; it had not provided a safe system of work.

In *Sutherland v Hatton* (2002) the Court of Appeal dealt with four separate appeals from employers where employees had been awarded damages after they were forced to stop working due to a stress induced psychiatric illness. Here, the court adopted a cautious approach to the award of damages in such cases. Three out of the four appeals were successful. The court stated that 'unless there was a real risk of breakdown which the claimant's employers ought reasonably to have foreseen and which they ought properly to have averted, there can be no liability'. In order for the employer to be liable the stress-induced injury must be sufficiently foreseeable to be plain enough for any reasonable employer to realise that he should do something about it.

The decision in *Hatton* (above) was approved by the House of Lords in the case of *Barber v Somerset County Council* (2004). However, in this case the House of Lords recognised that employers have a duty to be proactive and to take the initiative where an employee is suffering from stress, rather than simply adopt a 'wait and see position'. An employer may, therefore, be expected to do something to assist an employee who is suffering from workplace stress.

More recent cases have also debated the law on claims arising from stress at work and it can be seen that this remains a developing area of law. In *Hartman v South Essex Mental Health and Community Care NHS Trust* (2005) it was held that even where a claimant has suffered stress at work and their employer had allowed the situation to develop it does not necessarily mean that the claimant is able to establish a claim in negligence.

In *Hatton* the court had said that an employer who offers a confidential advice service, with referral options to an appropriate counselling service, was unlikely to be in breach of their duty of care. However, later cases have shown that each decision will be based on its own facts. In *Intel Corporation (UK) Ltd v Daw* (2007) the argument by an employer that the provision of a counselling service was enough to discharge their duty to take reasonable steps to prevent an overworked employee's breakdown failed. Here, the Court of Appeal upheld a decision to award £134.000 to a stressed employee who had made use of the counselling services provided by her employer.

See also: *Pratley v Surrey County Council* (2004), *Young v The Post Office* (2002), *Bonser v RJB Mining (UK) Ltd* (2004), *Green v D.B. Services Ltd* (2006), *Corr v IBC Vehicles Ltd* (2006).

Provision of safe work equipment

Employers have a duty to provide safe equipment for use in the workplace. This extends to the provision of safe vehicles, machinery, machine guards, safety harnesses, protective gloves, covers or overalls. What should be provided depends on the type of hazard that employees are likely to encounter. In *Tearle v Cheverton* (1970) it was held that the employer should have placed a hood over a waist-level starting button to prevent a machine from being started by accident.

Bradford v Robinson Rentals Ltd (1967)

A van driver was asked to make a delivery involving a very long drive in cold weather. His employer knew that the heater in the van was broken, but still asked the driver to use it. The temperature fell to below freezing during the journey, and the driver contracted frostbite.

Held The employer was liable for the driver's injury, having breached the duty to provide safe work equipment.

In *Pagano v HGS* (1976) an employer who, despite complaints from employees, had failed to maintain their vehicles in a safe condition was held not to have provided safe work equipment.

The Employer's Liability (Defective Equipment) Act 1969

The provision of safe equipment for use in the workplace is controlled by the Employer's Liability (Defective Equipment) Act 1969. Under this Act:

- if an employee suffers personal injury while at work, and this is:
- due to a defect in equipment provided by his employer;
- and the defect is wholly or partly due to the fault of a third party, for example, a supplier or manufacturer;
- the employer is liable for the injury – the employer is in breach of the duty to provide safe work equipment.

This rule was introduced to provide compensation for employees injured following the use of unsafe work equipment. Before 1969 employees could only claim from the original manufacturer, or supplier of the equipment. They are now able to claim directly from their employer. If an employer is sued on this basis, he can then recoup any damages paid to the employee by suing the manufacturer or supplier of the equipment.

Knowles v Liverpool County Council (1993)

Mr Knowles, an employee of the Council, was injured while laying a paving stone. The stone was defective.

Held The Council was liable for his injuries even though it had only purchased and not manufactured the paving stone.

Provision of safe work premises

Employers have a duty to ensure that their premises provide a safe place in which employees can work. See *Latimer* v *AEC* (above). This includes providing adequate light, ventilation and space, safe entrances and exits, and clear walkways. The court may also consider the methods used to deal with complaints regarding safety in the workplace and the reporting of accidents. This duty also applies where employees are sent to work on a different site.

General Cleaning Contractors v Christmas (1955)

GCC ran a window-cleaning business. It provided safety belts for employees, but on one building there were no hooks to attach to the belts. Mr Christmas was injured while cleaning windows on that building. A defective window sash fell on to his fingers; he lost his grip and fell. He sued GCC for failing to provide safe premises.

Held GCC had breached this duty. It was aware of the danger surrounding the lack of hooks on the building and should not have continued to send its employees to work there.

See also: *Smith* v *Austin Lifts* (1959), *King* v *Smith* (1994).

Non-delegable duty

The common law duty to take care of employee safety is non-delegable. This means that employers cannot avoid liability merely by showing that they delegated the selection of employees to someone else. This would cover the provision of staff by subcontractors or independent contractors. In *Morris* v *Breaveglen* (1993) it was held that the duty applies even where the employer has subcontracted the employees' labour to another contractor.

In *Wilsons and Clyde Coal Co Ltd* v *English* (1938) Mr Wilson's family sued his employer after he died in a mining accident. The company had employed another company to ensure that there was a safe system of work in the mine. This second company had failed to do this and the accident had occurred as a result of its negligence. The coal company was held to be liable for his death even though it had delegated its work to another company.

In *McDermid* v *Nash Dredging & Reclamation Co Ltd* (1987) Lord Hailsham stated that, 'a non-delegable duty does not involve the proposition that the duty cannot be delegated . . . but only that the employer cannot escape liability if the duty has been delegated and then not properly performed'.

9

Health and safety at work

Duty is owed to individual employees

Employers owe a duty to each individual employee. This means that if they are aware that a particular employee is more likely to have a serious accident, or be more seriously affected by that accident, employers should take special precautions to protect such an employee.

In *Paris* v *Stepney Borough Council* (below) the court held that:

> the special risk of injury is relevant consideration in determining the precautions which the employer should take in the fulfilment of the duty of care which he owes to the workman.

Paris v Stepney Borough Council (1951)

Mr Paris had lost his sight in one eye. He was cleaning the underneath of a bus with a chisel and was hit in the face by flying chippings. He then lost the sight in his 'good' eye resulting in total blindness. He sued SBC for failing to take care for his safety.

Held The employer SBC was liable; it should have taken more care to protect his eyesight. It knew that he was more likely to be seriously affected by any accident and should have done more in the circumstances to ensure that he wore safety goggles at all times

Breach can be of one or more of the duties

It can be seen from the above cases that an employee can bring a claim based on either part, or all of the general duties laid down in **Wilsons**. An employer who fails to provide competent fellow employees may also fail to provide a safe system of work, safe work equipment or premises. In any event, the claim is based on the same breach of common law duty or negligence.

BREACH OF STATUTORY DUTY

In addition to making a claim under the common law, employees may make a claim based on the fact that their employer breached a statutory duty. In negligence claims the employee has to prove that his employer acted negligently. When claiming breach of a statutory duty, the employee only has to show that his employer failed to do something required by a statute or regulation. For example, failure to provide a machine guard in breach of the Factories Act 1961.

The employee has to show that his employer's breach was the cause of his injury. In some cases an employee may claim that his employer was both in breach of the general duty of care and of a statutory duty. The employee then claims damages for both breaches.

In order to succeed in a claim for breach of statutory duty, the employee has to show that:

1 the statute places a statutory duty on the employer which is owed to the employee;

2 the employer has breached that statutory duty;

3 the employee has suffered an injury as a result;

4 the harm caused was of a kind contemplated by statute.

An employee cannot make a claim for breach of statutory duty in every case where an injury occurs. Usually the statute in question will state whether or not a civil claim is possible. For example, s 47 of the Health and Safety at Work Act 1974 states that breach of the general duties under ss 2–8 of the Act do not give rise to civil liability. A claim for breach of statutory duty cannot be made for a breach of the Act.

Unless they state otherwise, claims for breach of statutory duty may be made for a breach of the Health and Safety Regulations.

DEFENCES TO A COMMON LAW OR BREACH OF STATUTORY DUTY CLAIM

An employer facing a claim for damages from an injured employee may defend the action in any of three ways. The available defences are that:

- the accident was not caused by the employer's negligence;
- the employee was partly responsible for the accident, and so contributed to its occurrence; or
- the employee consented to the possibility of the accident occurring: *volenti non fit injuria*.

Accident not caused by employer's negligence

In order to succeed in a claim for damages the injured employee has to prove that the negligence of his employer caused his injury. If unable to show this, the claim will fail. The employer can defend the claim by showing that he did all that was reasonable in the circumstances (as in *Latimer v AEC*) to ensure the employee's safety.

Contributory negligence

Employees have a duty to take care for their own safety. The law does not expect employers to take full responsibility for accidents where they are caused by employee negligence. Here, the employer alleges that the injured employee was partly responsible for the accident.

In *Nance v British Columbia Electric Railway* (1951) Lord Simon stated that all that needs to be proved is that the employee 'did not in his own interest take reasonable care of himself, and contributed, by this want of care, to his own injury'.

If this defence is successful, the employee's claim for damages does not fail but any amount of money that the court may have awarded him will be reduced accordingly. It will be reduced on a percentage basis to reflect the level of the employee's responsibility for the accident.

The Law Reform (Contributory Negligence) Act 1945 states that the judge can reduce the amount of damages 'to such extent as the court thinks just and equitable having regard to the claimant's share in the responsibility for the damage'.

> **Example**
> *Peter spills oil on the factory floor and forgets to clean it up. Later in the day he slips on it and breaks his leg. He sues his employer for breach of duty, alleging that his employer failed to provide safe work premises. The court finds the employer liable but on the basis that Peter should have cleaned up the spillage, finds Peter to be 50 per cent responsible for the accident. The court would have awarded him £500, but he receives £250, due to his own negligence.*

9

Health and safety at work

Stapley v *Gypsum Mines Ltd* (1953)

Mrs Stapley claimed damages from the mine owners following an accident in which her husband had been killed. There had been a roof fall in the section of the mine in which he was working, and he was crushed. He and another worker had been told to bring the roof down to make the area safe. They had ignored this instruction and had continued to work knowing of the danger.

Held (HL) The employers were vicariously liable for the actions of the second employee who had been a senior worker. However, their Lordships also concluded that Mr Stapley would probably have agreed with this employee's decision to continue to work, and so held that his conduct amounted to contributory negligence. Consequently, the damages payable to his widow were reduced by 80 per cent.

● Volenti non fit injuria

An employer may raise the defence of *volenti non fit injuria*, alleging that he is not liable because his employee consented to the possibility of being injured. The basis of the defence is that the employee who consents to the possibility of harm cannot then complain when later injured.

Example

A boxer consents to being hit during a boxing match. He will also be aware that he could be severely injured or killed during the contest. He consents to the possibility of harm and so cannot sue his opponent if he is injured.

This is a general defence and is unlikely to succeed in many employment cases due to the fact that employees often have no choice but to work in hazardous environments. Just because an employee finds himself doing a dangerous job does not mean that he consents to being injured or killed.

This defence did succeed in *ICI* v *Shatwell* (below).

ICI v *Shatwell* (1965)

A group of shotfirers were told only to carry out detonations when they were safely behind cover. On one occasion the fuse wire they used was not long enough to enable them to get safely behind cover before the explosion. One employee left the site to look for more wire. The others decided to go ahead with the explosion without being safely behind cover and were injured.

Held The employer's defence of *volenti* succeeded. The employees had been fully aware that their actions might cause them injury. They had ignored this knowledge and by doing so had consented to injury.

VICARIOUS LIABILITY

Vicarious liability is a term used to describe the situation where an employer, although having committed no wrong himself, may be liable for the negligent actions of his employees.

Example
Conrad and Trinny both work for Readyfoods plc. Conrad knows that he is not supposed to leave boxes blocking corridors, entrances or exits. He nevertheless leaves five heavy boxes blocking the entrance to the factory. Trinny trips over the boxes, and they fall on top of her. She bangs her head and is unconscious.

In this case Readyfoods plc has done nothing wrong but would be vicariously liable for Conrad's actions and have to pay damages to Trinny. Vicarious liability also extends to injuries caused to non-employees and so Trinny could also make a claim if she did not work for Readyfoods plc but happened to be visiting the factory in some other capacity.

An injured person could also sue the employee who caused the accident, but as that person is unlikely to have the financial resources to pay damages, this may not be worthwhile. As the employer will have compulsory insurance, he is in a better position to pay damages to the injured person.

Vicarious liability does not arise in all situations. The basis of this claim is that employers should be liable for the negligent acts of their employees committed 'during the course of their employment'. In order for an employer to be vicariously liable for the actions of his employee, the employee must have been:

● acting in the course of his employment; and

● not on a frolic of his own.

In the course of his employment

The act that causes the accident must be done in the course of his employment. This means that the employee must be doing something that is authorised by his employer as part of his job.

Beard v London General Omnibus Co (1900)

A bus conductor was told not to drive the company's buses. He injured someone while reversing a bus into a depot.

Held He was not acting in the course of his employment; he had expressly been told not to drive the bus and so had performed an unauthorised act. The bus company was not vicariously liable for his actions.

An act is still done in the course of employment if, although authorised, it is done in an unauthorised way.

Century Insurance Co v NIRTB (1942)

A lorry driver was transferring petrol from his tanker into a petrol station store. He lit a cigarette and discarded it, causing a fire.

Held His employer was vicariously liable for the fire; he was acting in the course of his employment even though by discarding the cigarette he was doing an unauthorised act.

Rose v Plenty (1976)

A milkman was specifically told not to allow children on to his milkfloat to help him with deliveries. He employed a 13-year-old boy as an assistant. The child was injured while helping out on the float.

Held The employers were vicariously liable for the child's injuries; the employee had been doing his job even though he was not supposed to be doing it with the aid of a child assistant.

Limpus v London General Omnibus Co (1862)

A bus driver was racing against a rival bus operator. He injured a group of people standing in a bus queue when he negligently drove into them.

Held The bus company was vicariously liable for his actions; he was authorised to drive the bus and so was acting in the course of his employment, even though he was driving in an unauthorised manner.

Daniels v Whetstone Entertainments Ltd (1962)

A nightclub bouncer forcibly ejected Mr Daniels from the premises. Once outside the bouncer assaulted him.

Held The bouncer's employer was vicariously liable for the injuries caused when Daniels was removed from the premises, but not for those sustained in the later assault. The assault had been outside the scope of the bouncer's employment.

In some situations the employee may be performing his duties in the wrong way to such an extent that he will not be acting in the course of his employment. In **General Engineering Services Ltd v Kingston & St Andrews Corporation** (1989), a group of firemen instigated a go-slow policy when attending fires. They were in dispute with their employer over a pay claim. The go-slow meant that it took them twice as long to get to the site of a fire, and often people were injured and buildings burnt to the ground.

The firemen alleged that their employer was vicariously liable for their actions. The court dismissed this claim stating that their actions were outside the scope of their employment.

● Not on a frolic of his own

This phrase stems from the judgment of Parke J in **Joel v Morrison** (1834):

> if he [the driver] was going out of his way, against his master's implied commands, when driving on his master's business, he will make his master liable, but if he was going on a frolic of his own, without being at all on his master's business the master will not be liable.

If employees are doing something unconnected in any way to their work duties when the accident occurs, they are said to be on a 'frolic of their own'. In such situations their actions are outside the scope of their employment and their employers are not vicariously liable for any injuries.

Hilton v Thomas Burton (Rhodes) Ltd (1961)

Hilton's husband was killed when a works van in which he was travelling crashed on the way back from a café. The men were some distance away from their workplace and not on any of the routes authorised by their employer.

Held The employer was not vicariously liable for his death; the men were on a frolic of their own.

Jones *v* Tower Boot Co (1997)

This case highlights the way in which the rules on vicarious liability have been applied by the courts. Here, a 16-year-old employee of mixed race was subjected to severe racial harassment by fellow employees. The court held that Tower Boot was vicariously liable for the actions of these employees, even though they were not acting in the course of their employment.

The view here was that the attacks were so severe that the rules should not be used to relieve the employer of liability.

See also: *Credit Lyonnais Bank Nederland* v *ECGD* (1999), *Chief Adjudication Officer* v *Rhodes* (1999), *Dubai Aluminium Co Ltd* v *Salaam* (2003).

Lister *v* Hesley Hall (2001)

This more recent case highlights the modern view taken by the courts when applying the rules on vicarious liability.

Here, the owner of a school was held liable for acts of sex abuse against children carried out by a warden/housemaster. The school, Axeholme House, was part of a residential setting for maladjusted and vulnerable boys. Both a Mr Grain (the warden/housemaster) and his wife were employed by the school. During his employment Mr Grain sexually and physically abused three teenage boys. The boys did not bring an action against Mr Grain until they were adults. He was convicted in 1995. The adult 'boys' then sued Axeholme House for damages, claiming that the school was vicariously liable for the actions of their employee, Mr Grain.

The 'boys' were initially unsuccessful in their claim. However, the House of Lords later held that it was wrong to consider the claim from the traditional point of view of whether the employee used an unauthorised method to do a job he was authorised to do or was simply doing something which was unauthorised. Their Lordships held that that approach was not appropriate in cases such as *Lister* where an employer has a duty to take care of the persons who suffered as a result of their employee's acts. Consequently, the claimants were successful in their claim on the basis of vicarious liability.

INDEPENDENT CONTRACTORS

An employer owes the same duty of care to independent contractors as to their own employees. At common law employers are not usually liable for the actions of independent contractors unless they specifically instruct them to perform an action that results in injury to another.

STATUTORY CONTROL – THE HEALTH AND SAFETY AT WORK ACT 1974

The Health and Safety at Work Act 1974 (HSAWA 1974) regulates health and safety in the workplace by imposing general duties on employers, employees, designers, manufacturers, suppliers, importers and non-employees. Whereas the civil law aims to compensate injured employees, the 1974 Act creates criminal penalties for those who fail to meet health and safety standards. The ideal behind the Act is the promotion of health and safety in the workplace and the prevention of accidents.

Pre-1974 legislation

Before the implementation of the HSAWA 1974, the law regulating health and safety in the workplace existed in various statutes. For example, it could be found in the:

- Mines and Quarries Act 1954
- Factories Act 1961
- Offices, Shops and Railway Premises Act 1963.

The various Acts in force meant that the law was piecemeal. There was little consistency in the standards set and some occupations were not covered by it at all. The law was ineffective and too complicated. Some of these old statutes are still partially in force today. However, they are slowly being replaced by health and safety regulations.

The Robens Report

The government wanted to reform the way in which health and safety at work was regulated and to change the complicated structure that existed. In 1970 it set up a Royal Commission on Health and Safety at Work chaired by Lord Robens.

The Committee was set the task of investigating and commenting on the role of the then legislation, and reporting back with ideas for reform. The Robens Report (Cmnd 5034) was published in 1972 and was very critical of the existing law. The Report stated that the existing law was 'badly structured' and 'unintelligible'.

The Report recommended that the law be changed to provide:

> **a comprehensive and orderly set of revised provisions under a new enabling Act. The new Act should contain a clear statement of the basic responsibilities of safety responsibility. It should be supported by regulations and non-statutory codes of practice, with emphasis on the latter.**

The government adopted the recommendations of the Robens Report and enacted the Health and Safety at Work Act 1974. This Act provides the framework for health and safety legislation. It is an enabling Act which means that regulations and approved codes of practice can be made under its general provisions.

The HSAWA 1974 applies to all types of workplace, except those involving domestic employment. It makes the breach of the employer's common law duty of care a criminal offence. Employees cannot make a claim for breach of the Act. Enforcement is carried out by the Health and Safety Executive. The Act is used to punish those who do not provide adequate health and safety standards. Individuals, as well as, or instead of, organisations may be prosecuted for breaches of the Act.

Section 1 - The objectives of the HSAWA 1974

Section 1 of the Act states its objectives:

- to secure the health, safety and welfare of employees;
- to protect those who are not employees from health and safety risks that may arise due to the work being carried out;
- to control explosives, highly flammable or otherwise dangerous substances;
- to control the emission into the atmosphere of noxious or offensive substances.

The next section of this chapter discusses the first two general objectives, the remainder being beyond the scope of this text.

9

Health and safety at work

GENERAL DUTIES UNDER THE HSAWA 1974

The Act imposes duties with regard to health and safety provision on:

- employers
- employees
- designers
- manufacturers
- suppliers
- importers
- non-employees such as independent contractors.

Section 2 - employers' duties towards their employees

The general duties covered by s 2 of the Act mirror the common law duties discussed at pages 330 to 338

Section 2(1) states that:

it shall be the duty of every employer to ensure, so far as is reasonably practicable, the health, safety and welfare at work of all his employees.

Section 2(2) extends this duty to maintaining in particular:

(a) the provision and maintenance of plant and systems of work that are, so far as is reasonably practicable, safe and without risks to health;

(b) arrangements for ensuring, so far as is reasonably practicable, safety and absence of risks to health in connection with the use, handling, storage, and transport of articles and substances;

(c) the provision of such information, instructing, training and supervision as is necessary to ensure, so far as is reasonably practicable, the health and safety at work of his employees;

(d) so far as is reasonably practicable as regards any place of work under the employer's control, the maintenance of it in a condition that is safe and without risks to health and the provision and maintenance of means of access to and egress from it that are safe and without such risks;

(e) the provision and maintenance of a working environment for his employees that is, so far as is reasonably practicable, safe, without risks to health, and adequate as regards facilities and arrangements for their welfare at work.

In each case the duty only extends to doing what is reasonably practicable in the circumstances. As with the common law rules, the law does not demand the impossible and what is reasonably practicable will differ depending on the circumstances in each case.

● What is 'reasonably practicable'?

As with their common law duty, employers are able to balance the likelihood of harm occurring with the cost and inconvenience involved in preventing it. Section 40 of the 1974 Act states that an employer has to prove that his actions were reasonably practicable. If he can show that he has done all that was reasonable in the circumstances, the employer will not be liable under the Act. The following case highlights the often harsh interpretation of this duty.

Hawes v Railway Executive (1952)

Mrs Hawes sued the Railway Executive following the death of her husband, a railway employee. She alleged it was in breach of its duty to provide a safe system of work. He was killed while doing repairs near to a live rail. She established that the degree of risk and the likelihood of harm occurring was high. Her husband was inches away from the live rail at all times and one slightly wrong movement was very likely to result in serious harm or death. The only way to have avoided the risk completely would have been to switch off the current, and so stop the railway until the repairs were completed.

Held She lost her claim; the court felt that the cost and inconvenience to society of stopping the railway every time that repairs were needed outweighed the likelihood of harm occurring.

Associated Dairies v Hartley (1979)

Associated Dairies supplied their workers with safety shoes. They charged them £1 per week for the use of the shoes. Hartley argued that the Dairies were in breach of s 2 of the HSAWA 1974 because they did not provide safety equipment.

Held (CA) His claim was dismissed because the cost of providing the shoes outweighed the likelihood of minor or serious accidents occurring if they were not provided. It was not reasonably practicable to expect the employer to provide free shoes.

West Bromwich Building Society Ltd v Townsend (1983)

The Building Society was served with an improvement notice requiring it to install bandit screens to protect employees from attack. It appealed stating that it would prove to be too expensive to fit the screens, and that the risk of injury was low.

Held (High Court) The appeal was allowed as the risk had to be weighed against the cost.

It should be noted that an employer cannot be held liable for failing to take precautions which were not invented at the time of any incident or for failing to recognise and protect against any danger that 'science' had not recognised at that time, e.g. an unidentified disease.

● Section 2(3) – the provision of a health and safety statement

Section 2(3) of the HSAWA 1974 states that employers who employ five or more employees must prepare a written health and safety statement. Health and Safety Executive guidelines refer to the statement as a 'blueprint' on safety. It should state both the company's general health and safety policy, and detail what form and frequency inspections and assessments will take.

The statement should also provide the employee with details as to which member of the company has overall responsibility for health and safety matters. If possible, it should also outline which manager, and/or supervisor the employee should approach with any health and safety queries.

The statement should be brought to the attention of all employees. This can be done by including it in their written statement of terms and conditions of employment. The statement should be revised at regular intervals and employees must be informed of any changes made.

● Section 2(4), (5), (6) – duty to consult employees on health and safety matters

Employers have a duty to consult with their employees on health and safety matters. This is outlined in s 2(4), (5) and (6) of the HSAWA 1974 and the Health and Safety (Consultation with Employees) Regulations 1996.

Employers or unions may appoint employees to act as safety representatives. These representatives will represent the workforce in any consultation on health and safety issues. The duties of safety representatives include:

- being consulted on health and safety matters and making representation to employers;
- investigating hazards and risks;
- making safety inspections;
- considering employee complaints;
- accessing and consulting with Health and Safety Executive inspectors;
- being a member of any safety committee.

Section 2(7) states that if two or more safety representatives request it, the employer must set up a safety committee. The work of safety representatives and safety committees are regulated by the Safety Representatives and Safety Committees Regulations 1977. The safety committee should meet regularly and maintain a review of all health and safety matters.

An employer must consult the committee if he intends to introduce any new machinery or technology into the workplace. The committee should be provided with information on any safety risks or hazards likely to be created by the introduction of the new system.

Representatives may suggest ideas for safety improvements and are entitled to reasonable time off work to complete any health and safety tasks or for training. The dismissal of a representative for anything concerning health and safety is automatically unfair.

● Section 3 – the duty placed on employers and the self-employed to take care of the safety of non-employees

Section 3(1) of the HSAWA 1974 states that:

> It shall be the duty of every employer to conduct his undertaking in such a way as to ensure, so far as is reasonably practicable, that persons not in his employment who may be affected thereby are not thereby exposed to risks to their health and safety.

The self-employed have a duty to protect themselves and anyone likely to be affected by their work from health and safety risks. Both employers and the self-employed should provide any non-employee likely to be affected by their work with information on any risks or hazards that might exist.

This means that employers have a duty to take care for the safety of independent contractors working for them. Employers and the self-employed have a duty to take care of the safety of those visiting the workplace.

R v Swan Hunter Shipbuilders Ltd (1982)

A group of men working on the construction of HMS *Glasgow* died in a fire. The fire started during welding operations being carried out by a subcontracter, Telemeter. The fire was intense because there was too much oxygen in the air. Swan Hunter had warned its own employees about the dangers of working with oxygen in poorly ventilated areas, but had failed to provide the subcontractors with the same information.

Held (CA) Swan Hunter was liable under s 3(1) because it had failed to provide the contractors with information on possible health and safety risks and hazards.

R v Associated Octel Co Ltd (1997)

Associated Octel was convicted under s 3(1) of the HSAWA 1974 when a worker from a firm of independent contractors was seriously injured while working on Octel's site. He was badly burnt while cleaning and repairing the inside of a tank. The bulb of the light that he was using had smashed and ignited the substance that he was using. Octel appealed against the conviction arguing that it was not liable for the actions of the independent contractor as Octel had no control over how the independent contractor did his work.

Held Appeal dismissed; Octel was in overall control of the premises and was liable for the injuries resulting from the accident.

R v British Steel plc (1995)

British Steel employed two subcontractors to reposition a section of steel platform. British Steel's own engineer supervised the operation. After he had left the site the contractors rendered the platform unstable and it collapsed, killing one of them. British Steel was charged under s 3(1) and argued that the accident had occurred because the workers had not followed the British Steel engineer's instructions. British Steel said that it had done all that was reasonably practicable to ensure the safety of the men.

Held (CA) British Steel was liable for the death as it had not taken care for the safety of the contractors.

See also: *R v Mara* (1987), *Jones v Fishwick* (1989), *R v Nelson Group Services (Maintenance) Ltd* (1998).

Section 4 - duties on those in control of premises

Section 4 of the HSAWA 1974 places a duty on all occupiers of premises, except those in charge of domestic premises. The duty is to take care for the safety of persons who are not their employees but who work on their premises. This is the same as the duty imposed on employers and the self-employed in s 3(1), but relates only to those occupying or in control of premises.

In *Westminster CC* v *Select Managements* (1985) a company managing a block of flats was held to be liable for the safety of lifts and other common parts where people who were not their employees might work.

Section 6 - duties owed by designers, manufacturers, importers and suppliers

Section 6 imposes a duty on anyone who designs, manufactures, imports or supplies any article or substance for use in the workplace. The duty is to ensure, as far as is reasonably practicable, that the articles and substances are safe, and that they do not prove a risk to health and safety. The article or substance should be suitably tested and examined and adequate information provided on how it should or should not be used.

Section 7 - duties owed by employees

Section 7 of the HSAWA 1974 imposes a duty on employees to take care for their own safety and that of others in the workplace. Every employee has a duty to:

- take reasonable care for his own and other's health and safety;
- co-operate with employers or any other person to enable them to perform their statutory duties.

Examples of this duty would involve wearing protective clothing, using the safety equipment provided, and assisting the Health and Safety Executive with any investigation.

Section 8 - non-interference with anything provided for health and safety purposes

There is a duty on every person not to interfere with or damage anything that has been provided as an aid to health and safety in the workplace. This would include, for example, tampering with fire extinguishers or fire alarms.

Section 9 - employer's duty not to charge for health and safety provision

Employers have a duty not to charge employees for anything done, or provided, to comply with health and safety requirements. This would include, for example, the provision of safety goggles or training courses. Employers are free to charge for anything they provide beyond basic statutory requirements.

9

Health and safety at work

HEALTH AND SAFETY REGULATIONS

Regulations are made in addition to the requirements of the Health and Safety at Work Act 1974. As the 1974 Act is an enabling Act, regulations can be made under it which relate to almost anything concerning health and safety. Some regulations have been drafted to comply with European law and some to apply to specific problems such as noise at work or the provision of first aid.

The Framework Directive

On 12 June 1989 the European Community adopted a Framework Directive to encourage improvements in the health and safety of people at work. The Directive sets down general principles on the identification and control of occupational risks, the protection of health and safety and the informing, consulting and training of workers and their representatives.

The 'six-pack'

Many of the principles contained in the Framework Directive were introduced into English law by the Management of Health and Safety at Work Regulations 1992. These regulations have now been replaced by the Management of Health and Safety at Work Regulations 1999. Five other regulations were implemented in 1992 and together they are referred to as the 'six-pack'. The six-pack is now made up of:

- Management of Health and Safety at Work Regulations 1999 (as amended)
- Workplace (Health, Safety and Welfare) Regulations 1992
- Provision and Use of Work Equipment Regulations 1998
- Personal Protective Equipment at Work Regulations 2002
- Manual Handling Operations Regulations 1992
- Health and Safety Display Screen Equipment Regulations 1992.

Details of these and other regulations can be found on the Health and Safety Executive website at www.hse.gov.uk/legislation/statinstruments.htm.

Management of Health and Safety at Work Regulations 1999 (as amended 2006)

These regulations lay down general principles relating to the cleanliness and maintenance of the workplace. They apply to all workplaces.

The regulations introduced the concept of 'risk assessment'. All employers, except those of ships' crews must make:

> suitable and efficient assessments of the dangers facing their employees and anyone else likely to be affected by their work.

Risk assessment is used to help employers to identify any safety risks that exist in the workplace, and so highlight any changes or precautions that must be made to comply with safety standards. An assessment of risk is a careful examination of those things in the workplace that might cause harm.

If an employer employs more than five employees, risk assessment findings must be produced in a written document. Assessments must be kept under review and take place at reasonable intervals. Whilst these regulations introduced the concept of risk assessment, some of the others discussed below have also adopted the same procedures.

The regulations also state that employers must establish a procedure to be followed in an emergency. All employees should be instructed as to how this procedure should be implemented, and informed of any relevant hazards. Employees must be able to stop work and go to a place of safety if they are exposed to serious and immediate danger.

Employers must ensure that individual employees are capable of doing the work that they are given and that they have adequate health and safety training. Training must be given when an employee begins to work for the employer, at regular intervals, and if any new equipment or substances are to be used in the workplace. Employees must inform their employers or safety representatives of any serious dangers or failures in safety arrangements.

The regulations also state that employers should provide their workforce with adequate heating, lighting and ventilation.

The HSC has published a code of practice providing guidance on the 1999 regulations.

Workplace (Health, Safety and Welfare) Regulations 1992

These regulations expand the duties owed under ss 2 and 4 of the HSWA 1974. They apply to all workplaces apart from ships, building operations and sites for mineral extraction. They apply to employers or occupiers of premises. The regulations aim to protect the health and safety of everyone in the workplace and to ensure that adequate welfare facilities are provided.

The regulations state that the working environment should be kept at a reasonable temperature, adequately lit, ventilated, kept clean and provide safe means by which people can move around. For example, the provision of safe lifts, doors, floors, stairways and escalators. There should also be adequate vehicle routes outside the workplace. Equipment should be kept in good working order and there should be adequate toilet and washing facilities. Employers must also designate an area where employees can eat and take rest breaks. Places where any dangers or hazards exist should be clearly marked.

Provision and use of Work Equipment Regulations 1998

These regulations aim to ensure that machinery and other work equipment is safe and that it is used safely. The regulations are worded in general terms and cover all kinds of work equipment, except that on sea-going ships.

The regulations reinforce the obligations placed on designers, manufacturers, importers and suppliers specified in s 6 of the HSAWA 1974. The selection of work equipment should consider whether it will be safe to use, and once installed it should be routinely checked. Providers of equipment should provide written information and instruction on how it should be used.

Personal and Protective Equipment at Work Regulations 2002

These regulations aim to ensure that the personal and protective equipment used in the workplace is safe. Personal and protective equipment is defined as:

all equipment (including clothing affording protection against the weather) which is intended to be worn or held by a person at work, and which protects him against one or more risks to his health and safety.

This would include equipment such as safety helmets, gloves, eye protection, high visibility clothing, safety footwear and safety harnesses.

Likely hazards should be assessed and then equipment provided to protect workers from harm. Employees should also be trained in the use of protective equipment.

Manual Handling Operations Regulations 1992

These regulations affect the transporting or supporting of any loads in the workplace. This includes the lifting, putting down, pushing, pulling, carrying or moving of anything by hand or by bodily force. They apply to all workplaces except sea-going ships.

The regulations aim to reduce the high number of work-related back injuries that occur each year. The Health and Safety Executive booklet, Getting to Grips with Manual Handling, states that more than one-third of all over three-day injuries reported each year arise from manual-handling accidents.

The regulations require employers and the self-employed to do a risk assessment and to establish a hierarchy of safety measures. They should:

- avoid the use of hazardous manual-handling practices;
- assess the risks to health and safety where manual handling cannot be avoided;
- reduce the risk of injury by considering the size, shape and location of the load to be moved.

Risk assessment should be reviewed at regular intervals and the dangers reduced to the lowest possible levels.

Health and Safety Display Screen Equipment Regulations 1992

These regulations are concerned with the problems of fatigue, eye and muscle strain commonly arising from the use of display screens. They apply to those employees who spend most of the working day using such screens. The regulations state that employers should do a risk assessment, assessing the health and safety risks encountered by the use of display screens. Any risks to safety should then be reduced to the lowest possible levels.

Employers should do an assessment of the workstation where each employee sits whilst using the screen. They should look at the equipment and furniture provided, and assess whether the employee has enough space in which to work. Risks could be reduced by the provision of adjustable chairs, protective screen covers and good lighting.

If a screen user requests an eye test, the employer should provide a free test. If the employee needs special spectacles to enable him to continue to use the screen, these should be paid for by the employer. Employees may request eye tests at regular intervals.

Employers should provide training and information on the use of display screens and highlight any ways in which employees can act to protect their own safety.

OTHER REGULATIONS

There are over 50 other regulations relating to specific hazards or specific types of work. These include the:

- Control of Lead at Work Regulations 2002
- Health and Safety (First Aid) Regulations 1981
- Control of Asbestos Regulations 2006
- Control of Substances Hazardous to Health Regulations 2002

- Control of Noise at Work Regulations 2005
- Electricity at Work Regulations 1989
- Construction (Head Protection) Regulations 1989
- Construction (Design and Management) Regulations 2007
- Reporting of Injuries, Diseases and Dangerous Occurrences Regulations 1995
- Health and Safety (Signs and Signals) Regulations 1996
- Export and Import of Dangerous Chemicals Regulations 2005.

The Health and Safety (Miscellaneous Amendments) Regulations 2002 made minor amendments to many of these regulations. An outline of three of these regulations appears below.

Health and Safety (First Aid) Regulations 1981

These regulations state that employers should provide adequate and appropriate equipment, facilities and personnel to enable first aid to be administered in the workplace.

What is, for example, adequate equipment will depend on the size of the workforce. In some cases a suitably stocked first aid box and an employee appointed to deal with accidents will suffice. In others the employer may need to provide a first aid room and a nurse who is able to deal with all accidents.

The regulations apply to all workplace situations except those involving diving and some shipping and mining operations. Notices or other forms of communication must be used to tell employees where to go for first aid treatment and which member of staff is qualified to deal with accidents.

Control of Substances Hazardous to Health Regulations 2002 (COSHH)

These regulations lay down systematic rules to protect employees who use dangerous substances at work. A substance is hazardous if it is listed as toxic, very toxic, harmful, corrosive or irritant.

Employers should assess the risks involved in the use of hazardous substances and outline which precautions are needed to control their use. Employees should be trained on the safe use and storage of all substances that they are likely to come into contact with.

Reporting of Injuries, Diseases and Dangerous Occurrences Regulations 1995

These regulations relate to the reporting of accidents in the workplace. They cover all workplaces except domestic settings. Employers must report major workplace injuries and diseases to the Health and Safety Executive (HSE). If a death occurs as a result of an accident, or if there is a 'dangerous occurrence' in the workplace, employers must inform the HSE as soon as possible, and at least within seven days. The report can be made on a standard form and posted to the HSE.

Reportable major injuries include fractures of the skull, spine, pelvis, arm, wrist, leg or ankle, or anything that results in the victim being hospitalised for more than 24 hours.

Dangerous occurrences include the collapse of lifts, explosions, electrical short circuits, fires or the collapse of a scaffold. Reportable diseases include poisonings, skin and lung diseases.

9

Health and safety at work

ENFORCEMENT

The Health and Safety Executive is responsible for the enforcement of the Health and Safety at Work Act 1974 and the regulations. The HSE may also use local authority environmental health officers to either assist in or do inspections.

The HSE also appoints its own safety inspectors who have the authority to enter premises to carry out investigations. They also investigate when a serious accident has occurred. They may visit the workplace unannounced or by appointment. The HSE *Offences and Penalties Report* 2004/5 states that the HSE prosecuted 712 cases during 2004/5. Over 95 per cent of these cases resulted in a conviction. During the same year the HSE issued 8445 enforcement notices. These are the most recent HSE Statistics available at the time of writing.

Powers of health and safety inspectors

Health and Safety Executive safety inspectors have the power to:

- enter premises at any reasonable time;
- be accompanied by authorised persons and a police officer if obstructed;
- use equipment or materials necessary for investigation;
- take samples, measurements and photographs;
- direct that work areas be left undisturbed;
- take possession of articles, substances or equipment if believed to be a source of imminent danger;
- take statements from appropriate persons;
- examine and copy documents;
- issue an improvement notice;
- issue a prohibition notice.

Improvement and prohibition notices

Sections 21 and 22 of the Health and Safety at Work Act 1974 state that inspectors can serve improvement notices and prohibition notices on employers who are found to be in breach of the Act or any regulation.

If an inspector believes that an employer is not providing an adequate standard of health and safety provision, he can serve the employer with an improvement notice. This notice is a written explanation outlining what it is that the employer is doing wrong or failing to do. The notice will also outline what needs to be done in order to rectify the problem, and requires the employer to do this within 21 days.

If the inspector finds that there is an immediate risk of harm, he may serve the employer with a prohibition notice. This notice states that the employer must stop either all or part of the business operation until the problem is rectified.

Failure to comply with a prohibition notice, for example, continuing to use a machine when told not to, is punishable as an offence triable in the Crown Court. Prohibition notices are usually only given if the inspector thinks that there is a risk of serious injury.

Appealing against an improvement or prohibition notice

Section 24 of the Health and Safety at Work Act 1974 states that employers may appeal to an Employment Tribunal against either an improvement or prohibition notice. If an employer appeals against an improvement notice, it will be suspended until the appeal is heard. If the employer appeals against a prohibition notice, the notice remains in force until after the appeal is heard unless it is suspended by the tribunal. The tribunal can cancel or affirm a notice or modify its scope.

Offence to obstruct an inspector in the performance of his duties

Section 33 of the Health and Safety at Work Act 1974 states that it is an offence to obstruct an inspector in the performance of his duties.

Prosecution

If an employer who has received a prohibition or improvement notice does not appeal against the notice, or appeals and loses, he can be prosecuted if he:

- fails to make any improvement listed in an improvement notice; or
- continues to use or do something listed in a prohibition notice.

The HSE can institute prosecutions in either the Magistrates' Court or the Crown Court. The court used will depend on the seriousness of the offence and the penalty the HSE would like to see imposed. The Magistrates' Court and Crown Court have the power to impose different penalties. Note also that prosecutions can be instigated for breaches of the HSAWA 1974 or the regulations before the issue of any notice, for example, after a serious accident has occurred.

Penalties

The Magistrates' Court has the power to either fine the employer up to £5000, or up to £20 000 if there has been a breach of ss 2–6 of the 1974 Act or a breach of an improvement or prohibition notice. The court can also impose a sentence of up to six months' imprisonment for a breach of any notice.

The Crown Court has the power to impose an unlimited fine or up to two years' imprisonment.

THE WORKING TIME REGULATIONS 1998 (AS AMENDED)

The Working Time Directive 1993 introduced important health and safety measures to ensure that workers are, for example, protected from having to work very long hours. The Working Time Regulations 1998 came into force on 1 October of that year. These regulations implemented the 1993 Directive. Up until this time employers and employees had been able to negotiate on matters such as holiday entitlement, working hours, rest breaks and holiday pay. In most cases there was little negotiation with the employer dictating the terms on which the employee would work.

Whilst the 1998 regulations remain the main set of regulations on working time they have been subject to amendment. They were amended by the Working Time Regulations 1999 and the Working Time (Amendment) Regulations 2002. The 2002 amendment regulations became

9

Health and safety at work

law in April 2003 and implemented Directive 94/33/EC on the protection of young people at work. This is known as the Young Workers Directive. These amendment regulations provide better rights for young workers, that is those between the ages of 15 and 18.

A further set of amending regulations came into force in August 2003. The Working Time (Amendment) Regulations 2003 extended the protection of the 1998 regulations to all non-mobile workers in road, sea, inland waterways and lake transport, to all workers in the railway and offshore sectors, and to all aviation workers who are not already covered by the Aviation Directive. The regulations also applied to junior doctors as from 1 August 2004. Note also that the Working Time (Amendment) Regulations 2006 and the Working Time (Amendment) (No. 2) Regulations 2006 have also made their minor amendments to the 1998 regulations. Unless stated otherwise any following reference to 'the regulations' refers to the 1998 Regulations.

Main provisions - 1998 regulations

The main provisions of the 1998 regulations are that workers have the right:

- not to have to work more than 48 hours per week;
- to 11 hours of rest each day;
- to have at least one day off each week;
- to an in-work rest break if their working day is longer than six hours;
- to four weeks' paid holiday leave each year.

In addition the regulations provide that 'night workers' have the right:

- not to be required to work more than an average of 8 hours in any 24-hour period, and to
- free health assessments.

'Working time'

Regulation 2 defines working time as that when someone is 'working, at his employer's disposal and carrying out his activities or duties'. This would include, for example, time when a worker is travelling as part of their job or doing job-related training. Where a worker spends time 'on call' this time is to be regarded as being 'working time' if the employee is required to be present and available at their workplace. See: *Sindicato Medicas Publica* v *Valenciana* (2001), *Landeshauptstadt Kiel* v *Norbert Jaeger* (2004).

48-hour maximum working week

Regulation 4 provides that a worker cannot be required to work for more than an average of 48 hours per week. The average weekly working time is generally calculated over 17 weeks. This time is referred to as the 'reference period'. This period may be extended by up to 26 weeks. It may also be extended to 52 weeks if varied by a collective or workplace agreement. An employer would have to agree to any such extension. An employer has an obligation 'in keeping with the need for health and safety of workers' to ensure that the limit specified is adhered to. The average weekly working time is calculated by dividing the number of hours worked by the number of weeks over which the average working week is being calculated, for example, 17. Any overtime worked or leave taken should be included in the calculation. Figure 9.2 provides an example of a basic 'hours worked' calculation.

Jessica works for a local bookshop, Mystery Books. On average she is required to work 40 hours per week. Over the last 17 weeks she has worked five hours of overtime each week but has not taken any leave. The following calculation assesses how many hours she has worked within the last 17 weeks (the reference period):

worked hours: 40 per week $40 \times 17 = 680$
worked hours (overtime): 17 per week $5 \times 17 = 85$
                                              $\text{total} = 765$

Jessica has worked 765 hours during the 'reference period'.
Her average number of hours worked (total hours divided by number of weeks) is:

$$765 \div 17 = 45 \text{ hours a week}$$

Jessica's working hours are within the 48 maximum set by the regulations.

Figure 9.2 Basic 'hours worked' calculation

Under Regulation 5 workers have the option of agreeing to work more than 48 hours per week and so opt out of the protection provided by Regulation 4. Workers may agree to work as many hours as are required by their employer. However, before the employee opts out their employer should take reasonable steps to ensure that they are fully aware of their rights under Regulation 4. An employer cannot insist that an employee opt out of their rights under Regulation 4. Workers cannot be fairly dismissed or subjected to any detriment for refusing to sign an opt-out agreement.

If an employee agrees to opt out but later changes their mind they can end the agreement with their employer by giving them seven days' notice. Employers must keep a list of the names of those employees who have opted out.

Night work

Regulations 6 and 7 provide protection for those workers who work during the night. Regulation 2 defines night workers as those who 'work at least 3 hours of their daily working time during night time'. 'Night time' includes the period of time between midnight and 5 am. Night workers should not work more than eight hours in any 24-hour period. Nightly working time is calculated over a period of 17 weeks. Where a night worker's work involves special hazards or heavy physical or mental strain then there is a limit on them working not more than eight hours each day. Night workers are entitled to a free health assessment before they begin to work nights. This assessment should be repeated at regular set intervals. The assessment should take the form of a medical questionnaire and examination. If the worker suffers from any health problems which are exacerbated by them working nights then their employer should transfer them to daytime working.

Holidays

All workers (either full- or part-time) are entitled to four weeks' paid annual leave from their employer. This amount of leave is not additional to any provided under their contract of employment. The entitlement begins on the first day of employment. Employers may adopt an accrual system whereby during the first year of employment the proportion of leave that may be taken builds up over that year. There is no statutory entitlement to take leave on bank or other public holidays. An employee must inform their employer of the dates on which they would like to take annual leave. The employer may also stipulate certain dates on which annual leave must be taken.

In the case of *Davies v MJ Wyatt (Decorators) Ltd* (2000) an employer decided to cut the hourly rate of pay he paid to employees in order to help him recoup the cost of giving them four weeks' paid holiday leave. The Employment Appeal Tribunal held that this was unlawful; the workers were entitled to their normal rate of pay as well as their paid annual leave. In *Armstrong v Walter Scott Motors* (2003) Armstrong's dismissal was held to be automatically unfair. He had been dismissed because he had asserted in a letter to his employer that they had failed to give him the holiday leave to which he was entitled. He had been dismissed for asserting his rights under the regulations.

Note that at the time of writing the DTI has set out proposals to increase the current four weeks statutory minimum holiday entitlement. It is proposed that the increase will take place in two stages. If the proposals are implemented a full-time worker who works 5 days a week will be entitled to a minimum of 24 days' holiday per year (as from 1/10/2007) and 28 days holiday per year (as from 1/10/2008).

Exclusions

Regulation 18 provides that some workers are exempt from the regulations. These include those who work in the following sectors:

- sea fishing
- workers on board certain ships/hovercrafts.

Enforcement

There are several ways in which the regulations may be enforced. The entitlements to, for example, annual leave and rest periods are enforced by the Employment Tribunal. An employee who feels that they have not, for example, been given four weeks' paid annual leave as provided for under the regulations may make a complaint to the tribunal. They have three months within which to make the claim. Acas may also initially become involved in any action. They will seek to reach a settlement between the employer and employee before the case reaches the tribunal. If the claim is heard in the tribunal and they find in favour of the employee they will make a declaration to this effect. The tribunal may also award compensation on the basis of what is 'just and equitable' taking into account the employer's default of the regulations.

The working time limits are enforced both by the Health and Safety Executive and individual local authorities. The HSE is authorised to use the existing enforcement procedures contained in the Health and Safety at Work Act 1974. (See further pages 354 to 355.) Enforcement Officers may issue improvement notices requiring employers to rectify matters, for example to ensure that they stop requiring an employee to work more than 48 hours per week. Failure to comply with an improvement notice can lead to a fine of up to £20 000 and/or six months' imprisonment if the case is heard in the Magistrates' Court. If the case is tried in the Crown Court the judge may impose an unlimited fine and/or up to two years' imprisonment.

Local authorities are responsible for enforcement of the regulations where the offending 'employer' is involved in the provision of services to customers. This would include, for example, the owners of cafes and restaurants.

The working time limits set out in Regulation 4 take effect as implied contractual terms and so workers are also able to enforce their rights in the same way as they would following a breach of another contractual term. See: *Barber v RJB Mining (UK) Ltd* (1999).

SUMMARY CHECKLIST

- The law on health and safety at work is found in legislation, common law, regulations, approved codes of practice and guidance notes.
- Employers have a common law duty to take reasonable care for the safety of their employees.
- Employers only have to do what is reasonably practicable in the circumstances; they can balance risk with cost and inconvenience.
- All employers must have insurance to cover them against employee injuries or fatalities.
- Employers have a common law duty to provide competent fellow employees, a safe system of work, safe work equipment and safe work premises.
- Employees may also make a claim for breach of statutory duty.
- Defences to a common law claim are that the employer was not negligent, the employee contributed to the accident or that the employee consented to being injured.
- An employer will be vicariously liable for the acts of their employees if they were done in the course of their employment and not while they were on a frolic of their own.
- The Health and Safety at Work Act 1974 imposes duties on employers, employees, designers, manufacturers, suppliers, importers and non-employees, such as independent contractors.
- Employers have a duty to provide a safe plant/system of work, safety in handling, storage and transport of articles, substances, the provision of information and instructions, training and supervision, a safe place of work, safe entrances, exits, a risk-free working environment and adequate welfare facilities.
- The ideal behind the 1974 Act is the promotion of health and safety in the workplace and the prevention of accidents.
- The Act creates criminal penalties for non-compliance with health and safety standards.
- Employers only have to do what is reasonably practicable in the circumstances; as with the common law they are able to balance risk with cost and inconvenience.
- Employers who employ more than five people must produce a health and safety statement outlining their policies.
- Employers have a duty to consult with their employees on health and safety matters.
- Employers or unions may appoint safety representatives who will be consulted on health and safety matters.
- Employers and the self-employed have a duty to take care of the safety of those on work premises but who are not their employees.
- Designers, manufacturers, importers and suppliers of articles or substances must ensure that they do not pose a risk to health and safety.
- Employees have a duty to take care for their own safety and that of others in the workplace.
- Some health and safety regulations were made under the 1989 European Framework Directive and some under the HSAWA 1974.

- The provisions of the Framework Directive were implemented by the 'six-pack':

  1 Management of Health and Safety at Work Regulations 1999

  2 Workplace (Health, Safety and Welfare) Regulations 1992

  3 Provision and Use of Work Equipment Regulations 1998

  4 Personal and Protective Equipment at Work Regulations 2002

  5 Manual Handling Operations Regulations 1992

  6 Health and Safety Display Screen Equipment Regulations 1992.

- Other regulations relate to particular hazards or types of work.

- Enforcement is carried out by the HSE or environmental health officers of a local authority.

- They can issue improvement or prohibition notices and/or institute prosecution.

- The Magistrates' Court or Crown Court may fine or imprison anyone convicted of a breach of the HSAWA 1974, of a regulation or for not having followed the instruction of an improvement or prohibition notice.

- The Working Time Directive sets out provisions on working hours, holiday entitlement and shift work.

SELF-TEST QUESTIONS

1 What are the sources of health and safety law?

2 What common law duties does an employer owe to his employees?

3 What was decided in the case of *Walker v Northumberland County Council* (1995)?

4 What defences may an employer have to a claim for breach of common law or statutory duty?

5 Define the term 'vicarious liability'.

6 What are the general duties imposed on employers by s 2 of the Health and Safety at Work Act 1974?

7 What duties does the Health and Safety at Work Act impose upon employees?

8 What influence did the 1989 European Framework Directive have on national health and safety law?

9 How does the Health and Safety Executive enforce the provisions of the Health and Safety at Work Act 1974 and the regulations?

10 What penalties can the Magistrates' Court and Crown Court impose on an individual or company convicted of breaching the Health and Safety at Work Act 1974 or a regulation?

11 Summarise the main provisions contained in the Working Time Directive and Regulations.

CASE SCENARIOS

A

Rosie and Jenny work for Stress-Free World plc. The company manufactures and exports aids to relaxation such as candles, oil burners, meditation tapes and wind chimes. Their colleague, Henry, is a known practical joker. He is always leaving joke spiders at their workstations, and often leaves whoopee cushions on their chairs. Last Friday Rosie walked up to her machine and started to sneeze violently. She fell against her machine and injured her arm. Henry was seen laughing. He admitted to his friend Neil that he had poured sneezing powder all over Rosie's workstation.

Henry then left his workstation and went off in search of another friend, Brian. On his way, he runs and slips on some oil. Stress-Free World had tried to clean up the oil but could not find enough sawdust. Henry injured his ankle. He was not wearing his regulation office boots, but had on a thin-soled pair of trendy new boots. Brian, seeing Henry fall, loses concentration at his machine. There is no machine guard in place and he severs his hand. Stress-Free had previously refused to provide machine guards.

As Henry gets up Rosie appears and hits him with her unhurt hand. He falls, hitting his head and is unconscious.

Advise Rosie, Henry and Brian:

- *as to any possible common law claim that they may have against Stress-Free World plc;*
- *whether their employer has any defence to any claim;*
- *whether Henry will be able to claim any compensation following Rosie's attack on him.*

B

Janet and Tim have recently set up their own travel agency. Janet knows that they will have to comply with certain health and safety requirements. They plan to take on 30 employees. Janet buys a copy of the Health and Safety at Work Act 1974 and Tim tells her that some 'regulations' may also apply to their business. He jokes that they had better get 'clued up' before they get a visit from the Health and Safety Executive.

Briefly advise Janet and Tim on the main contents of:

- *the Health and Safety at Work Act 1974;*
- *the 'six-pack' of regulations;*
- *the enforcement powers of the Health and Safety Executive.*

C

Sandra and Scott work for a large chocolate making company, Gresham Chocolates. William Taylor runs the firm's factory. Scott works in the warehouse. His job involves heavy lifting, putting large boxes of chocolates on to trucks so that they can be distributed around the country. He normally works more than 50 hours per week. He recently decided that he wanted to spend more time with his family and so asked Mr Taylor if he could reduce his working hours. Mr Taylor said, 'No way – if you continue to make a nuisance of yourself I'll have you working more hours!'

Sandra works on the night shift at Gresham Chocolates. She picks chocolates from a conveyor belt and places them into their boxes ready for packing. She hates working nights. She suffers from backache as she stands for long periods while at work. She is also constantly exhausted as she does not sleep at all well during the day. She recently informed Mr Taylor that her health was suffering due to the fact that she worked nights. He was totally uninterested and told her to consult her own doctor.

Last week William Taylor informed both workers that they would be entitled to three weeks of paid annual leave each year. Both Scott and Sandra believe there to be a law which states that they are entitled to more than three weeks' holiday leave.

Advise Scott:

● *as to whether William Taylor can insist that he works more than 50 hours each week.*

Advise Sandra:

● *as to whether she can demand that her employer provide her with a medical assessment; and*
● *on whether she can demand that she be moved to daytime working due to her ill health.*

Advise Scott and Sandra:

● *as to whether William Taylor is correct in saying that they are entitled to only three weeks of paid annual leave each year;*
● *as to how they can complain about any breaches of the Working Time Regulations 1998. Your answer should take into account the enforcement powers of the Health and Safety Executive.*

Further reading

Stress at Work, ACAS Advisory Booklet, March 2004.

Health and Safety Regulation: A Short Guide, HSE leaflet, August 2003.

Health and Safety Law: What you should know, HSE leaflet, April 2006.

Your Guide to the Working Time Directive, DTI, March 2007.

Working Time, IDS Handbook, December 2002.

For legal updates on the material in this chapter please go to the Companion Website accompanying this book at **www.mylawchamber.co.uk/nairns**

10

Settling disputes – taking a case to the Employment Tribunal

Where a person feels that he has been, for instance, discriminated against or unfairly dismissed, he may pursue his claim in the Employment Tribunal. Most employment disputes are resolved in the Employment Tribunal. The roles of the Employment Tribunal, the Employment Appeal Tribunal (EAT) and the Advisory, Conciliation and Arbitration Service (Acas) are discussed in Chapter 1 (pages 6, 7 and 26 respectively). These sections should be read as an introduction to this chapter.

By using the unfair dismissal case scenario in Chapter 6, we can take Robert Brown through the stages involved in making his claim to the Employment Tribunal. We can also look at the ways in which Gerald plc will try to defend itself against his claim. Copies of the relevant tribunal forms are included in this chapter in Figures 10.3 and 10.4. These serve to illustrate the form 'filling and sending' stages that have to be completed before a date is set for a tribunal hearing.

This chapter begins by considering the role and administration of the Employment Tribunal and then goes on to discuss:

- tribunal composition, who decides the case;
- tribunal jurisdiction;
- funding a claim, representation;
- time limits, the importance of making a claim in time;
- the stages in tribunal procedure – from form ET1 to the EAT;
- how the employee/ex-employee makes a claim to the tribunal, completion of form ET1;
- how the employer responds to this claim, completion of the notice of appearance, form ET3;
- the role of Acas, negotiated settlements;
- the possible interlocutory stages, case management, pre-hearing review;
- the tribunal hearing, procedure;
- the tribunal decision, costs;
- the appeal procedure, the role of the EAT, Court of Appeal, House of Lords and the European Court of Justice.

THE ROLE OF THE EMPLOYMENT TRIBUNAL

Industrial Tribunals, as they were formerly called, were set up under the Industrial Training Act of 1964. They are now called Employment Tribunals and are governed by the Employment Tribunals Act 1996, the Employment Rights (Dispute Resolution) Act 1988, and the Employment Tribunals (Constitution and Rules of Procedure) Regulations 2004 (as amended). When the tribunal system was devised its aim was to provide:

> **an easily accessible, speedy, informal and inexpensive procedure for the settlement of . . . disputes . . .**

(Donovan Report, Report of the Royal Commission on Trade Union and Employers' Associations, 1968, Cmnd 3623, p. 578).

The 2004 regulations state that their overriding objective is to 'enable tribunals and chairmen to deal with cases justly'. Regulation 3 goes on to state that:

this includes so far as is practicable:

- **ensuring that the parties are on an equal footing,**

- **saving expense,**

- **dealing with the case in ways which are proportionate to the complexity or importance of the issues, and**

- **ensuring that it is dealt with expeditiously and fairly.**

The Employment Tribunal is a more informal setting than that of a courtroom, but the experience of being involved in a case can still be a daunting one for both employers and employees. The parties should not expect to find themselves sitting around a table and chatting about the case! Although they are not in a courtroom they may feel as though they are when attending for the first time.

In an attempt to promote informality, the parties, tribunal panel and any witnesses remain seated during the hearing. The tribunal is not bound by the same rules of evidence as the civil courts, and if any lawyers are involved they do not wear wigs and gowns. There has been an increase in the use of legal representation over recent years, and in some cases this has inevitably led to more formal proceedings. However, in the main the tribunal is a more accessible and informal setting than the courtroom.

Tribunals do offer a relatively quick form of justice, but the waiting times for cases to be heard differs between regions. The Employment Tribunal 'Charter Statement' states that the service will bring 75 per cent of single cases to a hearing within 26 weeks of receiving them. For a person who has just lost his job, even a six-month wait may seem too long.

In the tribunal the parties to the case are referred to as the:

- **Claimant → (employee or ex-employee making the claim)**

- **Respondent → (employer responding to the claim).**

This chapter also makes reference to tribunal forms. The main forms are the:

- **Originating Application/ET1 → (employee or ex-employee sets out their claim)**

- **Notice of Appearance/ET3 → (employer admits/denies that claim).**

ADMINISTRATION

The work of the tribunal system is administered by the Employment Tribunals Service (ETS).

The ETS replaced COIT (the Central Office of Industrial Tribunals) which previously administered the system for the former Regional Offices (ROITs) and Offices of the Industrial Tribunals (OITs).

All claims must now be presented to an Employment Tribunal office on form ET1. Claims may now be made online (via email on the service website at www.employmenttribunals.gov.uk). It is also possible to download and complete form ET1 via the service website. Alternatively, claims may still be sent to the service by post. Claimants must complete the prescribed ET1 form. The form must contain some specific information, namely:

- the name and address of the claimant;
- the name and address of the respondent/s;
- details of the complaint; and
- whether or not the claimant is or was an employee of the respondent.

If form ET1 is completed online then it will automatically be sent to the relevant tribunal office. If the form is completed in the downloadable PDF version then once it is submitted via the tribunal's service website it will be sent to the relevant tribunal office. If the claimant posts the form then they should send it to the tribunal office with the nearest postcode to the place where they normally work or worked. There is a 'venue finder' link on the service website which will assist the claimant if they are unsure of the location of the nearest office to their place of work. If the claimant has never worked for the respondent then they should identify the tribunal office postal address for the place where the matter complained about took place.

Once the form is received by an Employment Tribunal office the claimant will receive an email containing a unique reference/case number relating to their claim. If the claim is accepted the office will send a letter to the claimant to confirm this together with a booklet outlining the next steps in tribunal procedure. At the same time, the office will send the respondent a copy of the ET1 claim form together with a form for their response to the claim. This form is referred to as the 'Response to an Employment Tribunal Claim' or form ET3. In most cases a copy of both forms are also sent to Acas.

COMPOSITION – WHO 'JUDGES' THE CASE?

The case is normally heard by a panel of three tribunal members, a chairman and two lay persons. The chairman must have been a qualified solicitor or barrister for at least seven years. Each region is staffed by one full-time chairman and several part-time chairmen. All chairmen are appointed by the Lord Chancellor. Their role is to make a decision after hearing the case and then give reasons for that decision. They also preside over the hearing and if necessary can advise lay members on points of law and procedure.

The lay members of the panel are drawn from industry and are appointed by the Secretary of State for Trade and Industry. One is taken from a panel nominated by employers' associations, such as the Confederation of British Industry (CBI). The other is taken from a panel nominated by employee organisations, such as the Trades Union Congress (TUC). These representatives are able to use their industrial expertise to assist them in the work of the tribunal. The panel is often referred to as being an 'industrial jury'. There is also a self-nomination procedure, designed to attract women, ethnic minorities and persons with disabilities.

10

Settling disputes – taking a case to the Employment Tribunal

All three panel members have an equal vote. This means that the lay members are able to outvote the chairman. In some cases the chairman is able to hear a case sitting alone. A chairman is able to sit alone in cases involving, amongst other things:

- unlawful deductions from wages;
- questions of jurisdiction (subject to 3 exceptions);
- breach of contract;
- failure to provide a S1 statement of terms and conditions;
- time extensions;
- interlocutory stages of the claim.

The chairman can also sit alone, or with only one lay member, if the parties either request this, or have no objection to it.

JURISDICTION

The term jurisdiction relates to the 'power' that the tribunal has to hear some cases and not others. Employees can only make a claim to the tribunal if it has the jurisdiction to hear their case.

The Employment Tribunal can deal with claims concerning:

- unfair dismissal;
- redundancy pay;
- sex discrimination;
- race discrimination;
- disability discrimination;
- discrimination on the grounds of sexual orientation/religion or belief;
- sexual/racial harassment;
- unlawful deductions from wages;
- equal pay;
- the right to maternity leave, and to maternity pay;
- refusal of time off for ante-natal care, or other 'time off' rights;
- non-receipt of a section 1 written statement;
- trade-union membership and activity;
- the national minimum wage.

This list is not exhaustive but does cover the main areas in which the tribunal has jurisdiction to hear a case. Note that some employment disputes are dealt with in the ordinary courts.

Contractual jurisdiction

The Employment Tribunals Extension of Jurisdiction (England & Wales) Order 1994 extended tribunal jurisdiction to cover claims for breach of contract which are outstanding when employment ends. Previously breach of contract claims could only be dealt with in the civil courts. The contractual claim cannot be for more than £25 000 or relate to, amongst other things, personal injury, restraint of trade or intellectual property. The claim must be made within three months of the termination of employment.

The employer can then make a counterclaim within six weeks of receiving the ET1 from the ETS. The Employment Tribunal cannot deal with contractual claims where the employee is still employed. These should still be pursued in the County Court or High Court.

Claims made to the Employment Tribunal during 2005/6

Table 10.1 details the claims made to the Employment Tribunal during 2005/6. At the time of writing the Employment Tribunals Service Annual Report 2005/6 is the most recent available.

Table 10.1 Tribunal jurisdictions made in 2005/6

Type of claim	Number of claims made
Unfair dismissal	41 832
Unauthorised deduction of wages	32 330
Breach of contract	26 230
Sex discrimination	14 250
Working Time Directive	35 474
Redundancy pay	7214
Disability discrimination	4585
Redundancy – failure to inform and consult	4056
Equal pay	17 268
Race discrimination	4103
Written statement of terms and conditions	3078
Written statement of reasons for dismissal	955
Written pay statement	794
Transfer of an undertaking – failure to inform and consult	899
Suffered a detriment/Unfair dismissal – pregnancy	1054
Part-Time Workers Regulations	402
National minimum wage	440
Discrimination on grounds of Religion or Belief	486
Discrimination on grounds of Sexual Orientation	395
Others	5219
Total	201 514

Source: Employment Tribunals Service Annual Report 2005/6

FUNDING THE CASE

An employee cannot get government funded legal assistance to help him to finance his tribunal claim. 'Legal help' is not available to pay for tribunal representation. Possible sources of finance and representation include the employee's union, the Citizens' Advice Bureau or a local Law Centre. If the claim involves a discrimination issue, the Commission for Equality and Human Rights may finance the case and provide representation. However, as their resources are limited, they will be unable to assist in every case that is brought to their attention.

Some lawyers work on a part-time basis for organisations that provide free representation. The Citizens' Advice Bureau normally keeps details of any such schemes in its local area. If the employee is unable to get assistance from any of these organisations, he will have to finance the claim himself.

The 'legal help' scheme

An employee who is considering making a claim to the Employment Tribunal can apply for a basic 'legal help' award. This scheme is means tested, so there is no guarantee that the employee will be eligible. If he is eligible, the scheme entitles him to two hours of free legal advice. 'Legal help' is the term for what was referred to as 'legal aid'.

This advice is given by a solicitor or adviser who will be able to assist the applicant by helping him to write letters, or by making telephone calls on his behalf. The solicitor/advisor could also help the applicant to complete his ET1 form, and then give a general opinion on the strengths and weaknesses of the applicant's case.

The Legal Services Commission administers the 'legal help' scheme. The Commission also runs a telephone advice service in some parts of the country. Persons who are financially eligible are able to telephone the service and ask for advice on, for example, employment law problems.

Some firms also operate a fixed-fee interview system whereby a person might pay, for example, £25 for one hour of advice. In some cases the first interview may even be free.

Financing the defence to a claim will not normally be a problem for an employer. This will, of course, depend on the size and resources of the business. If there is a problem, then depending on the employer's line of work, he may receive assistance from a trade organisation.

The employer does not only have to take possible tribunal costs into account. The case may disrupt the daily running of their business. Other employees may need to be interviewed and then attend as witnesses. Personnel officers may have to spend a lot of their time working on the case.

REPRESENTATION

There is no requirement that either party be legally represented. Claimants can be represented by a solicitor or barrister, or can choose to represent themselves. They could also be represented by someone from their union, a Citizens' Advice Bureau or the Commission for Equality and Human Rights.

Employers can choose to represent themselves, hire a lawyer or send a representative from their firm or company. This is usually someone from their personnel or legal department. The use of non-lawyer representatives is thought to encourage informal hearings, but in reality many parties are represented by lawyers or other professionals who have expertise in tribunal work.

Note that once the relevant provisions of the Compensation Act 2006 come into force a 'Regulator' will be appointed to authorise persons to provide regulated claims management services. This means that companies offering to represent parties in Employment Tribunal cases will be regulated. It is likely that individuals will have to obtain a qualification in tribunal practice/employment law. There will be an exemption for persons who are already legally qualified. At the time of writing there is no information available as to when the relevant sections of the 2006 Act are likely to come into force.

TIME LIMITS – THE IMPORTANCE OF SENDING IN THE ET1 IN TIME

Anyone wishing to make a complaint to the Employment Tribunal must do so within the set time limit for that particular claim. If the claimant does not send his form ET1 to the ETS within the set time limit, his case will not be heard. Different time limits apply to different types of claim.

Example
Robert wants to make a claim for unfair dismissal. He was dismissed on 15 September 2005. The time limit for unfair dismissal claims is three months from the effective date of termination. Robert has to submit his ET1 before midnight on 14 December 2005.

Figure 10.1 highlights the different time limits attached to the main types of tribunal claim. (The rules on the effective date of termination are further discussed at page 229).

Extension of time limits

There is an automatic three-month extension to the normal time limits for filing a tribunal claim in circumstances where the statutory dispute resolution procedures apply (see generally Chapter 5). The aim of this extension of time is to encourage the parties to negotiate and/or settle their dispute without having to resort to a tribunal hearing.

Aside from in the situations outlined above, time limits are generally strictly enforced. There can be no extension of time in equal pay cases. However, in other cases the tribunal may be prepared to accept a claim after the time limit has expired. This will depend on the type of claim

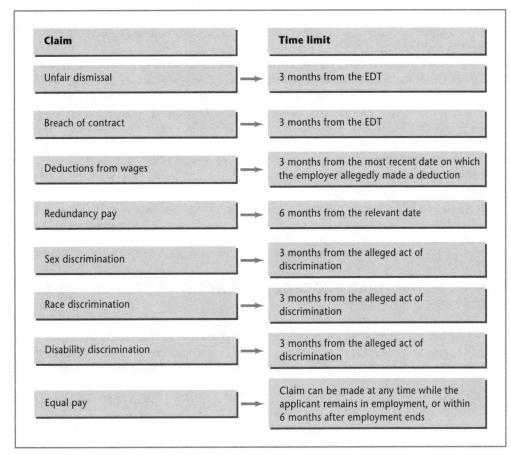

Claim	Time limit
Unfair dismissal	3 months from the EDT
Breach of contract	3 months from the EDT
Deductions from wages	3 months from the most recent date on which the employer allegedly made a deduction
Redundancy pay	6 months from the relevant date
Sex discrimination	3 months from the alleged act of discrimination
Race discrimination	3 months from the alleged act of discrimination
Disability discrimination	3 months from the alleged act of discrimination
Equal pay	Claim can be made at any time while the applicant remains in employment, or within 6 months after employment ends

Figure 10.1 Time limits relating to the main areas of complaint

10

Settling disputes – taking a case to the Employment Tribunal

involved and on whether the tribunal considers an extension to be 'just and equitable'. In some cases the tribunal may extend the time limit where it was 'not reasonably practicable' for the employee to make his claim in time.

'Just and equitable'

In discrimination claims the tribunal may extend the time limit if they think that it would be just and equitable to do so. The tribunal will not grant an extension where it is convinced that the claimant was responsible for the delay and that there was no reasonable excuse for this.

'Not reasonably practicable'

In claims for unfair dismissal, breach of contract or unlawful deductions from earnings, the tribunal may extend the time limit if:

- it was not reasonably practicable for the claimant to make his claim within that time limit; and
- the extension of time requested is reasonable.

Tribunals have extended claims on this basis where the claimant was unable to send in form ET1 due to serious illness, depression or a postal strike. Whether or not the extra time asked for is reasonable will depend on the circumstances in each case and how much extra time is required.

In *Jean Sorelle Ltd v Rybak* (1991) the claimant was given bad advice by both a Citizens' Advice Bureau and a member of the tribunal service. She was allowed to make her claim out of time based on the fact that she took their advice to be correct, and had thought that she still had time to make her claim.

In *London International College v Sen* (1992) the claimant had been given inaccurate advice by both a solicitor and a member of the tribunal service. It was held that it had not been reasonably practicable for her to make her claim in time. Consequently, she was allowed to make a claim after the time limit had expired. In *Schultz v Esso Petroleum Company Ltd* (1999) a dismissed employee who had suffered from depression at the time of his dismissal was allowed to make a claim to the tribunal outside of the three-month time limit. Here the Court of Appeal held that his illness had meant that he was not capable of submitting his claim in time. It had not been reasonably practicable for him to do so. See also: *Consignia Plc v Sealy* (2002), *Marks & Spencer plc v Williams-Ryan* (2005).

Claimants should not rely on the possibility of being given a time extension. There is no guarantee that the tribunal will agree to an extension and so all claimants should ensure that their ET1 form is sent to the ETS as soon as possible.

STAGES IN TRIBUNAL PROCEDURE - FROM THE COMPLETION OF FORM ET1 TO THE EAT

Figure 10.2 highlights the usual stages involved in the making of a claim to the Employment Tribunal. It begins with the stage at which the claimant completes form ET1 and concludes at the point where he may be able to challenge the tribunal decision in the Employment Appeal Tribunal.

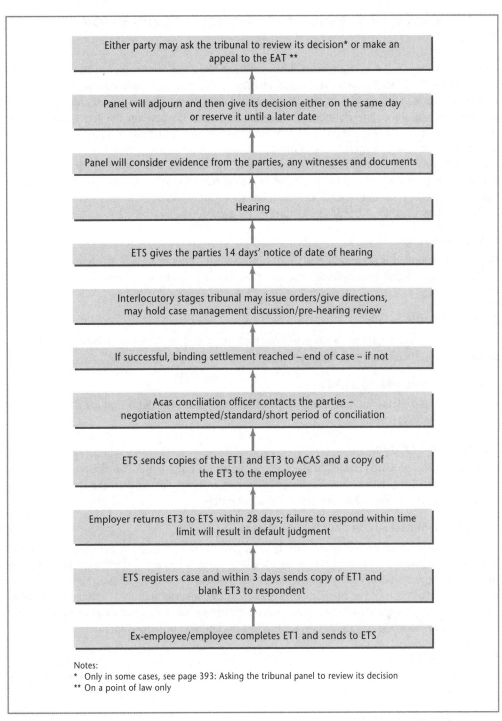

Figure 10.2 The stages involved in making a claim to the Employment Tribunal

THE CLAIMANT MAKES AN APPLICATION - COMPLETION OF FORM ET1

All tribunal claims begin with the completion of form ET1. As noted earlier in this chapter, this form may be completed online via the ETS website. The site also provides access to downloadable forms that can be emailed to the ETS or printed prior to completion and then posted to the relevant tribunal office. The claimant provides an outline of his case on this form and it is normally referred to as the ET1. The copy of form ET1 in Figure 10.3 has been completed using the case scenario details of Robert Brown from Chapter 6. It is a relatively straightforward form and only requires the claimant to provide basic personal information and an outline of his claim. He is also asked to specify the remedy that he is asking the tribunal to award. In most cases the claimant is seeking compensation for his employer's wrongdoing.

Robert Brown has completed his ET1 form as follows:

1 Your details

Robert has included his personal details, his name, address, telephone number and date of birth. He has also noted that he would like the ETS to deal with him by email and so he includes his email address.

2 Respondent's details

Robert has included the name of his previous employer, Gerald Plc. He also provides the address of this firm and their telephone number.

3 Action before making a claim

Robert has stated that he was the employee of the respondent. He states that his claim relates to a dismissal by the respondent.

4 Employment details

Here, Robert has provided details of the date on which his employment with Gerald Plc began. He has also provided details of when his employment with the firm ended, the job that he did, the hours that he worked each week, and his salary details.

5 Unfair dismissal or constructive dismissal

As Robert believes that he has been unfairly dismissed he has completed section 5 of the form. Here, he has provided details of the events leading up to his dismissal and explained why he thought that the dismissal was unfair. He states that he was a member of his employer's pension scheme and that he received an additional £2400 in benefits per annum. He has not yet been successful in acquiring another job. At 5.7 Robert notes that he would like to be reinstated in his old job and be awarded compensation for the fact that he was unfairly dismissed.

6 Discrimination

Robert has not completed this section of the form as his claim does not involve any discrimination issues.

7 Redundancy payments

Robert has not completed this section of the form as his claim does not involve any redundancy payment issues.

8 Other payments you are owed

Robert states that he was not allowed to work out his notice period or paid for the two months' notice that he was entitled to. He is claiming £3300 in lost wages.

9 Other complaints

Robert has not completed this section of the form as he does not have any additional complaint to add.

10 Other information

Robert has not completed this section of the form as he does not have any other information to add to his claim.

11 Disability

Robert has indicated that he is not disabled.

12 Your representative

Robert has an appointed representative who is going to assist him with his Employment Tribunal claim. He has provided details of the name and address of his representative.

13 Multiple cases

Robert has stated that to the best of his knowledge his claim is not one of a number arising from the same or similar circumstances.

Note that Robert has also signed and dated the form prior to sending it to the ETS.

Claim to an Employment Tribunal

Please read the **guidance notes** and the notes on this page carefully **before** filling in this form.

By law, your claim **must** be on an approved form provided by the Employment Tribunals Service and you must provide the information marked with ✳ and, if it is relevant, the information marked with ● (see 'Information needed before a claim can be accepted').

You may find it helpful to take advice **before** filling in the form, particularly if your claim involves discrimination.

How to fill in this form

All claimants **must** fill in **sections 1, 2 and 3**. You then only need to fill in those sections of the form that apply to your case. For example:

For **unpaid wages**, fill in **sections 4 and 8**.

For **unfair dismissal**, fill in **sections 4 and 5**.

For **discrimination**, fill in **sections 4 and 6**.

For a **redundancy payment**, fill in **sections 4 and 7**.

For **unfair dismissal** and **discrimination**, fill in **sections 4, 5 and 6**.

For **unfair dismissal** and **unpaid wages**, fill in **sections 4, 5 and 8**.

Fill in **section 10** only if there is some information you wish to draw to the tribunal's attention and **section 12** only if you have appointed a representative to act on your behalf in dealing with your claim.

If this claim is one of a number of claims arising out of the same or similar circumstances, you can obtain a Multiple Claim Form from the ETS Public Enquiry Line on 08457 959775 or from www.employmenttribunals.gov.uk. Alternatively you can give the names and addresses of additional claimants on a separate sheet or sheets of paper. If you do this you must make it clear that the relevant required information for all the additional claimants is the same as stated in the main claim.

Please make sure that all the information you give is as accurate as possible.

Where there are tick boxes, please tick the one that applies.

Please write clearly in black ink using CAPITAL LETTERS.

If you fax the form, do not send a copy in the post.

ET1 v02   ET1 v02

Figure 10.3 Example of completed Employment Tribunal claim form ET1

Note: This downloadable version of claim form ET1 is accessible via the ETS website at www.employmenttribunals.gov.uk

Source: Employment Tribunals Service

1   Your details

1.1   Title: Mr ✓   Mrs   Miss   Ms   Other

1.2* First name (or names):   Robert   Kevin

1.3* Surname or family name: Brown

1.4   Date of birth (date/month/year):   30 04 1958 Are you: male?   ✓ female?

1.5* Address: Number or Name   27
                     Street   Rodden   Square
              +   Town/City   Millfield
                     County   Oldtown
                     Postcode   OR7 9DX

1.6   Phone number (where we can contact   7172735
      you during normal working hours):

1.7   How would you prefer us to   E-mail ✓   Post   Fax
      communicate with you?
      (Please tick only one box)

      E-mail address: R.K.Brown@anyemail.
                                              co.uk

      Fax number:

2   Respondent's details

2.1* Give the name of your employer   Gerald   Plc
     or the organisation you are claiming
     against.

2.2* Address: Number or Name   Unit 9
                     Street   Factory   Place
                     Town/City   Industrial   Way
              +   County   Oldtown
                     Postcode   OJ9   2KH

     Phone number: 7279042

2.3 If you worked at an address   N/A
     different from the one you have
     given at 2.2, please give the
     full address and postcode.

     Postcode

     Phone number:

2.4● If your complaint is against more than one respondent please give the names, addresses and
     postcodes of additional respondents.

     N/A

ET1 v02 001   1   ET1 v02 001

Figure 10.3 continued

Note: This downloadable version of claim form ET1 is accessible via the ETS website at www.employmenttribunals.gov.uk

10

Settling disputes – taking a case to the Employment Tribunal

3   Action before making a claim

3.1* Are you, or were you, an employee of the respondent?   Yes ✓   No
If 'Yes', please now go straight to section 3.3.

3.2 Are you, or were you, a worker providing services to the respondent?   Yes   No
If 'Yes', please now go straight to section 4.
If 'No', please now go straight to section 6.

3.3● Is your claim, or part of it, about a dismissal by the respondent?   Yes ✓   No
If 'No', please now go straight to section 3.5.
If your claim is about constructive dismissal, i.e. you resigned because of something
your employer did or failed to do which made you feel you could no longer continue to
work for them, tick the box here **and** the 'Yes' box in section 3.4.

3.4● Is your claim about anything else, in addition to the dismissal?   Yes   No ✓
If 'No', please now go straight to section 4.
If 'Yes', please answer questions 3.5 to 3.7 about the
non-dismissal aspects of your claim.

3.5● Have you put your complaint(s) in writing to the respondent?

Yes   Please give the date you put it to them in writing.

No

If 'No', please now go straight to section 3.7.

3.6● Did you allow at least 28 days between the date you put your   Yes   No
complaint in writing to the respondent and the date you sent us this claim?
If 'Yes', please now go straight to section 4.

3.7● Please explain why you did not put your complaint in writing to the respondent or,
if you did, why you did not allow at least 28 days before sending us your claim.
(In most cases, it is a legal requirement to take these procedural steps. Your claim
will not be accepted unless you give a valid reason why you did not have to meet
the requirement in your case. If you are not sure, you may want to get legal advice.)

Figure 10.3 continued

Note: This downloadable version of claim form ET1 is accessible via the ETS website at www.employmenttribunals.gov.uk

4   Employment details

4.1   Please give the following information if possible.

When did your employment start?   1 3 · 0 8 · 2 0 0 4

When did or will it end?   1 5 · 0 9 · 2 0 0 5

Is your employment continuing?   Yes   No ✓

4.2   Please say what job you do or did.   Sales Representative
& Marketing Consultant

4.3   How many hours do or did you work each week?   4 0   hours each week

4.4   How much are or were you paid?

Pay before tax   £   2 3 , 7 0 0 . 0 0   Hourly
                                                           Weekly
Normal take-home pay (including   £   1 , 6 5 0 . 0 0   Monthly ✓
overtime, commission, bonuses and so on)   Yearly

4.5   If your employment has ended, did you work   Yes   No ✓
(or were you paid for) a period of notice?

If 'Yes', how many weeks or months did   weeks   months
you work or were you paid for?

5   Unfair dismissal or constructive dismissal

Please fill in this section only if you believe you have been unfairly or constructively dismissed.

5.1 ● If you were dismissed by your employer, you should explain why you think your dismissal
was unfair. If you resigned because of something your employer did or failed to do which
made you feel you could no longer continue to work for them (constructive dismissal)
you should explain what happened.

I was employed by Gerald Plc as a sales representative/marketing consultant from 13th August 2004 until 15th
September 2005. Gerald plc is a company which carries out the business of designing and selling clothes. They
also operate a clothing factory at Unit 19 Factory Place and together the Units employ approx. 800 people.

On 9th March 2005 I was promoted against my wishes to this more senior position. I was given no training on
how to perform my new duties. On 7th August 2005 I was told by Mr Smith (personnel officer) that the
management were not satisfied with my performance or sales figures. I asked him if I could go on a training
course and be given more time to settle into my new job. I even offered to go back to my old job, to go from being
the team leader to being part of the team. He did not agree to any of my suggestions.

On 15th September 2005 I was told by Mr Smith that I had been dismissed. I was given no notice of the
dismissal and was told that I would not be required to work out any notice period.

I had no further discussions with Mr Smith. I was not given the opportunity to appeal against the decision to
dismiss me. I believe that I was unfairly dismissed and claim reinstatement and/or compensation.

ET1 v02 003   3   ET1 v02 003

Figure 10.3 continued

Note: This downloadable version of claim form ET1 is accessible via the ETS website at www.employmenttribunals.gov.uk

5   Unfair dismissal or constructive dismissal continued

5.1 continued

5.2   Were you in your employer's pension scheme?   Yes ✓   No

5.3   If you received any other benefits from your employer, please give details.

bonuses of approx. £2,400:00 per annum

5.4   Since leaving your employment have you got another job?   Yes   No ✓
       If 'No', please now go straight to section 5.7.

5.5   Please say when you started (or will start) work.

5.6   Please say how much you are now earning (or will earn). £   ,   .

                                                                              each

5.7   Please tick the box to say what you want if your case is successful:

       a To get your old job back and compensation (reinstatement)   ✓

       b To get another job with the same employer and compensation (re-engagement)

       c Compensation only

ET1 v02 004   4   ET1 v02 004

Figure 10.3 continued

Note: This downloadable version of claim form ET1 is accessible via the ETS website at www.employmenttribunals.gov.uk

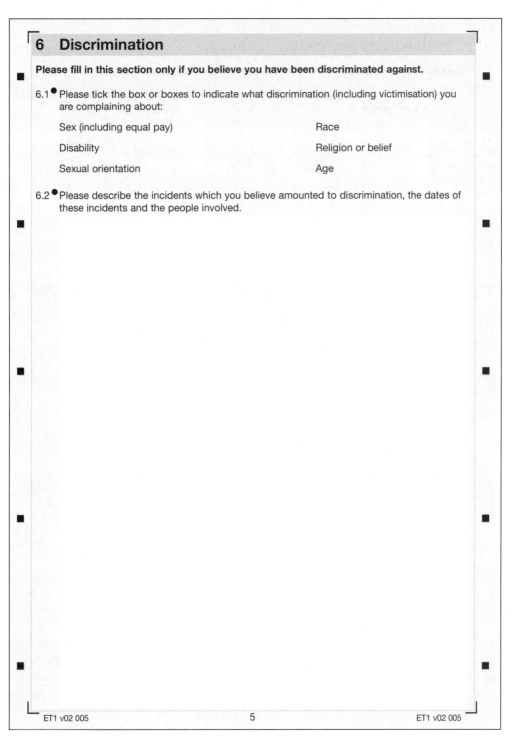

6   Discrimination

Please fill in this section only if you believe you have been discriminated against.

6.1 Please tick the box or boxes to indicate what discrimination (including victimisation) you are complaining about:

Sex (including equal pay)   Race

Disability   Religion or belief

Sexual orientation   Age

6.2 Please describe the incidents which you believe amounted to discrimination, the dates of these incidents and the people involved.

ET1 v02 005   5   ET1 v02 005

10

Settling disputes – taking a case to the Employment Tribunal

Figure 10.3 continued

Note: This downloadable version of claim form ET1 is accessible via the ETS website at www.employmenttribunals.gov.uk

7   Redundancy payments

Please fill in this section only if you believe you are owed a redundancy payment.

7.1 • Please explain why you believe you are entitled to this payment and set out the steps you have taken to get it.

8   Other payments you are owed

Please fill in this section only if you believe you are owed other payments.

8.1 • Please tick the box or boxes to indicate that money is owed to you for:

unpaid wages?	
holiday pay?	
notice pay?	✓
other unpaid amounts?	

8.2   How much are you claiming?   £   3,300.00

Is this: before tax?   after tax? ✓

8.3 • Please explain why you believe you are entitled to this payment. If you have specified an amount, please set out how you have worked this out.

I was not allowed to work my notice period and did not receive any payment. I was entitled to two months' notice and so am claiming two months' wages.

ET1 v02 006   6   ET1 v02 006

Figure 10.3 continued

Note: This downloadable version of claim form ET1 is accessible via the ETS website at www.employmenttribunals.gov.uk

9   Other complaints

Please fill in this section only if you believe you have a complaint that is not covered elsewhere.

9.1 ● Please explain what you are complaining about and why.
Please include any relevant dates.

10 Other information

10.1 Please do not send a covering letter with this form.
You should add any extra information you want us to know here.

ET1 v02 007   7   ET1 v02 007

Figure 10.3 continued

Note: This downloadable version of claim form ET1 is accessible via the ETS website at www.employmenttribunals.gov.uk

Settling disputes – taking a case to the Employment Tribunal

10

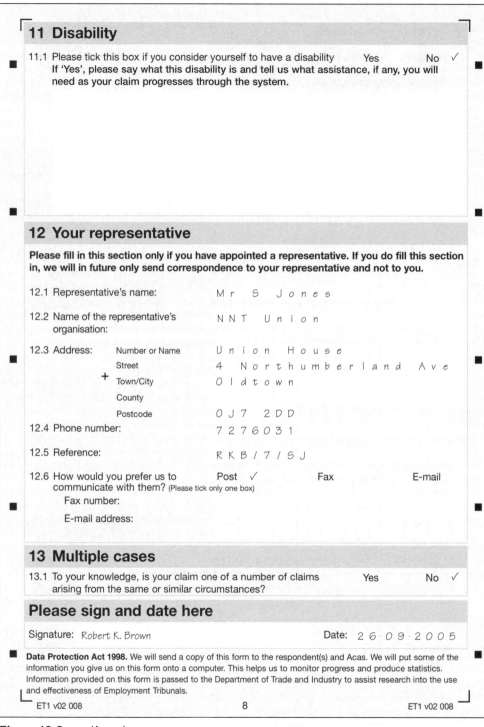

11 Disability

11.1 Please tick this box if you consider yourself to have a disability   Yes   No ✓
If 'Yes', please say what this disability is and tell us what assistance, if any, you will
need as your claim progresses through the system.

12 Your representative

Please fill in this section only if you have appointed a representative. If you do fill this section
in, we will in future only send correspondence to your representative and not to you.

12.1 Representative's name: M r   S   J o n e s

12.2 Name of the representative's   N N T   U n i o n
organisation:

12.3 Address: Number or Name   U n i o n   H o u s e
                     Street   4   N o r t h u m b e r l a n d   A v e
            +   Town/City   O l d t o w n
                     County
                     Postcode   O J 7   2 D D
12.4 Phone number: 7 2 7 6 0 3 1

12.5 Reference: R K B / 7 / S J

12.6 How would you prefer us to   Post ✓   Fax   E-mail
communicate with them? (Please tick only one box)
     Fax number:
     E-mail address:

13 Multiple cases

13.1 To your knowledge, is your claim one of a number of claims   Yes   No ✓
arising from the same or similar circumstances?

Please sign and date here

Signature: Robert K. Brown   Date: 2 6 · 0 9 · 2 0 0 5

ET1 v02 008   8   ET1 v02 008

Figure 10.3 continued

Note: This downloadable version of claim form ET1 is accessible via the ETS website at www.employmenttribunals.gov.uk

THE EMPLOYER RESPONDS TO THE APPLICATION – COMPLETION OF THE RESPONSE FORM ET3

The employer sets out his defence to the claim on form ET3 in Figure 10.4. The form is otherwise referred to as the 'response form'. If the employer does not send in an ET3 form, he will not be allowed to defend himself against the claim at a hearing.

Here, Gerald Plc intends to resist Robert's claim. The ET3 has been completed by the personnel manager, Mr Smith. He has included the following information:

On the front page of the Employment Tribunal response form Mr Smith has stated that the firm wish to respond to the claim. He has also completed details of the case number and the names of the parties.

1 Name of respondent company or organisation

Mr Smith has provided details of the name and address of his organisation, Gerald Plc. He has also stated that he is to be the contact name for this tribunal claim and asked if he be contacted by post in the future. Information on the operation of Gerald Plc has been completed, namely the fact that the firm mainly engages in manufacturing work, employs over 1000 employees in Great Britain, 800 of which are employed at the site where Robert Brown worked.

2 Action before a claim

Here, Mr Smith has admitted that Robert Brown was an employee of the company. He has also agreed that Mr Brown was dismissed and states that a letter outlining why the company was unhappy with his work was sent to him and that the company believe that they have used 'appropriate procedures'.

3 Employment details

Here, Mr Smith agrees that the dates of employment and job description given by Robert Brown are correct. However, he also states that Mr Brown was paid two months' salary in lieu of him working out his notice. There is no dispute over the earnings details provided by Mr Brown.

4 Unfair dismissal or constructive dismissal

There is no dispute over the details about either pension or other benefits provided by the claimant.

5 Response

Here, Mr Smith indicates that Gerald Plc intend to resist Robert Brown's claim for unfair dismissal. He sets out the grounds on which they intend to resist the claim.

6 Other information

Mr Smith has not completed this section of the form as he does not have any other information to add to the company's response.

7 Your representative

Mr Smith has not completed this section of the form as he is the representative of his company, Gerald Plc.

Note that Mr Smith has also signed and dated the form prior to returning it to the ETS.

The employer should return form ET3 to the ETS within 28 days of receipt. They will then send a copy of it to the claimant and to Acas.

Response to an
Employment Tribunal claim

IN THE CLAIM OF: *Robert Kevin Brown v Gerald Plc*

Case number: 12345
(please quote this in all correspondence)

This requires your immediate attention. If you want to resist the claim made against you, your completed form must reach the tribunal office within 28 days of the date of the attached letter. If the form does not reach us by you will not be able to take part in the proceedings and a default judgment may be entered against you.

Please read the **guidance notes** and the notes on this page carefully **before** filling in this form.

By law, you **must** provide the information marked with ✳ and, if it is relevant, the information marked with ● (see guidance on Pre-acceptance procedure).

Please make sure that all the information you give is as accurate as possible.

Where there are tick boxes, please tick the one that applies.

If you fax the form, do not send a copy in the post.

You must return the full form, including this page, to the tribunal office.

ET3

Figure 10.4 Example of completed Employment Tribunal response form ET3

Note: This downloadable version of response form ET3 is accessible via the ETS website at www.employmenttribunals.gov.uk

Source: Employment Tribunals Service

Case number: 1 2 3 4 5

1   Name of respondent company or organisation

1.1* Name of your organisation: G e r a l d   P l c

Contact name: M r   K   S m i t h

1.2* Address   Number or Name   P e r s o n n e l   D e p a r t m e n t

Street   F a c t o r y   P l a c e   U n i t s   9

Town/City   – 1 9   I n d u s t r i a l   W a y

County   O l d t o w n

Postcode   O J 9   2 K H

1.3   Phone number: 7 2 7 9 0 4 2   e x t   3 9 7 5

1.4   How would you prefer us to   E-mail   Post ✓   Fax
communicate with you? (Please tick only one box)
E-mail address:

Fax number:

1.5   What does this organisation mainly make or do?   Manufacturing

1.6   How many people does this organisation employ in Great Britain?   1 0 0 0

1.7   Does this organisation have more than one site in Great Britain?   Yes ✓   No

1.8   If 'Yes', how many people are employed at the place where the   8 0 0
claimant worked?

2   Action before a claim

2.1   Is, or was, the claimant an employee?   Yes ✓   No
If 'Yes', please now go straight to section 2.3.

2.2   Is, or was, the claimant a worker providing services to you?   Yes   No
If 'Yes', please now go straight to section 3.
If 'No', please now go straight to section 5.

2.3   If the claim, or part of it, is about a dismissal,   Yes ✓   No
do you agree that the claimant was dismissed?
If 'Yes', please now go straight to section 2.6.

2.4   If the claim includes something **other than** dismissal,   Yes   No
does it relate to an action you took on
grounds of the claimant's conduct or capability?
If 'Yes', please now go straight to section 2.6.

2.5   Has the substance of this claim been raised by the claimant   Yes   No
in writing under a grievance procedure?

2.6   If 'Yes', please explain below what stage you have reached in the dismissal and disciplinary
procedure or grievance procedure (whichever is applicable).
If 'No' and the claimant says they have raised a grievance with you in writing, please say
whether you received it and explain why you did not accept this as a grievance.

A letter outlining why we were unhappy with his work has been sent to Mr Brown.
We have used the appropriate procedures.

ET3 v02 001   1   ET3 v02 001

Figure 10.4 continued

Note: This downloadable version of response form ET3 is accessible via the ETS website at
www.employmenttribunals.gov.uk

3 Employment details

3.1 Are the dates of employment given by the claimant correct?   Yes ✓   No
If 'Yes', please now go straight to section 3.3.

3.2 If 'No', please give dates and say why you disagree with the dates given by the claimant.

When their employment started

When their employment ended or will end

Is their employment continuing?   Yes   No

I disagree with the dates for the following reasons.

3.3 Is the claimant's description of their job or job title correct?   Yes ✓   No
If 'Yes', please now go straight to section 3.5.

3.4 If 'No', please give the details you believe to be correct below.

3.5 Is the information given by the claimant correct about being   Yes   No ✓
paid for, or working, a period of notice?
If 'Yes', please now go straight to section 3.7.

3.6 If 'No', please give the details you believe to be correct below. If you gave them no notice or
didn't pay them instead of letting them work their notice, please explain what happened and why.

Mr Brown was paid two months' salary in lieu of him working his notice.

3.7 Are the claimant's hours of work correct?   Yes ✓   No
If 'Yes', please now go straight to section 3.9.

3.8 If 'No', please enter the details you believe to be correct.   hours each week

3.9 Are the earnings details given by the claimant correct?   Yes ✓   No
If 'Yes', please now go straight to section 4.

3.10 If 'No', please give the details you believe to be correct below.

Pay before tax	£	Hourly
		Weekly
Normal take-home pay (including overtime, commission, bonuses and so on)	£	Monthly
		Yearly

Figure 10.4 continued

Note: This downloadable version of response form ET3 is accessible via the ETS website at
www.employmenttribunals.gov.uk

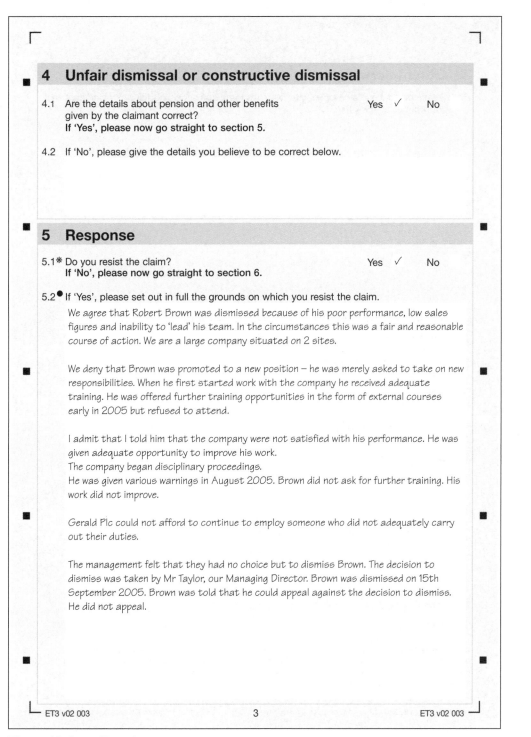

4   Unfair dismissal or constructive dismissal

4.1   Are the details about pension and other benefits   Yes   ✓   No
given by the claimant correct?
If 'Yes', please now go straight to section 5.

4.2   If 'No', please give the details you believe to be correct below.

5   Response

5.1* Do you resist the claim?   Yes   ✓   No
If 'No', please now go straight to section 6.

5.2● If 'Yes', please set out in full the grounds on which you resist the claim.

We agree that Robert Brown was dismissed because of his poor performance, low sales
figures and inability to 'lead' his team. In the circumstances this was a fair and reasonable
course of action. We are a large company situated on 2 sites.

We deny that Brown was promoted to a new position – he was merely asked to take on new
responsibilities. When he first started work with the company he received adequate
training. He was offered further training opportunities in the form of external courses
early in 2005 but refused to attend.

I admit that I told him that the company were not satisfied with his performance. He was
given adequate opportunity to improve his work.
The company began disciplinary proceedings.
He was given various warnings in August 2005. Brown did not ask for further training. His
work did not improve.

Gerald Plc could not afford to continue to employ someone who did not adequately carry
out their duties.

The management felt that they had no choice but to dismiss Brown. The decision to
dismiss was taken by Mr Taylor, our Managing Director. Brown was dismissed on 15th
September 2005. Brown was told that he could appeal against the decision to dismiss.
He did not appeal.

ET3 v02 003   3   ET3 v02 003

Figure 10.4 continued

Note: This downloadable version of response form ET3 is accessible via the ETS website at
www.employmenttribunals.gov.uk

10

Settling disputes – taking a case to the Employment Tribunal

6   Other information

6.1   Please do not send a covering letter with this form. You should add any extra information you want us to know here.

7   Your representative   If you have a representative, please fill in the following.

7.1   Representative's name:

7.2   Name of the representative's organisation:

7.3   Address   Number or Name

Street

+ Town/City

County

Postcode

7.4   Phone number:

7.5   Reference:

7.6   How would you prefer us to   E-mail   Post   Fax
communicate with them? (Please tick only one box)
E-mail address:

Fax number:

Please sign and date here

Signature: Mr K. Smith   Date: 3 1 0 2 0 0 5

Data Protection Act 1998. We will send a copy of this form to the claimant and Acas. We will put some of the information you give us on this form onto a computer. This helps us to monitor progress and produce statistics. Information provided on this form is passed to the Department of Trade and Industry to assist research into the use and effectiveness of Employment Tribunals.

ET3 v02 004 URN 05/1442   4   ET3 v02 004 URN 05/1442

Figure 10.4 continued

Note: This downloadable version of response form ET3 is accessible via the ETS website at www.employmenttribunals.gov.uk

THE ROLE OF ACAS

The Advisory, Conciliation and Arbitration Service operates independently from the tribunal service. Copies of every ET1 and ET3 form registered with the ETS are sent to Acas. Acas has an important role in the conciliation and early settlement of tribunal cases.

When Acas receives the ET1 form, it assigns a conciliation officer to the case. The conciliation officer has a duty to try to promote a settlement without the matter having to be dealt with by a tribunal. This officer acts as an impartial negotiator between the parties. The officer has no duty to advise on the possible success or otherwise of the case, or to recommend a particular settlement. The terms of the settlement are entirely the responsibility of the parties concerned.

The conciliation officer will contact the parties by telephone and try to get them to enter into negotiations. The aim is to reach a compromise or settlement of the case before the tribunal hearing. The parties do not have to agree to work with the conciliation officer. Negotiation is voluntary. The lack of funding for tribunal cases and the possibility of low awards means that the percentages of claims settled at this stage are high.

Table 10.2 highlights the number of cases that Acas conciliated in during 2005/6. It can be seen that most of the cases referred to Acas involve claims for unfair dismissal.

Table 10.2 Claims settled, withdrawn or sent to an Employment Tribunal 2005/6

Main jurisdiction	Total	Settled	Withdrawn	to ET hearing	Other outcomes
Unfair dismissal	31 375	11 989	10 631	7469	1286
Wages Act	14 168	5086	4411	4382	289
Breach of contract	5691	1962	1839	1726	164
Redundancy pay	2616	467	678	1422	49
Sex discrimination	7421	2229	3494	634	1064
Race discrimination	2521	1064	773	580	104
Disability discrimination	2550	1329	789	361	71
Working time	2642	1140	868	600	34
Equal pay	2210	874	1277	36	23
National minimum wage	181	31	29	19	102
Flexible working	63	36	19	7	1
Others	4696	889	2071	1317	419

Source: Acas Annual Report and Accounts 2005/6

Negotiated settlements

Following negotiations, the parties may agree to settle the case before the tribunal hearing.

Example
The parties may agree to settle the case on the basis that the employer will pay the ex-employee £8500 to withdraw his claim for unfair dismissal and reinstate him, or the employer will pay the employee £7000 to compensate for an act of discrimination.

10

Settling disputes – taking a case to the Employment Tribunal

If the case is settled in this way, there is no need for the parties to then attend a tribunal hearing. Claimants may often accept a settlement that may be less than they would have received had their case succeeded in the tribunal. This could be, for instance, because they do not want to attend the hearing, have no representation, or are worried about the payment of costs. Employers are often willing to settle claims because they do not want to incur costs, bad publicity or waste company time.

If a settlement is reached, the conciliation officer will record the terms on a settlement form, referred to as form COT3. A settlement reached with the involvement of ACAS is binding on the parties. Once it is signed, the parties cannot change their minds and pursue the case further. The case will be removed from the tribunal-hearing list. If either party fails to keep to the terms of the settlement, the other can sue that party in either the County Court or High Court.

The parties can continue to negotiate up until the time set for the hearing. They can settle 'at the door' before the hearing by the tribunal, or even ask for an adjournment part way through if they think that a settlement may be possible. Settlements can be agreed upon up until the time that the tribunal chairman delivers the panel's decision.

Compromise agreements

A settlement may also be reached under a compromise agreement. Such settlements are not binding unless they are in writing, and relate to particular proceedings. Prior to making the agreement the employee must have received advice on the terms of the agreement from a relevant independent adviser. A 'relevant independent adviser' may be a qualified lawyer, a trade union official or an advice worker.

Withdrawal of claim

Either party may choose to withdraw his tribunal application before the hearing. To do so, the party should write to the tribunal formally withdrawing the complaint or defence.

INTERLOCUTORY STAGES – CASE MANAGEMENT

Interlocutory or 'in-between' stages cover procedures that may take place after the ET1 and ET3 forms are completed, but before the case is heard. Use of these procedures is optional and whether they are used will depend on the facts of the case and the way in which the parties have completed forms ET1 and ET3.

Request for further and better particulars

This allows either party to ask the other for more information on something written on the ET1 or ET3 forms.

Example
Questions asking for further and better particulars of, for instance, a comment such as 'I was disciplined' might be phrased as 'Where the claimant states that he was disciplined – when, where and by whom?'

The purpose of this procedure is to ensure that each party is fully aware of all of the facts surrounding the claim before attending the hearing. In the above example the answers may help the employer to locate disciplinary records or interview other employees who may provide vital evidence.

Discovery and inspection of documents

This procedure allows either party to ask the other to list any non-confidential case documents that he has in his possession. Either party may also ask to inspect and/or copy any of these documents.

The parties often agree to exchange lists. The documents may relate to, for example, sickness records, disciplinary hearings or payroll information. If one party suspects that the other is withholding an important document, he can apply to the tribunal for an order forcing him to disclose it.

Witness orders

Witnesses may be required to attend the hearing to give evidence on behalf of either party. If the parties suspect that a witness will not attend, they can ask the tribunal to send them a witness order. This compels the witness to attend, and may also order a witness to take documents to the hearing. If an ordered witness does not attend, he will be fined.

In most cases witnesses will attend voluntarily and an order will be unnecessary. However, employees who are to give evidence for a colleague who was recently dismissed may prefer to be ordered to attend the tribunal. They may not want to appear to be voluntarily speaking out against their employer.

Pre-hearing review

After reading the ET1 and ET3 forms, the panel members may order a pre-hearing review of the case. This is a 'mini hearing' and may be conducted by a chairman sitting alone. It may also be held over the telephone. Either party can also request a pre-hearing review. A review is normally ordered where it appears that the case is unlikely to succeed. Its purpose is to discourage parties from continuing with their case where there is no reasonable chance of success.

During the review the chairman will consider written evidence and oral argument. The review focuses on whether there is a case to put to a full tribunal hearing. If the chairman decides that the case has no reasonable chance of success, he can advise either the claimant or respondent to withdraw his claim.

If they still want to proceed, the chairman can order them to pay up to £500 to the tribunal office. This is meant to ensure that they are serious about making or resisting the claim. If this deposit is not paid, the claim may be 'struck out', preventing the claimant from taking the case further.

The chairman may also strike out or amend all or part of a claim on the grounds that it is scandalous, vexatious, or has not been actively pursued.

In claims involving allegations of sexual misconduct or disability (where personal details are likely to be heard), the chairman may make a restricted reporting order. This order prohibits the reporting of details about the case, names of the parties etc. until after the conclusion of the main tribunal hearing.

THE TRIBUNAL HEARING

The ETS gives the parties at least 14 days' written notice of the date of the hearing. This should give them enough time to do final case preparation. If a claimant fails to attend the tribunal hearing the tribunal may dismiss the claim or adjourn the hearing to another date.

If one party is unable to attend due to, for example, illness or a sudden family emergency, he should ask the tribunal to set a new hearing date.

The tribunal is a public hearing. This means that anyone, including the press, can attend. A tribunal clerk is present at each hearing. The clerk is there to ensure that the hearing is administered efficiently.

At the hearing the parties, or their representatives, will address the panel. They will each outline their respective cases based on the information given on forms ET1 and ET3. Documents will be considered and witnesses may be called. Persons giving evidence are questioned and cross-examined in the same way as in a civil or criminal trial.

At the end of the hearing, the panel considers what it has heard and read, and retires to decide on the success or failure of the claim.

THE EMPLOYMENT TRIBUNAL'S DECISION

The tribunal decision is usually unanimous, but can be made by a two-thirds majority. There are two ways in which the panel can announce its decision. It may:

- tell the parties the decision at the end of the hearing, sending them a written summary of the decision at a later date; or
- reserve the decision to a later date, sending the parties a summary of that decision at that time.

A written decision is always signed by the chairman. The tribunal must always provide reasons for their judgment. These reasons will be provided in writing only if one of the parties requests written reasons. This request must be made within 14 days of receipt of the tribunal decision. The Employment Appeal Tribunal may also request that a tribunal provide written reasons for their decision.

A decision of the panel of an Employment Tribunal does not bind any other tribunal or court. This means that even though another tribunal may look at the reasoning of the decision, it does not have to follow it in any new cases.

When a tribunal finds in favour of the employee/ex-employee the main remedy awarded is compensation. The sum of money awarded is payable to him 'without further notice', unless the recoupment rules apply. These rules state that where he has received any state benefits during the period leading up to the hearing, the amount received must be deducted from the tribunal award.

If the employer does not pay the required amount of compensation, the would-be recipient of the compensation can enforce the order in the County Court.

Costs

Generally, both parties have to pay their own costs. In claims made in the courts the losing party may also have to pay the costs of the winner! This does not normally happen in the Employment Tribunal. However, a party may be ordered to pay the other's costs where the chairman had advised him not to continue with the case at a pre-hearing review. Also, a party may be ordered to pay the other's costs where the tribunal thinks that the party has acted 'frivolously, vexatiously, abusively, disruptively or unreasonably'.

APPEALING AGAINST A TRIBUNAL DECISION

There are two ways in which the parties can appeal against a tribunal decision. They can:

- ask the tribunal panel to review its decision; or
- make an appeal to the EAT.

Asking the tribunal panel to review its decision

Either party can ask the tribunal to review its decision only on the grounds that:

- one party did not receive notice of the hearing;
- new evidence has become available;
- the decision was made in the absence of one of the parties;
- there was an error by tribunal staff; or
- where the interests of justice require a review.

The parties have 14 days from the issue of the written panel decision to apply for a review. The tribunal can refuse an application to review if in their opinion it has no reasonable prospect of success.

If the tribunal agrees to review the case, it can then either confirm its earlier decision, or decide in favour of the other party. If the tribunal changes its original decision, the case is re-heard. It is important to remember that a review will only take place if triggered by one of the five situations listed above. A party cannot challenge a decision just because it was not made in his favour.

Appeal to the EAT

Either party wishing to appeal to the Employment Appeal Tribunal must do so within 42 days of the date on which the Employment Tribunal handed down its judgment. If a party wishes to appeal to the EAT they must complete EAT Form 1 and send it to the EAT within this 42-day period. A copy of this form can be printed direct from the EAT website at www.employmentappeals.gov.uk.

A blank copy of this form is given as Figure 10.5. Note that the form does not require as much information from the appellant as forms ET1 or ET3. However, note also that sections 5 and 6 require that additional documents be provided when the form is submitted to the EAT. EAT Form 1 and any additional details can be sent to the EAT by post, fax or email.

An appellant may be able to get free or reduced-cost legal advice on either the requesting of a review or an appeal. They may also receive free or reduced-cost representation at the EAT hearing. In order to request help with their claim, the applicant would need to show:

- that according to a test of their income and savings, they cannot afford to pay for representation themselves; and
- that their case is strong enough to make it worthwhile for them to be represented out of public funds.

Time limits are strictly enforced by the EAT. It should be noted that the Employment Tribunal judgment is not the same as the reasons for their decision. An applicant may begin to count the 42-day time limit for lodging his appeal from the date on which reasons are provided by the ET if:

- reasons were requested at the ET hearing;

- the appellant wrote to request reasons from the ET within 14 days of the date that the judgment was sent to them; or
- the Employment Tribunal reserved its reasons and subsequently provided them in writing.

The appellant must send a fully completed notice of appeal to the EAT. The following documents must accompany this form:

- the initial ET judgment, decision, direction or order against which they are appealing;
- the written reasons from the ET (if appeal is against a judgment);
- copies of forms ET1 and ET3 as submitted in the initial claim; and
- an application for review (if they have asked the ET for a review).

The EAT can only hear appeals that are based on a point of law. This means that an appeal can only be made where the party is alleging that the tribunal:

- wrongly applied the law at the hearing;
- misunderstood the law;
- misunderstood or misapplied the law to the facts; or
- the decision was 'perverse' in that no reasonable tribunal would have reached the same decision.

Here, the panel may have failed to ask the right legal questions, used the wrong sections of law, or failed to consider all of the issues raised in the case. These may be difficult things to prove and limit the amount of appeals that can be brought. Again, there can be no appeal based solely on the fact that one party is unhappy with the Employment Tribunal decision. It is important that the applicant sets out the point of law to be argued on EAT Form 1.

Once the EAT receives the form a copy of it will be sent to the other party in the initial claim. They will also be sent and asked to complete and return EAT Form 3, 'Respondent's Answer', which is accessible via the EAT website at www.employmentappeals.gov.uk. A blank copy of this form is given as Figure 10.6.

The EAT hearing is not a new hearing of the whole case. The parties' representatives are allowed to argue for or against the initial tribunal decision. The EAT does not have to follow its own previous decisions, but these must be followed by both the Employment Tribunal and the County Court.

The EAT can:

- refuse the appeal and uphold the original tribunal decision;
- allow the appeal and send the case back to the original tribunal, which then re-hears the case; or
- allow the appeal and change the original tribunal decision to its own, for example, changing a decision from a dismissal being fair to being unfair.

The EAT's judgments are usually given orally at the end of the hearing. The panel can reserve judgment, giving the decision at a later date. Written judgments are made available.

EAT Form 1

Notice of Appeal from Decision of Employment Tribunal

1   The appellant is (*name and address of appellant*).

2   Any communication relating to this appeal may be sent to the appellant at (*appellant's address for service, including telephone number if any*).

3   The appellant appeals from (*here give particulars of the decision of the employment tribunal from which the appeal is brought including the date*).

4   The parties to the proceedings before the employment tribunal, other than the appellant, were (*names and addresses of other parties to the proceedings resulting in judgment, decision or order appealed from*).

5   Copies of—
     (a)   the written record of the employment tribunal's judgment, decision or order and the written reasons of the employment tribunal;
     (b)   the claim (ET1);
     (c)   the response (ET3); and/or (*where relevant*)
     (d)   an explanation as to why any of these documents are not included;
     are attached to this notice.

6   If the appellant has made an application to the employment tribunal for a review of its judgment or decision, copies of—
     (a)   the review application;
     (b)   the judgment;
     (c)   the written reasons of the employment tribunal in respect of that review application; and/or
     (d)   a statement by or on behalf of the appellant, if such be the case, that a judgment is awaited;
     are attached to this Notice. If any of these documents exist but cannot be included, then a written explanation must be given.

Figure 10.5 The EAT Form 1

Source: Employment Appeal Tribunal, www.employmentappeals.gov.uk

10

Settling disputes – taking a case to the Employment Tribunal

7   The grounds upon which this appeal is brought are that the employment tribunal erred in law in that (*here set out in paragraphs the various grounds of appeal*).

Signed: ....   Date: ....

NB. The details entered on your Notice of Appeal must be legible and suitable for photocopying or electronic scanning. The use of black ink or typescript is recommended.

Figure 10.5 continued

EAT Form 3

Ref: ....

Appeal from decision of employment tribunal/certification officer

Respondent's Answer

Case name: .... **v** ....

1   The respondent is (*name and address of respondent*).

2   Any communication relating to this appeal may be sent to the respondent at (*respondent's address for service, including telephone number if any*).

3   The respondent intends to resist the appeal of (*here give the name of appellant*).

The grounds on which the respondent will rely are [the grounds relied upon by the employment tribunal/Certification Officer for making the judgment, decision or order appealed from] [and] [the following grounds]: (*here set out any grounds which differ from those relied upon by the employment tribunal or Certification Officer, as the case may be*).

Figure 10.6 The EAT Form 3

Source: Employment Appeal Tribunal, www.employmentappeals.gov.uk

4   The respondent cross-appeals from (*here give particulars of the decision appealed from*).

5   The respondent's grounds of appeal are: (*here state the grounds of appeal*).

Signed: ....   Date: ....

Figure 10.6 continued

Further appeals

If either party is unhappy with the EAT's decision, that party can either:

- ask the EAT to review its decision; this request must be made within 14 days of the hearing; or
- appeal to the Court of Appeal within two weeks of the decision.

An appeal to the Court of Appeal can only be made on a point of law, and in the same circumstances as those listed above. A party cannot appeal without 'leave', or permission, from either the EAT or the Court of Appeal.

Any further appeal would again be on a point of law only and be made to the House of Lords. If the case involves a question of European law, it can be referred to the European Court of Justice.

SUMMARY CHECKLIST

- Most employment law disputes are resolved in the Employment Tribunal.
- The employee or ex-employee bringing the case is referred to as the applicant or claimant.
- The employer defending the case is referred to as the respondent.
- The case is normally heard by three panel members, a legally qualified chairman and two lay members.
- The lay members are drawn from industry; one represents employers and the other employees; they are taken from lists provided from, for example, the CBI or the TUC.
- The panel is often referred to as the 'industrial jury'.
- Employees can only make a claim to the tribunal if it has the jurisdiction to hear their case.
- The tribunal can hear cases on, amongst other things, unfair dismissal, discrimination and equal pay.
- The tribunal can deal with breach of contract claims where the claimant is no longer employed and the claim is for no more than £25 000.
- 'Legal help' is not available for Employment Tribunal assistance or representation.
- Employees may be able to get financial help from, for example, their union, the Equal Opportunities Commission, the Commission for Racial Equality or the Disability Rights Commission; if not, they will have to fund the case themselves.
- Neither party has to be legally represented.
- The employee/ex-employee has to send in form ET1 within the specified time limit, for example three months in unfair dismissal cases.
- Time limits may only be extended in exceptional circumstances and never for equal-pay claims.
- Acas receives copies of all ET1 and ET3 forms; it assigns a conciliation officer to every case.
- The conciliation officer tries to negotiate a settlement between the parties.
- Negotiation is voluntary.

- Settlements negotiated with the help of Acas are binding on the parties.
- There may be a pre-hearing review where the case has no reasonable chance of success.
- At the hearing the panel listens to oral arguments from both parties and from witnesses, and it looks at any documentary evidence.
- The panel may announce its decision at the end of the hearing, sending a written summary at a later date, or reserve judgment to a later date, sending a written summary at that time.
- Either party may request a copy of the full written reasons for the decision.
- Parties have to pay their own costs.
- Parties wanting to appeal against the tribunal decision can, in limited circumstances, ask the tribunal to review its decision or appeal to the EAT.
- An appeal to the EAT can be made on a point of law only.
- Appeals from the EAT can be made to the Court of Appeal on a point of law only; the EAT or Court of Appeal has to give permission for an appeal to be made.
- Appeals from the Court of Appeal can be made on a point of law only to the House of Lords; the Court of Appeal or the House of Lords has to give permission for the appeal to be made.
- If the case involves a question of European law, it may be referred to the European Court of Justice.

SELF-TEST QUESTIONS

1   Describe the way in which the tribunal system is administered.

2   Who decides the case in the tribunal?

3   What types of case can the tribunal deal with?

4   How might an employee be able to finance his claim?

5   Do the parties have to be represented by lawyers?

6   In which circumstances might the tribunal hear a case when the ET1 form is not sent in within the required time limit?

7   What involvement does Acas have in the case?

8   When might there be a pre-hearing review?

9   When does the panel announce its decision?

10   How might a party appeal against a tribunal decision?

Reading about how a case is taken to the tribunal is no substitute for actually visiting a tribunal and seeing the procedures in action. The ETS can provide details of the types of case that are about to be heard in your area. A visit may help to make the information that you have read in this chapter 'come alive'. Details of the address of your local tribunal venue can be obtained from the ETS address noted in the Appendix of this book.

Further reading

Employment Tribunal Procedure: A user's guide to Tribunals and Appeals, 3rd edn, Jeremy McMullen, Rebecca Tuck and Betsan Criddle, Legal Action Group, 2004.

Making a claim to an Employment Tribunal, Employment Tribunal Service booklet, September 2006.

Responding to an Employment Tribunal claim, Employment Tribunal Service booklet, September 2005.

The Hearing – Guidance for claimants and respondents, Employment Tribunal Service booklet, April 2005.

For legal updates on the material in this chapter please go to the Companion Website accompanying this book at **www.mylawchamber.co.uk/nairns**

10

Settling disputes – taking a case to the Employment Tribunal

Appendix: Useful addresses

Advisory, Conciliation and Arbitration Service
Head Office
Brandon House
180 Borough High Street
London
SE1 1LW
Tel: (020) 7210 3613
Fax: (020) 7210 3645

Commission for Equality and Human Rights
Kingsgate House
66–74 Victoria Street
London
SW1E 6SW
Tel: (020) 7215 8415

Commission for Racial Equality
St Dunstan's House
201–211 Borough High Street
London
SE1 1GZ
Tel: (020) 7939 0000
Fax: (020) 7939 0001

Disability Rights Commission
Freepost MID02164
Stratford upon Avon
CV37 9BR
Tel: (08457) 622633

Employment Appeal Tribunal
Central Office
Audit House
58 Victoria Embankment
London
EC4Y 0DS
Tel: (020) 7273 1041
Fax: (020) 7273 1045

Employment Tribunals Service
Public enquiry line:
(0845) 7959775

Equal Opportunities Commission
Arndale House
Arndale Centre
Manchester
M4 3EQ
Tel: (0845) 6015901
Fax: (0161) 8388312

Health and Safety Commission/Executive
Rose Court
2–10 Southwark Bridge Road
London
SE1 9HS
Tel: (020) 7273 3000

Information Commissioner
Wycliffe House
Water Lane
Wilmslow
Cheshire
SK9 5AF
Tel: (01625) 545745
Fax: (01625) 524510

Legal Services Commission
85 Gray's Inn Road
London
WC1X 8TX
Tel: (020) 7759 0000

Low Pay Commission
6th Floor
Kingsgate House
66–74 Victoria Street
London
SW1E 6SW
Tel: (020) 7215 8459

Glossary

Atypical workers Those who do not work the 'normal' 9–5 routine under set employment contracts, e.g. casual workers, homeworkers.

Constructive dismissal Where there is no dismissal as such but the employee is forced to resign because of the conduct of his/her employer, that resignation is then taken to be constructive dismissal.

Contract of employment The agreement which forms the basis of the relationship between an employer and worker.

Contract of service The agreement made between an employer and employee.

Contract for services The agreement made between an employer and independent contractor.

Direct discrimination Where a person is treated less favourably because of, e.g., their sex, race or disability.

Effective date of termination The date on which the employee is said to have ceased to work for his or her employer.

Expected week of confinement The week in which a woman is due to give birth, used for assessing the timing of maternity benefits/absence from work.

Express terms Terms which are written into the contract of employment.

Genuine occupational qualifications Those which may be required without discriminatory effect in job advertisements, e.g. for reasons of authenticity.

Implied terms Terms implied into the contract of employment, either because their existence is obvious or needed to ensure the smooth running of the contract, e.g. the duty on the employer to treat the employee with mutual trust and confidence.

Indirect discrimination Where a person applies a condition or requirement to, e.g., a job description and, even though on first reading it would seem to apply to all persons, it in fact can only be complied with by a small proportion of potential applicants.

Male comparator The male worker required to act as a comparison in claims for equal pay.

Re-engagement A tribunal remedy which provides that a previously dismissed employee should be reinstated with his/her original employer, but employed in either a different capacity or on a different site.

Reinstatement A tribunal remedy which provides that a previously dismissed employee should be allowed to return to his/her original job.

Risk assessment The assessment undertaken by employers to highlight the risks to health and safety that exist in their workplace.

Statutory terms Terms incorporated into the contract of employment by statute, e.g. the equality clause from the Equal Pay Act 1970.

Summary dismissal Where the employee is dismissed with no notice, but which is not a wrongful dismissal because the employer has good cause to dismiss instantaneously, e.g. where the employee has committed gross misconduct.

Transfer of an undertaking The situation where a business or part of a business is sold or otherwise given to another.

Unfair dismissal Dismissal in breach of statute; the employer either dismisses for an automatically unfair reason or a potentially unfair reason.

Vicarious liability Where an employer may be held to be liable for the actions of employees done in the course of their employment.

Wrongful dismissal Dismissal that is in breach of the contract of employment because the employer has given no notice or inadequate notice, or has, e.g., breached the contract by failing to follow set disciplinary procedures.

Index

Index

Index

Index